This book belongs to
Ma'yan
The Jewish Women's Project
a program of the JCC
on the Upper West Side

PLEASE DO NOT REMOVE

American Jewish Liturgies

An I. Edward Kiev Library Foundation Book

Bibliographica Judaica 14

*A bibliographic series of the Library of
Hebrew Union College-Jewish Institute of Religion
3101 Clifton Avenue, Cincinnati, Ohio 45220
Edited by Herbert C. Zafren*

1. Rudolf Glanz. *The German Jew in America*. An Annotated Bibliography Including Books, Pamphlets and Articles of Special Interest. 1969

2. *Judaica*. A Short-Title Catalogue of Books, Pamphlets and Manuscripts Relating to the Political, Social and Cultural History of the Jews and to the Jewish Question, in the Library of Ludwig Rosenberger, Chicago, Illinois. 1971

3. Bernard Grossfeld. *A Bibliography of Targum Literature*. 1972

4. *Judaica*. Supplement [to No. 2 above]. 1974

5. Werner Weinberg. *How Do You Spell Chanukah?* A General-Purpose Romanization of Hebrew for Speakers of English. 1976

6. Martin H. Sable. *Latin American Jewry: A Research Guide.* 1978

7. Shimeon Brisman. *A History and Guide to Judaic Bibliography* (Jewish Research Literature, Vol. 1). 1977

8. Bernard Grossfeld. *A Bibliography of Targum Literature.* Volume Two. 1977

9. Vera Basch Moreen. *Miniature Paintings in Judaeo-Persian Manuscripts.* 1985

10. Nahum Waldman. *The Recent Study of Hebrew: A Survey of the Literature with Selected Bibliography.* 1989

11. Shimeon Brisman. *A History and Guide to Judaic Encyclopedias and Lexicons* (Jewish Research Literature, Vol. 2). 1987

12. *The Sino-Judaic Bibliographies of Rudolf Loewenthal.* 1988. (In association with the Sino-Judaic Institute)

13. Michael Pollak. *The Jews of Dynastic China: A Critical Bibliography.* 1993. (In association with the Sino-Judaic Institute)

14. Sharona R. Wachs. *American Jewish Liturgies.* A Bibliography of American Jewish Liturgy from the Establishment of the Press in the Colonies through 1925. 1997

Sharona R. Wachs

American Jewish Liturgies

A Bibliography of American Jewish Liturgy
from the Establishment of the Press in the Colonies
through 1925

Historical Introduction
Karla Goldman

Liturgical Introduction
Eric L. Friedland

Hebrew Union College Press
Cincinnati · 1997

Copyright ©1997 Sharona R. Wachs
All rights reserved.

Library of Congress Cataloging-in-Publication Data

Wachs, Sharona R.
American Jewish liturgies: a bibliography of American Jewish liturgy
from the establishment of the press in the colonies through 1925 / Sharona R. Wachs.
   p.   cm. — (Bibliographica Judaica, ISSN 0067-6853; 14)
Includes bibliographical references and index.
ISBN 0-87820-912-3
1. Judaism — United States — Liturgy — Texts — Bibliography — Catalogs.
I. Title. II. Series.
Z6371.L5W33   1997
[BM673.U5]   97-29994
016.2964'5'0973 — dc21   CIP

Design, typography and composition by Kelby and Teresa Bowers
Printed on acid-free paper. Manufactured in the United States of America

שַׁחַר אֲבַקֶּשְׁךָ צוּרִי וּמִשְׂגַּבִּי
אֶעְרֹךְ לְפָנֶיךָ שַׁחְרִי וְגַם עַרְבִּי
לִפְנֵי גְדֻלָּתָךְ אֶעֱמֹד וְאֶבָּהֵל
כִּי עֵינְךָ תִרְאֶה כָּל מַחְשְׁבוֹת לִבִּי
מַה-זֶּה אֲשֶׁר יוּכַל הַלֵּב וְהַלָּשׁוֹן לַעֲשׂוֹת
וּמַה-כֹּחַ רוּחִי בְּתוֹךְ קִרְבִּי
הִנֵּה לְךָ תִיטַב זִמְרַת אֱנוֹשׁ עַל-כֵּן
אוֹדְךָ בְּעוֹד תִּהְיֶה נִשְׁמַת אֱלוֹהַּ בִּי

Solomon ibn Gabirol

To my husband, Rabbi Donald P. Cashman,
for his patience and support

נַפְשִׁי קְשׁוּרָה בְּנַפְשְׁךָ

To my children,
Avraham, Eliana and Ayelet Wachs Cashman

אֵם הַבָּנִים שְׂמֵחָה

I. Edward Kiev Library Foundation

In memory of Dr. I. Edward Kiev, alike distinguished as Rabbi, Chaplain and Librarian of the Hebrew Union College-Jewish Institute of Religion in New York, his family and friends established in September 1976 a Library Foundation bearing his name, to support and encourage the knowledge, understanding and appreciation of books, manuscripts and other efforts of scholars in Judaica and Hebraica.
In cooperation with the Publications Committee of the Hebrew Union College-Jewish Institute of Religion, the Foundation offers the present work as an I. Edward Kiev Library Foundation Book.

Contents

- viii   Acknowledgements
- 1   Introduction
- 13   Historical Introduction
  Karla Goldman
- 23   Liturgical Introduction
  Eric L. Friedland
- 32   Abbreviations
- 33   Selected Bibliography
- 36   National Union Catalog Abbreviations
- 39   Bibliography
- 169   Geographical Index
- 172   Name Index
- 190   Title Index
- 213   Liturgical Index

Acknowledgements

No work can be done without the support and advice of others. In this regard I have been very fortunate.

I am indebted to my father, Dr. Saul P. Wachs, Rosaline B. Feinstein Professor of Education at Gratz College, for inititally introducing me to Jewish liturgy, both as a research topic, and as a vehicle for religious and spiritual expression.

I am thankful to the University at Albany, State University of New York Faculty Research Awards Program and the New York State/Union of University Professionals Professional Development and Quality of Working Life Committee, Librarian Study Leave for providing me with the time and the funding to travel to Judaica collections throughout the United States. I am also appreciative of the University Libraries' continued support of this project, in providing me with computer software (Multi Lingual Scholar 4.0), as well as the time to compile and edit this bibliography.

I am grateful to my fellow librarians and the staff of the various libraries which I have visited. The time, resources, expertise and incredible hospitality afforded to me in my travels has been extraordinary. Many of the librarians permitted me to search through uncataloged materials, or pointed to unknown resources. While it is impossible to thank every librarian who has helped me, I would like to acknowledge Michael Grunberger, formerly of Gratz College, now head of the Hebraica Section of the Library of Congress, for help given at the early stages of this research. I would also like to thank Peggy Pearlstein, of the Library of Congress, the staff of all three American campuses of the Hebrew Union College-Jewish Institute of Religion, the Jewish Division of the New York Public Library, the Jewish Theological Seminary of America, Gratz College, the University of Judaism, the American Jewish Historical Society and the Western Jewish Historical Center.

I am deeply appreciative of the help given to me by Professor Lawrence A. Hoffman of the Hebrew Union College-Jewish Institute of Religion, New York. Professor Hoffman's expertise in liturgy, particularly American Jewish liturgy, as demonstrated in his numerous essays and books on these subjects have been indispensible in my understanding the development of American Jewish liturgy.

I would also like to thank Professors Karla Goldman and Eric Friedland for their insightful articles which precede this bibliography. These informative essays provide the context for the religious and social development of American Jewish life during the nineteenth century. In addition, an examination of the forces which contributed to liturgical change and innovation is presented. Without these background essays, the significance of individual entries, as well as trends within the bibliography, would be hard to appreciate.

I am appreciative other the editors and readers at Hebrew Union College Press. Their careful reading of my manuscript, as well as their suggestions were very helpful and challenging.

Lastly, none of this work could have been done without the support of my husband, Rabbi Donald P. Cashman. I am particularly indebted for his editorial suggestions, as well as his good humor and forbearance. His belief in the value of this bibliography, and his deep commitment to Talmud Torah have seen this project to its completion.

Introduction

Scholars of American Jewish history have produced several bibliographies of American Jewish imprints. These bibliographies have usually been very general in scope. Some have focused on all literary works and documents which are related in some way to Jews and Judaism, and these have attempted to be comprehensive coverage. Other bibliographies have sought to be comprehensive within a specified time period or within a single library or group of libraries.

The American Jewish bibliographer Ephraim Deinard published three bibliographies documenting the literary output of American Jews. The first of these was entitled רשימת כל ספרי ישראל אשר נדפסו בשפת עבר and was published in 1904. The second work, published in 1913 was entitled, ספרת ישראל באמעריקא and it contained essays on American Jewish literature as well as a bibliography of American imprints in Hebrew from 1735 until 1913. Deinard's third and most comprehensive bibliographical work was published in 1926 and was called קהלת אמעריקא. It was an annotated bibliography of American Jewish imprints published from 1735 to 1925. This bibliography was intended to be comprehensive, but it was not so. Some of the problems with this bibliography will be discussed below.

Another bibliographical work which was more limited in terms years covered was that which was compiled by A.S.W. Rosenbach and published by the American Jewish Historical Society in 1926. This bibliography covered works of Jewish Americana published from the establishment of the press in the Colonies until 1850. Two supplements to Dr. Rosenbach's bibliography were published by the American Jewish Archives in Cincinnati, Ohio. The first was edited by Jacob R. Marcus, and it sought to complement Rosenbach's bibliography by listing all the items Rosenbach missed that are in the library of Hebrew Union College-Jewish Institute of Religion in Cincinnati. Dr. Marcus' work was continued in the second work by Allen E. Levine. This work lists Jewish Americana published from 1851 to 1875, which can be found in the library of Hebrew Union College-Jewish Institute of Religion in Cincinnati.

Two other bibliographies on Jewish Americana were compiled by Edwin Wolf (1958) and Nathan Kaganoff (1971). Kaganoff's work lists items found in the holdings of the American Jewish Historical Society in Waltham, Massachusetts.

Another bibliography, published in 1990, was compiled by Robert Singerman, of the University of Florida at Gainesville. Entitled *Judaica Americana: A Bibliography of Publications to 1900*, this work contains over 6,000 entries for American Jewish imprints published from 1676 to 1900. While this bibliography is comprehensive in scope, Dr. Singerman has indicated that not every re-issue of a item is listed in his bibliography. A given item is only listed anew, when there is a substantial change in the bibliographical description, such as a new publisher, or a revision or enlargement of the text.

The intention of this bibliography is to be as comprehensive as possible in a single area of Jewish Americana. This bibliography focuses on Jewish liturgy published in the United States from the establishment of the press in the Colonies (1638) through 1925. Such a bibliography has yet to be published.

The range of years covered roughly corresponds to that of Deinard's bibliography קהלת אמעריקא. Deinard's bibliography is replete with errors. Of particular interest is a section entitled "סדרי תפלות לרעפארמים באמעריקא" which is an annotated list of "Reform" prayer books published in the United States. This section contains several problems. It is not at all comprehensive in its documentation of Reform liturgy. More important, much of Deinard's work is inaccurate. For example, there are listings in Deinard's bibliography of Reform liturgy which can hardly be considered Reform, such as an 1852 edition of שפת אמת by Wolf Heidenheim (1757–1832), a German Hebrew grammarian and commentator on liturgy. This text, considered gramatically and textually correct, as well as typographically beautiful, enjoyed over one hundred and fifty printings, and has been considered to be a standard traditional, i.e., Orthodox, text.

Other problems include the absence of important bibliographical data in some entries. Some entries are entered twice in Deinard's bibliography, particularly if they are part of a multi-volume set. There are also some surprising omissions. Deinard focused on works published in Hebrew, while many of the new works of Jewish liturgy were written in, or contained significant sections in, German or English. In addition, many of those non-Hebrew items listed in Deinard's bibliography are entered in a Hebrew language format, regardless of the language of the title page.

Therefore, the goal of this bibliography is to correct Deinard's work, as well as to amplify it to include all works of Jewish liturgy published in the United States (Reform and non-Reform), published through 1925.

Why liturgy? Throughout the ages the *siddur* has been a mirror of the philosophical, theological, sociological and political reality of the Jewish community. The *siddur* is full of prayers reflecting the political or social realities of the various countries in which Jews have lived, as well as different theological or spiritual trends to which Jews have been exposed. As Abraham E. Millgram has written in *Jewish Worship* (Philadelphia: Jewish Publication Society, 1971, p. 391f)

> The Siddur is the Jewish book of piety. In it are reflected most clearly the Jews' intellectual and emotional attitudes to God ... This piety — or inwardness, as some call it — is based on a number of theological premises: the nature of God, the essence of sin, the efficacy of repentance, and similar articles of faith. These beliefs constitute the backdrop of Jewish piety, and they are fully and clearly expressed in the traditional prayers of the Synagogue.
>
> All prayer is based on a number of assumptions which represent the essential truths and highest good to which a person or people is committed. In the prayers of the Synagogue one can find the Jew's traditional ideals, beliefs, values, attitudes and feelings toward God, Israel, and mankind. These essentials of faith are authentic doctrines of rabbinic Judaism.

The importance of the text of the prayer book is noted by Lawrence Hoffman in his book *Beyond the Text* (Indiana University Press, 1987, p. 69), which considers the important question of the ways liturgy reflects the aspirations of a culture.

> It might be said, then that whatever worshipers presume to say to God, they are at the same time directing a message to themselves. The very act of worship takes on the function of identifying for the worshiper what it is that he or she stands for, what real life is like, what his or her aspirations are. The liturgical medium becomes the message.

As Jews settled in America their political and religious realities began to change. The early Sephardic immigrants created liturgy reflective both of their Sephardic traditions and of the community's assimilation into Colonial life. Later, many of the German immigrants of the mid-nineteenth century brought with them the reforming trends of their native country. Not finding the traditional prayer book adequate in expressing new ideals, many authors began creating new prayer books, some more radical than others. The *siddurim* published in the second half of the nineteenth century reflect a marketplace of different ideas and ideals, as well as a struggle with the choice of the language of prayer (Hebrew, German, English). Immigrants coming to the United States from Eastern Europe after 1800, who were not exposed to the reforming trends of Central Europe, published their own more traditional *siddurim*, both in Minhag Ashkenaz or Polin (German or Polish rite) as well as the newer Ḥasidic rite, sometimes called Nusaḥ Sefarad. Yiddish works also begin appearing in the last decade of the Nineteeth century. The intellectual struggle between Reform Jews and those who felt more traditional, but not completely Orthodox, evolved into Consevative Judaism, and this struggle also produced new liturgies.

In addition to *siddurim* and *maḥzorim*, prayer books were written for women, and also for children. Home prayer books, prayer books for a house of mourning, and other works were created. Synagogue dedication ceremonies, and liturgy for other single events were published. The introduction of musical instruments into Reform worhsip, created a whole category of music written expressly for synagogue worship. This work seeks to document the intellectual struggle of the Jew in this new land and the creativity Jews exhibited in confronting new realities.

Definitions

In this bibliography, liturgy is to be defined in the broadest of terms. The bibliography covers all *siddurim* and *maḥzorim*, as well as extractions from these liturgical works, such as an evening service (ערבית) from the daily worship, or a *siddur* for only the Sabbath or Festivals. The bibliography also covers the category of occasional prayers, such as those said in a house of mourning. Included are prayers designed to be said outside the synagogue, or designated for specific audiences, such as devotionals or prayer books for women, children, or soldiers. Also included are life-cycle rituals, as well as religious ceremonies and worship services held for a specific event, such as a dedication

Introduction

ceremony for a new synagogue, or a prayer service held to commemorate 250 years of Jewish settlement in the United States.

This bibliography contains both traditional liturgy of Sephardic, German, or Polish Rite, as well as the newer liturgies of Reform and Conservative Rite. (The years covered in the bibliography precede published Reconstructionist liturgy.) Standard *siddurim* and collections of traditional prayers are covered as well as modern prayers and prayer books by American authors. Also included are musical renditions of individual prayers and prayer services, (many were composed for the Union Prayer Book), as well as compilations of Jewish hymns. All relevant languages are included.

Haggadot, i.e., the liturgy of the Seder on Passover, or any extractions from *haggadot* are excluded from the bibliography. Haggadot have been documented in a systematic and scholarly fashion by Avraham Yaari in his ביבליוגרפיה של הגדות פסח as well as in supplements to this work. The inclusion of *haggadot* to this bibliography would be an unnecessary duplication.

Also excluded are one-time memorial services for individuals. The exception to this are entries for memorial services for famous or noteworthy persons, such as Moses Montefiore and Isaac Mayer Wise, or a President of the United States. It would be nearly impossible to document all such services, because most would never find their way into a library or archive. Such a service for an individual is entered into the bibliography, however, if it contained special prayers written or composed specifically for this event, such as a hymn composed by Alois Kaiser in memory of his mother Therese Kaiser.

Also excluded are prayers or prayer books in manuscript. The bibliography only contains published works. It does, however, contain works that are privately published. This bibliography also does not list works of liturgy published in newspapers or journals. Therefore, prayers published in *American Hebrew*, for example, are not listed, unless they are extracted and published separately.

An American imprint is defined as a work published in the United States, no matter what the origin of the work. The bibliography includes all reprints and reproductions of works originally published abroad, as long as they are reissued with an American place of publication. Also included are a few items published in the United States for synagogues out of the country, e.g., a synagogue dedication service published for Shearith Israel, in Montréal, published in New York.

Methodology

Initial research on this bibliography was carried out for a thesis written as part of the requirements for a Master of Arts in Judaic Studies from Brooklyn College of the City College of New York, under the direction of Sid Z. Leiman (1990). Four major Judaica collections in New York were searched for appropriate items. These libraries included the Jewish Theological Seminary of America Library, the Klau Library of the Hebrew Union College-Jewish Institute of Religion, the Jewish Division of the New York Public Library, and the Mendel Gottesman Library of Yeshiva University. The book catalogs of major Jewish collections were also searched, as well as the *National Union Catalog*. These included those of the Klau Library of the Hebrew Union College-Jewish Institute of Religion in Cincinnati, the *Catalogue of Hebrew Books and Judaica: Widener Library Shelflist*, 39 from Harvard University, and the *Dictionary Catalog of the Jewish Division*, of the New York Public Library. In addition the previously mentioned bibliographies were also consulted (Deinard, Kaganoff, Levine, Marcus, Rosenbach, Singerman and Wolf). Auction catalogs from recent sales of Judaica were also consulted. Score materials were checked against Alfred Sendrey's *Bibliography of Jewish Music*.

In addition, the on-line computer data bases of OCLC, Inc. and RLIN were searched. These are the two major commercial bibliographical utilities used by libraries to catalog books, serials and other items. All of the above-mentioned libraries have some of their holdings listed in OCLC, RLIN or both. Many libraries who do not necessarily have extensive Judaica collections have entered records for individual items, which may not be held by major Judaica libraries. This is particularly true of local items, such as synagogue dedication ceremonies.

In the academic year of 1990–1991, I was fortunate enough to receive two grants which enabled me to travel to several other major Judaica collections throughout the United States, in order to identify additional liturgical works, as well as to examine some of the items I had only identified in book catalogs. The University at Albany, State University of New York Faculty Research Awards Program and the New York State/Union of University Professionals Professional Development and Quality of Working Life Committee, Library Study Leave Award provided six weeks leave to travel across the country, as well as the funding to do so. During this leave I was able to visit these libraries: the Library of Congress in Washington, D.C.; Harvard University; the American Jewish Historical Society, Waltham, Mass; Gratz College, Melrose Park, Pa.; Hebrew Union College, Cincinnati, Ohio; University of California, Los Angeles; University of Judaism, Los Angeles; Hebrew Union College-Jewish Institute of Religion, Los Angeles; the Jewish Community Library of Los Angeles; the University of California, Berkeley; and the Western Jewish Historical Center, Berkeley. While I could have easily spent twice the time in the above libraries, and I would have liked to have visited a number of other collections, I was able to add significantly to my original bibliography.

Format

The bibliography is arranged chronologically from the earliest works through 1925. Within any given year, entries are arranged alphabetically by title. Entries in roman alphabet languages precede items with Hebrew or Yiddish titles. Titles containing both Hebrew and roman alphabets are entered under the language of the initial word in the title. Items which contain a Hebrew title page, as well as a roman alphabet title page, are entered under their Hebrew title.

Because most of the items in this bibliography would be entered under a uniform title for their liturgical form, if cataloged according to *Anglo-American Cataloging Rules 2nd ed. revised,* (AACR2 rev.) I chose not to enter items in an Author/main entry format. While there are many different forms of liturgy in this bibliography, most are *siddurim* or *mahzorim*. Therefore, a uniform title main entry was not deemed particularly helpful. Access to the liturgical form of the item, as well as its rite, is available through the Liturgical index at the back of the bibliography.

Each entry contains (if relevant and available) the following data: title and subtitle, including any parallel titles; author or editor; edition statement; place of publication; publisher; date of publication and/or copyright date; and languages of the item, if there are more than one. If an item is in only one language, one may assume that the text is in the same language as the title page. If this is not the case (e.g., English title, Hebrew text), this is indicated in the entry. Also included are notes regarding authorship, edition, translation or other important information not found on the title page.

Each item contains, if applicable, the entry number from any of the above-mentioned bibliographies (Deinard, Levine Marcus, Rosenbach, Sendrey, Singerman, Wolf). Each entry contains a field identifying, by National Union Catalog (NUC) symbol, those libraries which have a copy of this item. Occasionally there are items identified in Deinard, Singerman or Sendrey for which there were no copies located. These items have nonetheless been included in the bibliography.

Entries are described using the format of International Standard Book Description (ISBD). This is the format adopted under the *Anglo-American Cataloging Rules, 2nd ed. revised*, which is the most recent set of cataloging guidelines used in this country today. The format is as follows:

Title = Parallel title: Sub-title/Statement of responsibility. — Edition. — Place of publication: Publisher, Date.
   Pagination. Language. Notes. Entry number in external bibliographies. Copies:

An example of an entry in the bibliography is the following:

   277. עבדת הקדש = Service of the sanctuary for the Sabbath and Festivals: arranged for the use of the Congregation Beth Elohim, Charleston, S.C. / by David Levy, Minister of the Congregation. — New York: M. Thalmessinger, 5639–1879.
     168 p. English and Hebrew. Singerman: 2788. Copies: NN NNJ

At the end of the bibliography there is a section of undated items which are assumed to have been published through 1925. Some of these items are compiled, edited or composed by individuals who published in the above-stated time frame. Other items, particularly those published by the Hebrew Publishing Company, have identical items published with appropriate dates. There are likely to be errors in this section, but they are mostly errors of omission. If I did not feel comfortable with pre-1926 determination for a given item, I left it out of the bibliography. In the case of the Hebrew Publishing Company, an address (Delancey Street, Eldridge Street, etc.) often was printed on the title page, in both dated and undated items. These addresses roughly identify the span of the years of probable publication. Throughout the bibliography there are undated items which could be more more definitively identified with a particular decade. These items precede others in that decade (e.g., 189-? precedes 1890).

Indexes

At the end of the bibliography are four indexes. The first index is a geographical index. It contains all the places of publication, as well as any other place associated with an item. For example, in the sample entry listed above, index entries will be found under Charleston, S.C. and New York, N.Y.

The second index is a name index. It contains all personal and corporate names associated with an item, such as authors, editors, compilers, synagogues or sponsoring organizations. All entries are in roman alphabet. If a place of publication or a name appears in an entry in the Hebrew alphabet, a cross reference from the Hebrew form to the roman form appears at the end of the particular index. For example:

Adler, ראה, הכהן, אדלר, נפתלי בן מרדכי
Herbert M.
קליוולאנד, ראה Cleveland, Ohio

In the name index, synagogues are entered under the first significant word of their names. Synagogues are not entered under *Temple* or *Congregation,* unless the omission of such a word would make the nature of the institution unclear (Temple Israel, or Congregation Bikur Cholim). Cross references exist in the name index for institutions with more than one form of their name. Some cross references exist for synagogues which merged or changed names (from earlier to later forms, and vice versa). Initial articles in all languages are to be ignored. The Temple (Mobile, Ala.) is filed under Temple. Corporate bodies whose names appear only in Hebrew are systematically romanized using American Library Association/Library of Congress (ALA/LC) system of romanization. Cross references from the Hebrew are found at the end of the name index. The name index also contains selected references from individuals to relevant corporate bodies or to associated titles. For example, there are references from *Max Landsberg* to *Brith Kodesh* (Rochester, N.Y.) and to his works *Ritual for Jewish worship* and *Hymn book for Jewish worship.* These references are not reciprocal.

The form of personal name is that which appears on the title page. In cases of conflict of fullness, the fullest form of the name is chosen. In cases of conflict of spelling, the most common spelling is chosen. In cases of personal names only found in Hebrew, the form entered into the index is one that is romanized into the standard English version of the name (e.g., Aaron, not Aharon). Cross references from the Hebrew are found at the end of the name index.

The third index is a title index. Titles in roman alphabet precede titles in Hebrew alphabet. In works where there are both Hebrew and roman alphabet titles, references from the roman alphabet titles are made to the Hebrew titles. Spine titles, cover titles, and other significant titles are referenced to the main title.

The fourth index is a liturgical index. Unlike the previous three indexes which are alphabetical, this index is structural. The liturgical index attempts to divide and organize the sum total of liturgical forms found in this bibliography according to the innate structure of the *siddur*, the Jewish calendar, or life cycle events. This is complicated because certain liturgical forms cannot be categorized under a broader liturgical format. The liturgical index can be divided into several sections.

The first section contains the *siddur* and all of its subcomponents, e.g., the *siddur* for the Sabbath only, as well as the *maḥzor* and all of its subcomponents. This section is followed by special prayers or prayerbooks, such as prayers for the sick, devotionals, or children's prayer books. The next section includes life cycle events. The next section includes one-time events, such as a synagogue dedication ceremony. The next section lists individual prayers which cannot be categorized under a single section of the liturgy. For example, *Mi khamokha* (מי כמוך) is a prayer which appears in morning service, and the evening service (albeit, in a slightly different form), both in the daily service, the Sabbath service, or the Festival services. Because it does not fall into one category, it has its own entry. On the other hand, *Magen avot*, (מגן אבות), only occurs in the evening service of the Sabbath, is therefore listed under *Siddur. Sabbath. Evening Service. Magen avot.*

The final section contains the various liturgical rites listed in the bibliography. Not every item in the bibliography is indexed under rite. If an item expressly indicates its rite (Minhag Polin, Reform, etc.), it is indexed under the appropriate rite. If an item is a product of an institution or synagogue known

Introduction

to be associated with a given liturgical rite, then it is indexed under the appropriate rite. For example, items associated with Shearith Israel (New York, N.Y.) are Sephardic, items associated with Temple Emanu-El (New York, N.Y.) are Reform. If the rite of an item is not obvious, or not appropriate (e.g., Prayer said before the House of Representatives), no index entry is made. There are some *siddurim* or *maḥzorim*, which are either *Minhag Ashkenaz*, or *Minhag Polin*, but do not say so on the item, and these are not indexed by rite.

Items are indexed under the broadest possible category. If an item contains several components that cannot be lumped under a broader category, then the item will be indexed under more than one category. For example, a prayer book containing daily services and Sabbath services is indexed under *Siddur*. But a prayer book containing daily services, Sabbath services, and an appendix of hymns would be indexed under *Siddur* and under *Hymns/Gesänge/Songs/Anthems*. A hymnal for children will be indexed under *Hymns/Gesänge/Songs/Anthems* and under *Children's Prayer Books*. If the rite is identifiable, then an item will also be indexed under rite, so a children's hymnal written for a Reform congregation (such as those written by Isaac Moses or Louis Grossmann), would also be indexed under *Reform Rite*. If a *siddur* specifically highlights a prayer, set of prayers, or special category of prayers on its title page, an entry will be made under that category. For example, if a *siddur* highlights the presence of *yotserot* (יוצרות), or *seliḥot* (סליחות), then the item will be indexed under *Siddur* and under *Piyyuṭim. Yotserot* or *Piyyuṭim. Seliḥot*.

The following is an partial example of the structure of the liturgical index:

> Siddurim. (Including Siddur for the whole year, with Maḥzor)
> Siddur. Daily Prayers.
> Siddur. Daily Prayers. Evening Service.
> Siddur. Daily Prayers. Morning Service.
> Siddur. Daily Prayers. Sunday Service.
> Siddur. Sabbath.
> Siddur. Sabbath. Evening Service.
> Siddur Sabbath. Evening Service. Individual Prayers.
> Siddur. Sabbath Morning Service.
> Siddur. Sabbath. Musaf.
> Siddur. Sabbath. Musaf. Individual Prayers.

Romanization

The romanization of Hebrew and Yiddish may appear confusing to the user. In the body of the bibliography, titles appear exactly as the are on the title page. Therefore, Hebrew words may be rendered in a number of different spellings. For example, the prayer ושמרו is rendered as V'shomru, V, Schomru and V'shom'ru in the bibliography. In the index, Hebrew terms not established by the *Encyclopaedia Judaica* are romanized according to the American Library Association/Library of Congress (ALA/LC) system of romanization. Therefore, ושמרו is romanized as Ve-shamru, and is indexed under *Siddur. Sabbath. Evening Service. Ve-shamru*. Because the romanization system employed by the *Encyclopaedia Judaica* differs from that of ALA/LC, similar terms may be romanized differently. Judaica and Hebraica catalogers trying to conform to the confusing intricacies of AACR2 rev. and the Library of Congress Rule Interpretations, are painfully aware of these inconsistencies.

In summary, the focus of this bibliography is Jewish liturgy published in the United States from the establishment of the press through 1925. While the bibliography attempts to be as comprehensive as possible, recording nearly 1,300 separate items, it is inevitable that some items have been overlooked. Not having visited every library in the United States with an extensive Judaica collection has allowed for the omission of those items in other libraries which have not been entered in any of the book catalogs of major Jewish collections, the *National Union Catalog*, or even the computer data bases of OCLC and RLIN. My experience at the Library of Congress, as well as many of the other major Judaica collections indicated that liturgy is often uncataloged, and therefore, undocumented. In addition, many of the more ephemeral items of early American Jewish liturgy were probably lost before they could reach the protective hands of a library or archive, or exist only in someone's attic or basement.

In spite of the above-stated limitations, the value of this bibliography is that it is the first time such an extensive collection of like bibliographical items hase been brought together. This bibliography should be helpful in providing information of the history and sequence of the creation, evolution and distribution of American Jewish liturgy, as it elucidates where Jewish liturgy was produced, published and reprinted, and by whom, during the early years of American Jewish history.

Historical Introduction

The 165 years of liturgical creativity and diversity documented in Sharona Wachs's valuable bibliography encompass a time of continuing transformation as successive waves of Jewish immigrants made their way in the new world. Prayer liturgies constitute the primary published record of the evolving religious expression of America's Jews in this period. The present brief introduction seeks to demonstrate the utility of Wachs's bibliography by using it to examine the attempts of American Jews to adjust the experience and language of Jewish prayer to the conditions and rhythms of American life.

Whether preserved in its traditional form or brought forward in a radically modified version, Jewish liturgy — i.e. the language, structure, and content of the prayers — has provided a consistent touchstone for Jewish cultural and religious identity. Nineteenth- and twentieth-century Jews who had abandoned a traditional Jewish way of life continued to look to worship, whether traditional or modernized, to sustain their connection to the language and world of the Jewish past. As the consequences of Emancipation undermined personal observances which had structured the contours of Jewish existence for centuries, the centrality of synagogue worship in both European and American Jewish life became increasingly emphasized.

The *siddur* (pl. *siddurim*), containing the fixed, regular prayers for Jewish worship, has never been a static text. The traditional rites for Sephardic and Ashkenazic worship, for example, differ from each other in significant ways. Even the *amidah* prayers, which constitute the core of every worship service, have appeared in variant forms as determined by region, culture and historical moment. Various renderings of English translations for the liturgy in addition to the appearance of altered versions of the Hebrew text have multiplied the variations of the published prayer rituals which fill this bibliography. Wachs's work thus testifies to the profusion of attempts to provide American Jews with access to acceptable scripts for Jewish worship; in the process it portrays the broad outlines of American Jewish settlement and organization.

The earliest prayerbooks published in America emanated exclusively from New York, Philadelphia, and Charleston and were meant to serve those praying in communities favoring the Spanish-Portuguese (Sephardic) worship style. These liturgies, serving a small community centered in a few cities, mirrored the heritage of colonial America's earliest Jewish settlers. Indeed, despite the fact that Jews of Ashkenazic descent quickly came to outnumber Sephardic residents of the American colonies and early republic, the Sephardic style in American Jewish worship and liturgy persisted well into the nineteenth century. The first American liturgy published in accordance with "the custom of the German and Polish Jews" did not appear until 1848 [#30].

In the 1850s, however, as increasing numbers of Jews emigrating from German-speaking lands began to establish their own religious communities, American Jewish prayerbooks adjusted to reflect their religious experience. New liturgies offered a clear reflection of the growing community's prosperity, Americanization and spiritual evolution. With the surge of immigrants from Eastern Europe and Russia at the turn of the century, a profusion of traditional texts of the eastern Ashkenazi variety (*minhag Polin*) met the needs of the new arrivals and their congregations.

The earliest *siddurim* listed here, offering the traditional text of the "Sephardic rite" with English translation, were published in New York, presumably to correct what Isaac Leeser described in the introduction to his 1837 prayerbook [#17] as "the inadequate supply of prayer-books," on this side of the Atlantic. Leeser suggested that the provisional use of *siddurim* imported from England could not be depended upon to satisfy American audiences. In 1825, Solomon Henry Jackson, offering Jews what he described as the "best extant" prayerbook [#10], acknowledged that he had relied upon the British translation of David Levy, but declared his own superior. Moreover, with the exclusion of certain prayers addressed to the more oppressive conditions of other historical eras, Jackson claimed that his liturgy was better suited to the "republican institutions" of the United States.

Along with standard prayerbooks, Wachs's bibliography includes a new genre of liturgy that began to appear in the early years of the Republic. As Jewish congregations constructed or bought synagogue buildings, they celebrated their achievement with special dedication services [#7–9, #13, #21–23, #26–29, #31, #33, #35, #38–39, #41; see index for additional dedication services]. The publication of a special "order of service" on these occasions helped give a religious tenor to what would have otherwise been mainly secular ceremonies. The non-traditional nature of these events afforded the opportunity of creating public Jewish ceremonies that were not rigidly bound by traditional requirements. Thus, though mixed choirs of men and women would

Historical Introduction

never have been allowed to participate in the standard worship of these traditional communities, they did perform at dedication services, which were frequently attended by overflow crowds of sympathetic Christian friends.[1] The appearance of additional liturgical material designed to mark secular occasions such as national days of thanksgiving [#5] or the death of President William Henry Harrison in 1841 [#19] offers further evidence of the attempt to legitimate an Americanized Jewish identity through non-traditional religious statements.

The concern for public respectability revealed in these ceremonies also found expression in concerns about traditional worship. Early nineteenth-century attempts to Americanize synagogue ritual sought to bring order to the often chaotic style of traditional public worship. The solemn recital of prayers, either by a prayer leader, a male choir, or in decorous unison, marked many efforts to create an Americanized, but traditional, service.[2]

The Reform Society of Charleston, formed in 1824, proposed a more radical response to what its members saw as "the gradual decay" of Jewish worship by retaining "the most solemn portions" of the ritual, while excluding "everything superfluous."[3] Although the Charleston reformers were the first self-conscious American practitioners of liturgical change, the much-revised Sabbath liturgy issued by their short-lived society in 1830 [#12], which appeared in English, was not adapted elsewhere.

As time went on, however, many leaders in other communities also came to believe that the synagogue's respectability depended as much upon the content of prayer as upon the way in which worship was conducted. German-trained reformers at mid-century brought more systematic, informed, and long-lasting change to public Jewish devotion than the Charleston society had been able to offer. In 1855, Leo Merzbacher of Temple Emanu El in New York published the first full-scale Hebrew/English American Reform prayer-

---

1. For the development of consecration services and choirs in New York, see Hyman Grinstein, *The Rise of the Jewish Community of New York, 1654–1860* (Philadelphia, 1945), pp. 174–179, 278–282.

2. Jeffrey S. Gurock, "The Orthodox Synagogue," in Jack Wertheimer, ed., *The American Synagogue, a Sanctuary Transformed* (Cambridge Eng., 1987), pp. 41, 49–50; see also in the same volume, Marsha L. Rozenblit, "Choosing a Synagogue: The Social Composition of Two German Congregations in Nineteenth-Century Baltimore," pp. 332, 344, 348–349, 355.

3. From "Memorial," a petition to Congregation Beth Elohim, reprinted in L. C. Moise, *Isaac Harby* (n.p., 1931), p. 54.

book [#55] which according to Merzbacher retained, "all that tradition, authority, and usage have sanctioned" while excluding only "repetition, incongruities, and obvious abuses." Merzbacher's text was adopted by several other congregations. Other reforming liturgists, also anxious to adjust Jewish prayer and worship to match the evolving sensibilities of a modernizing constituency, were soon publishing their own revised prayerbooks. Isaac M. Wise [#66], David Einhorn [#76], and Benjamin Szold [#81], for instance, incorporated a broad spectrum of linguistic and ideological revisions in their efforts to provide texts that would hold relevance for modern worshippers.

It is important to note that those who first put forth alternative texts in an American setting were not overly concerned with meeting the expectations of traditional worshipers. Whereas European liturgies had to satisfy Jewish communities comprised of both traditional and liberal elements, American prayerbook editors could target more homogeneous communities. In fact, rabbis often produced texts for the use of their own congregations which may have already aligned themselves with their rabbi's personal spiritual direction. For instance in 1854, just months after the arrival of their new rabbi, Cincinnati's K. K. B'nai Yeshurun was already resolving "That the Minhag [custom, rite] of this congregation shall henceforth be the one proposed by the Rev. Dr. [Isaac M.] Wise."4

Wise's new prayerbook, first appearing in 1857, demonstrated [#66] that the community Wise envisioned was powerfully tied to tradition but not ruled by it. Wise's special concern, and even more the concern of his students who also became prayerbook revisers, was for the creation of a liturgy suited to the sensibilities of newly-minted and, later, fully-acculturated Americans. Certainly, many liturgists, like Wise with his *Minhag Amerika*, hoped that their worship service would eventually become the standard for a new and American Jewish tradition. These prayerbook editors sought to satisfy the desire of worshippers for connection to past practice and Jewish experience. At the same time, they focused on the important task of providing the worshipper with a liturgy that could comport with a modernized world view. Thus, in their prayerbooks, the broader effort to identify an acceptable American expression of Judaism was projected specifically into the effort to find an amenable and comfortable experience of worship.

4. *Israelite*, 1:7 (August 25, 1854): 54.

These liturgies, offered by some of America's most prominent rabbis, focused on rationalizing Jewish devotion within the synagogue sanctuary—where the authority of their authors was concentrated and where Jewish identity was increasingly localized. But in addition to documenting American Judaism's intensifying focus on the sanctuary, Wachs's bibliography also presents evidence of a competing, if complementary, trend towards providing American Jews with appropriate resources for personal and domestic devotion.

In 1852, *Rechama, Devotional Exercises for the Use of the Daughters of Israel* [#42] offered a selection of readings "intended for ... maidens, brides, wives, mothers, and on all other occasions, of joy, or of trial, incidental to their sex." This work, like many subsequent compilations of prayers intended for private prayer, was taken and translated from European devotional literature. Like Yiddish *t'khines* texts, these books offered "a suitable collection of Devotional exercises in the vernacular tongue, for the daughters of our people." This devotional genre is typified by *Imrei lev, Meditations and Prayers for every Situation in Life* attributed to Jonas Ennery, translated by Hester Rothschild and revised and corrected by Isaac Leeser, first published in 1864 [#116, for other examples see: #106, #153].

Scholars have tended to overlook these works, seeing them as less momentous than liturgies for public worship. Yet, many of these compilations appeared in numerous reprints straight through the chronology of Wachs's bibliography; an edition of *Imrei lev* appeared as late as 1923. The frequent reprinting of these devotional manuals testifies to a continuing demand for resources, drawn from less formal European liturgical sources, directed towards the personalized domestic devotion of women, even as other public worship became increasingly formal and abstracted from everyday life.

Towards the end of the nineteenth century, Americanized rabbis offered updated and spiritualized versions of this type of literature [see #s 368, 549]. These family-centered manuals, meant to facilitate Jewish practice in the home, were presumably still directed principally at women. However, they no longer attempted to address every occasion of a woman's life, including betrothal, marriage, childbirth, and sundry unhappy and happy moments. Gustav Gotheil's *Sun and Shield* of 1896 [#527], "a book of devout thoughts for every day use," for instance, included formal prayers for religious observance as well as reflections on the abstract subjects of God, Man, Israel, and Humanity. Despite these new contributions, the older American versions of female devotional literature continued to be reprinted. A new guide detailing the "Religious Duties of the Daughters of Israel" was published in 1902 to serve English-speaking daughters of recent immigrants who may have lost interest in European Yiddish devotional texts.

The bibliography also reveals the sudden emergence of another genre of liturgical material. Except for a few isolated texts [#87,#97] no specific material directed at children or for school use appears in the United States until the late 1860s. The 1870s, however, brought a plethora of catechisms, hymnbooks and prayerbooks produced specifically for Jewish religious schools. The apparently unprecedented attention to education indicated by the late appearance of this type of material suggests a noteworthy pattern that seems to govern the genesis and evolution of many of the different genres present in the bibliography. Concern for education among American Jews certainly predated the school manuals of the 1870s. Early educators, however, like early worshippers, made do with existing texts, which had been published for the existing community or which had been brought over from Europe. In the case of education such texts included Christian catechisms from which the explicitly Christian references had been blacked out. Once Jewish schoolbooks did appear, they quickly proliferated. German-Hebrew and German-English texts were rapidly supplemented and outnumbered by those in English and Hebrew or in English alone.

A similar pattern characterized the appearance of material for children of the late nineteenth-century immigration. German-Jewish philanthropists sponsored the frequent reprinting of a traditional prayerbook (Hebrew, "with English instructions," first published in 1874) [#234], as well as a Saturday-afternoon service (Hebrew and English, 1896) [#523] to serve the children of their impoverished and traditional co-religionists from Russia and Eastern Europe. However, no extant American-published texts directed at school-age Yiddish-speaking children emerged *from within* the immigrant community until 1903, when a Hebrew reader was published in Hebrew and Yiddish [#639]. English replaced Yiddish in an edition of this same reader in 1905, by which time, a myriad of other materials for both Anglicized [#677] and Yiddish-speaking children of the immigrant generation had become available.

Prayerbooks for adult worship which multiplied towards the end of the nineteenth century were dominated by the work of rabbis seeking appropriately acculturated versions of the worship ritual. These new prayerbooks were directed at an audience that increasingly lacked an intimate familiarity with the traditional Hebrew text. Early reformers had mostly omitted or adapted those prayers which they considered later accretions to the ancient text. Progressively, however, a growing liturgical ignorance among successive waves of Americanizing Jews meant that the insertion of only a few familiar and central Hebrew prayers could often provide a sufficient marker of continuity for American worshippers.

Many Reform rabbis, encouraged by their congregations, developed liturgies — offering a limited amount of Hebrew, a selection of extra (often responsive) English readings, and an abridged service — which were centered around a sermon. One striking example was the 1888 *Service Ritual* [#371] composed by Joseph Krauskopf, rabbi of Knesseth Israel in Philadelphia. Krauskopf hoped that his service, replete with "*free* translations from the Hebrew" could help communities worshipping on Sunday avoid "the monotony of weekly repetitions of the same prayers by giving *thirty* completely different *Services*." The potentially endless proliferation of these texts moderated somewhat with the appearance in 1894 of the *Union Prayer Book*, (*Tefilot Yisrael*) [#502] published and frequently reprinted by the Reform movement's Central Conference of American Rabbis.

A number of more traditional rabbis also joined in the project of prayerbook reform [see #s 125, 204, 337]. These editors sought to moderate the sometimes objectionable themes of the traditional text but avoided the more radical changes that Reformers were putting forward. Their texts removed many of the repetitions in the traditional ritual and altered or deemphasized a few particularly objectionable prayers.

Benjamin Szold's *Avodath Israel*, first published in 1864 [#125] for example, expurgated a number of references which seemed to celebrate God's cruelty to Israel's enemies. Among other changes, Szold removed explicit liturgical references to the slaying of the Egyptian first-born and, at least in the translation, to the drowning of Egypt's army. Szold also sustained his vision of a less vituperative God by omitting the traditional *Birkat Minim*, a paragraph of the *amidah* that calls for the obliteration of God's enemies. In addition, Szold transformed particularistic prayers of thanks for what God was wont to do for "your people Israel" into more universal acknowledgements of God's attention to all those who are in need. The rituals of America's proto-Conservative rabbis, like Szold, Adolf Huebsch, and Marcus Jastrow, often provided additional readings and a softened English translation which could make the text appear more ideologically and spiritually suited to the supposed needs of Americanized Jewish worshippers.

Meanwhile, traditional renditions of the liturgy continued to appear in the form of revisions and reprintings of editions published earlier in the century [#s 437(1890), 516(1895), 593(1900)], #604(1901), [#768(1909)]. The first decade of the twentieth century, however, marked a significant turning-point in the production of traditional liturgies. The few new editions of traditional liturgy published in the last decades of the nineteenth century were finally joined by a rush of new versions published to serve the burgeoning numbers of newly-arrived immigrants [see #s 573, 577, 626].

The immigrant generation that began to arrive in earnest in the early 1880s repeated the patterns established by earlier generations of American Jews. For instance, it took more than two decades for the newly-arrived Eastern European Jews to generate a locally-created liturgical literature of their own. By the time such liturgies did appear, many of the new immigrants were already firmly engaged in the throes of Americanization. It was not long before Hebrew-English editions of the traditional liturgy began to supplement Hebrew-Yiddish versions of the prayers. These translations were soon followed by the development of prayerbooks intended for more Americanized constituencies. Such prayerbooks, however, preserved a much more traditional focus than did the Americanized volumes typical of earlier generations.

With the *Union Prayer Book* and these more traditional texts filling the spectrum of early twentieth-century American Jewish liturgy, innovation in both the Reform and traditional communities focused on efforts to counteract the assimilationist pressures implicit in the rhythms of American life. Reform communities, for instance, began introducing services specially designed to attract children. For adults, Reformers offered public worship services formulated for late Friday night and Sunday morning which could replace the more customary, but now inconvenient, Sabbath services held early Friday evening and Saturday morning. Reformers also attempted to bring new life to traditional observances which had fallen into disuse. One "Manual of Exercises for Temple, Synagogue, or Sabbath School," was even entitled "Succoth Revived" [#794; see also #772].

Efforts to reach the more traditional, but nonetheless Americanizing, population of newer immigrants resulted in the creation of traditional liturgies especially designed for use on Friday night and Saturday afternoons. Like the Reform liturgies mentioned above, these services were intended for those who, because of work obligations, could not attend the customary Sabbath morning worship services. Even staunchly traditional texts often revealed an awareness of the seductive influence of more Americanized liturgies. Thus, the Hebrew title of a 1908 high holiday liturgy proudly advertised its full inclusion of "all the *piyyutim* in their proper order," along with its accompanying Yiddish translation [#739]. Other traditional renderings sought respectability by featuring "responsive readings" and "special English prayers" [#689].

At the close of the period covered in this bibliography, the American Jewish community was approaching the end of its own immigrant era. The quota laws of 1924 would abruptly cut off the Yiddish-speaking stream of new Americans. As a result, Jewish liturgies of the 1920s were serving a constituency, from the thoroughly Americanized native to the greenest immigrant, as diverse as it would ever be. Accordingly, the Jewish liturgical scene, as indexed by Sharona Wachs, featured a varied profusion of worship services.

During the first quarter of the twentieth century worshippers could choose from any number of liturgies from earlier decades. Old and new versions of texts ranging from the *Union Prayer Book* [#1200] to the prayerbook of Benjamin Szold as revised by Marcus Jastrow [#1204], which had first been published in 1864, continued to appear. In 1924, the "Standard Prayer Book" as adopted from the liturgy approved by England's chief rabbi was in its "44th thousand" American printing [#1198]. The latest revised edition of the *Daily Prayers with English instructions* [#1233] continued to tout the claim, first made in 1876 [#248] that it was still "as correct as any ed. ever published in *Rödelheim*."

New offerings during this period echoed earlier genres of American Jewish liturgy and offered hints of forms which would find future development. Musical scores to accompany diverse versions of the liturgy were continually created as they had been throughout much of the period under study. American Jews could find any number of specialized services to serve their spiritual needs. Offerings ranged from liturgies for *bar mitzvah* [#1007], confirmation [#1173] and the grace after meals [#1191] to a range of services for particular settings including homes, schools, Jewish camps [#'s 1184, 1209], the army [#1010] and deaf congregations [#1047]. Dedication services for synagogue centers and community centers marked the latest incarnation of the community's quasi-religious celebration of its own organization and existence. [#'s 1211, 1212].

Liturgies compiled by early twentieth-century rabbis of traditional but Americanizing congregations for the use of their communities echoed the liturgical efforts of nineteenth-century Reform rabbis. The appearance of liturgies like "Song and Praise for Sabbath eve" compiled by Israel Goldfarb and Israel Herbert Levinthal of the Brooklyn Jewish Center "for use at synagogue gatherings in connection with the late Friday evening sermon or discourse" [#1225] and of "Prayers of Israel for the Sabbath and the Festivals: arranged and revised with the latest English translation, and responsive readings" by Jacob Bosniak, rabbi of the Ocean Parkway Jewish Center and Tifereth Israel in Brooklyn [#1240] provided the necessary precursors to a unified Conservative prayerbook.

The broad range of liturgical preservation and creativity evident in this bibliography remains characteristic of the Jewish community in the United States. Denominational differences have now supplanted the initial distinctions of country of origin and of immigrant generation as the major source of liturgical diversity. Yet, the persistent desire of American Jews for prayerbooks suited to their own particular needs and occasions has guaranteed the continuing proliferation of Jewish liturgical material. The attempt, documented in this bibliography, to adjust Jewish worship to the sensibilities of a modernizing constituency continues to offer a sensitive barometer of the changing cultural and spiritual conditions of American Jewish life.

Karla Goldman
Cincinnati, Ohio

Liturgical Introduction

In the United States the last fifty years have witnessed bursts of unprecedented creativity in the area of Jewish liturgy, each decade having its own irreducibly unique style. What is generally not realized is that three-quarters of a century prior to that time was a period of at least as much productivity. Nearly all of the standard rites used in North America today are lineal or indirect heirs of those anterior liturgical efforts, principally from the mid-nineteenth century through 1925. That the European influence is dependably never far behind is evident from the works that were reprinted periodically on American soil, only to mention the critical editions of the *Siddur* (1823) and *Maḥzor* (1800–1805) by Wolf Heidenheim, the prodigiously annotated *'Avodat Yisrael* (1868) by Seligmann Baer and the princely Adler/Davis/Zangwill (1904–1920) and Singer (1898) volumes of the British, moderate Orthodox Ashkenazic rite. An invisible, but felt, presence was the pace-setting Reform *Seder ha-'Avodah/Ordnung der oeffentlichen Andacht fuer die Sabbath- und Festtage* (1819) of the Hamburg Temple.

The variety of liturgical manuals cited in the all-inclusive Wachs bibliography is rich indeed. It embraces prayerbooks designated for daily, Sabbath, Festival and High Holy Day worship; different *sifrey ḥayyim* (for those observances connected with sickness, dying, death and mourning); special synagogue dedication services; obsequies for a president or notable; musical scores for liturgical texts; hymnals; prayer textbooks for schoolchildren; and devotionals for private use. Circumstantially we catch more than a glimpse of what events were sacralized in the Jewish community at the time, of what made up a primary pedagogic concern (namely, learning the practical skills of joining in public worship), and of a doleful preoccupation in the not-so-distant past with the ever-present reality of death.

Of the making of prayerbooks for us in the synagogue there seemed to be no end. The very first ones to appear on the American continent were of Sephardic provenance, like the *Prayers for the Sabbath, Rosh-Hashanah, and Kippur* (New York, 1765 or 1766), translated by Isaac Pinto [#4]. Then, beginning in the second half of the nineteenth century, the proliferation of prayerbooks became very much an activity of Reform in all of its shadings, extending from the discernibly traditional to the essentially nonconformist. This multiplication of rites came about for two paramount reasons. First, readjusted rituals were then issued largely under the auspices of congregations that had the good fortune to be led by rabbis of theological acumen, liturgical scholarship and literary skill, and that also possessed the monetary means to publish. Secondly, synagogues issuing their own *siddurim* were in effect making a programmatic statement about where they were doctrinally and ritually. As often turned out to be the case, congregations in other cities and states adopted the rites of the originating congregations, sometimes even going so far as to take on the names of those congregations (e.g., Emanu-El or [Har] Sinai).

With the invaluable assistance of the exhaustive bibliography that follows, one should at least be able to trace with confidence the pedigree of virtually all the presentday American prayerbooks, from Reform to Orthodox, Sephardic to Ashkenazic, synagogal to domestic. For the purposes of this essay, as a kind of touchstone, it might be worthwhile to sketch here — very cursorily, to be sure — a historical overview of the American Reform and Conservative prayer manuals from their earliest days through the 1920s.

One of the first undertakings of the Reformed Society of Israelites, which broke away from K. K. Beth Elohim of Charleston, South Carolina in the 1820s, was the formulation of a ritual compatible with the Society's progressive principles, *The Sabbath Service and Miscellaneous Prayers* (Charleston, 1830) [#12;#952]. Isaac Harby and his associates, all of whom were of Sephardic background, living in a metropolis of the antebellum South and operating in a single cultural and literary milieu, were amenable to several influences that are reflected in their prayerbooks. All items drawn from the classical *siddur* are without exception in accord with the Sephardic *minhag*. While sharing neither the liturgical expertise nor the halakhic awareness of the Hamburg Temple prayerbook revisers, the Society's redactors found in the relatively recent Hamburg endeavor (1819) the needed justification for their own liturgical effort. The cadences and even an occasional usage, naturally in non-Christological terms, of the Anglican *Book of Common Prayer* insinuate themselves into the Society's prayerbook. Motifs of enlightenment, idealism and anticlericalism leaven the text. The fact that the lay-inspired and -framed *Prayerbook of the Reformed Society of Israelites* left no imprint on subsequent prayerbooks could well result from the fact of its being at a geographical remove from the mighty currents that swept Jewish life starting a decade later, and from the fact of the Society's short life (1824–1833).

Liturgical reform was inaugurated in 1855 with *Seder Tefillah/The Order of Prayer* [#55] by Leo Merzbacher, the first rabbi of Congregation Emanu-El of New York City. Seeking to apply the canons of liturgical change agreed upon by the German rabbinical conferences of the mid-1840s, Merzbacher recast a slender all-Hebrew rite that kept all the primary textual ingredients (*matbe'a shel tefillah/Stammgebete*), but eliminated those considered nonessential or of small importance. Structurally and lexically, the Hebrew side of *Seder Tefillah*, as revised in 1860, and again in 1864 by successor Samuel Adler [#93; #123–#124], was the rite to have the largest impact after David Einhorn's *Olath Tamid* (to be discussed below) on the *Union Prayer Book for Jewish Worship* of 1894/95 and all subsequent editions of the same [#1011–#1012; #1077–1078; #1108]. It is worthy of note that even though the congregation was German-speaking the translation of the prayer text was from the very outset in English. While the revised prayerbook was geared in the main to public worship, a page is allotted to private morning and nightly prayer (with the *Shema'—ve-ahavta* as the pivot). We find also a funeral service (*Tsidduq ha-Din*), with an *Evening Service for the House of Mourning* that was subsequently appended [#173]. So too, before long, there appeared as an appendix a selection of German hymns (and their singable English renditions) taken mostly from the Hamburg Temple *Gesangbuch*. In its earlier years Temple Emanu-El of San Francisco made the *Order of Prayer* its own too [#146].

Along with Isaac M. Wise, Isidor Kalisch and a certain Rothenheim, Merzbacher was originally part of the liturgical commission for the Cleveland Conference in 1855, which drafted a common prayerbook for all American Jews. Owing to Merzbacher's premature death, Wise became the prime mover of *Tefillot Beney Yeshurun: Minhag Amerika/The Daily Prayers of American Israelites* (Cincinnati, 1857) [#66; #69; #75]; 1862 [#102]; 1864 [#119–#120] and companion volumes for Rosh Hashanah and for Yom Kippur, 1866 [#148]; and 1872 [#201–#202]) which served not only his own Cincinnati congregation but many others across the country. *Minhag Amerika* is essentially a compromise effort to satisfy the spectrum of liturgical/ritual preferences from Traditionalist to Reform. On the surface, it is very much the established *Siddur*, but a closer look will reveal an emended Hebrew wording manifestly consonant with the principles of Reform. There are, by contrast, elements rare or not so ubiquitous in Reform/Liberal prayerbooks: *Kiddush ha-Levanah* ("At Seeing the New Moon"), *Hosha'not* (processions with the *lulav* and *etrog* on

Sukkot), and the full complement of *Birkat ha-Mazon* and Qallir's *Tal* and *Geshem* (prayers for dew and rain respectively). Oddly enough, Wise's *Kiddush* has no provision for wine and his otherwise-complete *Havdalah* none for light, wine or spices. Prohibition apparently had an early start for the masterbuilder of Reform Judaism in the United States. Despite some textual and compositional anomalies elsewhere in *Minhag Amerika*, features like Wise's still-moving Memorial Service "The eye is never satisfied with seeing; endless are the desires of the heart" found its way into all editions of the High Holy Day volume of the *Union Prayer Book* and is deservedly enjoying a long lifespan (*Gates of Repentance* [1978], p. 480).

The first Reform prayerbook to presuppose in a thoroughgoing manner the latest in historical and liturgical scholarship is *Olath Tamid/Gebetbuch fuer Israelitische Reform-Gemeinden* created and published by David Einhorn in 1856 for his Har Sinai Congregation in Baltimore [#58 and #76–#80]. The work rests foursquare on the theological doctrine that the Jewish people is divinely imbued with a mission of teaching and service to all humankind. Here and there the streamlined Hebrew text is lithely reconditioned to underscore this notion; and everywhere the expanded German paraphrase dwells on it. Moreover, the principles hammered out at the aforesaid rabbinic conferences (*Rabbinerversammlungen*) in Germany are applied consistently in this one-man literary *tour de force*. Einhorn's labor of love, as of artistic and religious genius, is a veritable *mahzor*, in the original sense of the word: a virtual all-purpose rite for every occasion — Shabbat, Festival, High Holy Day, fastday, weekday, life-cycle event, and personal use. *Olath Tamid* was twice slightly revised [#103] and twice translated into English, initially by savant Bernard Felsenthal [#207] of Chicago and at a later date by a rabbinic son-in-law, Emil G. Hirsch [#518; #862], with the Einhornian Hebrew text left substantially intact. The bulk of the English in the first edition of the *Union Prayer Book*, Volumes I and II came in a near straight line from *Olath Tamid's* rotund and effulgent German.

Those synagogues in what I call the proto-Conservative camp in nineteenth-century America were beginning to feel the exigency of an alternative rite that comported with the imperatives of modernity without yielding to the perceived extremes of Reform. Recoiling from the idiosyncrasies in wording and layout of *Minhag Amerika* and shunning the systematic radicalism of *Olath Tamid*, Benjamin Szold produced a series of prayerbooks very much along the lines of moderate Reform or the loosened traditionalism typical of Central European Liberal Judaism. For his congregation in Baltimore, Oheb Shalom, Szold first issued a supplementary volume, *Qodesh Hillulim/Pijutim, Gebete und Gesaenge* (1862) [#104–#105], chiefly for use in conjunction with a High Holy Day prayerbook. This served as the immediate precursor to the one-volume, Hebrew-German *Abodath Israel* (1864 [#125]; English translation: 1865 [#133]) for public worship all year round. Among the most far-reaching changes are 1) the replacement of the High Holy Day Ashkenazic *piyyutim* with graceful Sephardic ones, 2) principled and often barely noticeable verbal emendations, and 3) the removal of any petitions for the return of the ancient Temple cult. A companion volume for domestic use called *Hegyon-Lev/ Israelitisches Gebetbuch fuer haeusliche Andacht* (Baltimore, 1867 [#150; #153]; rev. ed., Philadelphia 1875 [#240]) contains not only prayers for specific occasions, but a stripped-down Passover *haggadah*, selections from *Pirqey Avot*, a kind of ethical and halakhic guide based on the Ten Commandments, and, wonderful to relate in this context, technical instructions on how to calculate calendrically the *molad* (the appearance of the new month). While keeping all of Szold's textual emendations and the basic structure and format of *Abodath Israel*, Marcus Jastrow of Rodeph Shalom in Philadelphia, introduced further revisions in phraseology that were in keeping with nineteenth-century Reform theology [#194–#195; #218; #337–#338; #750]. A number of derivatives of the Szold/Jastrow ritual arose through the first quarter of the century following, foremost among them those rites by Aaron Wise and Barnett A. Elzas. They range from Wise's also proto-Conservative, if negligibly more traditional, *Shalhevet Yah, The Temple Service for the Sabbath and the Festivals* (1891) [#453; #469; #1061] for his parsonage, Rodeph Shalom of New York City, to Barnett A. Elzas' unofficially Conservative 1) *Prayer Book for the Sabbath* (New York, 1914) [#890; #893; #1034], 2) *Festival Prayer Book* (New York, 1915; second, enlarged ed. 1923) [#914; #1145], and 3) *Prayer Book for New Year and Day of Atonement* (New York, 1927). Interestingly enough, the latter two, at least on the English side, show the undeniable influence of the Reform *Union Prayer Book*. All of the rites tracing to *Abodath Israel* had a hand in the shaping of the premier authoritative prayerbook of the Conservative movement, *The Festival Prayer Book*, published in 1927 under the aegis of the United Synagogue of America.

One more nineteenth-century prayerbook from New York City deserves particular mention, *Seder Tefillah/ Gebete fuer den oeffentlichen Gottesdienst der Tempelgemeinde Ahawath Chesed* (two volumes, 1872 [#204–#205]; 1875 [#241]). With a prototype for the High Holydays, 1869 [#167], edited by Adolph Huebsch, it is a prime example of what can be seen as a subtle gradation between Reform and Conservative liturgies. The congregation, the bulk of whose membership originated in Bohemia, was unshakably attached to certain liturgical and legal usages but quite willing to be guided in the direction of temperate Reform in other areas. Case in point: while adhering to the standard *matbe'a shel tefillah* of the preliminary benedictions, psalmodic section, the *Shema'* and its benedictions, and the *'Amidah* — to whatever degree they were recast — Huebsch dispensed altogether with the Additional Service for all days dictating it except for Yom Kippur (in part, no doubt, on account of its centerpiece of historical reminiscence, the *'Avodah*, the Service of the High Priest and, in part, because of the position of the ever-compelling *U-Netanneh Toqef*). Despite this radical excision, Huebsch's posthumous replacement at Temple Ahawath Chesed (later renamed the Central Synagogue) and translator of *Gebete*, Alexander Kohut, was one of the earliest proponents and spokesmen of Conservative Judaism — and staunch antagonist of Reform — in America. In 1889 Kohut rendered Huebsch's comely German prayers and hymns into English [#398; #467] with remarkable sensitivity and fidelity. When, as pastor of the synagogue now merged with another (Ahawath Chesed-Shaar Hashomayim), Isaac S. Moses redid — as late as 1916 — the English of the High Holy Day volume of Huebsch's *Gebete*, he brought in a handful of components from *Olath Tamid* and the *Union Prayer Book* [#945]. The many *ab initio* Hebrew alterations and the translational permutations notwithstanding, the Huebsch rite has, after all is said and done, a remarkably traditional aspect. The Huebsch/Kohut prayerbook was an influence on liturgiographer Moses [#455] as he set out to edit the first draft of the *Union Prayer Book* (1891), a decade and a half before he was to come out with his restrained adaptation/update of the Huebsch High Holy Day prayerbook for the New York congregation still attached to the 1872/1875 *boehmischer* Reform rite.

The next two decades of prayerbook creativity were mostly spinoffs of the aforementioned rites. Henry Berkowitz [#550–#551; #1092], Edward B. M. Browne [#327; #340], Edward N. Calisch [#487], Gustav Gottheil [#527–#528], Rudolph Grossman [#543–#544; #630], Kaufmann Kohler [#443–

#444; #546], Joseph Krauskopf [#718], Max Landsberg [#319; #336], J. Leonard Levy [#611–#612; #634], Isaac S. Moses [#325; #369; #472–#473; #479; #485–#486], David Philipson [#445] and others stood in the forefront of intergenerational change (from immigrant to native-born), favoring greater utilization of English in worship in place of German and, to widely varying degrees, Hebrew. There is even a *Jewish Home Prayer-Book: A Manual of Household Devotion* (New York/Cincinnati, 1887/1888) [#370] by the Jewish Ministers' Association of America, an unusual cross-denominational effort. In rare instances, a transitional prayerbook of the 1880s and 1890s would display considerable originality: Gustav Gottheil's *Morning Prayers* (New York, 1889 [#388], designed for worship on Sunday morning); or the several liturgies by Joseph Krauskopf: *The Service Ritual* (Philadelphia, 1888 [#371; #465, #622] for Sunday morning services), *The Service Manual* (Philadelphia, 1892 [#463] for Sabbath, the High Holy Days, the Pilgrim Festivals and Hanukkah, and *The Mourner's Service* (Philadelphia, 1895 [#509]). The Gottheil and Krauskopf volumes reveal Reform at its perhaps most Anglicized and Protestantized. The Hebrew language is reduced to a few select, mostly biblical, verses, while the substance of the liturgy is made up of often-topical readings, often-discursive prayers, responses (again, mostly biblical) and hymns. The *matbeʻa shel tefillah* becomes little more than a vague reminiscence or a faint echo. During services the role of the officiant ("Minister"), whether he is the same as the rabbi/preacher or not, is clearly the leading one. These late nineteenth-century literary efforts were in one way or another to affect the formation of the section in the *Union Prayer Book* devoted to weekday services [#502–#503].

In the meantime progress on the Conservative front continued steadily, if with comparably little fanfare. Congregations using *Abodath Israel* or any of its offshoots became divided between those eventually joining the ranks of Conservative Judaism and those affiliating with the Reform Movement. It is noteworthy that both Szold's and Jastrow's synagogues ultimately enrolled in the [Reform] Union of American Hebrew Congregations. The line of demarcation between liberalizing Conservatism and traditionalist Reform could at times be barely distinguishable.

Over a period of time the Szold-Jastrow *siddur/maḥzor* was slightly redacted to include antiphonal readings on the English side and to reinstate formerly expunged Hebrew prayers like the synagogal *Kiddush* and the *Birkat ha-Ḥodesh* ("Blessing of the Coming Month," replacing the previously broad

English paraphrase of the same), then in line with unfolding normative Conservative practice. One such revision was launched in 1921 [#1112; #1202] by a graduate of the [Conservative] Jewish Theological Seminary of America, Menachem Eichler, primarily on behalf of a traditionalist-leaning Boston Reform congregation, Ohabei Shalom. By the same token, for his Conservative Congregation Adath Jeshurun in Philadelphia, then still using *Abodath Israel*, Max D. Klein compiled a supplementary *Prayers for Use in the Jewish Home* (Philadelphia, 1921 [#1093]) replete with features unmistakably reminiscent of Reform ritual and both musical and textual practice.

Other Conservative rites evolved that were not as ambiguous as those based on Szold's and Jastrow's *Abodath Israel* but instead were materially Orthodox, even though they allowed for supplementary prayers in the vernacular, such as a prayer before the *Kaddish*, an invocation on behalf of the United States government, and an entreaty alongside the *Birkat ha-Hodesh*. The standard Hebrew texts are in no way impinged. Among such "unspoiled" prayerbooks of Conservative bent prior to those issued by the United Synagogue and/or the Rabbinical Assembly, are those edited by Jacob Bosniak, *Tefillot Yisrael/Prayers of Israel* (2 volumes, Brooklyn, N.Y., 1925) [#1238] and by Julius Silberfeld, *Tefillat Shabbat/The Sabbath Service* (New York, 1905) [#749; #856; #964]. As for those congregations wanting a service on Friday night after dinner that did not compete or conflict with the earlier *Qabbalat Shabbat* service, Israel Goldfarb and Israel H. Levinthal furnished a prayerbook containing fragments of the Sabbath Eve Service with English prayers and readings, and an assortment of synagogue hymns and *zemirot* ordinarily sung at home. The long-popular Conservative rite is called *Zemirot ve-Tishbahot le-Leyl Shabbat/Songs and Praise for Sabbath Eve* (Brooklyn, 1920) [#1070–#1072; #1225].

The two decades immediately following the conclusion of the Wachs's bibliography, and therefore not covered in it, were the start of a new era in prayerbook-making. In the thirties the major and prolific liturgiographer of Conservative Judaism, Morris Silverman, first made his mark with his *Tefillot le-Shabbat ve-Shalosh Regalim/Sabbath and Festival Services* (Hartford, Conn., 1936; rev. 1937), the immediate forerunner of the official *Seder Tefillot Yisrael le-Shabbat ule-Shalosh Regalim/Sabbath and Festival Prayer Book* (New York, 1946), under the joint auspices of the Rabbinical Assembly of America and the United Synagogue of America. Within the same time frame the *Union Prayer Book* underwent a major revision in favor of an increased traditionalism, the first volume in 1940 and the second in 1945. Meanwhile the youngest of the religious movements in American Judaism, Reconstructionism, came out with a *haggadah*, a *siddur* for Shabbat and a *maḥzor* for the High Holy Days respectively in 1942, 1946 and 1948. The new era also simultaneously betokened a clearer definition of boundaries, as well as a hefty and healthy cross-fertilization among the liturgies of the different branches of Judaism in the United States. To a substantial degree the practice, both knowingly and unawares, holds equally true even today.

Eric L. Friedland
Dayton, Ohio

Abbreviations

Deinard — Deinard, Ephraim. קהלת אמעריקא. St. Louis: Moinester Printing Co., 1926

Kaganoff — Kaganoff, Nathan. "Supplement III: Judaica Americana Printed Before 1851." In *Studies in Jewish Bibliography, History and Literature in Honor of I. Edward Kiev*, edited by Charles Berlin, 177–209. New York: Ktav, 1971.

Levine — Levine, Allen E. *An American Jewish Bibliography: A List of Books and Pamphlets by Jews or Relating to Them, Printed in the United States from 1851–1875, which are in the Possession of the Hebrew Union College-Jewish Institute of Religion in Cincinnati*. Cincinnati: American Jewish Archives on the Campus of the Hebrew Union College-Jewish Institute of Religion, 1959.

Marcus — Marcus, Jacob R. *Jewish Americana: A Catalogue of Books and Articles by Jews or Relating to Them, From the Earliest Days to 1850, and Found in the Posesion of the Hebrew Union College-Jewish Institute of Religion in Cincinnati, a Supplement to A.S.W. Rosenbach "An American Bibliography."* Cincinnati: American Jewish Archives on the Campus of the Hebrew Union College, 1954.

Rosenbach — Rosenbach, A.S.W. *An American Jewish Bibliography: Being a List of Books and Pamphlets by Jews or Relating to Them Printed in the United States From the Establishment of the Press in the Colonies Until 1850*. New York: American Jewish Historical Society, 1926.

Sendrey — Sendrey, Alfred. *Bibliography of Jewish Music*. New York: Columbia University Press, 1951.

Singerman — Singerman, Robert. *Judaica Americana: A Bibliography of Publications to 1900*. Sponsored by the Center for the Study of the American Jewish Experience, Hebrew Union College-Jewish Institute of Religion. New York: Greenwood Press, 1990. (2 vols.)

Wolf — Wolf, Edwin, 2nd. "Some Unrecorded American Judaica Printed Before 1851." In *Essays in American Jewish History: To Commemorate the Tenth Anniversary of the Founding of the American Jewish Archives under the Direction of Jacob Rader Marcus*, 187–245 [New York]: Ktav, 1975.

Selected Bibliography

Binder, A.W. "A History of American Jewish Hymnody." In *Studies in Jewish Music: Collected Writings of A.W. Binder*, edited by Irene Heskes, 255–269. New York: Bloch, 1971.

———. "A Perspective on Synagogue Music in America." In *Studies in Jewish Music: Collected Writings of A.W. Binder*, edited by Irene Heskes, 270–281. New York: Bloch, 1971.

Cohon, Samuel S. "The Theology of the Union Prayer Book." In, *Reform Judaism: A Historical Perspective: Essays from the Yearbook of the Central Conference of American Rabbis*, edited by Joseph Blau, 257–284. New York: Ktav, 1973. First published in *CCAR Yearbook* (1928).

Eisenstein, Judah David. "Prayer-books" In *The Jewish Encyclopedia*, Vol. 10, pp. 164–180. [New York]: Ktav, 1964.

Elbogen, Ismar. *Jewish Liturgy: A Comprehensive History*. Philadelphia: Jewish Publication Society, 1993. Translated from the original German by Raymond P. Scheindlin.

Encyclopaedia Judaica. Jerusalem: Encyclopaedia Judaica; New York: Macmillan, 1971–1972.

Evans, Charles. *American Bibliography: A Chronological Dictionary of all Books, Pamphlets and Periodical Publications Printing in the United States of America from the Genesis of Printing in 1639 Down to and Including the Year 1800*. Chicago, 1903–34; Worcester, 1955–59.

Friedland, Eric. *The Historical and Theological Development of the Non-orthodox Prayerbooks in the United States*. Ph.D. dissertation, Brandeis University, 1967. Ann Arbor: University Microfilms, 1967, c1968.

———. "Jewish Worship since its Canonization." In *The Making of Jewish and Christian Worship*. Edited by Paul F. Bradshaw and Lawrence A Hoffman. Notre Dame: University of Notre Dame Press, 1991.

———. "Olath Tamid by David Einhorn." *Hebrew Union College Annual* 45 (1974): 307–332.

Goldscmidt-Lehmann, Ruth P. *1784–1885*, משה מאנטיפיורי. Jerusalem: Misgav Yerushalayim, 1984.

Gordis, Robert. "A Jewish Prayer Book for the Modern Age." In his *Understanding Conservative Judaism*, 132–154. New York: Rabbinical Assembly, 1978.

Harvard University Library. *Catalogue of Hebrew Books.* Cambridge, Mass.: Harvard University Library, 1968 (Supplement, 1972)

———. *Judaica: Classification Schedule, Classified Listing by Call Number, Chronological Listing, Author and Title Listing.* Cambridge, Mass: Published by the Harvard University Library: Distributed by the Harvard University Press, 1971. (Widener Library Shelflist, 39)

Hebrew Union College-Jewish Institute of Religion. *HUC-JIR Alumni Directory.* Cincinnati: Rabbinic Alumni Association and Hebrew Union College-Jewish Institute of Religion, 1992.

Hebrew Union College-Jewish Institute of Religion. *Dictionary Catalog of the Klau Library. Cincinnati.* Boston: G. K. Hall, 1964.

Hirsch, Emil G. "Reform Judaism from the Point of View of the Reform Jew." In *The Jewish Encyclopedia*, Vol. 10, pp. 347–352. [New York]: Ktav, 1964.

Hoffman, Lawrence A. "American Jewish Liturgies." In his *Beyond the Text: A Holistic Approach to Liturgy.* Bloomington: Indiana University Press, c1987.

———. *The Canonization of the Synagogue Service.* Notre Dame, University of Notre Dame Press, 1979.

———. "The Language of Survival in American Reform Liturgy." *CCAR Journal*, Summer 1977, pp. 87–106.

Idelsohn, A. Z. "The Liturgy of Reform Judaism." In his *Jewish Liturgy and its Development.* New York: Schocken Books, c1932.

Jick, Leon A. *The Americanization of the Synagogue, 1820–1870.* Hanover, N.H.: Published for Brandeis University Press by the University Press of New England, 1976.

Korros, Alexandra Shecket and Sarna, Jonathan D. *American Synagogue History: A Bibliography and State-of-the-Field Survey.* New York: Markus Weiner, c1988.

Madison, Charles A. *Jewish Publishing in America: The Impact of Jewish Writing on American Culture.* New York: Sanhedrin Press, c1976.

Millgram, Abraham E. *Jewish Worship.* Philadelphia: Jewish Publication Society, 1971.

Meyer, Michael A. *Response to Modernity: A History of the Reform Movement in Judaism.* New York: Oxford University Press, 1988.

Nadel, Pamela S. *Conservative Judaism in America: A Biographical Dictionary and Sourcebook.* New York: Greenwood Press, 1988.

National Union Catalog, Pre-1956 Imprints. A Cumulative Author List Representing

Selected Bibliography

Library of Congress Printed Cards and Titles Reported by other American Libraries. Compiled and Edited with the Cooperation of the Resources and Technical Services Division, American Library Association. London: Mansell, 1968–1981.

New York Public Library. Reference Dept. *Dictionary Catalog of the Jewish Collection.* Boston: G. K. Hall, 1960.

Petuchowski, Jakob J. *Prayerbook Reform in Europe: The Liturgy of European Liberal and Reform Judaism.* New York: World Union for Progressive Judaism, c1968.

———. *Understanding Jewish Prayer.* New York: Ktav, 1972.

Philipson, David. *The Reform Movement in Judaism.* Reissue of new and revised edition. Introduction by Solomon B. Freehof. New York: Ktav, 1967.

———. "The Reform Prayer Book." *Journal of Jewish Lore and Philosophy* 1 (1919): 69–82, 211–223.

Schiller, Benjie-Ellen. "The Hymnal as an Index of Musical Change in Reform Synagogues." In *Sacred Sound and Social Change: Liturgical Music in Jewish and Christian Experience,* edited by Lawrence A. Hoffman and Janet R. Walton. Notre Dame: University of Notre Dame Press, c1992.

Silberman, Lou H. "The Union Prayer Book: A Study in Liturgical Development." In *Retrospect and Prospect,* edited by Bertram Wallace Korn. *New York: Central Conference of American Rabbis,* 1965.

Wiener, Theodore. "Addenda to Yaari's *Bibliography of the Passover Haggadah* from the Library of Congress Hebraica Collection." In *Studies in Jewish Bibliography, History and Literature in Honor of I. Edward Kiev,* edited by Charles Berlin, 511–516. New York: Ktav, 1971.

Wertheimer, Jack, ed. *The American Synagogue: A Sanctuary Transformed.* Cambridge [Eng.]; New York: Cambridge University Press, 1987.

Yaari, Abraham. ביבליוגרפיה של הגדות פסח מראשית הדפוס ועד היום. Jerusalem: Bamberger et Vahrman, [1960].

National Union Catalog Abbreviations

Symbols of selected libraries and collections most frequently represented in this bibliography are listed below. In addition, a few initialisms representing private collections are included.

AJK	Abraham J. Karp (Rochester, N.Y.)
CLHU	Hebrew Union College (Los Angeles, Ca.)
CLJ	University of Judaism (Los Angeles, Ca.)
CLU	University of California (Los Angeles, Ca.)
CU	University of California (Berkeley, Ca.)
CU-B	Bancroft Library, University of California (Berkeley, Ca.)
CSt	Stanford University (Stanford, Ca.)
CtY	Yale University (New Haven, Conn.)
DLC	Library of Congress (Washington, D.C.) *Includes uncataloged materials held by the Hebraic Section.*
DPC	Donald P. Cashman (Albany, N.Y.)
FU	University of Florida (Gainesville, Fla.)
GEU	Emory University (Atlanta, Ga.)
IaU	University of Iowa (Iowa City, Iowa)
ICJS	Spertus College of Jewish Studies (Chicago, Ill.)
ICN	Newberry Library (Chicago, Ill.)
ICU	University of Chicago (Chicago, Ill.)
InU	Indiana University (Bloomington, Ind.)
LNHT	Tulane University (New Orleans, La.)
MB	Boston Public Library (Boston, Mass.)
MH	Harvard University (Cambridge, Mass.)
MH-AH	Andover-Harvard Theological Seminary (Cambridge, Mass.)
MHi	Massachusetts Historical Society (Boston, Mass.)
MWA	Massachusetts Antiquarian Society (Worcester, Mass.)
MWalA	American Jewish Historical Society (Waltham, Mass.)
MWalB	Brandeis University (Waltham, Mass.)
MiU	University of Michigan (Ann Arbor, Mich.)
N	New York State Library (Albany, N.Y.)

NAlU	University at Albany, State University of New York (Albany, N.Y.)
NcD	Duke University (Durham, N.C.)
NcU	University of North Carolina (Chapel Hill, N.C.)
NhD	Dartmouth University (Hanover, N.H.)
NIC	Cornell University (Ithaca, N.Y.)
NjP	Princeton University (Princeton, N.J.)
NN	New York Public Library (New York, N.Y.)
NN-Br	New York Public Library, Branch System
NNC	Columbia University (New York, N.Y.)
NNHeb	Hebrew Union College-Jewish Institute of Religion (New York, N.Y.)
NNJ	Jewish Theological Seminary of America (New York, N.Y.)
NNUT	Union Theological Seminary (New York, N.Y.)
NNYI	Yivo Institute for Jewish Research (New York, N.Y.)
NNYU	Yeshiva University (New York, N.Y.)
NRU	Rochester University (Rochester, N.Y.)
OCAJA	American Jewish Archives (Cincinnati, Ohio)
OCH	Hebrew Union College (Cincinnati, Ohio)
OCl	Cleveland Public Library (Cleveland, Ohio)
OO	Oberlin College (Oberlin, Ohio)
OU	Ohio State University (Columbus, Ohio)
PHi	Historical Society of Pennsylvania (Philadelphia, Pa.)
PPAmP	American Philosophical Society (Philadelphia, Pa.)
PPAnR	Annenberg Research Institute (Philadelphia, Pa.) *Formerly Dropsie College: PPDrop, now the University of Pennsylvania, Center for Judaic Studies*
PPGratz	Gratz College (Melrose Park, Pa.)
PPL	Library Company of Philadelphia (Philadelphia, Pa.)
PU	University of Pennsylvania (Philadelphia, Pa.)
RPB	Brown University (Providence, R.I.)
RPJCB	John Carter Brown Library (Providence, R.I.)
SPW	Saul P. Wachs (Bala Cynwyd, Pa.)
TNJ	Joint University Libraries (Nashville, Tenn.)
TxU	University of Texas (Austin, Tex.)
UPB	Brigham Young University (Provo, Utah)
UU	University of Utah (Salt Lake City, Utah)
WJHC	Western Jewish History Center (Berkeley, Ca.)

Bibliography

1760

1. The form of the prayer which was performed at the Jews' synagogue in the city of New York, on Thursday October 23, 1760: being the day appointed by proclamation for a general Thanksgiving to Almighty God for the reducing of Canada to His Majesty's dominions/composed by Joseph Yeshurun Pinto in the Hebrew language; and translated into English by a Friend to truth. — New York: W. Weyman, 1760.

7 p. Rosenbach: 39. Singerman: 32. Copies: OCH PHi

1761

2. Evening service of Roshashanah, and Kippur, or the Beginning of the Year and the Day of Atonement. — New York: W. Weyman, MDCCLXI [1761].

52 p. English, with romanized prayer titles. Translated by Isaac Pinto. Rosenbach: 41. Singerman: 35. Copies: MH-AH MWalA NNJ OCH PPL PPRF

1765

3. Prayers for the Sabbath, Rosh-Hashanah, and Kippur, or the Sabbath, the Begining [sic] of the Year, and the day of Atonements: with the Amidah and Musaph of the Moadim, or solemn seasons: according to the order of the Spanish and Portuguese Jews/translated by Isaac Pinto. — New York: John Holt, A.M. 5526 [1765 or 1766].

iv, 190, i p. Rosenbach: 46. Singerman: 40. Copies: MB MH MWalA PMA.

4. Prayers for the Sabbath, Rosh-Hashanah, and Kippur, or the Sabbath, the Beginning of the Year, and the day of Atonements: with the Amidah and Musaph of the Moadim, or solemn seasons: according to the order of the Spanish and Portuguese Jews/translated by Isaac Pinto. — New York: John Holt, A.M. 5526 [1765 or 1766].

iv, 190, i p. Deinard: 472, 951. Rosenbach: 47. Singerman: 40. Copies: CtY DLC FU MH MiU-C MWA MWalA NHi NN OCH PPAnR PPL PPRF RPB RPJCB

1789

5. Religious discourse delivered in the synagogue in this city: on Thursday the 26th November, 1789: agreeable to the proclamation of the President of the United States of America, to be observed as a day of public thanksgiving and prayer/by the Reverend Mr. Gershom Seixas. — New-York: Printed by Archibald M'Lean, at Franklin's Head, MDCC,LXXXIX.

16 p. Prayers for the Government and a prayer for the Hazan: pp. 15–16. Rosenbach: 80. Singerman: 69. Copies: OCH PHi

18–

6. Friday evening service/by M. Goldstein. — [s.l.: s.n., 18–].

Score (13 p.) English and romanized Hebrew. For Cantor, chorus (SATB), with organ accompaniment. Copies: OCH

1816

7. Order of the service for Sabbath Evening פרשת יתרו 5576 being the celebration of the depositing of a ספר תורה in the היכל

of the ק"ק מקוה ישראל.— Philadelphia, 1816.

1 p. Includes the text of an acrostic hymn in Hebrew. Kaganoff: 21. Singerman: 262. Copies: MW MWalA

1817

8. Form of the service at the dedication of the new synagogue of "Kahal Kadosh Shearith Israel"/M.L.M.Piexotto, E.S.Lazarus, Aaron Levy, Committee of Arrangement. — New York: J.Seymour, 5578 [1817 or 1818].

24 p. English and Hebrew. Includes a hymn composed by Rabbi Pique. Rosenbach: 197. Singerman: 289. Copies: MWalA NN OCH PPAnR

1824

9. אלה השירים והפסוקים מהקפות מהספרים לחנוכת בית הכנסת ,מקוה ישראל, דק"ק פילאדעלפיא בשנת [תקפ"ה]
Form of the service at the dedication of the new synagogue of the "Kahal Kadosh Mickvi Israel" in the city of Philadelphia. — New York: S.H.Jackson, 5585 [1824 or 1825].

18, 18 p. English and Hebrew. Deinard: 48. Rosenbach: 278. Singerman: 427. Copies: NN NNJ NNYU (Sephardic Reference Room) OCH PPAmp PPAnR PPGratz PPL

1825

10. סדר התפילות כמנהג ק"ק ספרדים יז"א: מתוקן בסדר נאה ויפה והוגה/ה/ע"י המדקדק אליעזר ב' שמואל. – נו-יארק: נדפס על ידי שלמה בן צבי הירש מלונדון, שנת [תקפ"ו].
The form of daily prayers according to the custom of the Spanish and Portuguese Jews as read in their synagogues and used in their families/translated into English from Hebrew by Solomon Henry Jackson; the Hebrew text carefully revised by E.S. Lazarus. — 1st ed. — New York: Printed by S.H.Jackson at the Hebrew and English Printing Office, A.M. 5586 [1825 or 1826].

234, 234, 11 p. English and Hebrew. Deinard: 953. Rosenbach: 284. Singerman: 436. Copies: CLamB MH MH-AH MWalA NjNbs NNJ OCH PPGratz PPL ViAlTh

1826

11. Compendium of the order of the burial service, and rules for the mournings, &c: compiled by the desire, and published on the account of the חברה חסד ואמת of the ק"ק ספרדים שארית ישראל. — New York, 5587 [1826 or 1827].

12, 18, 18 p. English and Hebrew. Deinard: 267, 687. Rosenbach: 291. Singerman: 447. Copies: MWalA NN NNC NNJ NNYU (Sephardic Reference Room) OCH (photostat) PPL

1830

12. The Sabbath service and miscellaneous prayers adopted by the Reformed Society of Israelites: founded in Charleston, South Carolina November 21, 1825. — Charleston: J.S.Burges, 1830.

68 p. Isaac Harby, Abraham Moïse and David Nuñes Carvalho are unnamed compilers. Rosenbach: 327. Singerman: 488. Copies: Gu NN

1834

13. אלה השירים והפסוקים מהקפות הספרים לחנוכת בית הכנסת שארית ישראל=
Form of the Service at the dedication of the new synagogue of Kahal Kadosh Shearith Israel in Crosby-Street, New

York ... — [New York]: S. H. Jackson, 5594 [1834].

12, 12 p. English and Hebrew. Rosenbach: 382. Singerman: 583. Copies: MWalA NN

1837

14. The feast of Tabernacles: a poem for music in two parts / by Henry Ware. — Cambridge: J. Owen, 1837.

x, 38 p. Pt. I. The morning service. — Pt. II. The evening service. Without the music of Charles Zeuner. Kaganoff: 54. Singerman: 639. Copies: CSmH DLC MB MH MWA MWalA NhD NN NNC OU RPB ViU

15. The feast of Tabernacles: an oratorio / the music by Charles Zeuner; the words by Henry Ware; performed at the Odeon by the Choir and Orchestra of the Boston Academy of Music. — [Cambridge: J. Owen], 1837.

12 p. Kaganoff: 55. Singerman: 642. Copies: CtY MdBJ MH MWalA NN NcU

16. The feast of Tabernacles: an oratorio in two parts: morning and evening sacrifice / the words by Henry Ware; the music by Ch. Zeuner. — [Cambridge, Mass: Printed by G. A. and J. Curtis, c 1837.]

Score (87 p.). Holdings: CtY

17. סדור שפתי צדיקים ... כמנהג ק"ק ספרדים / הוגה בשקידה מרבה מאתי הקטן יצחק בן אורי ן' אליעזר ש"ץ דק"ק מקוה ישראל בפילאדעלפיא. — פה פילאדעלפיא: בבית הדפוס של המשתתפים הזוויל, במצות ובהוצאת המחבר, בשנת 5597-5598.

The form of prayers according to the custom of the Spanish and Portuguese Jews / edited, and with former translations carefully compared and corrected by Isaac Leeser, Reader of the Congregation Mikveh Israel of Philadelphia. — Philadelphia: Haswell, Barrington, and Haswell, 5597-5598, [1837-1838].

6 v. English and Hebrew. V.1. Daily prayers. — V.2. New Year service. — V.3. Day of Atonement service. — V.4. Tabernacle service. — V.5. Passover and Pentecost service. — V.6. Fast Day service. Deinard: 950. Rosenbach: 411. Singerman: 630. Copies: CU DLC (uncat) Jewish Community Library of Los Angeles MWalA NjPT NN NNYU (Sephardic Reference Room) OCH PPAnR OO (V.4) PPGratz PPL PU

1838

18. Rebecca Gratz prayers. — Philadelphia: Hebrew Sunday School Society, 1838.

2 p. Singerman: 647. Copies: PPAnR (lost)

1841

19. Order of service in the synagogue of the Congregation שארית ישראל Crosby-Street, New York: 14th day of May 5601 ... in consequence of the death of the late President, Wm. H. Harrison. — [New York, 1841].

1 p. English and Hebrew. Includes a Kinah. Deinard: 264. Singerman: 752. Copies: MWalA

1842

20. Hymns written for the service of the Hebrew Congregation, Beth Elohim, Charleston, S.C. — [Charleston]: Levin & Tavel, 1842.

iv, [1], 6–80 p. Most hymns are signed P.M. [i.e. Penina Moïse]. Rosenbach: 494. Singerman: 770. Copies: DLC (microfilm) GDC ICN MWalA NN OCH PPAnR PPL

21. סדר חנוכת הבית והשירים אשר שרו קהל בית אל ביום חנוכת בית מקדש מעט בית תפילתינו פה אלבני =
Order of the consecration of the synagogue Beth-El at Albany. — New York: S.H. Jackson, 5602.

2, 4–12, 4–12 p. Hebrew and English. Marcus: 179. Singerman: 768. Copies: OCH

1843

22. Gesänge und Gebete zu der Am Adar ראשון ג (Februar 3,) statthabenden Einweihung der neuen Synagogue Rodoph Scholom zu New-York: In hebräischer und deutscher Sprache, New York, 5603. — New-York: Jackson, Printer, 1843.

17 p. German and Hebrew on facing pages. Rosenbach: 504. Singerman: 818. Copies: MWalA

23. Order of service at the consecration of the synagogue Roudafe Sholum, of Philadelphia, on Wednesday 12th of Nissan 5603, 12th of April 1843. — Philadelphia: C. Sherman, 5603.

24 p. English and Hebrew. Deinard: 47. Rosenbach: 515 (Entry says Roudef, facsimile says Roudafe). Singerman: 824 (Entry says Roudef). Copies: A.S.W. Rosenbach and Cyrus Adler had personal copies.

24. אדון עולם: adapted to a favourite air of Bertoni/arranged for the voice, with piano accompaniment by E. Roget. — Philadelphia: The Occident, 1843.

Score (p.143–144) Romanized Hebrew. "Dedicated to the Portuguese Congregation of Philadelphia." Extracted from the *Occident* v.1, no.3. Sendrey: 7122. Copies: PPGratz

1845

25. סדור שפתי צדיקים ... כמנהג ק"ק ספרדים/ הוגה בשקידה מרבה מאתי הקטן יצחק בן אורי ן' אליעזר ש"ץ דק"ק מקוה ישראל בפילאדעלפיא. — פה פילאדעלפיא: נדפס שנית בבית הגביר קונגר שרמן במצות ובהוצאת המסדר.

The form of prayers according to the custom of the Spanish and Portuguese Jews/ edited, and with former translations carefully compared and corrected by Isaac Leeser, Reader of the Congregation Mikveh Israel of Philadelphia. — 2nd ed. rev. — Philadelphia: Printed by C. Sherman for the editor, 5606–5610 [1845 or 1846–1849 or 1850].

6 v. English and Hebrew. V.1. Daily prayers. — V.2. New Year service. — V.3. Day of Atonement service. — V.4. Tabernacle service. — V.5. Passover and Pentecost service. — V.6. Fast Day service. Rosenbach: 590. Singerman: 939. Copies: CtY (V.1) NNJ NNYU OCH (V.1. only)

1847

26. Order of service at the consecration of the synagogue Rodef Sholum, of Philadelphia, on Wednesday, Elul 27th, 5607, September 8th 1847. — Philadelphia: C. Sherman, 5607 [1847].

23 p. Rosenbach: 614 (Entry says Roudafe, facsimile says Rodef). Singerman: 997 (Entry says Rodef). Copies: A.S.W. Rosenbach personal copy MW

27. סדר חנוכת הבית והשירים אשר ישוררו קהל שערי תפלה לאל חי שישפכו לפני ה' ביום חנוכת בית מקדש מעט, וואוסטער סטריהט, נוא-יארק יום ע"ש ק' י"א תמוז פרשת חקת ובלק בשנת [1847]. — נוא-יארק: נדפס על ידי יעקב בן שלמה.

סדר חנוכת הבית = Order of the service: to be performed at the consecration of the new synagogue "The Gates of Prayer," Wooster Street, New-York, on Friday, Tammuz the 11th, corresponding with June 25th 5607 [1847]. — New York: J. M. Jackson.

23 p. Hebrew and English. Rosenbach: 615. Singerman: 983. Copies: MH MWalA

1848

28. Auswahl deutscher Gesänge zum Gebrauche im Tempel der Imanu-El Congregation in New-York. — Nebst Anhang. — New-York: J. Mühlhäuser, [1848?].

82, [1] p. Kaganoff: 166. Singerman: 1042. Copies: MWalA NNJ

29. Translation of the order of the service at the consecration of the synagogue Bayth Ahabah, of Richmond, Va.: on Thursday, Elul 23d, 5608, September 21st 1848. — Richmond: Printed by I. Lyon, 1848.

8 p. Singerman: 1051. Copies: Vi ViR Val

30. סדור דברי צדיקים: כולל סדר התפלות מכל השנה כמנהג ק״ק אשכנז ופולין/הוגה ונעתק ללשון אנגליא מאתי הקטן יצחק בן אורי בן אליעזר, ש״ץ דק״ק מקוה ישראל בפילאדלפיא. — פה פילאדעלפיא: בבית ובדפוס של קונגר שרמן במצות המסדר, בשנת [תר״ח]. The book of daily prayers for every day in the year according to the custom of the German and Polish Jews/edited by Isaac Leeser, Minister of the Congregation Mikveh Israel of Philadelphia. — Philadelphia: Printed by C. Sherman for the editor, 5608 [1848].

243, 243 p. English and Hebrew. Deinard: 959. Rosenbach: 636. Singerman: 1024. Copies: CBGTU CLHU CLJ CtY DLC ICU MBAt MH MWA MWalA NIC NjNbs NN NNYI OCH PPAnR PPGratz

31. סדר חנוכת הבית והשירים אשר ישררו קהל בית יעקב ביום חנוכת בית מקדש מעט בית תפלה פה אלבני: יום ו' עש״ק כ״ה ניסן שנת ופתחו שעריך לפ״ק. — נוא יארק: נדפס על ידי יעקב בן שלמה, תר״ח. Order of consecration service of the Congregation Beth Jacob, at Albany: on the eve of the Sabbath, Nissan 25, 5608. — New-York: J. M. Jackson, 5608.

18 p. English and Hebrew. Deinard: 591. Rosenbach: 624. Singerman: 1009. Copies: MWA N NHi NN OCAJA

32. תפלות ישראל = Prayers of Israel with an English translation. — New York: H. Frank, 5609 [1848 or 1849].

243, 229 p. English and Hebrew. Pt. 1. יום טוב, ראש השנה. — Pt. 2. שבת וחול. יום כפור. Deinard: 921–923? Singerman: 1023. Copies: NNJ OCH

1849

33. סדר חנוכת הבית = Order of service to be performed at the consecration of the synagogue Beth Israel, Crown Street, Philadelphia: on Thursday, Nissan the 6th, corresponding with March 29th 5609. — New York: J. M. Jackson, 5609.

24 p. Rosenbach: 657. Singerman: 1090. Copies: NNJ PPAnR

34. סליחות ליום כפור = Order of Selihot to be recited on Yom Kippur. — New York: Ya'akov ben Shelomoh: Printed for Congregation Sha'are Tefilah (Gates of Prayer), 5610, [1849 or 1850].

1 p. English and Hebrew. Kaganoff: 187. Singerman: 1073. Copies: OCH

1850

35. Order of service at the consecration of the synagogue Nefutsoth Jehudah of New-Orleans on Tuesday, May 14th, 1850,

5610. — New Orleans: J. Cohn, Printer, 1850.

8 p. Rosenbach: 678. Wolf: 225. Singerman: 1142. Copies: MWalA PPAnR TxU

36. הזכרת נשמות = Gebete und Gesänge zur Seelenfeier: Begangen am Versöhungstage in der Imanu-El Gemeinde zu New York. — New York: Druck von J. Mühlhaüser und H. Frank, 1850.

16 p. German and Hebrew. Marcus: 226. Singerman: 1130. Copies: OCH

37. תפלות החולה = Kranken Gebete des Hebra Bikur Holim Vekadisha. — New York, 1850.

21 p. Singerman: 1131. Copies: NNJ

1851

38. Order of service and the consecration of the synagogue Shangarai Chesed, on Rampart Street, New-Orleans: Wednesday, Second Adar 1st, 5611 (March 5th 1851). — New Orleans: Printed at the Job Office of J. Cohn, 1851.

8 p. Singerman: 1201. Copies: MWalA

39. Order of service on laying the first stone of the synagogue K.K. B'ne Jeshurun, Greene Street: on Tuesday the 23rd of Adar Rishon, 5611, February 25th, 1851. — New York: J.M. Jackson, [1851].

12 p. Singerman: 1204. Copies: MWalA

1852

40. סדור שפת אמת/מאת וואלף ב"ר שמשון דוב איש היידנהיים. — מהד' י"ז. — New York: H. Frank, 1852.

214 p. Deinard: 935. He claims 1842, but edition is correct. Levine: 23. Singerman: 1240. Copies: DLC (uncat) NNJ OCH

41. סדר חנוכת בית הכנסת בית ישראל בעיר ווילימסבארג, יום א' ט"ז אב.
Order of consecration of the synagogue "House of Israel" Williamsburgh, 1st Day of August, 5612/arranged by David Barnard. — New York: J.M. Jackson, 1852.

12 p. English and Hebrew. Deinard: 323. Singerman: 1229. Copies: MWalA NN

42. רחמה = Devotional exercises for the use of the daughters of Israel: intended for public and private worship on the various occasions of woman's life/compiled and translated with emendations from the German of Letteris, Miro & Stern, and edited by M.J. Raphall. — New York: L. Joachimssen, 1852.

139, iii p. Levine: 27. Singerman: 1260. Copies: MWalA NN NNJ OCH PPL

1853

43. מחזור...כמנהג אשכנז: מסודר בשלימות הסדור ומדויק בתכלית הדיוק/מאת וואלף בר שמשון דוב איש היידנהיים. — נוא יארק: בבית ובדפוס חיים פראנק.
Form of prayers for the... according to the custom of the German Jews: with English translation. — New York: H. Frank, 5614 [1853 or 1854].

2 v. English and Hebrew. V.1 New Year. — V.2. Day of Atonement. Deinard: 467 (V.1). Levine: 57. Singerman: 1284. Copies: MWalA (V.2) NNJ OCH

44. מחזור...כמנהג פולין: מסודר בשלימות הסדור ומדויק בתכלית הדיוק/מאת וואלף בר שמשון איש היידנהיים. — נוא יארק: בבית ובדפוס חיים פראנק.
Form of prayers for the... according to the custom of the Polish Jews: with English translation. — New York: H. Frank, 5614 [1853 or 1854].

2 v. English and Hebrew. V.1 New

Year. —V. 2. Day of Atonement. Levine: 58. Singerman: 1285. Copies: CtY NNJ OCH PPAnR

45. סדור שפתי צדיקים...כמנהג ק״ק ספרדים / הוגה בשקידה מרבה מאתי הקטן יצחק בן אורי נ׳ אליעזר. — פה פילאדעלפיא: במצות ובהוצאת המסדר, בשנת [תקפ״ג]. The form of prayers according to the custom of the Spanish and Portuguese Jews / edited by Isaac Leeser. — 2nd ed. — Philadelphia: Stereotyped by Slote & Mooney, 1853.

6 v. English and Hebrew. V. 1. Daily prayers. —V. 2. New Year service. —V. 3. Day of Atonement service. —V. 4. Tabernacle service. —V. 5. Passover and Pentecost service. —V. 6. Fast Day service. Copies: CLJ (V. 5–6) CU (V. 1, V. 6) MWalA PPGratz (V. 4–6)

46. סדור שפתי צדיקים...כמנהג ק״ק ספרדים / הוגה בשקידה מרבה מאתי הקטן יצחק בן אורי נ׳ אליעזר. — פה פילאדעלפיא: במצות ובהוצאת המסדר, בשנת [תקפ״ג–תקפ״ז]. The form of prayers according to the custom of the Spanish and Portuguese Jews / edited by Isaac Leeser. — 2nd ed. — Philadelphia: Stereotyped by Slote & Mooney, 1853–1857.

6 v. English and Hebrew. V. 1. Daily prayers. —V. 2. New Year service. —V. 3. Day of Atonement service. —V. 4. Tabernacle service. —V. 5. Passover and Pentecost service. —V. 6. Fast Day service. Deinard: 933. Levine 45. Copies: MWalA (V. 3 only 1857) NNJ NNYU (Sephardic Reference Room) OCH (V. 2–6) RPB (V. 3 only 1857)

47. תפלות ישראל = Prayers of Israel with an English translation. — 2nd ed. — New York: H. Frank, 1853.

1 v. (various pagings) English and Hebrew. Levine 702 (Not the same as Levine 44). See Singerman: 1023. Copies: OCH

48. תפלות ישראל = Prayers of Israel with an English translation. — 2nd ed. — New York: H. Frank, 1853.

243, 229 p. English and Hebrew. Levine: 44. See Singerman: 1023. Copies: CLHU (uncat) OCH

49. תפלות ישראל = Prayers of Israel with an English translation. — 2nd ed. — New York: H. Frank, 1853.

183, 172 p. See Singerman: 1023. Copies: OCH

1854

50. Gesänge zur feierlichen Einweihung des Versöhnungstages, 1854. — [Albany, N.Y.: South Pearl Street Synagogue, 1854].

7 p. Signed at end: Dr. E. Cohn, Rabbiner; Jos. Sporberg, Präs. Synagogue was named Anshe Emeth. Singerman: 1309. Copies: MH

51. Programme of the dedication service of the synagogue Emmanu-El... Broadway above Stockton St.: Thursday September 14, 5615. — San Francisco: Whitton Towne & Co., Printers, 1854.

8 p. Levine: 65. Singerman: 1356. Copies: OCH (photostat copy)

52. תפילות החולה = Kranken-Gebete für die חברה אחים רחמנים Gesellschaft Brüder der Barmherzigeit. — New York: Gedruckt bei S. S. Buchsweiler, 1854.

22 p. German and Hebrew. Deinard: 908. Singerman: 1336. Copies: DLC MH NN

1855

53. ...מחזור = Form of prayers... according to the custom of the German and

Polish Jews: with English translation. — New York: H. Frank, 5616.

    5 v. English and Hebrew. V.1. New Year. — V.2. Day of Atonement. — V.3. Feast of Tabernacles. — V.4. Feast of Passover. — V.5. Feast of Pentecost. Deinard: 465, 469. Levine: 118. Singerman: 1385. Copies: DLC (uncat) FU MH (V.3–5) MWalA (V.1, V.3) MWalB (V.5) PPAnR

54. סדר העבודה ביום חנוכת בית חולים אשר ליהודים בנוא יארק, ערב ר"ח סיון תרט"ו. Order of service at the inauguration of the Jews' Hospital, New York: on Thursday 17th May 5615 A.M. — New York: J. M. Jackson, 1855.

    15 p. English and Hebrew. Deinard: 594. Levine: 89. Singerman: 1399. Copies: MH MWalA OCH

55. סדר תפלה = The order of prayer for divine service / revised by Dr. L. Merzbacher, Rabbi at the Temple "Emanu-El." — New York: J. Mülhaüser, printer, 1855.

    2 v. English and Hebrew. [V.1.] Daily prayers. V.II. Prayers for the Day of Atonement. Deinard: 927, 967. Levine: 90. Singerman: 1384. Copies: CtY DLC NNJ OCH

1856

56. The dedication of the Home for Jewish Widows and Orphans of New Orleans. — New Orleans: Sherman and Wharton, 1856.

    19 p. Levine: 121. Singerman: 1448. Copies: Au L-M LNHT OCH PPAnR

57. Form of the service at the consecration of the synagogue Mishkan Israel, Court Street, New Haven, Conn.: on Friday June 6th 5616. — New York: H. Frank, 5616.

    16 p. English and Hebrew. Added t.p. in Hebrew. Singerman: 1447. Copies: CtY

58. Gebetbuch für israelitische Reform-Gemeinden: im Verlag der Har-Sinai Gemeinde zu Baltimore. — New York: H. Frank, 1856.

    64 p. German and Hebrew. Copyright secured by Abraham Nachman. "I. Heft: Die Gebeten für den Sabbath und die drei Haupt-Feste." Deinard [912]. Singerman: 1433. Copies: DLC MH NN OCH

59. Gesänge zum Gebrauche beim Gottesdienst der Reform-Gemeinde "Keneseth Israel" zu Philadelphia. — [Philadelphia]: R. Stein, 1856.

    27 p. Levine: 122. Singerman: 1456. Copies: OCH

60. Hymns written for the use of Hebrew Congregations. — 2nd ed. rev. and enl. — Charleston, S.C.: Congregation Beth Elohim: A.M. 5616, [c 1856].

    xv, 212 p. Written primarily by Penina Moïse. Levine: 106. Singerman: 1424. Copies: DLC MWalA NNJ NNUT OCH ScU

61. סדר חנוכת הבית דקהלה החדשה כנסת ישראל = Form of service at the consecration of the new synagogue Kenaises Israel, Grape Street, Syracuse, N.Y. / the consecration sermon by H. A. Henry, Minister of the Congregation "Rodeph Shalom," New York; the usual prayers will be read by the Minister of the Congregation, Simon Zelig. — New York: J. Mühlhaüser, 1856.

    10 p. Hebrew and English. Levine: 130. Singerman: 1462. Copies: OCH

62. רינה ותפילה = Order of service at the dedication of the Congregation Beth El, 33rd St. near 8th Ave.: 28th Alul (28 of September) 5616 / arranged by M. S. Cohen. — New York: [s.n.], 1856.

10 p. Deinard: 752. Singerman: 1463. Copies: NNJ

63. תפלת ישראל = Israelitisches Andachtsbuch: hebraeisch und deutsch mit neuen deutschen Gebeten (תחינות)/von W. Schlessinger. — New York: Frank, 1856.

240, 224, 34 p. German and Hebrew. Singerman: 1432. Copies: NNJ OCH

64. תפלת ישראל = Prayers of Israel with an English translation. — 5th ed. — New York: H. Frank, 1856.

240, 229 p. English and Hebrew. Deinard: 923. Copies: MWalA NN PPPD

65. תפלת ישראל = Prayers of Israel with an English translation. — 5th ed. — New York: H. Frank, 1856.

183, 172 p. English and Hebrew. Copies: Iou MH NNJ

1857

66. The daily prayers. Pt. 1./revised and compiled by the Committee of the Cleveland Conference; translated by Isaac M. Wise. — Cincinnati: Bloch, 5617.

120 p. Bound with: תפלות בני ישורון, מנהג אמעריקא, 1857 (Entry 75). Some copies bound with: Gebet-buch für den öffentlichen Gottesdienst und die Privat-Andacht, 1857 (Entry 69). Deinard: 911. Levine: 151. Singerman: 1489. Copies: English, German and Hebrew edition: DLC MH NNJ OCH PU. English and Hebrew edition: OCH

67. Dedication of the new synagogue Beth-El Emeth: on Thursday the 14th day of Elul, 5617 (September 3d, 1857): also the address of Solomon Jacobs, on the Sabbath following. — Philadelphia: Barnard & Jones, 5618.

34 p. Singerman: 1480. Copies: MWalA OCH PPAnR

68. Dedication service for the new synagogue Beth-El Emeth (The House of the True God) of Philadelphia, on Thursday the 14th day of Elul, 5617 (September 3d, 1857) — Philadelphia: Barnard & Jones, 5617.

8 p. Levine: 155. Singerman: 1502. Copies: MWalA OCH

69. Gebet-Buch für den öffentlichen Gottesdienst und die Privat-Andacht. Th. 1./geordnet und übersetzt von der in der Cleveländer Conferenz ernannten liturgischen Commission den Rabbinern Kalisch, Rothenheim und Wise. — Cincinnati: Bloch, 1857.

171 p. Deinard: 911. Levine: 152. Singerman: 1488. Bound with: תפלות בני ישורון, מנהג אמעריקא, 1857 (Entry 75). Some copies bound with: The daily prayers, 1857 (Entry 66). Copies: English, German and Hebrew edition: DLC MH NNJ OCH PU. German and Hebrew edition: OCH

70. Order of prayers established by the Congregation אנשי מעריב, Chicago, Illinois. — Cincinnati: Bloch, 5618 [1857 or 1858].

8 p. Synagogue was known as K.A.M. (Kehilath Anshe Ma'ariv). Singerman: 1476. Copies: MWalA (uncat).

71. Order of service at the consecration of the new synagogue of the Congregation "B'nai Israel," Philadelphia. — [Philadelphia]: R. Stein, 1857.

17 p. English and Hebrew. Levine: 149. Singerman: 1504. Copies: OCH PPAnR

72. Order of service at the dedication of the synagogue Nefutsoth Jehudah of New-Orleans: on Wednesday, Nissan 7, 5617

(April 1st, 1857). — New Orleans: E.C. Wharton, 1857.

11 p. Singerman: 1497. Copies: NN

72a. Order of service to be performed at the consecration of the synagogue, Washington Street, Newark, N.J. on Wednesday, Alul the 27th, corresponding with September 16, 5617. — Newark: O.S.C. Atkinson, [1857]

23 p. For Congregation B'nai Jeshurun, Newark, N.J. In Hill, Frank Pierce. *Books, pamphlets and newspapers printed at Newark, New Jersey, 1776–1900: a list.* [Newark, 1902] Entry 361. Copies:

73. סדור שפתי צדיקים... כמנהג ק״ק ספרדים / הוגה בשקידה מרבה מאתי הקטן יצחק בן אורי ן׳ אליעזר. — מהד׳ ג׳. — פה פילאדעלפיא, במצות ובהוצאת המסדר, בשנת [תרי״ז-תרכ״ד].

The form of prayers according to the custom of the Spanish and Portuguese Jews / edited by Isaac Leeser. — 3rd ed. — Philadelphia: Stereotyped by Slote & Mooney, 5617–5624, 1857–1864.

6? v. English and Hebrew. Levine: 153. Copies: MWalA (V.1.) NNJ (V.1, V.3 in 2 parts, V.5) OCH (V.1) PPGratz (V.1) RPB (V.1)

74. סדר הסליחות ליום ב׳ פרשת שמות להחברה ביקור חולים וקדישה, מהקונטרס של מנהג פוזנא [sic!]. — [New York: H. Frank, 1857].

20 p. Singerman: 1491. Copies: MWalA OCH

75. תפלות בני ישורון, מנהג אמעריקא. חלק א׳ / סדרו והעתיקו בפקודת האסיפה הגדולה בק״ק קליוולאנד, הרבנים יצחק מאיר ב״ר יהודה, בנימין ב״ר יצחק, ישראל בן שמחה בונם. — צינצינאטי: בדפוס בלאך, תרי״ז.

144 p. Some copies bound with: The daily prayers, 1857 (Entry 66). Some copies bound with: Gebet-buch für den öffentlichen Gottesdienst und die Privat-Andacht, 1857 (Entry 69). Deinard: 911. Levine: 150. Singerman has this bound with: 1488 and 1489. Copies: English, German and Hebrew edition: DLC MH NNJ OCH PU. English and Hebrew edition: OCH. German and Hebrew edition: OCH. Hebrew only edition: OCH

1858

76. עלת תמיד = Gebetbuch für israelitische Reform-Gemeinden. — Baltimore: C.W. Schneidereith, 1858.

viii, 492 p. German and Hebrew. Edited by David Einhorn. Levine: 167. Singerman: 1534. Copies: DLC ICU MWalA NIC NNJ OCH

77. עלת תמיד = Gebetbuch für israelitische Reform-Gemeinden. — New York: Thalmessinger & Cahn, 1858.

viii, 492 p. German and Hebrew. Edited by David Einhorn. Deinard: 949. See Singerman: 1534. Copies: CLJ CU DLC (uncat) MWalA NN OCH PPAnR

78. עלת תמיד = Gebetbuch für israelitische Reform-Gemeinden. — 4. Aufl. — New York: For sale at the Office of the Sexton of the Congregation Temple Beth El: Printed by Thalmessinger & Co., c1858.

viii, 492 p. German and Hebrew. Edited by David Einhorn. Copies: CtY MnCs MWalA NcD NN NNJ OCH

79. עלת תמיד = Gebetbuch für israelitische Reform-Gemeinden. — 5. Aufl. — New York: For sale at the Office of the Sexton of the Congregation Temple Beth El, N.Y.: M. Thalmessinger, c1858.

viii, 492 p. German and Hebrew. Edited by David Einhorn. Copies: CU DLC (says n.d., but same ed.) MH MWalA NIC PPAnR

80. עלת תמיד = Gebetbuch für israelitische Reform-Gemeinden. — 6. Aufl. — New York: For sale at the Office of the Sexton of the Congregation Temple Beth El, N.Y.: E. Thalmessinger, c 1858.

viii, 492 p. German and Hebrew. Edited by David Einhorn. Copies: MWalA NN NNHeb OCH

1859

81. Gebete und Gesänge zur Seelenfeier / Benjamin Szold. — Baltimore: [s.n], 1859.

22 p. Singerman: 1604. Copies: NNJ

82. מחזור... כמנהג אשכנז: מסודר בשלמות הסדור ומדויק בתכלית הדיוק / מאת וואלף בר שמשון דוב איש היידנהיים. — נוא יארק: בבית ובדפוס חיים פראנק.

Form of prayers ... according to the custom of the German Jews: with English translation. — New York: L. H. Frank, 5620 [1859 or 1860].

v. Copies: NNJ (V.1)

83. מחזור... כמנהג אשכנז: מסודר בשלמות הסדור ומדויק בתכלית הדיוק / מאת וואלף בר שמשון דוב איש היידנהיים. — נוא יארק: בבית ובדפוס חיים פראנק.

Form of prayers ... according to the custom of the German and Polish Jews: with English translation. — New York: L. H. Frank, 5620 [1859 or 1860].

5 v. Copies: NNJ (V. 1, 5)

84. מחזור... כמנהג פולין: מסודר בשלמות הסדור ומדויק בתכלית הדיוק / מאת וואלף בר שמשון דוב איש היידנהיים. — נוא יארק: בבית ובדפוס חיים פראנק.

Form of prayers ... according to the custom of the Polish Jews: with English translation. — New York: L. H. Frank, 5620–5621 [1859 or 1860–1860 or 1861].

2 v. V.1. ליום כפור — V.2. לראש השנה. Possibly Deinard: 470. Copies: CLHU (V.1) MH (V.2)

85. סדור שפת אמת / מאת וואלף בר שמשון דוב איש היידנהיים. — מהד' ל"ב. — רעדעלהיים, תר"ך.

Sephat emeth. — New York: L. H. Frank, 1859.

172 [i.e. 102] p. Hebrew only. Singerman: 1582. Copies: DLC MWalA NN OCH

1860

86. Inauguration of the Hebrew Orphans' Asylum in Charleston, S.C.: January 8th 1860 (Tebet 13th, A.M. 5620). — Charleston, S.C.: Welch, Harris, 1860.

23 p. Includes oration by Asher D. Cohen and a prayer and ode by H. S. Jacobs. Singerman: 1642. Copies: NN PPAnR

87. Order of prayers for חפציבה Hebrew School: temporarily compiled for the devotions of the school on the Solemn holidays & Succoth of the year 5621. — San Francisco: [s.n.], 1860.

114 p. English and Hebrew. Attributed to Julius Eckman. WJHC copy in folder attributed to Temple Emanu-El, San Francisco. Singerman: 1666. Copies: NNJ PPAnR WJHC (photocopy)

88. Prayer at the opening of the House of Representatives at Washington, D.C.: on Wednesday, February 1st, 1860 / Morris Jacob Raphall. — New York: T. E. Isaaks, [1860].

1 p. Also in *Congressional Globe*. 36th Congress, 1st session. Pt. 1. pp. 648–649. Singerman: 1684. Copies: MWalA

1860

89. אלה המזמורים אשר שרו להקת המשוררים בחנוכת בית הכנסת שבנו היחידים בשם ק"ק שארית ישראל פה נוא-יארק ביום ד' כ"ה אלול בשנת [תר"ך] — [נוא-יארק]: נדפס על ידי יעקב בן שלמה =

Form of service for the dedication of the new synagogue of the Portuguese Hebrew Congregation "Shearith Israel": in West 19th Street, near Fifth Avenue: consecrated on Wednesday, the 25th Elool, 12th Sept. 5620. — New York: J. M. Jackson, 5620.

13, 13 p. English and Hebrew. Singerman: 1679. Copies: MWalA NNJ PPAnR

90. אלה המזמורים אשר שרו להקת המשוררים לחנוכת בית הכנסת של ק"ק מקוה ישראל: פה פילאדילפיא ביום ג' לחדש סיון, בשנת [תר"ך] =

Form of service for the dedication of the new synagogue of the Portuguese Congregation "Mikve Israel": in Seventh Street above Arch: consecrated on the 24th of May, 1860. — Philadelphia: Barnard & Jones, 5620.

11, 11 p. English and Hebrew. Deinard: 46. Singerman: 1682. Copies: MWalA NN NNJ PPL NNYU (Sephardic Reference Room)

91. מחזור לכל מועדי השנה: מוגה ומדויק אין מחסור כל דבר: מתורגם אשכנזית מחדש מפרש ושום שכל/על ידי יחיאל מיכל זקש ... כמנהג פולין בעהמען מעהרען ואונגארן. — מהד' ד'. — בערלין: ל. גערשעל, תר"ך =

Festgebete der Israeliten: mit vollständigem sorfältig durchgesehenem Texte: Neu Übersetzt und erläutert/von Michael Sachs. — New York: M. Ellinger & Co.; Berlin: L. Gerschel, 1860.

9 v. in 5. German and Hebrew. Levine: 219. Singerman: 1669. Copies: DLC MH OCH

92. סדור תפלת ישראל: דבר יום ביומו אין מחסור כל דבר: מסודר בסדר נכון ומוגה בעיון דק, מתורגם אשכנזית מחדש מפורש ושום שכל/על ידי מיכל זקש. — בערלין: בהוצאת ל. גערשעל, תר"ך =

Das Gebetbuch der Israeliten: mit vollständigem sorfältig durchgesehettenem Texte: Neu übersetzt und erläutert/von Michael Sachs. — Berlin: L. Gerschel; New York: M. Ellinger & Co., 1860.

475 p. German and Hebrew. Levine: 216. Copies: NNJ OCH

93. סדר תפלה = The order of prayer for divine service./revised by Dr. L. Merzbacher, Rabbi at the Temple "Emanu-El"... 1855 — 2nd. ed./rev. by S. Adler, 1860. — New York, Thalmessinger, Cahn & Benedicks, c1860.

2 v. English and Hebrew. [V.I] Daily prayers. — V.2. Prayers for the Day of Atonement. Singerman: 1667. Copies: OCH (V. 1)

94. תפלת ישראל = Israelitsches Andachts-Buch: nebst deutscher Übersetzung neuen deutschen Gebeten (תחינות)/ von W. Schlessinger. — 6. Aufl. — New York: Frank, 1860.

240, 224, 32 p. German and Hebrew. Final section has separate t.p.: תחינות בנות ישורון = Religiöse Betrachtungen und Gebete für Israels Frauen und Mädchen. Levine 217–218. See Singerman 1432. Copies: OCH

95. תפלת ישראל = Prayers of Israel with English translation. — 5th ed. — New York: L. H. Frank, 1860.

240, 229 p. English and Hebrew. Levine: 215. Singerman: 1668. Copies: NNJ OCH PPAnR

1861

96. Hymnen: gesammelt und herausgegeben auf Kosten der Sinai-Gemeinde in Chicago. — Chicago: G. Feuchtinger, 1861.

30 p. Singerman: 1706. Copies: OCH

97. Order of prayers for חפציבה Hebrew School (Sutter St., near Stockton): temporarily compiled for the use of the school. — San Francisco: [s.n.], 1861.

84 p. English and Hebrew. Arranged by Julius Eckman. Singerman: 1713. Copies: NNJ

98. סדר העבודה = Order of service for the day of solemn fast and humiliation: Friday, 22 Tebeth, 5621 A.M., 4th January, 1861, at the synagogue of the Congregation B'nai Jeshurun, Greene Street, New York. — New York: J. Davis, Printer: "Jewish Messenger" Office, 1861.

13 p. English and Hebrew. Levine: 239. Singerman: 1717. Copies: OCH

1862

99. Form of service at the consecration of the synagogue Beth Elohim, Brooklyn, N.Y.: on Sunday, Adar Scheni, corresponding with March 30, 1862 / address in English by S. M. Isaacs; address in German by Jos. Saxe; the prayers chaunted by G. Brandenstein, Minister of the Congregation, accompanied by choir and orchestra. — New York: C. A. Alvord, 1862.

15 p. English and Hebrew. Deinard: 903. Singerman: 1736. Copies: NN (microfiche)

100. Gedenkbuch ... für alle ihre verstorbenen Mitglieder ... alljährlich soll am Versöhnungstage ... eine Seelenfeier begangen werden. — Baltimore: Oheb Shalom, 1862.

12 p. Singerman: 1734. Copies: NNJ

101. Gesänge für den öffentlichen jüdischen Gottesdienst aus verschiedenen Liedersammlungen zusammengetragen: im Verlage der Kneseth-Israel-Gemeinde in Philadelphia. — Philadelphia: Stein & Jones, 1862.

93, 1 p. Levine: 251. Singerman: 1749. Copies: ICJS OCH PP PU

102. מנהג אמעריקא תפלות בני ישורון = Daily prayers. — 3rd ed. — Cincinnati: Bloch & Co., Office of the Israelite and Deborah, 1862, c1857.

138, 144 p. English and Hebrew. Compiled by Isaac M. Wise. Levine: 248. Singerman: 1741. Copies: CLHU MWalA NNJ OCH

103. עלת תמיד = Gebetbuch für israelitische Reform-Gemeinden. — 2. Aufl. — Baltimore: C. W. Schneidereith, 1862, c1858.

viii, 492 p. German and Hebrew. Compiled by David Einhorn. Deinard: 949. Levine: 249. Copies: CU NNHeb OCH

104. קדש הלולים = Pijutim, Gebete und Gesänge zum Gebrauche, nebst dem allgemeinen Israel: Gebet-buche bei dem geregelten öffentlichen Gottesdienste in der Synagogue der Oheb-Schalom-Gemeinde zu Baltimore. — Baltimore: C. W. Schneidereith, 1862.

203, 72 p. German and Hebrew. Compiled by Benjamin Szold. Deinard: 714. Singerman: 1740. Copies: MWalA NNJ PU

105. קדש הלולים = Pijutim, Gebete und Gesänge zum Gebrauche, nebst dem allgemeinden Israel: Gebet-buche bei dem geregelten öffentlichen Gottesdienste in

der Synagogue der Oheb-Schalom-Gemeinde zu Baltimore. — Baltimore: [s.n.], 1862.

180, 72 p. German and Hebrew. Compiled by Benjamin Szold. See note, Singerman: 1740. Copies: CLHU OCH

1863

106. Stunden der Andacht: Ein Gebet-und Erbauungsbuch für Israels Frauen und Jungfrauen zur öffentlichen und häuslichen Andacht: so wie für alle Verhältnisse des weiblichen Lebens / von W. Schlessinger und anderen Schriftstellern und mit meheren Aufsätzen von Fanny Neuda, geb. Schmiedl. — 3.Stereotyp.-Ausgabe. — New York: L. H. Frank, 1863.

96 p. Singerman: 1787. Copies: MWalA NN

107. זמירות ישראל = Auswahl israelitisch religiöser Lieder in Musik gesetzt / Wilhelm Fischer. — Philadelphia: The Composer at L. N. Rosenthal, [1863].

160 p. Sendrey: 6130. Singerman: 1772. Copies: OCH

108. סדר תפלה = The order of prayer for divine service / revised by Dr. L. Merzbacher, Rabbi at the Temple "Emanu-El"... 1855 — 2nd.ed./rev. by S. Adler, 1860. — New York, Thalmessinger and Cahn, 1863.

2 v. English and Hebrew. Singerman: 1780 (V.2 only). Copies: MB (V.2) MH (V.2) NNJ (V.2) OCH (V.2) PPAnR (V.2) PSt PU

109. תפלת ישראל = Prayers of Israel with an English translation. — 6th stereotype ed. — New York: L. H. Frank, 1863.

182, 172 p. English and Hebrew. Levine: 267. Singerman: 1668. Copies: NNJ OCH PPAnR

1864

110. Form of service at the consecration of the new synagogue Benai Israel, Sacramento Cal.: on Sunday May 22, 5624 (1864) / the consecration sermon by H. A. Henry, Rabbi Preacher of Congregation Sherith Israel, San Francisco. — San Francisco: "The Hebrew," 1864.

12 p. English and Hebrew. Singerman: 1837. Copies: C

111. Form of service at the consecration of the synagogue Adereth El, 29th St., bet. Lexington & Third Av.: on Sunday Elul 24th 5624, corresponding with Sunday September 25th, 1864 / addresses by Rev. Dr. Raphell [sic!], S. M. Isaacs ... and others; prayers chaunted by M. R. De Leeuw, and choir. — New York: D. Wolf, 1864.

16 p. English and Hebrew. Deinard: 324, 904. Singerman: 1854. Copies: NN (microfiche)

112. Programm für das Einweihungsfest des neuens Tempels der Reform-Gemeinde "Keneseth Israel": am Freitag und Sabbath, den 22. u. 23 Ellul, 5624 A.M. (23 und 24. September 1864). — Philadelphia: Stein & Jones, 1864.

11 p. Singerman: 1858. Copies: OCH PPAnR

113. Programme of the exercises on the occasion of laying the corner-stone of the new synagogue of the Congregation "B'nai Jeshurun" on לג בעמר 18th day of Iyar, May 24th, 1864. — New York: J. F. Rosenbaum & Weil, 1864.

8 p. Singerman: 1853. Copies: MWalA

114. The sacred harp of Judah: a choice collection of music for the use of synagogues, schools and home. Part I. Sabbath

1864

liturgy/by G. M. Cohen. — Cleveland: S. Brainard, c1864.

    Score (49 p.) English, German and romanized Hebrew. For 1–2 voices or chorus (SATB). Sendrey: 6932. Singerman: 1825. Copies: OCH PPGratz

115. Stunden der Andacht: Ein Gebet- und Erbauungsbuch für Israels Frauen und Jungfrauen zur öffentlichen und häuslichen Andacht: so wie für alle Verhältnisse des weiblichen Lebens/von W. Schlessinger und anderen Schriftstellern und mit meheren Zusätzen von Fanny Neuda, geb. Schmiedl. — 4. Stereotyp. Ausgabe. — New York: L. H. Frank, 1864.

    iv, 96 p. Levine: 297. Copies: OCH

116. אמרי לב = Meditations and prayers for every situation in life/translated and adapted from the French by H. Rothschild; revised and corrected by I. Leeser. — American stereotype ed. — Philadelphia: [s.n.], 5624–1864.

    xvi, 260 p. Original in French by Jonas Ennery. Levine: 283. Singerman: 1832. Copies: CLU NN NNJ NNYU (Sephardic Reference Room) OCH PPL

117. מחזור... = Form of prayers ... with English translation. — 2nd. ed. — New York: L. H. Frank, 1864–5624 — 1865–5625.

    5 v. English and Hebrew. Deinard: 471. Levine: 228. Singerman: 1844. Copies: MH MWalA (V.2, 5.) OCH

118. מחזור לראש השנה ויום כפור: מסודר ומדויק בתכלית הדיוק/מאת וואלף בר שמשון דוב איש היידנהיים = Machsor. — New York: L. H. Frank, 1864.

    1 v. (various pagings) Hebrew only. Levine: 289. Singerman: 1847. Copies: MH MWalA NNJ OCH PPAnR NNHeb

119. מנהג אמעריקא תפלות בני ישורון = Daily prayers. — 4th ed. — Cincinnati: Bloch, 1864, c1857.

    146, 139 p. English and Hebrew. Compiled by Isaac M. Wise. Levine: 290. Copies: DLC NNJ OCH

120. מנהג אמעריקא תפלות בני ישורון = Gebet-buch für den öffentlichen Gottesdienst und die Privat-Andacht. — 2. verbesserte deutscher Ausgabe. — Cincinnati: Bloch, 1864, c1861.

    139, 144 p. German and Hebrew. Compiled by Isaac M. Wise. Levine: 291. Singerman: 1846. Copies: CLHU NNJ OCH

121. סדור שפתי צדיקים ... כמנהג ק״ק ספרדים הוגה בשקדה מרבה/מאתי הקטן יצחק בן אורי ן׳ אליעזר. — פה פילאדילפיא: במצות ובהוצאת המסדר = Form of prayers according to the custom of the Spanish and Portuguese Jews/edited by Isaac Leeser. — 4th ed. — Philadelphia: Stereotyped by Slote and Mooney, 5624–5627.

    6 v. English and Hebrew. V.1. Daily prayers. — V.2. New Year service. — V.2. Day of Atonement service. — V.4. Tabernacle service. — V.5. Passover and Pentecost service. — V.6. Fast Day service. Levine: 293, 377 (for V.2. 1867). Singerman: 1779. Copies: CLHU (V.1) MH NNJ MWalA OCH (V.1–2) PPGratz (V.1–2)

122. סדר תפלה = The order of prayer for divine service/revised by L. Merzbacher. — New York: Thalmessinger & Cahn, 1864.

    xvii, 229 p. English and Hebrew. Daily prayers. Copies: COMC DLC NN WJHC

123. סדר תפלה = The order of prayer for divine service/revised by L. Merzbacher,

Rabbi of the Temple Emanu-El, 1855. — 3rd ed. rev. and corr./by S. Adler. — New York: Thalmessinger and Cahn, 1864.

xv, 181 (32), (17) (71) p. English and Hebrew (181 p) German (32 p.). Some copies include German Hymns (32 p.). Some copies include: Hymns for divine service in Temple Emanu-El/[compiled by James K. Gutheim et al.]. (71 p.) (Entry 186). Some copies include: Order of prayer in the house of mourners (17 p.) (Entry 188). Deinard: 966, 968. Levine: 292. Singerman: 1845. Copies: With German hymns only: DLC. With English hymns only: OCH. With German hymns and Order of prayer in the house of mourners: DLC (uncat). With English hymns and Order of prayer in the house of mourners: MWalA. With German hymns, English hymns and Order of prayer in the house of mourners: MH NN NNJ

124. סדר תפלה = The order of prayer for divine service/revised by L. Merzbacher. — 3rd ed. rev. and corr./by S. Adler. — New York: Thalmessinger & Co., 1864.

xv, 181, 71, 17 p. English and Hebrew. Includes Hymns for divine service in Temple Emanu-El (Entry 186) and Order of prayer in the house of mourners (Entry 188). Copies: OCH

125. עבודת ישראל = Israelitisches Gebetbuch für den öffentlichen Gottesdienst im ganzen Jahre/geordnet und übersetzt von Benjamin Szold, Rabbiner der Oheb Schalom-Gemeinde in Baltimore. — Baltimore: W. Polmyer, 1864.

viii, 618, 31 p. German and Hebrew. Deinard: 943?, 945? Singerman: 1843. Copies: NNJ OCH PPAnR TNJ

126. תפלת ישראל = Prayers of Israel with an English translation. — 7th stereotype ed. — New-York: L. H. Frank, 1864, c1862.

240, 229 p. English and Hebrew. Levine: 287. Copies: NNJ OCH

1865

127. Order of exercises at the consecration of the new synagogue of the Congregation Shaar Hashomajim, Rivington Street between Ludlow and Orchard Streets: on Friday March 31, 1865. — New York: [s.n.], 1865.

12 p. Singerman: 1908. Copies: NNJ

128. Order of service at the consecration of the new synagogue of Congregation Bnai Jeshurun, Thirty-fourth Street: on Thursday, Sept. 14th, 1865 (corresponding with the 23rd day of Ellul, 5625)/the consecration sermon will be delivered by M. J. Raphall ... — New York: J. Davis, 5625–1865.

12 p. English and Hebrew. Singerman: 1906. Copies: NNUT

129. Programm für das Einweihungs-Fest der neuen Synagoge der Gemeinde Beth El: Freitag und Sabbath 22 & 23 Tebeth 5625 A.M. (20. und 21. Januar 1865). — Albany: A. Miggael, 1865.

8 p. English and German. Singerman: 1868. Copies: N NN

130. Programm für das Einweihungs-Fest des Tempels der Reform-Gemeinde "Temple Beth Zion": am Freitag den 26 Mai 1865, 5625 A.M. = Programm of the ceremonies of the consecration of the Temple of the Reformed Congregation "Temple Beth Zion": Friday, May 26th, 1865, 5625 A.M. — Buffalo: Brunck & Held, 1865.

9 p. English and German. Singerman: 1879. Copies: NBuHi

131. Service and sermon held on the day of lamentation: June 1st 1865, in memory of our late beloved President Abraham Lincoln: at the Congregation Adath J'Shurun … /Herman M. Bien. — New York: [s.n.], 1865.

7 p. Singerman: 1872. Copies: MWalA

132. זמירות ישראל = Auswahl israelitisch religiöser Lieder in Musik gesetzt/Wilhelm Fischer. — 2. Aufl. — Philadelphia: Schaefer & Koradi, 1865.

160 p. Levine: 307. See Singerman: 1772. Copies: OCH PPGratz

133. עבודת ישראל = The order of prayer for the Israelitish divine service on every day of the year/revised and translated by Benjamin Szold. — Baltimore: W. Polmyer, 1865.

vi, 618, 27 p. English and Hebrew. Deinard: 942. Singerman: 1896. Copies: DLC MH OCH

134. תפלת ישראל = Prayers of Israel with an English translation. — 7th stereotype ed. — New York: L. H. Frank, 1865.

183, 170 p. English and Hebrew. Levine: 313. Copies: OCH

135. תפלת ישראל = Prayers of Israel with an English translation. — 7th stereotype ed. — New York: L. H. Frank, 1865, c1864.

240, 229 p. English and Hebrew. Levine: 314. Copies: MH NNJ OCH

1866

136. Consecration service … Bnai Israel, Philadelphia … the 26th Elul 5626. — Philadelphia: Vonstrellen, 1866.

8 p. English and Hebrew. Deinard: 905. Singerman: 1964. Copies: Uk

137. Gesänge für den öffentlichen jüdischen Gottesdienst, aus verschiedenen Liedersammlungen zusammengetragen: im Verlage des Temple Adath Jeshurun in New York. — New York: Waldheimer & Zenn, 1866.

93 p. Reprinted from: Philadelphia: Reform Congregation Keneseth Israel, 1862. (Entry 101). Levine: 345. Sendrey: 6008. Singerman: 1962. Copies: MWalA NN NNJ OCH PU

138. Hours of devotion: a book of prayers and meditations for the use of the daughters of Israel, during public service and at home for all the conditions of woman's life/translated from the German "Stunden der Andacht" by M. Mayer. — New York: L. H. Frank, 5626–1866.

105 p. Original German by Fanny Schmiedl Neuda. Singerman: 1958. Copies: NN

139. Hours of devotion: a book of prayers and meditations for the use of the daughters of Israel, during public service and at home for all the conditions of woman's life/translated from the German "Stunden der Andacht" by M. Mayer. — 5th ed. — New York: J. L. Werbelowsky, c1866.

105 p. Original German by Fanny Schmiedl Neuda. Copies: MH KyWat NN OCl

140. Hours of devotion: a book of prayers and meditations for the use of the daughters of Israel, during public service and at home for all the conditions of woman's life/translated from the German "Stunden der Andacht" by M. Mayer. — 5th ed. — New York: Hebrew Pub. Co., c1866.

105 p. Original German by Fanny Schmiedl Neuda. Probably published after 1901, as the Hebrew Publishing

Company did not form until about 1901. Cf. Charles Madison. *Jewish Publishing in America.* New York: Sanhedrin Press, c1976, p. 77. Singerman: 1958. Copies: CLJ Jewish Community Library of Los Angeles MWalA NN NjP NNJ OCH

141. Hymns written for the use of Hebrew Congregations. — 3rd ed., rev. and corr. — Charleston: Published by the Congregation Beth Elohim; Philadelphia: Printed by W.W. Jones, 5627, 1866, c1856.

xiv, 214 p. Written primarily by Penina Moïse. Singerman: 1933. Copies: CLHU NNJ PPASnR PPGratz

142. Programme of ceremonies at the dedication of the Temple K. K. Bene Yeshurun, of Cincinnati: Friday, August 24th. — Cincinnati: Bloch, 1866.

16 p. English and Hebrew. Levine: 335. Singerman: 1934. Copies: MWalA OCAJA

143. אמרי לב = Meditations and prayers for every situation in life/translated and adapted from the French by H. Rothschild; revised and corrected by I. Leeser. — American stereotype ed. — Philadelphia, 1866.

xvi, 260 p. Original in French by Jonas Ennery. Levine: 328. Copies: CU DLC NN OCH OrP

144. מחזור...כמנהג פולין = Form of prayers ... with English translation. — 3rd ed. — New York: L.H. Frank, 1866–5626, c1864.

5 v. English and Hebrew. V.1. New Year. — V.2. Day of Atonement. — V.3. Feast of Tabernacles. — V.4. Feast of Passover. — V.5. Feast of Pentecost. Levine: 340. Copies: DLC (uncat) NNHeb OCH PPAnR (V.1, V.4–5)

145. מחזור לפסח שבועות וסוכות: מסודר בשלמות הסדור ומדויק בתכלית הדיוק/מאת וואלף בר שמשון דוב איש היידנהיים = Machsor. — New York: L. H. Frank, 5626–1866, c1864.

1 v. (varous pagings) Hebrew only. Copies: NNJ

146. סדר תפלה = The order of prayer for divine service/as revised by L. Merzbacher and adopted by Congregation "Emanu-El" of San Francisco. — San Francisco: San Francisco Abend Post Print, [1866?]

2 v. English and Hebrew. [V.1] Daily prayers. — V.2: Prayers for the Day of Atonement. See Singerman: 1781 (claims 1863–1866). Copies: CU NN (V.2) OCH (V.2)

147. ספר החיים = Andachtsbuch zum Gebrauche bei Krankheiten und Sterbfällen bei der Leichenfeier, im Trauerhause und auf dem Friedhofe/von Benjamin Szold. — Baltimore: W. Polmyer, 1866.

vi, 78 p. Deinard: 306. Levine: 339, 349. Singerman: 1951. Copies: DLC (uncat) OCH PPAnR

148. תפלות בני ישורון כפי מנהג אמעריקא = The divine service of American Israelites/ Isaac M. Wise. — Cincinnati: Bloch, 5627, 1866.

2 v. Text in English and Hebrew, Hymns in German. V.1. New Year. — V.2. Day of Atonement. Levine: 341 (V.1), 342 (V.2). Singerman: 1949 (V.1), 1952 (V.2). Copies: CarP (V.1) CLHU CoDu CU (V.1) DLC FU IU KyLoS (V.2) MdCP MH MoS MWA MWalA MWalB NNJ OC (V.2) OCH PP (V.1) PPAnR TxDaM-P

149. תפלת ישראל = Prayers of Israel with an English translation. — 8th stereopye ed. — New York: L. H. Frank, 1866, c1864.

240, 229 p. English and Hebrew. Levine: 337. Copies: NN OCH

1867

150. Andachtsbüchlein für israelitische Kinder für Haus und Schule: in hebräischer, deutscher und englischer Sprache/ entworfen von Benjamin Szold. — Baltimore: W. Polmyer, 1867.

32 p. English, German and Hebrew. Levine: 338. Singerman: 2020. Copies: NNJ OCH

151. Gesänge für israelitische Reform Gemeinden aus verschiedenen Liedersammlungen zusammengetragen: im Verlage der Keneseth Israel Gemeinde in Philadelphia. — Neue vermehrte Aufl. — Philadelphia: Stein und Jones, 1867.

136 p. Levine: 383. Singerman: 2037. Copies: MWalA NN NNJ OCH PPAnR PPG PU

152. Hymns written for the use of Hebrew Congregations. — 4th ed. — Charleston, S.C.: Congregation Beth Elohim, 5627, [1867].

xii, 212 p. Written primarily by Penina Moïse. Levine: 356. Copies: OCH

153. הגיון לב = Israelitisches Gebetbuch für die häusliche Andacht/geordnet von Benjamin Szold, Rabbiner der Oheb-Schalom-Gemeinde in Baltimore. — Baltimore: W. Polmyer, 1867.

xi, 264, 11 p. German and Hebrew. Deinard: 247. Singerman: 2019. Copies: DLC NN NNHeb NNJ OCH PPGratz (Music) PPL

154. מנהג אמעריקא תפלות בני ישורון = Daily prayers. — 6th rev. stereotype ed. — Cincinnati: Bloch, 1867.

316 [i.e. 158] p. Hebrew only edition. Compiled by Isaac M. Wise. Copies: MH

155. תפלת ישראל = Prayers of Israel with an English translation. — 8th stereotype ed. — New York: L. H. Frank, 1867.

183, 172 p. English and Hebrew. Deinard: 921. Copies: DLC (uncat) NNJ

1868

156. Confirmant's guide to the Mosaic religion / E. Eppstein. — Detroit: F. A. Schober & Bro., 1868.

iv, 55 p. Pages 49–55 contain prayers in English and German. Singerman: 2067. Copies: MiDW MiU OO

157. Dedication of the new Temple Adas Israel, corner Sixth & Broadway, Louisville, Ky.: programme of ceremonies, Friday, Sept. 4, 1868. — Louisville, Ky.: Hull & Brother, [1868].

10 p. English and German. Includes text of "Einweihungs-Hymne"/by Minna Kleeberg (Reprinted in שירו לה׳ שיר חדש = Hymns, Psalms & prayers. Cincinnati, 1868. Entry 165). Singerman: 2084. Copies: NN (microfilm)

158. Hours of devotion: a book of prayers and meditations for the use of the daughters of Israel, during public service and at home for all the conditions of woman's life/translated from the German "Stunden der Andacht" by M. Mayer. — 2nd ed. — New York: L. H. Frank, 1868.

105 p. Original German by Fanny Schmiedl Neuda. Levine: 421. Copies: C NN OCH PPGratz

159. Hours of devotion: a book of prayers and meditations for the use of the daughters of Israel, during public service and at home for all the conditions of woman's

life/translated from the German "Stunden der Andacht" by M. Mayer. — 5th ed. — New York: Hebrew Pub. Co., c1868.

    105 p. Original German by Fanny Schmiedl Neuda. Probably published after 1901. Copies: DLC MB NjP NN OCH

160. Der israelitische Confirmand: oder Glaubens- und Pflichtenlehre für den Schul- und den Privatgebrauch in Reformgemeinde: bearbeitet und mit Zusätzen, Anmerkungen und neuen Liederversen/ S. Herxheimer; versehen von S. Hecht. — Evansville: Selbstverlag; Cincinnati: Bloch, 1868.

    69 p. Singerman: 2074. Copies: MWalA MwalB OCH

161. Order of service at the re-opening celebration of the Temple Anshi Chesed, Norfolk Street: on Friday, May 22, 1868 = Programm zur Wiederöffnungs-feier des Gotteshauses der Gemeinde "Anshi Chesed" am 1ten Sivan, 5628. — New York: Thalmessinger, 1868.

    13 p. English and German. Singerman: 2093. Copies: NNJ OCH

162. Order of service for the consecration of the Temple Emanu-El ... on Friday, Sept. 11, 1868. — New York: M. Thalmessinger, 1868.

    22, 1 p. English and Hebrew. Singerman: 2094. Copies: NN NNJ

163. מנהג אמעריקא תפלות בני ישורון = Daily prayers. — 6th rev. stereotype ed. — Cincinnati: Bloch, 1868, c1857.

    316 p. English and Hebrew. Compiled by Isaac M. Wise. Deinard: 914. Levine: 415. Copies: DLC (uncat) NNJ OCH

164. עבודת ישראל = The order of prayer for the Israelitish divine service on every day of the year/revised and translated by Benjamin Szold. — Baltimore: W. Polmyer, 1868.

    vi, 618, 27 p. English and Hebrew. Copies: OO

165. שירו לה׳ שיר חדש = Hymns, Psalms & prayers in English and German/by Isaac M. Wise and others. — Cincinnati: Bloch, c1868.

    263 p. English and German. Levine: 428. Singerman: 2109. Copies: CLHU DLC ICJS IU MWalA MH NN NNHeb NNJ NNYI OCH OO PPGratz RPB

166. תפלת ישראל = Prayers of Israel with an English translation. — 10th stereotype ed. — New York: L. H. Frank, 1868, c1864.

    240, 229 p. English and Hebrew. Deinard: 922. Levine: 414. Copies: DLC MH NNJ OCH

1869

167. Gebete-Ordnung der Congregation Ahawath Chesed für ראש השנה und יום כפור des Jahres 5630. — New York: J. Mühlhäuser, 1869.

    23 p. German and Hebrew? Compiled by Adolph Huebsch. Singerman: 2152. Copies: MWalA OCH

168. Gesänge für den öffentlichen jüdischen Gottesdienst, aus verschiedenen Liedersammlungen zusammengetragen: im Verlage des Temple Adath Jeshurun in New York. — New York: Waldheimer & Zenn, 1869.

    93 p. Levine: 452. Singerman: 2151. Copies: MWalA OCH

169. Gottesdienst-Ordnung der Gemeinde Mischkan Israel in New Haven, Conn. — New York: L. H. Frank, 1869.

    1 leaf printed on 3 sides. Singerman: 2149. Copies: OCAJA

1869–1870

170. "A prayer for peace"/Samuel Yates Levy.

    2 p. In: Brock, Sallie, ed. *The Southern Amaranth.* New York: Wilcox and Rockwell, 1869. pp. 628–629. Singerman: 2144. Copies: CSt CU-A FU IaU McA (microfilm) MnU NNC NNU (microfilm) RPB

171. Proceedings of the laying of the cornerstone for the synagogue of the Congregation Rodef Shalom, at Broad and Vernon Sts., Philadelphia: July 20th, 1869. — Philadelphia: R. Stein, 1869.

    40 p. English, German and Hebrew. Singerman: 2157. Copies: MWalA PPAnR PU

172. [חנוכת הבית סדר] = Synagogue dedication service.] — New York: [s.n.], 1869.

    17 p. For Congregation Shaaray Tefilah, New York, N.Y. Deinard: 906. Singerman: 2153. Copies:

173. סדר תפלה = The order of prayer for divine service/revised by L. Merzbacher. — 3rd ed. rev. and corr./by S. Adler. — New York: M. Thalmessinger, 1869.

    xv, 181, 32, 17 p. English, German and Hebrew. Includes German hymns (32 p.). Includes: Order of prayer in the house of mourners. 1871 (17 p.) (Entry 188). Copies: DLC

187-?

174. Der Herr ist Koenig = The Lord is ruler: Psalm 93 in Musik gesetzt/Samuel Welsch. — New York: E. Schuberth, [187-?]

    Score (6 p.) English and German. For Cantor and chorus (SATB). Sendrey: 6902. Singerman: 2198. Copies: OCH

175. The priestly blessing: traditional דוכן arranged from Naumbourg's ותערב/by G. S. Ensel. — [Paducah, Ky? s.n., 187-?]

    Score (6 p.). Singerman: 2190. Copies: OCH

1870

176. The American-Jewish ritual: as instituted in Temple Israel, Brooklyn/by Raphael D'C Lewin. — New York: L. H. Frank, 1870.

    xvii, 273 p. English and Hebrew. Levine: 480. Singerman: 2215. Copies: CtY DLC MWalA NN NNHeb NNJ OCH

177. Einweihung der Synagoge der Gemeinde Rodef Schalom = Programme of the consecration services of the synagogue of the Congregation Rodef Shalom. — Philadelphia: The Congregation: H. Stein, Printer, 1870.

    8, 8 p. English and German. Singerman: 2235. Copies: OCH

178. Hours of devotion: a book of prayers and meditations for the use of the daughters of Israel, during public service and at home for all the conditions of woman's life/translated from the German "Stunden der Andacht" by M. Mayer. — 2nd. ed. — New York: L. H. Frank, 1870.

    105 p. Original German by Fanny Schmiedl Neuda. Levine: 486. Copies: NN OCH OCl

179. הזכרת נשמות = Service for the dead: written and arranged for Congregation B'nai Jeshurun ... / H. Vidaver. — New York: [s.n.], 1870.

    p. English and Hebrew. Singerman: 2216. Copies: NNJ (Lost?)

180. מנהג אמעריקא תפלות בני ישורון = Daily prayers. — 7th ed. — Cincinnati, Ohio: Bloch, 1870.

pp. 10–316 (Even numbers only). Hebrew only edition. Compiled by Isaac M. Wise. Levine: 479. Copies: MWalA MWalB (photocopy) OCH

181. ... [sic!] סדר חנוכת הבית החדשה = Form of the service at the consecration of the new synagogue Sherith Israel, San Francisco, Cal.: on Friday Aug. 26, 5630 (1870). — San Francisco: Hebrew Observer Print, 1870.

9, 9 p. English and Hebrew. Singerman: 2240. Copies: ICRL

182. תפלת ישראל = Prayers of Israel with an English translation. — 11th stereotype ed. — New York: L. H. Frank, 1870, c1864.

240, 229 p. English and Hebrew. Levine: 478. Copies: MWalA NNJ OCH

1871

183. The Christian marriage ceremony: its history, significance and curiosities: ritual, practical and archaeological notes: and the text of the English, Roman, Greek and Jewish ceremonies / J. Foote Bingham. — New York: A. D. F. Randolph & Co., 1871.

3, 10–322 p. Copies: McA MWA NNU OCH UpB

184. Confirmant's guide to the Mosaic religion / by E. Eppstein, Minister of the Congregation B'ne Jeshurun, Milwaukee, Wis. — 2nd ed. — Milwaukee: "Herold" Steam Book and Job Print, 1871.

iv, 55 p. English and German. Pages 49–55 contain prayers in English and German. Singerman: 2270. Copies: CLHU NNJ OCH PPAnR

185. Gesänge und Gebete für den öffentlichen Gottesdienst der Israeliten. — [Baltimore: s.n., 1871].

104 p. Compiled by Benjamin Szold.

Bound with: עבודת ישראל = Israelitische Gebetbuch für den öffentlichen Gottesdienst ... 1871. (Entries 193–195). Deinard: 945. Singerman: 2280. Copies: DLC MWalA NN OCH PPGratz

186. Hymns for divine service in Temple Emanu-El. — New York: M. Thalmessinger, 1871.

71 p. English and German. Hymns are by James K. Gutheim, M. Mayer and Felix Adler. Found alone and Bound with V.1. of: סדר תפלה = Order of prayer for divine service / rev. by L. Merzbacher. (Entries 123–124, 259). Sometimes bound with: Order of prayer in the house of mourners. 1871 (Entry 188) Levine: 521. Singerman: 2295. Copies: CtY FiU MH-AN NN NNJ NNU-W OCH PPGratz

187. Hymns for divine service in the Temple Emanu-El / [James K. Gutheim et al. ...] — San Francisco: Congregation Emanu-El], 1871.

71 p. English and German. Copies: CU-B

188. Order of prayer in the house of mourners. — New York: M. Thalmessinger, 1871.

17 p. English and Hebrew. Bound with V.1. of: סדר תפלה = Order of prayer for divine service / Rev. L Merzbacher. (Entries 123–124, 173, 192, 259). Sometimes bound with: Hymns for divine service in Temple Emanu-El. (Entry 186) Levine: 514–515. Copies: CtY DLC (uncat) MH MWalA NN NNJ OCH

189. Ordnung der Gebete beim Gottesdienst der Gemeinde Anshi Chesed an ראש השנה und יום כפור. — New York: L. H. Frank, 1871.

8 p. Levine: 520. Singerman: 2281. Copies: NNJ

190. Predigt-Lieder gesammelt zum Gebrauche beim Gottesdienst der Gemeinde Anshi Chesed: im Anhage: stilles Gebet der Leidtragenden vor Kaddisch zu sprechen. — New York, [s.n.], 1871.

    22 p. Singerman: 2282. Copies: NNJ NNUT

191. Stunden der Andacht: Ein Gebet- und Erbauungsbuch für Israels Frauen und Jungfrauen zur öffentlichen und häuslichen Andacht: so wie für alle Verhältnisse des weiblichen Lebens/von W. Schlessinger und anderen Schriftstellern und mit meheren Zusätzen von Fanny Neuda, geb. Schmiedl. — 8. Stereotyp. Ausgabe. — New York: L. H. Frank, 1871.

    iv, 96 p. Copies: NN

192. סדר תפלה = The order of prayer for divine service/revised by L. Merzbacher. — 3rd ed. rev. and corr./S. Adler. — New York: M. Thalmessinger, 1871.

    181 p. English and Hebrew. Bound with: Order of prayer in the house of mourners, 1871. (Entry 188). Copies: MH

193. עבודת ישראל = Israelitisches Gebetbuch für den öffentlichen Gottesdienst im ganzen Jahre/geordnet und übersetzt von Benjamin Szold, Rabbiner der Oheb Schalom-Gemeinde in Baltimore. — 2. Aufl. — Baltimore: Deutsch und Golderman, 1871.

    vii, 590 p. German and Hebrew. Bound with: Gesänge und Gebete für den öffentlichen Gottesdienst der Israeliten, 1871 (Entry 185). Singerman: 2280. Copies: CLHU DLC (uncat) MH MWalA NNHeb OCH

194. עבודת ישראל = Israelitisches Gebetbuch für den öffentlichen Gottesdienst im ganzen Jahre/geordnet und übersetzt von Benjamin Szold, Rabbiner der Oheb Schalom-Gemeinde in Baltimore. — 3. Aufl. revidirt von M. Jastrow, Rabbiner der Rodef-Schalom Gemeinde zu Philadelphia und H. Hochheimer, Rabbiner der Oheb Israel-Gemeinde zu Baltimore — [Baltimore]: Mühsam und Siemers, 1871.

    vii, 590 p. German and Hebrew. Bound with: Gesänge und Gebete für den öffentlichen Gottesdienst der Israeliten, 1871 (Entry 185). Deinard: 945. Singerman: 2280. Copies: NN NNJ PPGratz

195. עבודת ישראל = Israelitisches Gebetbuch für den öffentlichen Gottesdienst im ganzen Jahre/geordnet und übersetzt von Benjamin Szold, Rabbiner der Oheb Schalom-Gemeinde in Baltimore. — 3. Aufl. revidirt von M. Jastrow, Rabbiner der Rodef-Schalom Gemeinde zu Philadelphia und H. Hochheimer, Rabbiner der Oheb Israel-Gemeinde zu Baltimore. — Baltimore: H. F Siemers, c 1871.

    vii, 590 p. German and Hebrew. Bound with: Gesänge und Gebete für den öffentlichen Gottesdienst der Israeliten, 1871 (Entry 185). Copies: OCH

196. תחינות בנות ישורון = Religiöse Betrachtungen und Gebete für Israels Frauen und Mädchen/von W. Schlessinger. — New York: Frank, 1871.

    32 p. Levine: 513. Copies: OCH

1872

197. Der XXIV Psalm (hebräischer und deutscher text) für gemischten Chor und Solo: mit obligater Orgelbegleitung in Musik gesetzt/Morris Goldstein. — New York: The Composer, c 1872.

    Score (7 p.) For Cantor and chorus (SATB). Sendrey: 6822. Singerman: 2327. Copies: OCH

198. Hours of devotion: a book of prayers and meditations for the use of the daughters of Israel, during public service and at home for all the conditions of woman's life/translated from the German "Stunden der Andacht" by M. Mayer. — 3rd. ed. — New York: L. H. Frank, 1872.

105 p. Original German by Fanny Schmiedl Neuda. Levine: 551. Copies: NNJ OCH

199. Order of service for the consecration of the Temple Ahawath Chesed, cor. Lexington Ave. & 55th St.: on Friday April 19th, 1872. — New York: The Congregation, 1872.

10 p. English, German and Hebrew. Singerman: 2351. Copies: NNJ OCH

200. ... מחזור = Form of prayers ... with English translation. — 4th ed. — New York: L. H. Frank, 1872–5632.

5 v. English and Hebrew. Copies: NNJ

201. מנהג אמעריפא = Daily prayers for American Israelites: as revised in Conference. — Cincinnati: Bloch, c 1872.

271, 48 p. English and Hebrew. Compiled by Isaac M. Wise. Appendix: Select prayers for various occasions in life. Deinard: 918, 961. Levine: 546. Singerman: 2337. Copies: CLHU CSt CtY DLC FU MWalA MWalB N NN NNJ OCH

202. מנהג אמעריקא = Daily prayers for American Israelites: as revised in Conference. — Cincinnati: Bloch, c 1872.

270 [i.e. 135] p. Hebrew only edition. Compiled by Isaac M. Wise. Singerman: 2338. Copies: DLC MH MWalA NN OCH

203. מנהג אמעריקא = Daily prayers for American Israelites: as revised in Conference. — School ed. — Cincinnati: Bloch, c 1872.

270 [i.e. 135] p. Hebrew only ed. Compiled by Isaac M. Wise. Singerman: 2339. Copies: AJK

204. סדר תפלה = Gebete für den öffentlichen Gottesdienst der Tempelgemeinde Ahawath Chesed/geordnet von A. Huebsch, Rabbiner derselben. — New York: L. H. Frank, 5632–1872.

2 v. German and Hebrew. V.1 לשבת שלש רגלים וחול — V.2 .לראש השנה ויום הכפורים. Deinard: 913, 926. Levine: 547. Singerman: 2335. Copies DLC (V.2 uncat) ICN (V.1) MH NN NNHeb NNJ OCH (V.1)

205. סדר תפלה = Gebete für den öffentlichen Gottesdienst der Tempelgemeinde Ahawath Chesed/geordnet von A. Huebsch, Rabbiner derselben. — New York: A. Sommers, 1872.

2 v. German and Hebrew. V.1 לשבת שלש רגלים וחול — V.2 .לראש השנה ויום הכפורים. Deinard: 926. Singerman: 2336. Copies: MH (V.2) NNJ OCH (V.2)

206. סליחות ותפלות ליום ט״ו כסלו...כפי מנהג חברה קדישא גמילות חסדים: עם מנהגים ודינים מלוקטים משו״ע ... השייכים לחולה ולגוסס. — נויארק: מ. ח. לאוונער, תרל״ג.

[1872 or 1873]

13 p. Deinard: 600. Singerman: 2341. Copies:

207. עלת תמיד = Book of prayers for Israelitish Congregations. — New York: For sale by the sexton of the Congregation Adath Jeshurun.; Baltimore: Printed by Deutsch & Golderman, 1872.

394 p. English and Hebrew. Compiled by David Einhorn, with emendations

by B. Felsenthal. Singerman: 2340. Copies: DLC (uncat) NN OCH

208. עלת תמיד = Book of prayers for Israelitish Congregations. — 5th ed. — New York: E. Thalmessinger, c1872.

394 p. English and Hebrew. Compiled by David Einhorn. Copies: CLHU DLC NN NNJ OCH

209. תפלת ישראל = Israelitsches Andachtsbuch: nebst deutscher Übersetzung neuen deutschen Gebeten (תחינות)/ von M. [i.e. W.] Schlessinger. — New York: Frank, 1872.

240, 224, 34 p. German and Hebrew. Final 34 p.: תחנות בנות ישורון = Religiöse Betrachtungen und Gebeten für Israels Frauen und Mädchen. Deinard: 924. Copies: MH

210. תפלת ישראל = Prayers of Israel with an English translation. — 13th stereotype ed. — New York: Frank, 1872, c1864.

240, 229 p. English and Hebrew. Levine: 544. Copies: NiNbs NNJ OCH

1873

211. Gesänge und Gebete für den öffentlichen Gottesdienst der Israeliten. — Baltimore: C. W. Schneidereith, 1873.

104 p. Compiled by Benjamin Szold. Bound with: עבודת ישראל = Israelitische Gebetbuch für den öffentlichen Gottesdienst, 1873 (Entry 217). Copies: MdBHC MH PPAnR PPGratz

212. Hymnen für den öffentlichen Gottesdienst der Templegemeinde Ahawath Chesed/herausgegeben von A. Huebsch. — New York: A. Sommers, 1873.

64 p. Levine: 573. Sendrey: 6966. Singerman: 2394. Copies: CoDU MH-AN MWalA NN OCH PPGratz

213. The order of service: consecration of the Temple Anshi-Chesed, Sept. 12, 1873. — New York: [s.n.], 1873.

p. Singerman: 2406. Copies: NNJ

214. Songs and prayers and meditations for divine services of Israelites/compiled by B. Szold; translated from the German by M. Jastrow. — Philadelphia: M. Jastrow, 1873.

iv, 104 p. Found separate and bound with: עבודת ישראל = Israelitish prayer book for all the public services of the year, 1873 (Entry 218). Deinard: 946. See Singerman: 2399. Copies: Separate: PPGratz. With עבודת ישראל: DLC MH NN NNJ NNUT OCH PPAnR

215. זמרת יה = Zimrath Yah: liturgic songs consisting of Hebrew, English and German Psalms and hymns systematically arranged for the Jewish rite: with organ accompaniment/edited and published by M. Goldstein, A. Kaiser, S. Welsch, I. L. Rice. — New York: The Cantors, 1873–1886.

4 v. of music. Text in English, German or romanized Hebrew. V.1. Sabbath service (1873). — V.2. For the Three Feasts (1875). — V.3. Liturgic songs (1877). — V.4. New Year and Day of Atonement (1886). Levine: 587 (V.1). Sendrey: 6958 (V.2), 7004 (V.3) 6973 (V.4). Singerman: 2429. Copies: AzTeS CLU (V.1) MH (V.2,4) NNJ (V.1–2) OCH (V.4) PPGratz (V.1–3)

216. סדר תפלה = The order of prayer for divine service/revised by L. Merzbacher. — 3rd ed./rev. by S. Adler. — New York: Thalmessinger & Co., 1873.

2 v. English and Hebrew. [V.1] Daily prayers. — V.II. Prayers for the Day of Atonement. Copies: OCH

217. עבודת ישראל = Israelitisches Gebetbuch für den öffentlichen Gottesdienst im ganzen Jahre/geordnet und übersetzt von Benjamin Szold — 3. Aufl. — Baltimore: C.W. Schneidereith, 1873.

590 p. German and Hebrew. Bound with: Gesänge und Gebete für den öffentlichen Gottesdienst der Israeliten, 1873 (Entry 211). Copies: MdBHC MH OCH PPAnR PPGratz

218. עבודת ישראל = Israelitish prayer book for all the public services of the year/originally arranged by Benjamin Szold, of Baltimore.: 2nd ed. (Hebrew and German) revised by M. Jastrow, of Philadelphia, and H. Hochheimer, of Baltimore. — Hebrew and English ed., in text and typographical arrangement fully corresponding with the revised Hebrew-German ed./by M. Jastrow, Rabbi of the Congregation Rodef Shalom. — Philadelphia: M. Jastrow, 1873.

590 p. English and Hebrew. Bound with: Songs and prayers and meditations for the divine services of Israelites, 1873 (Entry 214). Deinard: 946. Singerman: 2399. Copies: DLC MH NN NNJ NNUT OCH PPAnR PPGratz

219. ראשית דעת = Catechism designed for the religious instruction of Israelitish children/by Benjamin Szold. — Baltimore: C.W. Schneidereith, 1873.

46 p. English and Hebrew. Copies: MH

220. ראשית דעת = Catechism designed for the religious instruction of Israelitish children/by Benjamin Szold. — Baltimore: H.F. Siemers, c 1873.

76 p. English and Hebrew. Includes music. Includes Szold's Hebrew primer and Alois Kaiser's Tunes for the Israelitish school (Levine 575). Deinard: 745. Singerman: 2419. Copies: DLC OCH

221. ראשית דעת = Catechism designed for the religious instruction of Israelitish children/by Benjamin Szold. — Baltimore: Mühsam & Siemers, c 1873.

76 p. English and Hebrew. Includes music. Includes Szold's Hebrew primer and Alois Kaiser's Tunes for the Israelitish school (Levine 575). Deinard: 745. See Singerman: 2419. Copies: OCH

222. ראשית דעת = Catechism designed for the religious instruction of Israelitish children/by Benjamin Szold. — [Baltimore: s.n., c 1873].

30 p. English and Hebrew. Copies: AJHS

223. תפלות ישראל = Gebete der Israeliten in Amerika = מנהג אמעריקא: Verbessert von der Conferenz. — Cincinnati, Ohio: Bloch, c 1873.

271, 65 p. German and Hebrew. Compiled by Isaac M. Wise. Second section has title: Gebete zur öffentlichen und häuslichen andacht: Sammlung von Gebeten für all Verhältnisse Lebens für Frauen und Mädchen. Levine: 579. Copies: CLHU MiDW NNJ OCH

224. תפלת ישראל = Prayers of Israel with an English translation. — New York: L.H. Frank, 1873, c 1864.

240, 229 p. English and Hebrew. Levine: 578. Copies: OCH

1874

225. 2 [Zwei] Lieder vor nach der Confirmation/Text von A. Huebsch; in Musik gesetzt und Confirmanden des Tempels "Ahawath Chesed" in New York gewidmet von S. Welsch. — New York: [s.n.], 1874.

Score (3 p.). Levine: 615. Singerman: 2482. Copies: OCH

226. Kommt, Söhne der Allmacht = Come, sons of the mighty: Psalm XXIX: chorus with German and English word with organ accompaniment/Alois Kaiser. — [Baltimore, Md.: s.n.], 1874.

Score (10 p.) English and German. For chorus (SATB), with organ accompaniment. Levine: 599. Singerman: 2452. Copies: OCH

227. [This entry has been deleted.]

228. Order of service for ראש השנה ויום כפור and הזכרת נשמות, 1874–5635. — San Francisco: M. Weiss, Oriental Printing House, 1874–5634.

16 p. English and Hebrew. For Congregation Sherith Israel, San Francisco, CA. = ק״ק שארית ישראל. Singerman: 2475. Copies: MWalA WJHC

229. Stunden der Andacht: Ein Gebet- und Erbauungsbuch für Israels Frauen und Jungfrauen zur öffentlichen und häuslichen Andacht: so wie für alle Verhältnisse des weiblichen Lebens/von W. Schlessinger und anderen Schriftstellern und mit meheren Zusätzen von Fanny Neuda, geb. Schmiedl. — 10. Stereotyp. Ausgabe. — New York: L. H. Frank, 1874.

iv, 96 p. Levine: 611. Copies: OCH

230. זמירות ישראל = Jewish hymns for Sabbath schools and families. Part I./ Simon Hecht. — Evansville, Ind.: S. Hecht, 1874.

29 p. English and German. Singerman: 2444. Copies: OCH

231. ... מחזור = Form of prayers ... with English translation. — 5th ed. — New York: L. H. Frank, 1874–5634, c1864.

5 v. English and Hebrew. Levine: 605. Copies: MH (V.2) NNJ (V.1, 4) OCH OrP (V.1–2)

232. מעין הישועה = Source of salvation: a catechism of Jewish religion: with an appendix of the confirmation-service/ Isaac Mayer. — New York: L. H. Frank, 1874–5634.

106 p. English and Hebrew. Levine: 607. Singerman: 2460. Copies: MH MWalA OCH PU

233. מעין הישועה = Source of salvation: a catechism of Jewish religion: with an appendix of the confirmation-service / Isaac Mayer. — Brooklyn: Hebrew Pub. Co, c1874.

106 p. English and Hebrew. Levine: 608. Published after 1901. Copies: OCH

234. סדור שפת אמת/מאת וואלף בר שמשון דוב איש היידנהיים= Daily prayers with English instructions: published for the Hebrew Free Schools of New York. — New York: L. H. Frank, 1874.

292 p. Levine: 604. Singerman: 2450. Copies: OCH

235. ראשית דעת = Catechism designed for the religious instruction of Israelitish children/by Benjamin Szold. — Baltimore: C. W. Schneidereith, 1874.

56 p. [10] leaves. Includes music. Includes Alois Kaiser's Tunes for the Israelitish School. Singerman: 2478. Copies: AJK

1875

236. Gebete für Kinder für Haus und Schule/entworfen von Benjamin Szold; revidirt von M. Jastrow. — Philadelphia: Im Verlage des Herausgegebers, 1875.

20 p. Found separate and bound with: הגיון לב = Israelitisches Gebetbuch für die häusliche Andacht, 1875 (Entry 240). Deinard: 962. Levine: 633. Singerman: 2510. Copies: Separate: OCH

Bound with הגיון לב: CLU CtY DLC MWalA NNJ

237. Hours of devotion: a book of prayers and meditations for the use of the daughters of Israel, during public service and at home for all the conditions of woman's life/translated from the German "Stunden der Andacht" by M. Mayer. — 3rd. ed. — New York: L. H. Frank, 5635–1875.

    105 p. Original German by Fanny Schmiedl Neuda. Copies: NN

238. Hymns written for the use of Hebrew Congregations. — 4th ed. rev. corr. — Charleston, S.C.: Congregation Beth Elohim; Edward Perry, Printer, 1875.

    xii, 212 p. Written primarily by Penina Moïse. Singerman: 2497. Copies: CU MWalA NNJ OCH ScCF

239. Temple Emanu-El hymn book for schools/[words selected by G. Gottheil; music partly composed and arranged by A. J. Davis, partly chosen from the collection used in the Temple]. Part. 1. — New York: W. A. Pond, c1875.

    15 p. For chorus (SATB). Levine: 637. Sendrey: 6936, 6999. Singerman: 2524. Copies: NNJ OCH PPPrHi

240. הגיון לב = Israelitisches Gebetbuch für die häusliche Andacht/geordnet von Benjamin Szold, Rabbiner der Gemeinde Oheb-Schalom zu Baltimore. — 2. gänzlich umgearbeitete Aufl./herausgegeben von M. Jastrow, Rabbiner der Gemeinde Rodef-Schalom. — Philadelphia: Im Verlage des Herausgegebers, 1875.

    163 p. German and Hebrew. Bound with: Gebete für Kinder für Haus und Schule, 1875 (Entry 236). Deinard: 962, 963. Singerman: 2510. Copies: CLU CtY DLC MWalA NNJ OCH

241. סדר תפלה = Gebete für den öffentlichen Gottesdienst der Tempel-Gemeinde Ahawath Chesed/geordnet von A. Huebsch, Rabbiner derselben. — New York: Rubens & Freund, 5635–1875, c1872.

    2 v. German and Hebrew. Deinard: 926. Levine: 634. Singerman: 2511. Copies: CtY MH MWalA (V.2) NN NNHeb NNJ OCH

242. ראשית דעת = Catechism designed for the religious instruction of Israelitish children/by Benjamin Szold. — Baltimore: C. W. Schneidereith, 1875.

    77, [18] p. Includes music. Includes Alois Kaiser's Tunes for the Israelitish school. Singerman: 2532. Copies: OCH

243. שירי חנוך = Shirai chinooch: confirmation hymns with English and German words/Alois Kaiser. — Baltimore: [s.n.], 1875.

    19 p. English and German. Levine: 627. Singerman: 2512. Copies: OCH

1876

244. Consecration of the Jewish synagogue, Richmond Street, Toronto, Canada: 23rd Tebeth, 5636, 20th January, 1876. — New York: L. H. Frank, 1876.

    17 p. English and Hebrew. Singerman: 2598. Copies: CaOOIHM CaOONL CSt

245. Israelitische Tempel-Gesänge: Hymnen für Sabbath- und Fest-Tage mit deutschem und englischem Text in Musik gesetzt/von Otto Lob. — Chicago: E. Rubovits, 1876.

    Score (56 p.) English and German. Sendrey: 7105. Singerman: 2570. Copies: DLC NNJ OCH

246. אמרי לב = Meditations and prayers for every situation in life/translated and

adapted from the French by H. Rothschild; revised and corrected by I. Leeser. — American stereotype ed. — Philadelphia: Sherman, 5637–1876.

xvi, 260 p. Original in French by Jonas Ennery. Copies: OCH

247. סדור שפת אמת/מאת וואלף בר שמשון דוב איש היידנהיים =
Daily prayers with English instructions: published for the Hebrew Free Schools of New York: as correct as any edition ever published in רעדעלהיים — New York: L. H. Frank, 1876.

292 p. Copies: OCH

248. סדר גמלות חסדים: נקבצו בו התפלות בעד החולה ולבית החיים ולבית האבלים =
Gemilus chasodim. — Chicago: B. J. Ettelson, 5637. [1876 or 1877]

43 p. Singerman: 2634. Copies: AJK

249. קרבן אהרן = Gebet-Buch fuer Sabbath, Pesach, Schebuoth, Succoth, und Rosh Hashana/von Aaron Hahn, Rabbiner der Tifereth Israel Gemeinde, Cleveland, Ohio. — Cleveland, O.: Kultchar & Hartley, c1876.

33 p. German and Hebrew. Bound with: Hahn, A. פרי עץ הדעת. Cleveland, 1876. Singerman: 2562. Copies: DLC MH NNHeb OCH

250. ראשית דעת = Catechism designed for the religious instruction of Israelitish children/by Benjamin Szold. — Baltimore: C. W. Schneidereith, 1876.

77, [18] p. Includes music. Includes Alois Kaiser's Tunes for the Israelitish school. 1875. Copies: PPAnR

251. תפלת ישראל = Prayers of Israel with an English translation. — 15th stereotype ed. — New York: L. H. Frank, 1876.

240, 229 p. English and Hebrew. Copies: MWalA

1877

252. Gebet-Ordnung für die Todten-Bestattung/entworfen von Benjamin Szold, Rabbiner der Gemeinde "Oheb Schalom" zu Baltimore. — Baltimore: S. Rauders, 1877.

13 p. German and Hebrew. Deinard: 907. Singerman: 2633. Copies: NNJ

253. Der israelitische Confirmand: oder Glaubens- und Pflichtenlehre für den Schul- und den Privatgebrauch in Reformgemeinde: bearbeitet und mit Zusätzen, Amnerkungen und neuenLiederversen/S. Herxheimer. — Evansville, Ind.: [s.n.], 1877.

79 p. See Singerman: 2074. Copies: ICN MH NN OCH

254. Order of service Thanksgiving Day, November 29th 1877: by the Congregations Shearith Israel and Shaaray Tefila, of New York, in the Nineteenth Street Synagogue. — New York: [s.n.], 1877.

7 p. Singerman: 2629. Copies: NNJ

255. Prayer and singing-book for the use of the rising generation of Hebrew Congregations/compiled by E. Eppstein. — Milwaukee: B. Loewenbach & Son, 1877.

38 p. English and German. Singerman: 2631. Copies: OCH

256. מחזור ... = Form of prayers ... with English translation. — 6th ed. — New York: L. H. Frank, 1877–5637.

5 v. English and Hebrew. Copies: CU (V.1–2) NNJ (V.1) OCH (V.1)

257. סדור שפתי צדיקים ... כמנהג ק"ק ספרדים כאשר נדפס על ידי המגיה והמעתיק/ דוד בן אהרן די סולה ... והמעתיק יצחק ליסר ... ועתה נדפס בתוספות חדשות מועילות ושתים מהן השכבה לילד ותפלה וברכה ליום שמחת

בר מצוה מאת בנימין ארטום, ראש ק"ק הספרדים בברטניא, הכל מסודר תחת הרב הנ"ל על ידי אברהם בן דוד די סולה, דורש טוב לעמו בק"ק שארית ישראל בעיר מנטריאל. — פה פילאדילפיא: נדפס על ידי שרמן וחביריו, בשנת [תרל"ח]=.

Form of prayers according to the custom of the Spanish and Portuguese Jews ... new edition based on the versions of the the late revs. D. A De Sola and Isaac Leeser / edited and revised by Abraham De Sola, Minister of the Portuguese Congregation, to which are added prayers and blessings for the ceremony of religious majority, with reflections, also a prayer on the death of a child, by and printed with the authority of Benjamin Artom, Chief Rabbi of the Spanish and Portuguese Congregations of England. — Philadelphia: Sherman & Co., 5638 [1877 or 1878].

6 v. English and Hebrew. Singerman: 2628. Copies: Beth Ahabah Museum and Archives Trust, Richmond, Va. CLU DLC (V.1, uncat) MH (V.1) MWalA (V.1–3) NNJ (V.4) OCH (V.1) PPGratz (V.1–3) (V.2–3) UU (V.2)

258. סדר להדרת קדש: כולל תפלות כל השנה =. Form of blessings of Israel with an English translation. — New York: Harris B. Germansky, 1877.

507 p. English and Hebrew. Singerman: 2632. Copies: DLC

259. סדר תפלה = The order of prayer for divine service / revised by L. Merzbacher ... 1855. — 3rd ed. rev. and corr. / by S. Adler, 1864. — New York: Industrial School Hebrew Orphan Asylum, 1877.

2 v. English and Hebrew. [V.I]. Daily prayers. — V.II. Prayers for the Day of Atonement. [V.I] Bound with: Hymns for divine service in the Temple Emanu-El, 1871 (Entry 186) and Order of prayers in the house of mourners, 1871 (Entry 188). Deinard: 927. Singerman: 2630. Copies: CtY (V.1) MH NN OCH

1878

260. Form of the service for the consecration of the new synagogue of the Congregation Mickva Israel, Savannah Ga.: consecrated on Thursday 8th Nissan, 5638 [11th April, 1878]. — Savannah; J. Stern, 5638.

14 p. Singerman: 2722. Copies: GU-De

261. The orpheus, or musical recreations for the family circle and public worship: with piano and organ accompaniment: an entire new collection of songs, duets, choruses, hymns and prayers / composed by G. M. Cohen. — [Cleveland: S. Brainard's sons,] c 1878.

Score (88 p.). The text is "mostly taken from the hymns of the Congregation Beth Elohim, Charleston, S.C., also from Dr. Wise's Hymn Book, L Stein's and others ..." — preface. Sendrey: 6930. Singerman: 2685. Copies: OCH PPGratz (Music)

262. Psalm CXII. Heil dem Manne (Blesst the man): chorus and soli, with English and German words: composed and dedicated to Julius Stiefel, Esq. at the Twenty fifth anniversary of his presidency of Oheb Shalom Congregation of Baltimore, MD / Alois Kaiser. — New York: Hounslow, 1878.

Score (7 p.) English and German. For Soli and chorus (SATB). Singerman: 2699. Copies: OCH

263. Psalm CXXV. We sich auf Gott verlässt (He who in God confides): chorus and quartet with English and German words: composed for the Twenty fifth anniversary of the Oheb Shalom Congrega-

tion of Baltimore, Md./Alois Kaiser; words by Benjamin Szold. — New York: Hounslow, 1878.

Score (9 p.) English and German. Sendrey: 6839. Singerman: 2700. Copies: OCH

264. זמירות ישראל = Jewish hymns for Sabbath-schools and families (English and German)/Simon Hecht. — [2nd ed.] — Cincinnati: Bloch, c1878.

55 p. English and German. Includes music. Edition implied from preface. Deinard: 292? Singerman: 2689. Copies: MH OCH PU

265. סדור שפת אמת/מאת וואלף בר שמשון דוב איש היידנהיים = Daily prayers with English instructions: published for the Hebrew Free Schools of New York: as correct as any edition ever published in רעדעלהיים — New York: L.H. Frank, 1878–5638.

293 p. Copies: NNJ

266. ספר החיים = The book of life: a complete formula of the service and ceremonies observed at the death-bed, house of mourning and cemetery: together with prayers on visiting the graves/elaborated and revised by H. Vidaver. — Cincinnati; Chicago: Bloch, 1878.

194 p. English and Hebrew. Deinard: 308. Copies: OCH

267. ספר החיים = The book of life: a complete formula of the service and ceremonies observed at the death-bed, house of mourning and cemetery: together with prayers on visiting the graves/elaborated and revised by H. Vidaver. — New York: L.H. Frank, 1878.

194 p. English and Hebrew. Singerman: 2698. Copies: DLC (uncat) ICU MeLB MWalA NjNBS NNYU OCH OCL OYU

268. ספר החיים = The book of life: a complete formula of the service and ceremonies observed at the death-bed, house of mourning and cemetery: together with prayers on visiting the graves/elaborated and revised by H. Vidaver. — New York: Hebrew Pub. Co., c1878.

194 p. English and Hebrew. Probably published after 1901. Copies: WJHC

269. תפלת ישראל = Prayers of Israel with an English translation. — 16th stereotype ed. — New York: L.H. Frank, 1878, c1864.

240, 229 p. English and Hebrew. Copies: ABAu NNHeb OCH

1879

270. Confirmation service/Alois Kaiser. — Baltimore: A. Kaiser, 1879.

Score (4 p.) English and German. For Chorus (SATB). Singerman: 2790. Copies: OCH

271. Gottesdienst für Sabbath, Fest- und Wochentage und Gebete für Kinder: zum Gebrauch für die Schule der Gemeinde B'nai Jeshurun in Newark, N.J. — Philadelphia: Heymann & Scholvien, 1879.

79, 21 p. English, German and Hebrew. Second section has title: Anhang: Gebete für Kinder. Deinard: 940. Singerman: 2787. Copies: DLC

272. Hymns/Polonies Talmud Torah School. — New York: Kahrs & Cowen, 1879.

21 p. Singerman: 2809. Copies: CtY

273. Prayers, hymns and exercises: for the Hebrew and Religious School of the Congregation Sherith Israel, San Francisco. — San Francisco: Weiss, 5640–1879.

16 p. Singerman: 2815. Copies: MWalA OCAJA OCH

1879–1880

274. הזכרת נשמות = Requiem for the Day of Atonement: devoted in filial affection to the memory of his deceased mother, Mrs. Therese Kaiser/composed and arranged for soli and chorus with English and German words, and organ accompaniment by Alois Kaiser. — Baltimore: A. Kaiser, 1879.

>Score (31 p.) English, German and romanized Hebrew. Sendrey: 7450. Singerman: 2791. Copies: NNJ OCH

275. מעין הישועה = Source of salvation: a catechism of Jewish religion: with an appendix of the confirmation-service/Isaac Mayer. — New York: H. Sakolski's Hebrew Book Store, 5639–1879, c 1874.

>106 p. English and Hebrew. Singerman: 2800. Copies: MWalA NStBU

276. סדר תפלה = The order of prayer for divine service/revised by L. Merzbacher, 1855. — 3rd ed. rev. and corr./by S. Adler, 1864. — New York: John Mendole & Son, 1879, c 1860.

>xviii, 181, 17, 67 p. English, German and Hebrew. Includes: Hymns for divine Service in Temple Emanu-El and Order of Prayer in the house of mourners. Deinard: 927. Copies: MH NNJ

277. עבודת הקדש = Service of the sanctuary for the Sabbath and Festivals: arranged for the use of Congregation Beth Elohim, Charleston, S.C./by David Levy, Minister of the Congregation. — New York: M. Thalmessinger, 5639–1879.

>168 p. English and Hebrew. Singerman: 2788. Copies: NN NNJ

188-?

278. The crown of a good name: service of confirmation for Shebuot/arranged by H. Berkowitz. — New York: Bloch, [188-?]

>20 p. Copies: NN NNJ PPGratz

279. אותך אדרש = Traditional hymn for the Day of Atonement: alto or bariton solo with chorus/arranged by Gustavus Ensel. — [Paducah, Ky., 188-?]

>Score (3 p.). Singerman: 2848. Copies: OCH

280. שירי ישראל = Sherai Israel: a collection of sacred music, Psalms and hymns, with accompaniment for organ adapted for public worship/Morris Goldstein. — Cincinnati: Bloch, [188-?]

>Score (58 p.). Title taken from pasted label. Includes "Sabbath song"/by Simon Hecht. Singerman: 2854. Copies: OCH

1880

281. Gesänge für den öffentlichen jüdischen Gottesdienst aus verschiedenen Liedersammlungen zusammengetragen: im Verlage des Temple Beth El in New York. — New York: W. Cahn, 1880.

>135 p. English, German and Hebrew. Singerman: 2941. Copies: NN (Microfilm) NNJ OCH

282. Hymn book for Jewish worship. — Rochester, N.Y.: Daily Union and Advertiser Company's Book and Job Print., 1880.

>108 p. Compiled by Max Landsberg and Solomon Wile. Sendrey: 6977. Singerman: 2929. Copies: NNJ OCH

283. ...מחזור = Form of prayers ... with English translation. — 6th ed. — New York: H. Sakolski, 1880–5640.

>5 v. English and Hebrew. V.1. For the New Year. — V.2. For the Day of Atonement. — V.3. Feast of Tabernacles. — V.4. Feast of Passover. — V.5. Feast of Pentecost. Singerman: 2918. Copies: NNJ (V.5) OCH

284. ‎מחזור‎ ... = Form of prayers ... with English translation. — 7th ed. — New York: H. Sakolski, 1880–5640.

5 v. English and Hebrew. V.1. For the New Year. — V.2. For the Day of Atonement. — V.3. Feast of Tabernacles. — V.4. Feast of Passover. — V.5. Feast of Pentecost. Copies: CLHU (V.2) NNHeb (V.3–5) NNJ (V.3)

285. ‎מלמד להועיל‎ = Hebrew first reader: a progressive method of learning to read Hebrew correctly and to accentuate accurately: with an appendix of prayers for children's Sabbath service/compiled by ‎אבירא ל ן׳ שלום‎. — San Francisco: M. Weiss, 5640–1880.

40 p. Hebrew with English instructions. Attributed to Abraham Solomon. Singerman: 2952. Copies: DLC (microfilm) OCH PPGratz WJHC

286. ‎סדר תפלה‎ = The order of prayer for divine service/revised by L. Merzbacher, Rabbi of the Temple Emanu-El 1855. — 3rd ed. rev. and corr./by S. Adler, 1864. — New York: J. Mendole & Son, 1880.

2 v. English and Hebrew. [V.I.] Daily prayers. — V.II. Prayers for the Day of Atonement. Singerman: 2919. Copies: OCH

287. ‎שערי חסד‎ = Order of services at the house of mourning, burial and setting of tombstones/arranged by I. L. Leucht. — New Orleans: Jewish South Pub. House, 5640–1880.

21 p. English and Hebrew. Deinard: 823. Singerman: 2923. Copies: CLHU DLC (uncat) MH MWalA NN (microfilm) OCH PPAnR PU

288. ‎תפלת ישראל‎ = Prayers of Israel with an English translation. — 17th stereotype ed. — New York: H. Sakolski, 1880, c1864.

240, 229 p. English and Hebrew. Singerman: 2920. Copies: OCH

1881

289. Hymns of the Beth El Emeth Congregation, Franklin Street. — Philadelphia: The Congregation, 5641–1881.

22 p. Singerman: 3012. Copies: MWalA NNJ NNYU (Sephardic Reference Room) OCH PPL

290. ‎למען ילמדו‎ = (Lema'an yilmedu): a second Hebrew reader for Jewish schools and private instruction. — Chicago: M. Stern, Goldsmith & Co., 1881.

41 p. Hebrew. Compiled by B. Felsenthal. Pages 20–37 contain prayers. Deinard: 412. Singerman: 2984. Copies: OCH

291. ‎סדור שפת אמת/מאת וואלף בר שמשון דוב איש היידנהיים‎ = Daily prayers with English instructions: published for the Hebrew Free Schools of New York: as correct as any edition ever published in ‎רעדעלהיים‎ — New York: H. Sakolski, 1881–5640.

293 p. Singerman: 3000. Copies: OCH

292. ‎סדר להדרת קדש:כולל תפלות כל השנה‎ = Form of blessings of Israel with an English translation. — New York: J. H. Kantrowitz, 1881.

507 p. English and Hebrew. Singerman: 2998. Copies: DLC (uncat) MH MWalA OCH

293. ‎סדר להדרת קדש:כולל תפלות כל השנה‎ = Form of blessings of Israel with an English translation. — New York: Hebrew Pub. Co, c1881.

507 p. English and Hebrew. Probably published after 1901. Copies: OCH

294. סדר תפלה = The order of prayer for divine service/revised by L. Merzbacher, 1855.— 3rd ed. rev. and corr./by S. Adler, 1864.— New York: J. Mendole & Son, 1881.

    2 v. (V.1 181, 17, 71 p.) V.2 (389 p.) English and Hebrew. [V.I] Daily prayers. Includes: Hymns for divine service in the Temple Emanu-El. and Order of prayer in the house of the mourners. — V.II. Prayers for the Day of Atonement. Deinard: 927, 957. See Singerman: 2919. Copies: DLC MH MWalA (V.1) NNJ OCH

295. סדר תפלה = The order of prayer for divine service: as adapted by the Congregation Emanu-El of San Francisco.— San Francisco: G. Spaulding & Co. Mining and Scientific Press Printing Office, 1881.

    xv, 299 p. English and Hebrew. Introduction adapted from the siddur of Temple Emanu-El of New York. Singerman: 2999. Copies: NNJ

1882

296. The Hebrew text for schools from the prayerbook of B. Szold.— Baltimore: [s.n.], 1882.

    59 p. Hebrew. Singerman: 3076. Copies: OCH

297. Hours of devotion: a book of prayers and meditations for the use of the daughters of Israel, during public service and at home for all the conditions of woman's life/translated from the German "Stunden der Andacht" by M. Mayer. — 5th ed. — New York: H. Sakolski, 5642–1882, c1866.

    105 p. Original German by Fanny Schmiedl Neuda. Copies: NNHeb OCH PP

298. Hymns and anthems/[Temple Emanu-El, New York, N.Y.].— New York: Industrial School of the Hebrew Orphan Asylum, 1882.

    19 leaves. Singerman: 3091. Copies: OCH (lost)

299. Stunden der Andacht: Ein Gebet- und Erbauungsbuch für Israels Frauen und Jungfrauen zur öffentlichen und häuslichen Andacht: so wie für alle Verhältnisse des weiblichen Lebens/von W. Schlessinger und anderen Schriftstellern und mit meheren Zusätzen von Fanny Neuda, geb. Schmiedl. — 9. Stereotyp. Ausgabe.— New York: Sakolski, 1882–5642.

    iv, 96 p. Singerman: 3089. Levine: 611. Copies: NN OCH

300. סדור שפת אמת/מאת וואלף בר שמשון דוב איש היידנהיים = Daily prayers with English instructions: published for the Hebrew Free Schools of New York: as correct as any edition ever published in רעדעלהיים — New York: H. Sakolski, 1882–5642.

    293 p. Copies: OCH

301. ספר החיים = The book of life: a complete formula of the service and ceremonies observed at the death-bed, house of mourning and cemetery: together with prayers on visiting the graves/elaborated and revised by H. Vidaver. — New York: H. Sakolski, 5642–1882, c1878.

    194 p. English and Hebrew. OCH's copy has label: Bloch & Co., Cincinnati, O. pasted over imprint. Singerman: 3077. Copies: CFIS CU MiDW MWalA NNHeb OCH

302. תפלת ישראל = Israelitisches Andachts-Buch: nebst deutscher Übersetzung mit neuen deutschen Gebeten [תחנות]/von W. Schlessinger. — Neue

verbesserte Stereotyp-Ausgabe. — New York: H. Sakolski, 1882–5642.

240, 228, 32 p. German and Hebrew. Final section: תחנות בנות ישורון = Religiöse Betrachtungen und Gebete für Israels Frauen und Mädchen. Deinard: 924. Copies: DLC (ucat) NNHeb

303. תפלת ישראל = Prayers of Israel with an English translation. — 17th stereotype ed. — New York: H. Sakolski, 1882.

240, 229 p. English and Hebrew. Copies: OCH

1883

304. Coll nidrey by Rabbi J'Hudo Halewi from the city of Prague, Bohemia / Simon Adler. — New York: T. Lohr, 1883.

Score (5 p.) romanized Hebrew. With piano accompaniment. Sendrey: 7165. Singerman: 3115. Copies: NN

305. Dedication of the Temple Gates of Hope, 86th Street bet. Lexington and Park Aves.: Sunday January 28th, 1883: with the sermon preached on the occasion, the Evolution of religion / by the Rev. Dr. Browne. — New York: Jewish Herald Pub. Co., 1883.

29 p. Singerman: 3125. Copies: MWalB NN (microfilm) NNJ OCH

306. Hymnen für den öffentlichen Gottesdienst der Tempel-Gemeinde Ahawath Chesed / herausgegeben von A. Huebsch. — New York: A. L. Goetzl, 1883.

64 p. Sendrey: 6966. Singerman: 3153. Copies: DLC (microform) NN (microfilm) OCH

307. Selected hymns and prayers for divine service, Congregation Hand in Hand (יד ביד) of Harlem. — New York: A. L. Goetzl, 5644, 1883.

31 p. Singerman: 3175. Copies: NNJ

308. סדר תפלה = Gebete für den öffentlichen Gottesdienst der Temple-Gemeinde Ahawath Chesed / geordnet von A. Huebsch, Rabbiner derselben. — New York: A. L. Goetzl, 5643–1883, c1872.

2 v. German and Hebrew. Deinard: 926 (V.2), 969 (V.1). Singerman: 3161. Copies: DLC (uncat) MH (V.1) MWalA (1883– 1887) NN NNJ

309. קרבן תודה = Sunday services for Jewish Reform congregations / by D. Stern. — Philadelphia: E. Hirsch, 1883.

37 p. English and Hebrew. Compiled for The Reform Congregation at Wilkes-Barre, Pa., now Congregation B'nai Brith of Wilkes-Barre, Kingston, Pa. Deinard: 729. Singerman: 3160. Copies: AJK OCH

310. תפלת ערבית לבית האבל = Evening service for the house of mourning: arranged for the use of the Congregation B'nai Jeshurun / by Henry S. Jacobs, Minister of the Congregation. — New York: F. Lewine, 5644. [1883 or 1884].

1 v. (unpaged) English and Hebrew. Deinard: 929. Singerman: 3162. Copies: DLC MH NNJ ViU

1884

311. Centennial anniversary: Sir Moses Montefiore: united Hebrew services at Rodef Sholom Synagogue, Philadelphia. — Philadelphia: S. W. Goodman, printer, [1884].

17 p. Singerman: 3213. Copies: MWalA NNYI OCH PPAmP PPAnr PPL NNYU

312. Gebete bei Leichenbegängnissen auf dem Friedhof der Oheb-Israel-Gemeinde zu Baltimore. — Baltimore: [s.n.], 1884.

11 p. Singerman: 3252. Copies: NNJ

1884

313. The Hebrew reader for schools: from the prayer book of B. Szold / revised by Jastrow and Hochheimer. — Philadelphia: The editors, 1884.

    59 p. Hebrew. Singerman: 3249. Copies: NNJ OCH PPAnR

314. Order of children's service for Jewish Sabbath schools / published by Isaac S. Moses. — Milwaukee: I. S. Moses, 1884.

    18 p. English and Hebrew. Singerman: 3250. Copies: NNJ OCH

315. Order of service in honor of the hundredth birthday of Sir Moses Montefiore, Bart.: held at the synagogue "Gates of Prayer" New Orleans, Louisiana: Chesvan 7th 5645, October 26th, 1884. — New Orleans: [s.n.], 1884.

    4 p. Singerman: 3276. Copies:

316. Order of service in honor of the one hundredth bithday of Sir Moses Montefiore, Bart.: held at the Touro Synagogue, New Orleans, October 26th 1884. — New Orleans: [s.n.], 1884.

    8 p. Singerman: 3277. Copies: NNJ

317. Psalm I. verses 1, 2, and 3: chorus and solo, with English and German words / Alois Kaiser. — Baltimore: O. Sutro, c1884.

    17 p. English and German. At head of title: To his friend Benjamin Szold on his Twenty-fifth ministerial anniversary. Sendrey: 6863. Singerman: 3256. Copies: NNJ OCH

318. Pure words: a collection of special prayers / by Isaac P. Mendes, Minister of the Hebrew Congregation "Mickva Israel," Savannah Ga. — Savannah, Ga. — M. S. Byck, 1884.

    56 p. Singerman: 3272. Copies: DLC GHi GU-De NN NNHeb NNJ OCH

319. Ritual for Jewish worship. — Rochester, N.Y.: C. Mann, 1884, c1883.

    47 p. Compiled by Max Landsberg for use at Rochester's Temple Brith Kodesh. Singerman: 3246. Copies: DLC OCH

320. Service of prayer and thanksgiving as used in all the synagogues of the British empire: as adopted for use in the United States on the occasion of Sir Moses Montefiore, completing his hundredth year, Sunday 26th October, 5645–1884. — New York: C. S. Nathan, 1884.

    3 p. English and Hebrew. Singerman: 3295. Copies: NNJ

321. Service on the occasion of the one hundredth birthday of Sir Moses Montefiore: held at Temple Beth Elohim, Brooklyn, Sunday October 26, 1884.

    4 p. Singerman: 3275. Copies:

322. Sir Moses Montefiore, Centennial: [a service] / Congregation Mickve Israel, Savannah, Ga. [Savannah, Ga.: The Congregation, 1884].

    p. Singerman: 3293. Copies: NNJ

323. Sir Moses Montefiore Centennial celebration.: Union Thanksgiving services by the Israelites of Milwaukee, held at Temple Emanu-El, October 26, 1884. — Milwaukee: Cramer, Aikens & Cramer, 1884.

    4 p. English only. Includes: "Hymn to Moses Montefiore" and "Prayer written for the occasion by the Chief rabbi of London." Singerman: 3296. Copies:

324. ספר החיים = The book of life: a complete formula of the service and ceremonies observed at the death-bed, house of mourning and cemetery: together with prayers on visiting the graves / elaborated and revised by H. Vidaver. — New York: F. Lewine, 1884–5645.

194 p. English and Hebrew. Singerman: 3253. Copies: NNJ

325. תפלה למשה = Order of prayers and responsive readings for Jewish worship/ published by Isaac S. Moses, Rabbi of Congregation "Emanu-El" Milwaukee, Wis. — Milwaukee, Wis.: I. S. Moses, 1884.

116 p. English and Hebrew. Singerman: 3247. Copies: NN NNHeb NNJ OCH PPGratz

326. תפלת ישראל = Prayers of Israel with an English translation. — 17th stereotype ed. — New York: H. Sakolski, 1884, c1864.

240, 229 p. English and Hebrew. Copies: MH NNHeb

327. תפלת ישראל כולל התפלות מכל השנה כמנהג ק״ק שערי תקוה/מאת משה בן יעקב ברוין, רב ודרשן דק״ק הנ״ל. — מהד׳ חדשה — נעוו-יארק, תרמ״ה.
תפלת ישראל = Prayers of Israel arranged for the American Reform services in Temple "Gates of Hope"/by Dr. Browne. — New York: [s.n.], 1884.

160 p. English and Hebrew. Singerman: 3248. Copies: NNG NNJ OCH

1885

328. Dedication of the new synagogue [Congregation B'nai Jehudah]: Friday and Saturday, September 4th and 5th, 1885. — Kansas City: I. P. Moore, Printer, 1885.

1 folded leaf printed on 4 sides. Singerman: 3356. Copies: OCAJA

329. Order of service at the dedication of the synagogue of Congregation "B'nai Jeshurun" of Madison Avenue: Wednesday, March 25th, 1885, 9th Nissan, 5645. — New York: Hebrew Journal Print, 1885-5645.

9 p. Singerman: 3371. Copies: MWalA

330. Sacred memorial services in memory of the late משה מאנטיפיורי Sir Moses Montefiore: held in Boston at the Church Street Synagogue, Zion's Holy Prophets: on Sunday Ab 20, A.M. 5645/by Alfred A. Marcus. — New York: Hebrew Journal Print, 5645.

26 p. Singerman: 3362. Copies: CtY DLC MB NNJ OCH RPB

331. A service of the synagogue in the time of Jesus Christ: for the Sabbath/by R. Henry Ferguson. — Newton Centre, Mass.: R. H. Ferguson, 1885.

12, 2, 9 p. Includes music by Henry F. Dexter (9 p. at end), Preface by Rabbi S. S. Kohn. Singerman: 3333. Copies: DLC FU ICU MB MiU Nh NRCR RPB

332. A service of the synagogue in the time of Jesus Christ: for the Sabbath/by R. Henry Ferguson. — 3rd rev. ed — [Newton Centre, Mass.: R. H. Ferguson], 1885.

2 p. Without the music by Henry F. Dexter. See Singerman: 3333. Copies: NRCR RPB

333. Songs and prayers and meditations for divine services of Israelites/compiled by Benjamin Szold; translated from the German by M. Jastrow. — Philadelphia: M. Jastrow, 1885.

iv, 104 p. Found separate and bound with: עבודת ישראל = Israelitish prayer book, 1885 (Entries 335, 336). Deinard: 946. Copies: Separate: PPGratz Bound with: עבודת ישראל :CLHU CoU DLC FU MH MWalA NN NNJ OCH OCl PPAnR RPB ViU

334. בית תפלה = Synagogue service for the use of the Congregation "Shaaray Tefilla." — New York: F. Lewine, 1885.

3 v. English and Hebrew. V.1. New Year. — V.2. Day of Atonement. — V.3.

Sabbath and Festivals. Preface signed: F. de Sola Mendes, David Davis, Louis Levenson, Ritual Committee. Singerman: 3350. Copies: DLC MWalA MWalB NNJ OCH (V.3)

335. ‏... מחזור‎ = Form of prayers ... with English translation. — 8th ed. — New York: F. Lewine, 1885–5646.

5 v. English and Hebrew. Singerman: 3351. Copies NNHeb (V.1) OCH

336. ‏סדר תפלות כל השנה‎ = Ritual for Jewish worship. — Rochester, N.Y.: C. Mann, 1885, c1884.

vi, 69, 150 p. English. Edited by Max Landsberg for Congregation Brith Kodesh, Rochester, N.Y. Singerman: 3353. Copies: CPA CtY CU DLC NAlU NN NNYU NRCR OCH PPGratz

337. ‏עבודת ישראל‎ = Israelitish prayer book for all the public services of the year/ originally arranged by Benjamin Szold. — 2nd ed. (Hebrew and German) revised by M. Jastrow and H. Hochheimer. Hebrew and English ed., in text and typographical arrangement fully corresponding with the revised Hebrew-German ed./ by M. Jastrow. — Philadelphia: M. Jastrow, 1885.

2 v. English, German and Hebrew. V.1. Prayers for Sabbaths and Festivals. — V.2. Prayers for the New Year. Spine title: Abodath Israel. Bound with: Songs and prayers and meditations, 1885 (Entry 331). Deinard: 946. Copies: CLHU (V.2, uncat) DLC (uncat) FU MWalA NN NNJ OCH OCl PPAnR RPB

338. ‏עבודת ישראל‎ = Israelitish prayer book for all the public services of the year/ originally arranged by Benjamin Szold. — 2nd ed. (Hebrew and German) revised by M. Jastrow and H. Hochheimer. Hebrew and English ed., in text and typographical arrangement fully corresponding with the revised Hebrew-German ed./ by M. Jastrow. — Philadelphia: M. Jastrow, 1885.

590 p. in 4 pts. English and Hebrew. Bound with: Songs and prayers and meditations, 1885 (Entry 331). Copies: CLHU CoU MH NN ViU

339. ‏קול זמרה‎ = Kol zimroh: a hymn book for Temples and Sabbath schools: and adapted for choirs and congregational singing/ M. Goldstein. — Cincinnati: Bloch, 1885.

Score (144 p.) For Cantor and chorus (union or SATB), with organ accompaniment. Sendrey: 6957. Singerman: 3334. Copies: CLHU NNJ OCH PPGratz

340. ‏תפלת ישראל: התפלות מכל השנה כמנהג ק״ק שערי תקוה/ מאת משה ברוין. — מהד. חדשה. — נעוו-יארק, תרמ״ה‎ = Prayers of Israel: containing the divine services of the entire year: arranged for the American Reform services in the Temple "Gates of Hope"/ by Edward B. M. Browne, Rabbi of the Congregation. — 2nd ed. — New York: The Congregation, 1885.

168, 168 p. English and Hebrew. Deinard: 970. Singerman: 3352. Copies: MWalA NN OCH

1886

341. Hours of devotion: a book of prayers and meditations for the use of the daughters of Israel, during public service and at home for all the conditions of woman's life/ translated from the German "Stunden der Andacht" by M. Mayer. — 5th ed. — New York: Lewine & Rosenbaum, 1886–5646.

105 p. Original German by Fanny Schmiedl Neuda. Singerman: 3481. Copies: MWalA NNYU

1886

342. Hymns and anthems adapted for Jewish worship/selected and arranged by Gustav Gottheil. — New York: [s.n.], 1886.

xii, 219, xii p. Spine title: Hymns for Jewish worship. Singerman: 3431. Copies: MWalA ViU

343. Hymns for Jewish worship: adopted for Temples and Sabbath schools. No. 1. — [Baltimore]: D. Binswanger, 1886.

53 p. English and German. Singerman: 3441. Copies: OCH

344. The order of service at the dedication of the Temple of Congregation Bikur Cholim: Wykoff Avenue bet. Fulton & Atlantic Aves., Brooklyn: Sunday September 26th, 1886. — New York: J. Lanzit, 1886.

9 p. Singerman: 3416. Copies: OCH

345. הזכרת נשמות = Prayers for the sick and the dead: arranged for the use of the Congregation B'nai Jeshurun/by Henry S. Jacobs. — New York: Lewine & Rosenbaum, 1886.

10 p. English and Hebrew. Singerman: 3460. Copies: OCH

346. זמרות ושירות = Order of service at the consecration of the new synagogue "Shaar Hashomayim": on McGill College Avenue, on Wednesday, the 15 Elul 5646/15 Sept. 1886, at 2:30 p.m. Montreal. — New York: Jewish Gazette Print, 1886.

23 p. English and Hebrew. Singerman: 3479. Copies: Jewish Public Library, Montreal (File for Shaar Hashomayim, Jewish Canadiana Collection)

347. זמרות ישראל = Jewish hymns for Sabbath-Schools and families (English and German)/by Simon Hecht. — [2nd ed.] — Cincinnati: Bloch, 1886, c1878.

55 p. English and German. Includes music. Edition statement taken from preface. Copies: CLHU

348. למען ילמדו = (Lema'an yilmedu): Hebrew reader for Jewish schools and private instruction. — Rev. 2nd stereotype ed. — Chicago: M. Stern, 1886.

47 p. Hebrew. Written by B. Felsenthal. Pages 20–37 contain excerpts from the prayer book. Deinard: 412. Singerman: 3429. Copies: NN OCH PPAnR PPGratz

349. מחזור ... = Form of prayers ... with English translation. — Rev. ed. — New York: Lewine & Rosenbaum, 1886–5646.

5 v. English and Hebrew. Singerman: 3452. Copies: MWalA (V.5) NNJ (V.3) OCH (V.1–2, 4)

350. סדור שפת אמת/מאת וואלף בר שמשון דוב איש היידנהיים =.

Daily prayers with English instructions: published for the Hebrew Free Schools of New York: as correct as any edition ever published in רעדעלהיים. — New York: Lewine & Rosenbaum, 1886–5646.

293 p. Hebrew with English instructions. Singerman: 3455. Copies: NNJ

351. סדר תפלה = The order of prayer for the divine service/revised by L. Merzbacher, 1855. — 3rd ed. rev. and corr./by S. Adler, 1863. — New York: J. Mendole, 1886–1888, v.1, 1888.

2 v. English and Hebrew. Deinard: 927. [V.1] Daily prayers. — V.2. Prayers for the Day of Atonement. [V.1] includes: Hymns for divine service in the Temple Emanu-El. Copies: CFlS Cst CtY DLC ICRL (V.1) MWalA NN (V.1) NNU (V.2) NNHeb NNU-W (V.1) OCH (V.2)

352. סליחות ותפלות ליום ט״ו כסלו לער׳ ח׳ שבט וליום ז׳ אדר: מדויק היטב כפי מנהגי החברה קדישא גמילות חסדים של אמת. — New York: Jewish Gazette, 1886.

32 p. Singerman: 3462. Copies: AJK

353. צדוק הדין = Service for the burial of the dead: arranged for the use of the Congregation B'nai Jeshurun / by Henry S. Jacobs. — New York: Press of Stettinger, Lambert, 1886.

> 10 p. English and Hebrew. Singerman: 3461. Copies: CtY

354. תפלות בני ישורון ליום הכפורים כפי מנהג אמעריקא = The divine service of American Israelites for the Day of Atonement / Isaac M. Wise, with an appendix. — Cincinnati: Bloch, 1886.

> 307, 55 p. English and Hebrew. Copies: NN

355. תפלת ישראל = Prayers of Israel with English translation. — 17th stereotype ed. — New York: Lewine & Rosenbaum, 1886–5646.

> 240, 229 p. English and Hebrew. Singerman: 3454. Copies: MH NNJ OCH

356. תפלת ישראל = Prayers of Israel with English translation. — New York: Lewine & Rosenbaum, 1886–5646.

> xiv, 183, 172 p. English and Hebrew. Singerman: 3453. Copies: MH MWalA OCH

1887

357. Hymns and anthems adapted for Jewish worship / selected and arranged by Gustav Gottheil. — New York: G. P. Putnam's 1887, c1886.

> ix, 191 p. Singerman: 3531. Copies: ATLA (microform) CBGTU (microform) CLHU CtY-D (microform) CU GEU-T InNd MB MiDW MWalA NN NNJ NNUT (microform) OCH PPBI PPF PPGratz PPP PU RPB

358. Israelitische Tempel-Gesänge: Hymnen für Sabbath und Fest-Tage mit deutschem und englischem Text in Musik gesetzt / von Otto Lob. — 2. Aufl. — Chicago: E. Rubovits, 1887.

> 56 p. English and German. Includes music. Sendrey: 7105. See Singerman: 2570. Copies: DLC NNJ PPGratz

359. Music to the hymns and anthems for Jewish worship by G. Gottheil / composed and selected by A. J. Davis. — New York: K. Kakeles, 1887.

> Score (2 v., 108, 56 p.) For chorus (SATB) For use at Temple Emanu-El, New York. Part. 2. Photo lith. O. Lobner. Sendrey: 6935. Singerman: 3523. Copies: MH-AN (V.1) MWalA (V.1) NN (V.1) NNJ (V.1) OCH PPGratz (V.1)

360. A service of the synagogue in the time of Jesus Christ: for the Sabbath / by R. Henry Ferguson. — Newton Centre, Mass.: R. H. Ferguson, 1887.

> 9, 2, 9 p. Includes the music of Henry F. Dexter (9 p. at end). Singerman: 3333. Copies: ICU

361. Synagogue and school: hymns, songs and religious memoranda for Jewish congregations / F. de Sola Mendes. — New York: F. de Sola Mendes: Press of P. Cowen, 5647–1887.

> 35 p. Singerman: 3568. Copies: CtY DLC MWalA NNJ OCH NNYU (Sephardic Reference Room)

362. מנהג אמעריקא = The daily prayers for American Israelites, as revised in Conference. — Cincinnati: Bloch, 1887.

> 271, 48 p. English and Hebrew. Compiled by Isaac M. Wise. With appendix: Select prayers for various occasions in life. Copies: OCH

363. מנהג אמעריקא = The daily prayers for American Israelites, as revised in Conference. — Cincinnati: Bloch, 1887.

270 [i.e. 135] p. Hebrew only version. Compiled by Isaac M. Wise. Deinard: 919. Copies: DLC (uncat) OCH

364. סדור שפת אמת/מאת וואלף בר שמשון דוב איש היידנהיים =
Daily prayers with English instructions: published for the Hebrew Free Schools of New York: as correct as any edition ever published in רעדעלהיים.— New York: Lewine & Rosenbaum, 1887–5647.

293 p. Hebrew with English intructions. Copies: OCH

365. סדר להדרת קדש: כולל תפלות כל השנה וכל הברכות הנהנין, וברכות המצות, וברכות הראיה והריח וכו' הנדרכים לדעת לכל איש יהודי: בהעתקת לשון ענגליש =
Form of prayers and blessings of Israel with an English translation.— New York: J. H. Kantrowitz, 1887.

507 p. English and Hebrew. Singerman: 3544. Copies: NNJ OCH

366. סדר תפלה לראש השנה ויום הכפורים = Gebete für den öffentlichen Gottesdienst Temple Gemeinde Ahawath Chesed/ geordnet von A. Huebsch, Rabbiner Derselben.— New York: A. L. Goetzl, 5647–1887.

512 p. German and Hebrew. Deinard: 913. Copies: DLC (uncat) MH MWalA (V. 2 of set, 1883–1887) MWalB NNHeb NNJ OCH

367. ספר החיים = Andachtsbuch zum Gebrauche auf dem Friedhofe und in Trauerhause für Israelitische Gemeinde. — Baltimore: C. W. Schneidereith, 5647–1887.

27 p. German and Hebrew. Bound with: ספר החיים = Ritual for funerals and prayers in the house of mourning, 1887 (Entry 368). Deinard: 307. Singerman: 3546. Copies: CtY NNHeb OCH

368. ספר החיים = Ritual for funerals and prayers in the house of mourning and at the graveside for Israelitish congregations. — Baltimore: C. W. Schneidereith, 5647–1887.

27 p. English and Hebrew Bound with: ספר חיים = Andachtsbuch zum Gebrauche auf dem Friedhofe und in Trauerhaus, 1887 (Entry 367). Deinard: 307. Singerman: 3547. Copies: CtY NNHeb OCH

369. תפלת ישראל = Order of prayers and responsive readings for Jewish worship/ arranged by Isaac S. Moses, Rabbi of Congregation Emanu-El, Milwaukee, Wis. — 2nd rev. and corr. ed.— Milwaukee, Wis.: I. S. Moses, 1887, c 1884.

131, 71 p. English and Hebrew. Singerman: 3545. Copies: CU DLC NNJ PPGratz OCH

1888

370. The Jewish home prayer-book: a manual of household devotion/edited by a committee of the Jewish Ministers' Association of America.— New York: Published for the Jewish Ministers' Association by P. Cowen; Cincinnati: Bloch, 1888, c 1887 by F. de Sola Mendes.

viii, 144 p. English and Hebrew. Singerman: 3670. Copies: ATLA (microform) CLHU MiDu MWalA NNHeb NNJ NNUT OCH

371. The service ritual/compiled by Joseph Krauskopf. — Philadelphia: J. B. Lippincott, 1888.

205 p. English with Hebrew. Deinard: 916. Singerman: 3669. Copies: CtY DLC MH MWalA NN NNHeb NNYI OCH OCl

372. Services at the installation of David Philipson as Rabbi of Congregation B'ne Israel, Cincinnati, Ohio: November 3, 1888. — [Cincinnati: B'ne Israel, 1888].

16 p. Singerman: 3632. Copies: OCH PPAnR

373. Shire Yehudah = Songs of Judah: a collection of sacred songs for soli and chorus, with organ accompaniment: for Sabbath morning & evening services/ composed and published by Fr. E. Kitziger. — New Orleans: F. E. Kitziger, 1888–1889.

Score (4 v. in 5) English and romanized Hebrew. Singerman: 3677. Copies: DLC LN MH (V.2) NN OCH PPGratz (Music)

374. Songs of the synagogue for Sabbath morning service according to the ritual of D. Einhorn/Carl Retter. — New York: E. Schubert, c1888.

Score (15 p.) English, German or romanized Hebrew. For Cantor and chorus (SATB). Sendrey: 6369. Singerman: 3737. Copies: OCH

375. Trial issue of the new ritual for "Temple Israel" St. Louis. — St. Louis: [Temple Israel], 1888.

4, 126 p. English and German. Compiled by S. H. Sonneschein. Cover title: Temple Israel — New ritual. Deinard: 920. Singerman: 3673. Copies: NN NNYU OCH Temple Israel, St. Louis

376. זמרות ישראל = Jewish hymns for Sabbath schools and families (English and German)/Simon Hecht. — Cincinnati: Bloch, 1888.

55 p. English and German. Includes music. Copies: OCH

377. ... מחזור = Form of prayers ... with English translation. — Rev. ed. — New York: Lewine & Rosenbaum, 1888–5648.

5 v. English and Hebrew. Copies: MWalA NNJ (V.1–2,5)

378. סדר להדרת קדש: כולל תפלות כל השנה וכל הברכות הנהנין, וברכות המצות, וברכות הראיה והריח וכו' הנדרכים לדעת לכל איש יהודי: בהעתקת לשון ענגליש = Form of prayers and blessings of Israel with an English translation. — New York: J. H. Kantrowitz, 1888.

507 p. English and Hebrew. See Singerman: 3544. Copies: NNJ

379. תפלת ישראל = Prayers of Israel with English translation. — 17th stereotype ed. — New York: Lewine & Rosenbaum, 1888–5648, c1881.

240, 229 p. Hebrew and English. Copies: OCH

380. תפלת ישראל = Prayers of Israel: תפלות לכל השנה containing the divine services of the entire year: arranged for the American Reform services in the "Temple Gates of Hope" שערי תקוה. — New York: Jewish Gazette Print, 1888.

543 p. English and Hebrew, with German hymns. Compiled by Edward B. M. Browne. Singerman: 3671. Copies: NNHeb

1889

381. Beth Emeth Sunday school hymns. — Albany, N.Y.: [Beth Emeth], 1889.

8 leaves. Singerman: 3758. Copies: OCH

382. Children's prayers for all ages: reprinted from the "Jewish home prayer book" by the Jewish Ministers' Association of America. — New York: Jewish Ministers' Association, 1889.

6 leaves. Singerman: 3806. Copies: NN (microform)

383. [Dedication service, Congregation

Moses Montefiore, New York, N.Y.]
— New York [The Congregation], 1889.

  p. Singerman: 3837. Copies: NNJ

384. A Hebrew reader containing the daily prayers of the Jewish ritual/published by Isaac S. Moses.— Chicago: E. Rubovits, 1889.

  38 p. Hebrew. Singerman: 3808. Copies: NNJ

385. Hours of devotion: a book of prayers and meditations for the use of the daughters of Israel, during public service and at home for all the conditions of woman's life/translated from the German "Stunden der Andacht" by M. Mayer.— 5th ed. — New York: J. Rosenbaum, 1889–5650, c1866.

  105 p. Original German by Fanny Schmiedl Neuda. Copies: CU NN NNHeb OCH

386. Hymns and anthems adapted for Jewish worship/selected and arranged by Gustav Gottheil.— New York: G. P. Putnam's sons, 1889, c1886.

  ix, 191 p. Copies: CLJ NN OCH OCl PPAnR

387. Min hamezar: Psalm 118/M. Haas. — [Cleveland: M. Haas], c1889.

  Score (7 p.) romanized Hebrew. For Cantor and chorus (SATB) with organ accompaniment. Sendrey: 6826. Singerman: 3789. Copies: OCH

388. Morning prayers/arranged by Gustav Gottheil, Temple Emanu-El, New York. — New York: P. Cowen, 1889.

  48 p. Singerman: 3804. Copies: CU NN NNHeb OCH

389. Order of children's service for Jewish Sabbath schools/published by Isaac S. Moses.— Chicago: Rubovits, 1889.

  24 p. English and Hebrew. Singerman: 3807. Copies: NNJ OCH

390. Prayers and hymns for the use of religious school attached to the Congregation B'nai Jeshurun, Madison Avenue, N.Y.: H. S. Jacobs, Superintendent, Morris S. Wise, Principal.— New York: P. Cowen, 5650–1889.

  20 p. Singerman: 3805. Copies: NN

391. Programme of the dedication services at the Temple of Congregation Shomer Emunim, of Toledo, Ohio: Friday Sept. 20th, 1889.— [Toledo: Shomer Emunim, 1889].

  14 p. Singerman: 3866. Copies: OCH

392. ונתנה תוקף = Unsane taukef/Joachim Kurantmann.— New York: J. Kurantmann, c1889.

  Score (11 p.) Romanized Hebrew. For voice and piano. Singerman: 3824. Copies: OCH

393. חנוך בית הכנסת בית המדרש הגדול אנשי אונגארן: באלול תרמ״ט/ע״י מאריס וועקסלער, עם תרגום אשכנז.— נויארק = Order of service at the dedication of the synagogue, Hungarian Congregation Beth Hamedrash Hagadol בית המדרש אנשי אונגארן, 70 Willet Street, New York: Sunday Sept. 22nd '89 יום א׳ אלול תרמ״ט/ Morris Wechsler. — New York: [The Congregation], 1889.

  22 p. English, German and Hebrew. Deinard: 318. Singerman: 3836. Copies: NN

394. ... מחזור = Form of prayers ... with English translation.— New York: J. Rosenbaum, 1889–5650.

  5 v. English and Hebrew. Singerman: 3803. Copies: CLHU (V.1) OCH PPLT (V.1)

1889 — 189–?

395. מחזור ליום כפור כמנהג אשכנז ופולין: מסודר בשלמות הסדור ומדויק בתכלית הדיוק כמש״נ ברעדעלהיים = Machzor (Form of prayers) for the Day of Atonement with English translation. — New York: Sarasohn and son, publishers, 5650–תר״ן.

769, 37 p. English and Hebrew. Deinard: 466. Singerman: 3814. Copies: NNJ OCH

396. מנהג אמעריקא = The daily prayers for American Israelites, as revised in Conference. — Cincinnati: Bloch, 1889, c1872.

271, 48 p. English and Hebrew. Compiled by Isaac M. Wise. With appendix: Select prayers for various occasions in life. Copies: MH MtU NN NNJ OCH

397. סדר תפלה = The order of prayer for the divine service/revised by L. Merzbacher (1855). — 3rd ed. rev. and corr./ by S. Adler (1863). II. Volume. Prayer for the Day of Atonement. — New York: J. Mendole, 1889.

397 p. English and Hebrew. Copies: MH

398. סדר תפלה = Prayers for the divine services of Congregation Ahawath Chesed/arranged by A. Huebsch; translated by Alexander Kohut. — New York: A. L. Goetzl, 1889.

2 v. English and Hebrew. V.1. שלש, לשבת לראש השנה ויום — V.2. רגלים וחול הכפורים. Deinard: 956. Singerman: 3809. Copies: CarP CtY DLC FU MH MWalA NN NNHeb NNJ NRCR OCH

399. ספר החיים = The book of life: a complete formula of the service and ceremonies observed at the death-bed, house of mourning and cemetery: together with prayers on visiting the graves/elaborated and revised by H. Vidaver. — New York: J. Rosenbaum, 1889–5649.

194 p. English and Hebrew. Singerman: 3815. Copies: MH OCH

400. עבדת הקדש = The synagogue service arranged for the Congregation B'nai Jeshurun of New York/by Henry S. Jacobs, Minister of the Congregation. — New York: [B'nai Jeshurun], 1889.

4 v. English and Hebrew. V.1. New Year's service. — V.2. Day of Atonement. — V.3. Festivals service. — V.4. Sabbath service. Singerman: 3802. Copies: MWalA MWalB (V.1) NN NNHeb OCH (V.4)

401. שמחת תורה = Simchath Torah: cantata for soli and chorus: with Hebrew and English words/by Alois Kaiser. — Baltimore, 1889 (Philadelphia: Printed by Brophy Bros.)

Score (17 p.) English and romanized Hebrew. For soli and chorus (SATB) with organ accompaniment. Sendrey: 7232. Singerman: 3819. Copies: DLC OCH PPGratz (Music)

402. תפלות בני ישורון ליום הכפורים כפי מנהג אמעריקא = The divine service of American Israelites for the Day of Atonement/Isaac M. Wise, with an appendix. — Cincinnati: Bloch, 1889.

307, 55 p. English and Hebrew. Copies: CLolC OCH

189-?

403. Draft of a revised ritual for Temple Emanu-El, New York. — [New York: Emanu-El, 189-?].

26 p. Singerman: 3935. Copies: OCH

404. Order of the memorial service at the Plum Street Temple, Cincinnati, Ohio. — [Cincinnati]: May & Kreidler, [189-?].

12 p. For Bene Yeshurun. Singerman: 3938. Copies: FU OCH

189–?

405. Prayers in commemoration of the dead. — [San Francisco: Emanu-El?, 189-?].

11 p. English and Hebrew. "Property of the Congregational [sic] Emanu-El." Singerman: 3939. Copies: OCH

406. The Psalmists: three choruses for the synagogue/A. Fellner. — New York: Smith & McDougal, [189-?].

Score (6 leaves). Cover title. Copies: OCH

407. Sabbath hymn ... Hark, my soul ... / Morris Goldstein. — Cincinnati: [M Goldstein, 189-?].

Score (11 p.) For Solo and chorus (SATB) with organ accompaniment. Sendrey: 7051. Copies: OCH

408. Select prayers for the New Year and Atonement days: adapted from the Hebrew and arranged/by J. Bogen, Rabbi of Hebrew Union, Greenville, Miss. — Cincinnati: Bloch, [189-?].

28 p. English with Hebrew headings. Singerman: 3933. Copies: NNHeb NNJ OCH (claim 19 — ?)

409. A service of the synagogue in the time of Jesus Christ. For the Sabbath/ R. Henry Ferguson. — [Newton Centre, Mass.?: R. H. Ferguson, 189-?].

2 leaves. Without the music of Henry Dexter. Copies: NN (microform)

410. [Torah service/Alois Kaiser. — Baltimore: A. Kaiser, 189-?].

Score (14 p.) English and romanized Hebrew For Cantor and chorus (SATB), with organ accompaniment. Singerman: 3942. Copies: OCH

411. זמרות ישראל = Jewish hymns for Sabbath schools and families (English and German)/Simon Hecht. — Cincinnati: Bloch, [189-?].

55 p. English and German. Includes music. Copies: OCH

412. ... מחזור = Form of prayers ... with English translation. — Rev. ed. — New York: J. L. Werbelowsky, [189-?].

5 v. English and Hebrew. Singerman: 3931. Copies: OCH

413. ... מחזור = Form of prayers ... with English translation. — Rev. ed. — New York: Rosenbaum & Werbelowsky, [189-?].

5 v. English and Hebrew. Singerman: 3932. Copies: MWalA (v.1–2) OCH

414. סדור שפת אמת/מאת וואלף בר שמשון דוב איש היידנהיים =

Daily prayers with English instructions: published for the Hebrew Free Schools of New York: as correct as any edition ever published in רעדעלהיים. — New York: J. L. Werbelowsky, [189-?].

292 p. Hebrew with English intructions. Singerman: 3936. Copies: DLC (uncat) MH MWalA NNJ OCH

415. סדר תפלות ובקשות על החולה ר"ל ומקשה לילד ר"ל וספר מעבר יבק: כולל סדר הוידוי לחולה, עניני המיתה, הטהרה והקבורה. — ניו יארק: בהוצאת בית מסחר הספרים של אליהו קופטשיק. — New York: E. Kupchik, [189-?].

32 p. Hebrew with Yiddish instructions ספר מעבר יבק by Aaron Berechiah ben Moses. Copies: MWalA

416. סליחות לימים נוראים כמנהג אונגארן, מעהרען, בעהעמען, שלעזיען וכל גלילות ... — Brooklyn, N.Y.: R. G. & W. Inc, [189-?].

107 p. Copies: OCH

417. תפלה זכה חדשה לימים נוראים ולכל ימות השנה. — New York: Anshe Temime Derekh, [189-?].

83

15 p. Hebrew and Yiddish. Singerman: 4007. Copies: OCH

418. תפלת ישראל = Prayers of Israel with English translation. — New York: J. L. Werbelowsky, [189-?].

183, 172 p. English and Hebrew. Singerman: 3934. Copies: OCH

419. תפלת ישראל = Prayers of Israel with English translation. — New York: Rosenbaum & Werbelowsky, [189-?].

183, 172 p. English and Hebrew. Copies: OCH

1890

420. The burial of the dead: a hand book for Ministers/prepared by a committee of the Jewish Ministers' Association of America. — New York: The Association, 1890.

18 p. English and Hebrew. Singerman: 4080. Copies: DLC NN (microform) NNJ OCH

421. Confirmation manual: designed for the service in Jewish congregations: consisting of catechisms on the tenets of the Jewish religion, and on the history of the Jewish nation: addresses with appropriate prayers and recitations: also préces for a Barmitzvah, etc., etc./J. Mendes de Solla. — Cincinnati: Bloch, 1890, c1889.

128, iii p. Singerman: 4062. Copies: MH NNJ OCH

422. Confirmation service: as sung at Touro Synagogue: consisting of six hymns, responses, etc.: for solo, trio and chorus/ published by Fred E. Kitziger. — New Orleans: F. E. Kitziger, c1890.

Score (22 p.) English or romanized Hebrew. With organ accompaniment. Sendrey: 7456. Singerman: 4092. Copies: NNJ OCH PPGratz

423. Evening prayers for the house of mourning: with thoughts on immortality. — New York: P. Cowen, 1890.

46 p. English and Hebrew. Copyright by the Temple Emanu-El, New York. Singerman: 4088. Copies: CtY NN NNUT OCH

424. Hymn book for Jewish worship. — Rochester, N.Y.: Union and Advertiser Press, 1890.

3, 96 p. English and German. Includes music. Compiled by Max Landsberg and Solomon Wile. Singerman: 4099. Copies: NNUT OCH PPGratz (Music)

425. The order of services for the dedication of Temple Beth Zion: September 12, 1890, Buffalo, N.Y. — Buffalo, N.Y.: Matthews, Northrup, 1890.

7 p. Singerman: 4044. Copies: OCH

426. Selected hymns for Hebrew Sunday school. — [Philadelphia: s.n.], 1890.

29 p. Singerman: 4130. Copies: MWalA

427. The service-ritual/Joseph Krauskopf. — 2nd ed. — Philadelphia: Lineaweaver & Wallace, 1890, c1888.

205 p. English with Hebrew. Copies: NNJ OCH

428. The Temple Beth-El hymn book for the use of religious schools: with an appendix containing prayers and readings. — New York: A. L. Goetzl, 1890.

iv, 6–62 p. Sendrey: 6998. Singerman: 4117. Copies: NN OCH

429. ... מחזור = Form of prayers ... with English translation. — Rev. ed. — New York: Lewine & Rosenbaum, 1890–5650.

5 v. English and Hebrew. Singerman: 4081. Copies: DLC (V.1–2 cat, V.3–5 uncat) MWalA (V.1, 5) OCH (V.2)

430. ... מחזור = Form of prayers ... with English translation. — Rev. ed. — New York: Rosenbaum & Werbelowsky, 1890–5650.

5 v. English and Hebrew. Copies: DLC MWalA (V.1–2) NNJ (V.1, 5) Or (V.2) PPLT (V.3–5)

431. מעריב של שבת = Sabbath eve service: Congregation "Emanuel" Denver, Col. — Cincinnati: Bloch, 1890.

24 p. English and Hebrew. Singerman: 4089. Copies: NN NNJ OCH

432. מעריב של שבת = Sabbath eve service: Congregation B'nai Israel, Little Rock, Ark. — Cincinnati: Bloch, 1890.

24 p. English and Hebrew. See Singerman: 4089. Copies: OCH

433. סדור שפת אמת/מאת וואלף בר שמשון דוב איש היידנהיים = Daily prayers with English instructions: published for the Hebrew Free Schools of New York: as correct as any edition ever published in רעדעלהיים. — New York: Rosenbaum & Werbelowsky, 1890–5650.

293 p. Hebrew with English instructions. Singerman: 4087. Copies: FU OCH

434. סדר חנוכת הבית = Order of the service for the consecration of the new Stanly Street Synagogue: on Elul 15th, August 31st, 5650. — [New York: s.n., 1890].

20 p. For Shearith Israel, Montreal, Québec, Canada. Sermon was given by H. Pereira Mendes. Singerman: 4109. Copies: CaOONL

435. שיר חדש /לה' שירו = Hymns and prayers in English and German/by Isaac M. Wise and others. — Cincinnati: Bloch, 1890.

263 p. English and German. Spine title: Hymns, Psalms and prayers. Singerman: 4082. Copies: CLHU MH OCH PPGratz

436. תפלת ישראל = Israelitisches Andacht-Buch nebst deutscher Uebersetzung: mit neuen deutschen Gebete תחנות/von W. Schlessinger. — neue verbesserte Stereotyp.-Ausg. — New York: J. Rosenbaum, 1890–5560.

240, 228, 32 p. German and Hebrew. Final section has title: תחנות בנות ישורון = Religiöse Betrachtungen und Gebete für Frauen und Mädchen. Singerman: 4083, 4090. Copies: MWalA NNJ OCH

437. תפלת ישראל = Prayers of Israel with English translation. — New York: Rosenbaum and Werbelowsky, 1890–5650.

183, 172 English and Hebrew. Singerman: 4084. Copies: OCH OCl

438. תפלת ישראל = Prayers of Israel with English translation. — 17th stereotype ed. — New York: Rosenbaum and Werbelowsky, 1890–5650.

240, 229 p. English and Hebrew. Singerman: 4062. Copies: MH NNJ OCH

439. תפלת ישראל = Prayers of Israel with English translation. — 18th stereotype ed. — New York: J. Rosenbaum, 1890.

240, 229 p. English and Hebrew. Singerman: 4086. Copies: NNJ OCH

1891

440. Dedication of the Temple Beth-El, 5th Ave. and 76th St., New York: Friday, September 18th, 1891. — [New York: Beth-El, 1891].

22, [2] p. Singerman: 4254. Copies: MWalA OCH

441. Hymns/Polonies Talmud Torah School. — New York: G. M. Allen & Co., 1891.

    28 p. Singerman: 4253. Copies: NNJ NNYU

442. Programme of the dedication services at the Temple of Congregation Emanu-El of Helena, Montana: Sunday April 19th, 1891. — Helena: [Emanu-El], 1891.

    11 p. Singerman: 4203. Copies: OCH

443. Sabbath eve service, Temple Beth-El, New York. — New York: P. Cowen, 1891.

    13 p. English and Hebrew. Opens with "Mah tovu." Compiled by Kaufmann Kohler. Deinard: 930 Singerman: 4225. Copies: MH MWalA OCH ViU

444. Sabbath eve service, Temple Beth-El, New York. — New York: P. Cowen, 1891.

    16 p. English and Hebrew. Opens with "Sabbath hymn." Compiled by Kaufmann Kohler. Singerman: 4226. Copies: MH NOCH

445. Services for Sabbath and holidays. — Cincinnati: Bloch, 1891.

    112 p. English and Hebrew. Compiled by David Philipson for K. K. Bene Israel, of Cincinnati. Deinard: 931. Singerman: 4221. Copies: CLHU DLC ICU MH NNJ NNUT OCH

446. Shire Yehudah: Songs of Judah: a collection of sacred songs for soli and chorus, with organ accompaniment: for Sabbath morning and evening services/ published by Fred. E. Kitziger, organist of Touro Synagogue. — New Orleans, La.: F. E. Kitziger, 1891.

    Score (2 v.) English and romanized Hebrew. Copies: MH (V.2)

447. The Temple Beth-El hymn book for the use of religious schools: with an appendix containing prayers and readings. — New York: A. L. Goetzl, 1891.

    iv, 62 p. English and Hebrew. Singerman: 4255. Copies: OCH

448. Temple service for New Year and Day of Atonement/arranged by Franz Wald. — Chicago: F. Wald, 1891.

    Score (144 p.) English and romanized Hebrew. Holograph note on copy in OCH indicates that this musical service is intended for use with the Einhorn prayerbook (עלת תמיד) at the Sinai and Zion Congregations in Chicago. Sendrey: 5986. Singerman: 4290. Copies: OCH

449. סדר תפלה = The order of prayer for the divine service/revised by L. Merzbacher, 1855. — 3rd ed. rev. and corr./by S. Adler, 1863. — New York: J. Mendole, 1891.

    2 v. English and Hebrew. [V.1] Daily prayers. — V.2. Prayers for the Day of Atonement. [V.1] includes: Hymns for divine service in the Temple Emanu-El. Copies: DLC (uncat) MWalA (V.1) MWalB NNJ (V.2) OCH

450. סדר תפלה = Order of prayers adopted by the Congregation Mickva Israel, Savannah, Georgia, organized 1733–chartered 1790. V.I. — Savannah, Ga.: J. Stern; New York: Sarasohn & Son, 1891.

    267 p. English and Hebrew. Deinard: 971. Singerman: 4220. Copies: NNJ

451. ענף יוסף = Prayer-book for Sabbath, Pesach, Shebuoth and Succoth: arranged under the auspices of and dedicated to the "Hebrew Union Congregation"/by Jos. Bogen, Greenville, Miss. — Cincinnati: Bloch, 1891.

64 p. English and Hebrew. Singerman: 4219. Copies: NNJ OCH

452. קול רינה = Kol rinah: Sabbath evening service: in accordance with B. Szold's and A. Huebsch's prayer books/Max Braun. — Newark, N.J.: M. Braun, c1891.

Score (22 p.) English and romanized Hebrew. Sendrey: 5875. Singerman: 4167. Copies: OCH

453. שלהבת יה = The Temple service arranged for the Congregation Rodeph Sholom of New York/by Aaron Wise. — New York: "Jewish Gazette" Print, 5651–תרנ"א, 1891.

2 v. English, German and Hebrew. V.I. For Sabbath and Festivals. — V.II. For the New Year's Day and the Day of Atonement. V.I. includes 173 p. of prayers for Women in English and German. V.II arranged by Rudolph Grossman. Deinard: 932. (V.I) Singerman: 4222. Copies: MH (V.I) NNHeb NNJ OCH (V.I)

454. תפלות בני ישורון... כפי מנהג אמעריקא = The divine service of American Israelites/I.M. Wise. — Cincinnati: Bloch, 1891.

2 v. English, German and Hebrew. Copies: CLHU GEU-T (V.I) MWalA (V.I) MWalB (V.2) OCH (V.I) UU (V.I)

455. תפלת ישראל = The Jewish prayer book: order of worship for Sabbath and holidays/by Isaac S. Moses. — Chicago: [s.n.], 1891.

124 p. English and Hebrew. "Printed as manuscript for the Ritual Committee appointed by the Rabbinical conference held at Baltimore, Md. July, 1891." Singerman: 4223. Copies: NN (microfilm) OCH

1892

456. Ceremonies of the laying of the corner stone of the Temple of Oheb Shalom Congregation, Eutaw Place and Lanvale St., Baltimore, Md.: Wednesday June 29th, 1892... — Baltimore: [Oheb Shalom], 1892.

18, [2] p. English and German. Singerman: 4302. Copies: OCH

457. Consolation: hymn for contralto or baritone/Alois Kaiser. — Baltimore: G. Willig, c1892.

Score (3 p.). Singerman: 4363. Copies: OCH

458. The Hebrew text for schools from the prayerbook of B. Szold/revised by Drs. Jastrow & Hochheimer. — Baltimore: H.F. Siemers, 1892.

[58] p. Hebrew with German instructions. Copies: NNJ

459. Hymns collected from various sources and selections from the Psalms: for the use of the Congregation and the Religious school of Temple Israel of Harlem. — New York: DeLeeuw, Oppenheimer & Co., 1892.

48 p. Singerman: 4408. Copies: NNJ OCH ViU

460. Order of Thanksgiving service/conducted by J. Leonard Levy, in commemoration of the 400th anniversary of the discovery of America, Columbus Day, Friday Oct. 21, 1892. — Sacramento: Congregation B'nai Israel, 1892.

12 p. English. Singerman: 4425. Copies: NN

461. Programme of the dedication services of Reform Congregation Keneseth Israel at the new Temple, Broad Street above

Columbia Avenue: September 9, 10, & 11, 1892. — Philadelphia: S. W. Goodman, 1892.

21 p. Cover title: Dedicatory exercises. Singerman: 4412. Copies: C OCH

462. Sabbath afternoon service/arranged by the Advisory Board of Jewish Ministers for the use of the pupils attending the Hebrew Free Schools of New York. — New York: P. Cowen, 1892.

37, 13 p. Final section contains: Hymns. Singerman: 4361. Copies: MWalA

463. The service manual/by Joseph Krauskopf, of the Reform Congregation Keneseth Israel. — Philadelphia: E. Stern, 1892.

95, 256–564 p. English with Hebrew. Singerman: 4355. Copies: CU FU MeLB MWalA N NNJ OCH PBL PPGratz

464. The service manual/by Joseph Krauskopf, of the Reform Congregation Keneseth Israel. — 2nd ed. — Philadelphia: E. Stern, 1892.

95, 256–564 p. English with Hebrew. Copies: NN NNJ

465. The service-ritual/compiled by Joseph Krauskopf. — 2nd ed. — Philadelphia: E. Stern, 1892, c1888.

205 p. English with Hebrew. Singerman: 4356. Copies: IaDuT MWalA NN NNYU OCH PP PU

466. Shire Yehudah = Songs of Judah: a collection of sacred songs for soli and chorus, with organ accompaniment: for Sabbath morning & evening services/composed and published by Fred. E. Kitziger. — 2nd rev. and aug. ed. — New Orleans: F. E. Kitziger, 1892.

v. English and romanized Hebrew. Sendrey: 6223. Copies: OCH

467. אלון בכות = Prayers for mourners: English and German/compiled by Alexander Kohut, Rabbi, Congregation Ahawath Chesed. — New York: A. L. Goetzl, c1892.

vi, 111 p. English, German and Hebrew. Singerman: 4360. Copies: CtY DLC NNHeb OCH

468. מנהג אמעריקא = The daily prayers for American Israelites, as revised in Conference. — Cincinnati: Bloch, 1892, c1872.

271, 48 p. English and Hebrew. Compiled by Isaac M. Wise. Copies: CLHU OCH

469. ספר החיים = Ritual for funerals and prayers in the house of mourning and at the grave: arranged for Temple Rodoph Sholom of New York/by Aaron Wise. — New York:"Jewish Gazette" Print, 1892, 5652.

67 p. English and Hebrew. Singerman: 4224 Holdings: NN (microform)

470. שירי תהילה = Shirai tehilloh: a collection of sacred music, Psalms and hymns: with accompaniment for the organ. — Cincinnati: Bloch, 1892.

Score (76 p.) English and romanized Hebrew. For chorus (SATB) with organ accompaniment Sendrey: 7132. Singerman: 4434. Copies: OCH PPGratz (Music)

471. תפלות בני ישורון ... כפי מנהג אמעריקא = The divine service of American Israelites/Isaac M. Wise. — Cincinnati; New York: Bloch, 1892.

2 v. English, German and Hebrew. V.1 New Year. — V.2. Day of Atonement. Copies: OCH

472. תפלות ישראל = Jewish prayer book/edited under the auspices of the Central Conference of American Rabbis,

by the Ritual Committee. — Chicago: [s.n.], 1892.

216, 140 p. English and Hebrew. Printed as a manuscript for the Rabbinical Conference/revised by I.S.Moses.With an appendix: Responsive readings of Psalms and scriptural selections and ethical readings. Copies: NN OCH PPGratz

473. תפלות ישראל = Union prayer book: as adopted by the Central Conference of American Rabbis/published by the Ritual Committee. — Chicago, Ill.: E.Rubovits; Cincinnati: For sale at Bloch; New York: B.Westerman, 1892.

260, 140 p. English and Hebrew. Revised by I. S. Moses. Pt. 1. Sabbath, the Three Festivals, and the daily prayers. Deinard: 965. Singerman: 4357. Copies: CLHU DLC MH MWalA NN NNHeb OCH OO

1893

474. Additions to the ritual/arranged by A.Guttmacher for the "Baltimore Hebrew Congregation." — Baltimore, Md.: [s.n.], 1893.

11 p. OCH's copy bound with: תפלות ישראל = Union prayer-book Pt. 1. Chicago, 1892 (Entry 473) Singerman: 4535. Copies: OCH

475. Children's prayers for use in the school and home/Ella Jacobs. — Philadelphia: [s.n.], c1893.

1 folded leaf printed on 4 sides. Singerman: 4539. Copies: NN (microform) NNJ

476. Children's prayers for use in the school and home/Ella Jacobs. — 2nd. ed. — Philadelphia: [s.n.], c1893.

4 p. Singerman: 4539. Copies: NN (microform)

477. A collection of principal melodies of the synagogue: from the earliest time to the present/compiled by Alois Kaiser and William Sparger. — Chicago: T.Rubovits, 1893.

Score (xvii, 197, 2 p.) English, with some Hebrew subtitles. Cover title: Songs of Zion: Souvenir of the Jewish Women's Congress, Chicago. Deinard: 703. Sendrey: 6190. Singerman: 4544. Copies: AzU CL CLJ CLobs CtY DLC HU ICJIQ KyLo LN LNT MdBPC MH-Mu MWalA MWalB NN NNHeb NNJ NNYU OCH PPAnR PPGratz RPB TxDaM WM

478. Evening service at the house of mourning. — Chicago, Ill.: Ritual Committee, 1893.

p. 193–205. English and Hebrew. Reprinted from: תפלות ישראל = The Union prayer book: as adopted by the Central Conference of American Rabbis, 1892 (Entry 473). Singerman: 4541. Copies: OCH

479. Hanukkah festival: a song service for the Feast of Lights/arranged by I.S.Moses. — Chicago: American Hebrew Pub. Co., 1893.

14, [5] p. English and Hebrew. Includes music. Singerman: 4567. Copies: IU MWalA NN OCH

480. Hebrew reader containing the daily prayers of the Union prayer book. — Chicago: I.S. Moses, 1893.

48 p. Hebrew. Singerman: 4536. Copies: DLC (microform) NN

481. Hymns and anthems adapted for Jewish worship/selected and arranged by Gustav Gottheil. — 4th ed. — New York: W.R. Jenkins, 1893.

ix, 191 p. Singerman: 4512. Copies: CtY MWalA NNJ OCH PP

482. Stunden der Andacht: Ein Gebet- und Erbauungsbuch für Israels Frauen und Jungfrauen: zur öffentlichen und häuslichen Andacht so wie für alle Verhältnisse des weiblichen Lebens/von W. Schlessinger und anderen Schriftstellern, und mit Zusätzen von F. Neuda. — 9. Ausg. — New York: Rosenbaum & Werbelowsky, 1893.

iv, 96 p. Singerman: 4542. Copies: OCH

483. זמרות ישראל = Jewish hymns for Sabbath-schools and families (English and German)/Simon Hecht. — Cincinnati: American Hebrew Pub. House, 1893.

55 p. English and German. Includes music. Copies: NN OCH

484. ספר החיים = The book of life: a complete formula of the service and ceremonies observed at the death-bed, house of mourning and cemetery: together with prayers on visiting the graves/elaborated and revised by H. Vidaver. — New York: Rosenbaum & Werbelowsky, 1893–5653, c1878.

194 p. English and Hebrew. Deinard: 308. Singerman: 4542. Copies: FiU NN OCH

485. תפלות ישראל = Union prayer book: printed as manuscript for the Central Conference of American Rabbis/by the Ritual Committee. — Chicago, Ill.: [s.n.], 1893.

335 p. English and Hebrew. Revised by I. S. Moses. Pt. II. New Year's Day and the Day of Atonement. Singerman: 4538. Copies: OCH

486. תפלות ישראל = Union prayer book: printed as manuscript for the Central Conference of American Rabbis/by the Ritual Committee. — Chicago, Ill.: [s.n.], 1893.

212 p. English and Hebrew. Revised by I. S. Moses. Pt. 2. Copies: OCH

487. תפלת בית אהבה = A book of prayer for Jewish worship/compiled by Edward N. Calisch, Rabbi of the Congregation Beth Ahaba, Richmond, Va. — Richmond, Va.: Ezekiel & Bass, 1893.

108, 95, iii p. Second section entitled: Hymns for divine service. Deinard: 909. Singerman: 4537. Copies: NN NNJ OCH OCU

1894

488. 20 hymns for Jewish worship: for solo and chorus with accompaniment of the organ/composed, arranged and published by Fred. E. Kitziger. — New Orleans: F. E. Kitziger, 1894.

Score (58 p.) For soli and chorus (SATB) Sendrey: 7094. Singerman: 4707. Copies: MH-MU NNJ PPGratz (Music)

489. Anthems, hymns and responses for the Union prayer book. — New York: Cantors Association of America, 1894.

vi, 63 p. "Introductory note" signed by Alois Kaiser [et al.]. Singerman: 4647. Copies: OCH

490. Hebrew reader containing the prayers and Psalms of the Jewish ritual/Isaac S. Moses. — Chicago: Bloch, 1894.

48 p. Hebrew. Singerman: 4735. Copies: NNJ OCH

491. Hymns and responses from Jastrow's prayer book: especially adopted for congregational singing in Congregation Rodeph Shalom/William Loewenberg. — [Philadelphia: s.n.], 1894.

30 p. Singerman: 4723. Copies: OCH

492. Opening services of the Temple, Wilson & Central Aves.: Tifereth Israel

Congregation, Moses J. Gries, Rabbi: September 21, 22, 23, 24, 1894. — [Cleveland: s.n., 1894].

12 p. Singerman: 4653. Copies: OCH

493. A prayer of repentance for the afternoon service of the Day of Atonement/by Max Heller. — Chicago: Bloch, 1894.

15 p. English and Hebrew. Printed left to right. Singerman: 4686. Copies: NN NNJ OCH

494. A prayer of repentance for the afternoon service of the Day of Atonement/by Max Heller. — Chicago: Bloch, 1894.

12 p. English and Hebrew. Printed right to left. See Singerman: 4686. Copies: OCH

495. Sabbath eve services and hymns and anthems for Sabbath and holidays/compiled and arranged for Congregation Sherith Israel by Jacob Nieto. — San Francisco: Weiss, 5655, [1894 or 1895].

41 p. English and Hebrew. Copies: WJHC

496. Sabbath-school hymnal: a collection of songs, services and responses for Jewish schools and homes/arranged and published by I.S. Moses. — Chicago: Bloch, [1894].

194 p. English and romanized Hebrew. Includes music. Singerman: 4736. Copies: OCH

497. Sabbath-school hymnal: a collection of songs, services and responses for Jewish schools and homes/arranged and published by I.S. Moses. — 2nd rev. ed. — Chicago: Bloch, c1894.

194 p. English and romanized Hebrew. Includes music. See Singerman: 4736. Copies: NN NNHeb

498. Sabbath-school hymnal: a collection of songs, services and responses for Jewish schools and homes/arranged and published by I.S. Moses. — 3rd ed. — Chicago: I.S. Moses, c1894.

218 p. English and romanized Hebrew. Includes music. Sendrey: 6985. Copies: GEU-T NN RPB

499. The school service/by Joseph Krauskopf. — Philadelphia: O. Klonower, 1894.

47 p. English with Hebrew. [4] p. of Hymns. Singerman: 4701. Copies: CU DLC (micrform) NN NNHeb NNJ OCH PPGratz

500. זמרות ישראל = Responses, Psalms and hymns for worship in congregations and schools/edited by Louis Grossmann and F.L.York. — Detroit: J.F. Eby, 1894.

75 p. English and Hebrew. Singerman: 4675. Copies: CU MH OCH OCl PPGratz

501. זמרות ישראל = Responses, psalms and hymns for worship in congregations and schools/edited by Louis Grossmann and F.L.York. — Detroit: J.F. Eby, 1894.

12 p. English and Hebrew. Advance sheets. See Singerman: 4675. Copies: OCH

502. סדר תפלות ישראל = The Union prayer-book for Jewish worship/edited and published by the Central Conference of American Rabbis. — Cincinnati: CCAR; [Chicago: S. Ettlinger], 1894–1895 (V.1 1895)

2 v. English and Hebrew. Pt. 1. Prayers for the Sabbath, the Three Festivals, and the week days. — Pt. 2. Prayers for the New Year and the Day of Atonement. Deinard: 965. Singerman: 4700. Copies: CBGTU CLHU FU (V.1)

GEU-T MH MWalA NN NNJ NNUT OCH PPGratz TxDaM-P

503. סדר תפלות ישראל = The Union prayer-book for Jewish worship/edited and published by the Central Conference of American Rabbis. — Cincinnati: CCAR; [Chicago: T. Rubovits], 1894–1895 (V.1 1895)

2 v. English and Hebrew. Pt. 1. Prayers for the Sabbath, the Three Festivals and the week days. — Pt. 2. Prayers for New Year's Day, Day of Atonement. Copies: CoGrU CSdP IEN FU MeB MH OCH OCl OO PPBI TCleL

504. ספר שיר ציון: בו מזמורי שבת הנהוגים בישראל לזמרם... וגם מזמורים למוצאי שבת, וברכת המזון עם פירוש חדש/שלמה אהרן ווערטהיימער. — New York: Gross, 1894.

104 p. Information taken from a 1970 reprint cataloged by NNJ. Copies:

1895

505. Evening and morning service for the week days: reprint from the Union prayer book/edited and published by the Central Conference of American Rabbis. — Cincinnati, O.: CCAR; Chicago: S. Ettlinger, 1895.

pp. 231–277, 104–107, 52–53, 108. English and Hebrew. Deinard: 965. Copies: NNHeb NNJ OCH

506. Evening prayers for the house of mourning: with thoughts on death and immortality. — New York: P. Cowen, 1895, c1890 by Temple Emanu-El, New York.

46 p. English and Hebrew. See Singerman: 4088. Copies: NN NNHeb NNJ OCH RPB

507. Memorial hymn (Why are thou cast down): devoted in filial affection to the memory of his father Cantor Josef Stark/composed & arranged for soli and double chorus, with cello and harp obligato, and organ accompaniment by Edward Joseph Stark. — San Francisco: L. Roesch, c1895.

Score (9 p.) Sendrey: 7474. Singerman: 4924. Copies: OCH

508. Minhammezar: Psalm 118, v. 5–24.: voice with organ accompaniment/Jacques Fromental Halévy; English words by Wm. Noelsch. — Philadelphia: J.E. Ditson, 1895.

Score. Sendrey: 6827a. Copies:

509. The mourner's service/by Joseph Krauskopf. — Philadelphia: O. Klonower, 1895, c1894.

15 p. English with Hebrew. Singerman: 4857. Copies: NN NNHeb NNJ OCH

510. Order of service at the dedication of the synagogue of Cong. Sharay Tefila... May 26th, 1895. — New York: L. Lederer, 1895.

8 p. For Congregation Sharay Tefila, East Orange, N.J. Singerman: 4829. Copies: OCH

511. Sabbath-school hymnal: a collection of songs, services and responses for Jewish schools and homes/arranged and published by I.S. Moses. — 2nd rev. ed. — Chicago: Bloch, c1895.

194 p. English and romanized Hebrew. Includes music. Copies: DLC

512. The Temple service: containing all the music required for the Union prayer-book for Jewish worship: as prepared and adopted by the Central Conference of American Rabbis/published by Morris Goldstein. — Cincinnati: Bloch, c1895–1896.

Score (3 v.) English and romanized Hebrew. For Cantor and chorus (SATB), with organ accompaniment. V.1. New Year and Day of Atonement. — V.2. Evening and morning services for the Three Festivals, Pesah, Shabuoth, Succoth. — V.3. Evening and morning services for the Sabbath. Sendrey: 5903. Singerman: 4835. Copies: NRU-Mus OCH PPGratz (Music, V.1)

513. זמרות ישראל = Jewish hymns for Sabbath schools and families (English and German) / Simon Hecht. — Cincinnati: Bloch, c1895.

55 p. English and German. Includes music. Copies: OCl

514. מעין הישועה = Source of salvation: a catechism of the Jewish religion: with an appendix of the confirmation-service / Isaac Mayer. — New York: Rosenbaum & Werbelowsky, 5656–1895.

106 p. English and Hebrew. Singerman: 4878. Copies: MWalA NN

515. סדר להדרת קדש: כולל תפלות כל השנה וכל הברכות הנהגין, וברכות המצות, וברכות הראיה והריח וכו' הנדרכים לדעת לכל איש יהודי: בהעתקת לשון עגלש = Form of prayers and blessings of Israel with an English translation. — New York: Rosenbaum & Werbelowsky, 1895.

507 p. English and Hebrew. Singerman: 4856. Copies: NNYI OCH

516. סדר תפלות ישראל = The Union prayer-book for Jewish worship. Pt. I. Prayers for the Sabbath, the Three Festivals and the weekdays. — Cincinnati: CCAR, 1895.

110 p. English and Hebrew. Deinard: 964. Copies: NNJ

517. תפלת ישראל = Prayers of Israel with English translation. — 18th stereotype ed. — New York: Rosenbaum & Werbelowsky, 1895.

240, 229 p. English and Hebrew. Copies: DLC (uncat) NNJ OO

1896

518. Dr. David Einhorn's עלת תמיד: book of prayers for Jewish congregations: new translation after the German original. — Chicago: [S. Ettlinger], 1896.

v, 166, 279 p. English with Hebrew. Pt. I. Sabbath, Festivals and days of the week. — Pt. II. New Year's Day and Day of Atonement. Translated by Emil Hirsch. Deinard: 948. Singerman: 5021. Copies: AzU CLHU CoD CoDU DLC (uncat) FMFIU FAUC ICU MiU MoS MoSpCB NN NNJ OCH OSteC OU PPiU TCT TNJ TxDaTS

519. Hours of devotion: a book of prayers and meditations for the use of the daughters of Israel, during public service and at home for all the conditions of woman's life / translated from the German "Stunden der Andacht" by M. Mayer. — 5th ed. — New York: Rosenbaum & Werbelowsky, 1896–5656.

105 p. Original German by Fanny Schmiedl Neuda. Copies: PPGratz

520. Hymns collected from various sources and selections from the Psalms: for use of the Congregation and the Religious school of Temple Israel of Harlem. — New York: W.C. Poppers, 1896.

62 p. Singerman: 5060. Copies: MH-AH RPB

521. Memorial service of the Hebrew Union-Veterans Association: held at Temple Emanu-El, New York, on May 29th, 1896. — [New York: s.n., 1896.]

1 folded leaf printed on 4 sides. Singerman: 5010. Copies: MWalA (uncat)

522. The order of the burial of the dead and service in the house of mourning. — Chicago: Furth, c1896.

    30 p. Reprinted from David Einhorn's: עלת תמיד. (Entry 518). Copies: OCH

523. Sabbath afternoon service: Hebrew Orphan Asylum, Brooklyn. — New York: [s.n.], 1896.

    38 p. English and Hebrew. Singerman: 5023. Copies: NNJ

524. Sabbath music: complete evening and morning service according to the Union prayer book: for soprano, alto, tenor and bass, with organ accompaniment/ Sebastian B. Schlesinger. — Cincinnati: Bloch, c1896–1904.

    Score (3 v.) English and romanized Hebrew. V. 3. published New York. Singerman: 5086. Copies: MH (V.1) OCH (V.1, 3)

525. The service-ritual/compiled by Joseph Krauskopf. — 3rd ed. — Philadelphia: E. Stern, 1896, c1888.

    205 p. English with Hebrew. Copies: KyWAT NNHeb NNJ OCH

526. The song book for Jewish worship: adapted for congregational singing as well as for the Sabbath school and the home/ arranged and published by Isaac S. Moses. — Chicago: I.S. Moses, 1896.

    62 p. English and romanized Hebrew. Includes music. Sendrey: 6986. Singerman: 5049. Copies: NNJ OCH OCl PPGratz

527. Sun and shield: a book of devout thoughts for every day use/written and selected by Gustav Gottheil. — Chicago: Bloch, c1896.

    3, xx, 1, 466 p. Copies: NNC OCH

528. Sun and shield: a book of devout thoughts for every day use/written and selected by G.G. [i.e. Gustav Gottheil] — New York: Brentano, c1896.

    xx, 466 p. Singerman: 5002. Copies: CLJ CtY CU DLC NN NNJ OCH OU PP PPYH

529. Why art thou cast down my soul?: hymn for memorial service in memory of Mr. and Mrs. Joseph Schwartzchild/ Herman Goldstein. — New York: O. Loebner, c1896.

    Score (8 p.) For soli and chorus (SATB) with organ accompaniment. Sendrey: 7437. Singerman: 5001. Copies: OCH

530. זמרות ישראל = Jewish hymns for Sabbath schools and families (English and German)/Simon Hecht. — [2nd ed.] — Cincinnati: American Hebrew Pub. House; New York: Bloch, 1896.

    55 p. English and German. Includes music. Sendrey: 6964. Copies: PPGratz (Music)

1897

531. How goodly are thy tents/Max Helfère. — New York: Luckhardt & Belder, c1897.

    Score (5 p.) For alto or baritone, with piano accompaniment. Sendrey: 7059. Singerman: 5179. Copies: OCH

532. How goodly are thy tents, O Jacob, the dwellings, O Israel. Lift up the cup of salvation and call upon the name of the Lord: according to the new Union prayer-book, p. 36, for the third Sabbath evening services: solo and duo for soprano and alto, with accompaniment of organ or piano/Fred. E. Kitziger; adapted from F. Mendelssohn. — New Orleans: F. E. Kitziger; Philadelphia: printed by W. H. Keyser, c1897.

Score (4 leaves). Sendrey: 7096. Singerman: 5202. Copies: OCH

533. Memorial service (Seelenfeier) for the Day of Atonement: according to the new Union ritual / published by Fred. E. Kitziger. — New Orleans: F. E. Kitziger, c1897.

Score (34 p.) English and romanized Hebrew. For Cantor and chorus (SATB) with organ accompaniment. Sendrey: 7457. Singerman: 5203. Copies: NN NNJ OCH PPGratz (Music)

534. Ritual for Jewish worship / compiled by Max Landsberg. — Rochester, N.Y.: C. Mann, 1897, c1884.

229 p. English and Hebrew. Copies: NNHeb NRU OCH

535. The Sabbath school hymnal: a collection of songs, services and responsive readings for the Jewish Sabbath school and home / arranged and published by I. S. Moses. — 4th rev. and enl. ed — Chicago: I. S. Moses, 1897, c1894.

218 p. English and romanized Hebrew. Includes music. Copies: MH-AN NNHeb

536. Selected hymns for Hebrew Sunday-schools. — Philadelphia: Billstein, 1897.

29 p. Singerman: 5268. Copies: DLC (microfilm) NN OCH

537. Union hymnal / text edited by the Central Conference of American Rabbis; music selected and arranged by the Society of American Cantors. — [s.l.]: CCAR; New York: Bloch, c1897.

218 p. Includes music. Sendrey: 6972, 7002? Singerman: 5139. Copies: CU FU ICJS LN NN MH NNUT OCH OO

538. Union hymnal / text edited by the Central Conference of American Rabbis; music selected and arranged by the Society of American Cantors. — [s.l.]: CCAR (New York: Press of C. Popper, 1897)

218 p. Includes music. Copies: CBGTU (microform) CtY-D (microform) CO CU GEU-T (microform) NNHeb NNUT (microform) PPGratz RPB

539. הזכרת נשמות = Memorial service for the dead: arranged for the use of the Congregation Ohabai Shalome / by Isidore Myers, Rabbi of the Congregation. — San Francisco, Cal.: Levison Printing Co., 1897–5658.

8 p. Cover title. Copies: WJHC (Box for Ohabai Shalome 69/2)

540. חג השבועות תרנ״ז = Order of service for Shabuoth and confirmation in Congregation "Shaar Hashomayim" (Fifteenth Street Temple): Sunday June 6th, 1897–5657. — [New York: Shaar Hashomayim], 1897.

1 folded leaf printed on four sides. Singerman: 5229. Copies: OCH

541. סדר העבודה לחנוכת הבית לק״ק שארית ישראל = Consecration service: synagogue of the Spanish and Portuguese Congregation Shearith Israel, in the city of New York: Iyar 18 5657–May 19, 1897. — New York: P. Cowen, 1897.

15 p. English and Hebrew. Deinard: 595. Singerman: 5230. Copies: MWalA NN (microfilm) NNYU (Sephardic Reference Room) OCH PPAnR

542. ספר ברית יצחק: כולל א) דיני אירוסין ונשואין... ב) דיני מילה... ג) דיני פדיון הבן... ד) בר מצוה ה) דרושים... יבואו בהעתקת אנגלית / מלוקט ע״י יצחק יהודה ליב קאדרושין המוהל. — ניו יארק: א.ח. ראזענברג, 1897.

Brith Itzhak: a manual comprising the riti of marriage, circumcision, redemption of the first born, and confirmation and the usual prayers for these ceremonies: also speeches designed for such occasions/by I. L. Kadushin. — New York: A.H. Rosenberg, 1897.

> 81, 43 AB p. English and Hebrew. Second part has title: ספר ציון:חלק שני מספר ברית יצחק = Zion. Part II of Brith Itzhak: prayers and speeches designed for holidays and all other occasions. — New York: Goldmann, 1898. Deinard: 101 (pt. 1) 693 (pt. 2). Singerman: 5198. Copies: CLU (Bloch label over imprint) DLC FU MH NN NNHeb NNJ NNYI NNYU OCH

543. שלהבת יה = The Temple service ... : arranged for the Congregation Rodeph Sholom/by Aaron Wise; revised by Rudolph Grossman. — New York: D. A. Huebsch & Co., c 1897.

> 2 v. English and Hebrew. V.1. For the Sabbath and Festivals. — V.2. For the New Year's Day and the Day of Atonement. Copies: MWalA (V.2) NNHeb

544. שלהבת יה = The Temple service ... : arranged for the Congregation Rodeph Sholom/by Aaron Wise; revised by Rudolph Grossman. — New York: P. Cowen, 1897.

> 2 v. English and Hebrew. V.1. For the Sabbath and Festivals. — V.2. For the New Year's Day and the Day of Atonement. Copies: MWalA (V.2) DLC MH OCH

1898

545. Day of God = Tag des Herrn: hymn for soprano solo & chorus, with flute, violin, cello, harp & organ accompt./E.J.Stark. — [San Francisco?: E.J.Stark, c 1898].

> Score (23 p.) English and German. Based on Kol nidre. Sendrey: 7219. Singerman: 5480. Copies: OCH

546. The door of hope: a manual of prayers and devotional readings upon visiting the cemetery/prepared by the New York Board of Jewish Ministers, 5658–1898. — New York: P. Cowen, 1898.

> 98 p. Written primarily by Kaufmann Kohler. Singerman: 5428. Copies: CU FU MWalA NN OCH

547. Evening service for the synagogue: according to the Union prayer book/ A.J.Davis. — Boston: O. Ditson, c 1898.

> Score (35 p.) English and romanized Hebrew. With organ accompaniment. Sendrey: 5879. Singerman: 5331. Copies: MnS OCH PPGratz (Music)

548. Fünfzigjähriges Stiftungsfest der Gemeinde Ahabeth Achim (Bruderliebe): Programm, Geschichte der Gemeinde, Namensverzeichniss der Mitglieder und Fest-Hymne. — Cincinnati: Ahabeth Achim, 1898.

> [16], 15 p. Includes a program, including "Fest-Hymne." Also includes "Hymne von Joel Steinberg zur Feier des Fünfzigjährigen Jubilaeums der Gemeinde Ahabeth Achim "Bruderliebe" Cincinnati, O./componiert von Hermann Gerold. Singerman: 5322 Holdings: NNJ OCH OCU

549. The Jewish year: a collection of devotional poems for Sabbaths and holidays throughout the year/translated and composed by Alice Lucas. — London; New York: Macmillan, 1898.

> xix, 187 p. Copies: CLU CtY DLC FU MWalB NcU NSiCS OCH OCl PPAnR PPGratz TNJ

550. Kiddush, or Sabbath sentiment in the home/H. Berkowitz; with special illustrations by Katherine M. Cohen. — Philadelphia: [s.n], 1898.

70, [4] p. Includes "Sabbath songs" without music. Singerman: 5310. Copies: CoDu CtY CU DLC KyLou MB MiU MWalA MWalB NcU NN OCl PPAnR PPGratz

551. Kiddush, or Sabbath sentiment in the home / H. Berkowitz; with special illustrations by Katherine M. Cohen. — 2nd thousand. — Philadelphia: [s.n], 1898.

70, [6] p. Includes music. Copies: OCH RPB

552. New Festival service: specially composed for the Reformed Hebrew ritual used at Har Sinai Temple, Baltimore, Md. / by S. Archer Gibson. — [Baltimore: S.A Gibson], 1898.

Score (9 p.) English and romanized Hebrew. For chorus (SATB), with organ accompaniment. Copies: MdBPC

553. Special prayer during the time of our war with Spain: arranged for Temple Emanu-El. — New York: [Emanu-El], 1898?

4 p. Singerman: 5438. Copies: NNJ

554. Three Psalms, Nos. 77, 121, 129: for voice with pianoforte accompaniment / music by J. D. Sapir; German text by Moses Mendelssohn; English text by Cambell. — New York: J. D Sapir, 1898.

Score (11 p.) English and German. Singerman: 5468. Copies: OCH

555. ספר החיים = The book of life: a complete formula of the service and ceremonies observed at the death-bed, house of mourning and cemetery: together with prayers on visiting the graves / elaborated and revised by H. Vidaver. — New York: J. Rosenbaum, 1898.

194 p. English and Hebrew. Copies: NNCoCi OCH

556. עבודת ברית שלום = Services of the B'rith Shalom Congregation. 1st part. Sabbath and Festivals. — Louisville: [B'rith Shalom], 5658–1898.

167 p. English and Hebrew. No more published. Singerman: 5391. Copies: NNJ OCH

1899

557. Dedication ceremonies: Temple Emanuel, Dallas Texas: Thursday, November Thirtieth, Eighteen Hundred and Ninety-nine, 5660. — [Dallas: Emanuel, 1899].

12 p. Includes dedicatory hymn by George Alexander Kohut. Singerman: 5537. Copies: CtY MWalA (uncat) NNJ

558. Dedication of the synagogue of the Congregation Sons of Jacob, Haverstraw, N.Y.: September 3rd, 1899. — New York: [s.n.], 1899.

11, 1 p. Singerman: 5579. Copies: NNJ

559. Dedicatory services of Orach Chaim synagogue: Sunday, March 19th, 1899. — New York: P. Cowen, 1899.

15 p. English and Hebrew. Deinard: 401? Singerman: 5632. Copies: NN

560. In Thee, O God, do I put my trust (Psalm 71): sacred song for alto. Op. 48 / Max Spicker. — New York: G. Schirmer, c1899.

Score (7 p.) With piano accompaniment. No. 5 in a volume lettered: Songs. Copies: CSt IEdS

561. Memorial service for the Day of Atonement: according to the Union prayer book: for 4 voices and organ accompaniment / S. Schlesinger. — Mobile, Ala.: S. Schlesinger, 1899.

Score (1, 15 p.) English and romanized

1899 — 190-?

Hebrew. Sendrey: 7470. Singerman: 5663. Copies: OCH

562. Prayer of the repentant / Isadore H. Weinstock. — Philadelphia: J.W. Jost, c1899.

Score (5 p.) For voice and piano. Singerman: 5686. Copies: OCH

563. Sabbath evening service No. 1.: for the synagogue, according to the Union prayer book / Franklin Pierce Fisk. — New York: Bloch, 1899.

Score (22 p.?) English and romanized Hebrew. Sendrey: 5893. Copies:

564. Shire Yehudah = Songs of Judah: a collection of sacred songs for soli and chorus, with organ accompaniment: for sabbath morning and evening services / composed by Fr. E. Kitziger. — 3rd rev. and greatly augm. ed. — New Orleans: F. E. Kitziger, 1899, c1888.

Score ([3] v.) English and romanized Hebrew. Includes Sendrey: 5934. Copies: OCH

565. Sunday service: Temple Beth-El, New York. — New York: P. Cowen, 1899.

13 p. Compiled by Kaufmann Kohler. Singerman: 5599. Copies: IaDuW MWalA

566. ברכת כהנים = Birchas [sic!] Cohanim / Joachim Kurantmann. — New York: Katzenelenbogen & Rabinowitz, c1899.

Score (5 p.) For Cantor and chorus, with piano accompaniment. Sendrey: 6537. Singerman: 5609. Copies: OCH

567. פסוקי דזמרה: מספר תהלים מסודרים בעשרה מאמרות ומתורגמים בתרגום חדש בלשון אנגלית ולתועלת בני נעורים בבית הספר / על ידי יהודה דוד אייזנשטיין = The classified Psalter arranged by subjects: the Hebrew text with a new English translation on opposite pages: a reader for Hebrew schools / by J.D. Eisenstein — New York: Press of A. Ginsberg, 1899–5659.

16, 123 4 p. English and Hebrew. Deinard: 672. Singerman: 5523. Copies: DLC FU MH MWalA NN NNJ PPBI

568. קבוץ סליחות ותפלות ליום חמשה עשר לחדש כסלו: כפי מנהג החברה קדישא גח"א דווילנא: גח"א בבהכנ"ס קהל עדת ישורון ... — פה נוארק: הובא לדפוס ע"י הגבאים דחברה קדישא (דפוס ה. פאגן און זאהן) תר"ס [1900 or 1899].

91 [i.e. 16] p. For Adath Jeshurun, New York, N.Y. Deinard, 601, 704. Singerman: 5778. Copies: MH MWalA NNJ

190-?

569. [Children's Sabbath service. — Washington, D.C: s.n., 190-?].

7 p. Copies: OCH (unfound)

570. Evening service at the house of mourning: from the Union prayer book. — Cincinnati: Published by the Central Conference of American Rabbis, [190-?].

15 p. English and Hebrew. Copies: MWalA NNHeb

571. New Year's hymn / Fred. E. Kitziger. — New York: Bloch, [190-?].

Score (p.) English and German. For chorus, with organ accompaniment. Sendrey: 7095. Copies:

572. Prayers for the house of mourning. — San Francisco: Published for the use of Congregation Emanu-El, [190-?].

16 p. English and Hebrew. Copies: CU-B OCH

573. מחזור ליום א' וב' של ראש השנה (ליום כפור): כמנהג אשכנז: עם פרשיות הפטרות ושיר היחוד. — New York: Hebrew Pub. Co., [190-?].

2 v. in 1 (224, 256 p.) Hebrew with Yiddish instructions. Copies: MWalA PPAnR

574. מענה לשון: הוא סדר תחנות על בית עלמין: לבקש ולחנן על קברי צדיקים וקדושים... = דיעזען מענה לשון האבין מיר געדרוקט אויף עברי-טייטש... אויך האבין מיר צוגעגעבען די פאלגענדע תחנות און תפלות "השבעתי" "ויעבר" "הצור תמים פעלו" און קדיש יתום ...
— New York: Hebrew Pub. Co, [190-?].

192 p. Hebrew and Yiddish Attributed to Eliezer Liebman ben Loeb. Cover title: מענה לשון עברי טייטש. Copies: DLC (uncat) MH MWalA

575. סדור חנוך תפלה עם חנוך לנער, כל התפלות לכל השנה: נוסח אשכנז: באותיות גדולות מאד. — נויארק: היברו פאב. קא., [190-?].

265 p. Copies: OCH

576. סדור קרבן מנחה: נוסח אשכנז: עברי-טייטש. — ניו יארק: היברו פאב. קא., [190-?].

1 v. (various pagings) Hebrew and Yiddish. Copies: MWalA NNYI

577. סדר סליחות לימים נוראים כמנהג פולין גדול ופולין קטן ...
— New York: L. Flohr, [190-?].

63 p. Copies: MH OCH

1900

578. Evening service at the house of mourning: also for private reading: arranged for Temple Israel of Harlem. — New York: [s.n.], 1900.

44 p. Singerman: 5775. Copies: OCH

579. Fear not, O Israel: anthem (Jer. 6)/ Max Spicker. — New York: G Schirmer, 1900.

Score (8 p.) For 4 soli, chorus (SATB), with piano or organ accompaniment. Sendrey: 7138. Copies:

580. Fiftieth anniversary services of the Temple, Cleveland, Ohio, Tifereth Israel Congregation, Moses J. Gries, Rabbi: October 26, 27, 28, 29, 1900. — Cleveland, O.: [Tifereth Israel], 1900.

26 p. Singerman: 5714. Copies: MWalA NN OCH OClWHi

581. The Hebrew reader for schools: from the prayer book of B. Szold/revised by Drs. Jastrow and Hochheimer. — Philadelphia: [s.n.], 1900.

59 p. Hebrew. Deinard: 596. Singerman: 3249. Copies: MH NNJ OCH Philadelphia Jewish Archives

582. Hymns and prayers for the religious school of Congregation Ahawath Chesed-Shaar Hashomayim, New York/by David Davidson and Th. Guinsburg. — New York: [s.n.], 1900.

47 p. Singerman: 5771. Copies: NNJ

583. Meditations of the heart: a book of private devotion for old and young/collected, adapted, composed by A.J.L. [Annie Josephine Levi]; with an introduction by G. Gottheil. — New York: G. Putnam's Sons, 1900.

xvii, 166 p. Singerman: 5790. Copies: DLC NN NNJ NNYU OCH PPAnR

584. Memorial service after Dr. Einhorn's prayer book: Temple Beth-El, New York. — New York: [Beth-El], 1900.

26, 2 p. Singerman: 5776. Copies: CtY MWalA NNJ OCH

585. Prayers and hymns for divine service: New Year and Day of Atonement. — Newark, N.J.: Congregation B'nai Jeshurun, 1900.

24 p. Singerman: 5773. Copies: OCH

586. Sabbath eve services and hymns and anthems for Sabbaths and holidays/ compiled and arranged for Congregation Sherith Israel by Jacob Nieto. — San Francisco: Weiss, 5661, [1900 or 1901].

68 p. English and Hebrew. Singerman: 5777. Copies: OCH WJHC

587. The school service/by Joseph Krauskopf. — Philadelphia: O. Klonower, 1900.

52 p. Copies: NNJ

588. Services for children: prepared and collected for the use of religious schools — San Francisco: Standing Committee on Religious Education of the Congregation Emanu-El, 1900.

56 p. "Note introduction" by Jacob Voorsanger. Singerman: 5772. Copies: OCH

589. Temple music/issued by the publishers of this work [S. Welsch, A. Kaiser]. — New York: S. Welsch, A. Kaiser, [c1900].

Score (156 p.) English and romanized Hebrew. Copies: NNJ

590. Temple music: a song service in accordance with the Union prayer book: for the evening and the morning of the Sabbath: arranged from Lewandowski's "Kol rinnah ut'fillah": for one and two voices and congregational choir/Isaac S. Moses. — Chicago: I.S. Moses, 1900.

Score (3 v.) English and romaninzed Hebrew. Sendrey: 5940. Singerman: 5812. Copies: NNJ (V.3) OCH PPGratz (V.3)

591. אלון בכות = Divine consoler: prayers for house and home: a true conductor for mourners at the house and upon the grave/ arranged by Adolph L. Goetzl. — New York: A.L. Goetzl, 1900.

32 p. English and Hebrew. Singerman: 5774. Copies: NN OCH

592. אמרי לב = Meditations and prayers for every situation and occasion in life/ translated and adapted from the French by Hester Rothschild; revised and corrected by Isaac Leeser. — Cincinnati: Bloch, 1900.

ix, 260 p. Original in French by Jonas Ennery. Singerman: 5729. Copies: OCH

593. תפלת ישראל = Prayers of Israel with English translation. — 19th stereotype ed. — New York: J.L. Werbelowsky, 1900–5600.

240, 229 p. English and Hebrew. Copies: NNJ OCH

1901

594. Complete musical service for Day of Atonement: evening, morning, afternoon, memorial and concluding: according to the Union prayer book/by S. Schlesinger. — New York; Cincinnati: Bloch, c1901.

Score (169 p.) English and romanized Hebrew. For Cantor and chorus (SATB), with organ accompaniment. Sendrey: 5961. Copies: DLC NN-Br OCH OCl PPGratz PPL UU

595. Complete musical service for New Year: evening and morning: according to the Union prayer book/by S. Schlesinger. — New York: Bloch, c1901.

Score (64 p.) English and romanized Hebrew. For Cantor and chorus (SATB) with organ accompaniment. Sendrey: 5963. Copies: LNT NN-Br PPGratz PPi UU WaU

596. Evening prayers for the house of mourning: with thoughts on death and immortality. — New York: P. Cowen, 1901.

46 p. English and Hebrew. Copyright by the Temple Emanu-El, New York. Copies: MeB NN-Br NN NNJ OCH

597. Friday evening religious exercises of the Young Men's Hebrew Association, New York. — New York: P. Cowen, 1901.

53 p. English and Hebrew. Copies: NNHeb

598. Hymns collected from various sources and selections from the Psalms: for use of the Congregation and the Religious school of Temple Israel of Harlem. — New York: W. Popper, 1901.

62 p. Copies: NN

599. Memorial service held in honor of our dearly beloved and much lamented President William McKinley: held on September Nineteenth, 1901, at Temple Beth-El, Fifth Avenue and 76th Street, New York City. — New York: Bloomingdale Bros., 1901.

16 p. Copies: DLC

600. Morning prayers/arranged by Gustav Gottheil, Temple Emanu-El, New York. — New York: P. Cowen, 1901, c1890 by Temple Emanu-El.

1–12, 12a–12l, [13]–48 p. Copies: NNHeb OCH

601. Rest in the Lord, my soul: anthem for mixed chorus/Abraham Wolf Binder. — New York; Chicago: O. Ditson, 1901.

Score (4 p.). Sendrey: 7020. Copies:

602. Tov le hodos/ Max Spicker and William Sparger. — New York: G. Schirmer, 1901.

Score (8 p.) romanized Hebrew. For Cantor, chorus (SATB), with organ accompaniment. Psalm 92. Sendrey: 6430. Copies:

603. Wm. McKinley memorial service: Congregation Rodeph Shalom, Pittsburgh, Pa: September 19th, 1901. — [Pittsburgh: Rodeph Shalom, 1901].

32 p. Order of Service written by J. Leonard Levy. Copies: OCH

604. ...מחזור = Form of prayers ... with English translation. — Rev. ed. — New York: Hebrew Pub. Co, 5662–1901.

2 v. English and Hebrew. Copies: CLHU (V.2) NNJ PPGratz

605. ...מחזור = Form of prayers ... with English translation. — Rev. ed. — Brooklyn: Hebrew Pub. Co., 1901.

2 v. English and Hebrew. Copies: DLC (uncat) ICU (V.1) MWalA NNJ PPGratz (V.2) WJHC

606. סדר להדרת קדש: כולל תפלות כל השנה וכל הברכות הנהנין, וברכות המצות, וברכות הראיה והריח וכו' הנדרכים לדעת לכל איש יהודי: בהעתקת לשון ענגליש = Form of prayers and blessings of Israel with an English translation. — Brooklyn: Hebrew Pub. Co., 5662–1901, c1881.

507 p. English and Hebrew. Deinard: 939. Copies: DLC (uncat) NNJ OCH OCl OO PPAnR

607. ספר החיים = The book of life: a complete formula of the service and ceremonies observed at the death-bed, house of mourning and cemetery: together with prayers on visiting the graves/elaborated and revised by H. Vidaver. — Brooklyn: Hebrew Pub. Co., 1901.

194 p. English and Hebrew. Deinard: 308. Copies: CLU DLC (uncat) PPAnR

608. ספר החיים = The book of life: a complete formula of the service and ceremonies observed at the death-bed, house of mourning and cemetery: together with prayers on visiting the graves/elaborated and revised by H. Vidaver. — New York: Hebrew Pub. Co., 1901.

194 p. English and Hebrew. Copies: MH

609. עמנואל = The synagogical service/ edited, and in part composed by Max Spicker (musical director) and the Rev. William Sparger (Cantor) of Temple Emanu-El. — New York: G. Schirmer, c1901.

Score (2 v.) English and romanized Hebrew. Pt. I. Service for Sabbath eve. — Pt. II. Service for Sabbath morning. Some copies have עמנואל red ink. Sendrey: 5971. Copies: AzTes CSmH DLC FMU-Mu ICJS IRivFT MiKW MiRochOU MnSCC MoS MoKu NB NBu NFQC NcElon NMu NN NN-Br NNJ OCH OCl PPGratz (Music) RPB TxDA TxDN TxFs ViRU WM

1902

610. Adon olam / Max Spicker and William Sparger. — New York: G. Schirmer, 1902.

Score (12 p.) romanized Hebrew. For Cantor, alto solo and chorus (SATB) with organ accompaniment. Sendrey: 7139 Holdings:

611. Book of prayer / by J. Leonard Levy. — Pittsburgh: Publicity Press, 1902.

281, A–U p. English with Hebrew. Copies: ATLA (microform) CBG-TU (microform) CtY-D (microform) NNUT (microform)

612. Book of prayer / by J. Leonard Levy. — 2nd ed. — Pittsburgh: Publicity Press, 1902.

281, A–V p. English with Hebrew. Copies: DLC NNJ OCH OCl

613. Children's service for use in religious schools / J. Leonard Levy. — 2nd ed. — [Pittsburgh: s.n.], c1902.

259 p. Copies: NN

614. Complete musical service for the Three Festivals: Pesa'h (Passover), Shabuoth (Weeks), Succoth (Tabernacles): according to the Union prayer book / by S. Schlesinger. — New York: Bloch, c1902.

Score (74 p.) English and romaninzed Hebrew. For Cantor and chorus (SATB). Sendrey: 5962. Copies: DLC MoKU OCH PPGratz (Music)

615. Golden jubilee services and dedication ceremonies: Temple Beth-Or, Montgomery, Ala., June 6th, 1902. — Montgomery, Ala.: Beth-Or, 1902.

12 p. Copies: OCH

616. Memorial service for the Day of Atonement: written for Congregation Rodeph Shalom / by J. Leonard Levy. — Pittsburgh: [s.n.], 1902.

59 p. Copies: NNHeb OCH

617. Order of services at the dedication of the new synagogue First Roumanian-American Congregation "שערי שמים": December 24th, 25th, and 28th 1902 כסלו כ״ד, כ״ה, כ״ח תרס״ג. — New York: R. Auerbach, 1902.

18 p. English and Hebrew. Copies: NN NNJ

618. Order of services for the house of mourning / arranged and compiled by Jacob Nieto for Congregation Sherith Israel. — San Francisco: Sherith Israel, 1902–5662.

11 p. English and Hebrew. Copies: WJHC

619. Religious duties of the daughters of Israel: the three most important duties viz Niddah, Challah, Hadlakah: we have also added laws concerning the salting of meat, prayers and meditations, and duties for parents in training children / compiled by Abraham E. Hirschowitz, Rabbi of Congregation "Sons of Israel" Anshei Kalwarier. — New York: [s.n.], c1902.

77 p. English with Hebrew. Prayers and meditations: pp. 45–77. Copies: DLC NjP NNJ

620. Sabbath morning service/Arthur Foote. — Boston: A.P. Schmidts 1902.

Score (p.) English with romanized Hebrew? Sendrey: 5895. Copies:

621. Sabbath service of the Reformed Hebrew ritual/W.G. Owst. — Boston: O. Ditson, 1902.

Score (24 p.) English and romanized Hebrew. For Cantor, chorus (SATB), with organ accompaniment. Sendrey: 5949. Copies: DLC KyLoS OCH PPGratz (Music)

622. The service-ritual/compiled by Joseph Krauskopf. — 4th ed. — Philadelphia: E. Stern, 1902, c1888.

205 p. English with Hebrew. Copies: OCH

623. Two responses: mixed voices/Arthur Foote. — [Boston]: A.P. Schmidt, 1902.

Score (4 p.) English. For chorus (SATB). 1. Response to silent prayer. — 2. How goodly are thy tents. Reprinted from: עזי וזמרת יה = My strength and song is the Lord (Entry 629). Copies: NRU-Mus

624. Why art thou cast down, O, my soul?: sacred song/Max Spicker. — New York: G. Schirmer, 1902.

Score (7 p.). Copies: OrU

625. ... מחזור = Form of prayers ... with English translation. — Rev. ed. — Brooklyn: Hebrew Pub. Co., 1902–1903.

5 v. English and Hebrew. Copies: CLamB (V.1) MH MWalA (V.1–2) NNJ (V.4) PU (V.3, 5)

626. מחזור לראש השנה ויום הכפורים עם באורים בית לוי: מבאר ... המלות ... גם מראה מקורן ... בתנ״ך, בתלמוד ומדרשים: מטה לוי מבאר כוונת המאמרים/חברם אהרן בהרב יחיאל מיכל דמיקיילישאק, עם העתקה בלשון עברי טייטש ... והוספנו לקוטי צבי ... עם עברי טייטש. — Brooklyn: Hebrew Pub. Co., 1902.

400 p. Hebrew and Yiddish. Copies: OCH

627. סדור שפת אמת/מאת וואלף בר שמשון דוב איש היידנהיים=. Daily prayers with English instructions: published for the Hebrew Free Schools of New York: as correct as any edition ever published in רעדעלהיים. — Brooklyn, N.Y.: Hebrew Pub. Co., 1902–1903.

292 p. Hebrew with English instructions. Copies: NNJ

628. סדור שפת אמת/מאת וואלף בר שמשון דוב איש היידנהיים=. Daily prayers with English instructions: published for the Hebrew Free Schools of New York: as correct as any edition ever published in רעדעלהיים. — New York: Hebrew Pub. Co., 1902–1903.

292 p. Hebrew with English instructions. Copies: MWalA OCH

629. עזי וזמרת יה = My strength and song is the Lord, Psalm 118:14: music for the synagogue/by Arthur Foote. — Boston: A.P. Schmidt, c1902.

Score (40 p.) English and romanized Hebrew. For solo and chorus (SATB) with organ accompaniment. Friday night service including: Tov l'hodos — Bor'chu — Sh'ma Jisrael — Bo-ruch — Michomocho and Adonai jimloch — Kedushoh — Response to silent prayer — S'u sh'orim — L'cho Adonoi — J'hal'lu — Ez chayim — wa'anachnu — En kelohenu — Adon olam — W'shomru — How goodly are thy tents. Sendrey: 5895?, 6132. Copies: OCH

630. שלהבת יה = The Temple service: arranged for the Congregation Rodeph Sholom/by Aaron Wise; revised by Rudolph Grossman. — 3rd ed. — New York: P. Cowen, 1902–1903, c1897.

    2 v. English and Hebrew. V.1. For Sabbath and Festivals. — V.2. For the New Year's Day and the Day of Atonement. Copies: OCH

1903

631. Evening and morning service for week days: reprint from the Union prayer book/edited and published by the Central Conference of American Rabbis. — Chicago: T. Rubovits, 1903, c1895.

    64 p. English and Hebrew. At head of title: Pamphlet I. Copies: NN OCH

632. Evening service for week-days and the Sabbath: for the use of the Field Secretary of the Union of American Hebrew Congregations, and of the Central Conference of American Rabbis. — [Cincinnati]: The Publications Committee, CCAR, 1903.

    42 p. English and Hebrew. Reprinted from the סדר תפלות ישראל = The Union prayer book. Copies: OCH

633. For little children: prayers and benedictions for various occasions: compiled for the members of Temple Emanu-El, Montreal/Isaac Lamdan. — Cincinnati: [s.n.], 1903.

    27 p. Copies: OCH

634. Home service for Hanukkah/J. Leonard Levy. — [Pittsburgh?: s.n.], 1903.

    33 p. Copies: NNJ

635. Hymns and anthems for Jewish worship/edited by I.S. Moses. — New York: [s.n.], 1903.

    32 p. Copies: OCH

636. A ritual for children's Sabbath services and Sabbath school devotions/Leo M. Franklin. — Detroit: Jewish American Pub. Co., 1903.

    27 p. Compiled for Temple Beth El, Detroit, Mich. by its Rabbi. Copies: OCH

637. Sabbath service for children/Solomon Foster. — New York: American Hebrew, 1903.

    8 p. Copies: OCH

638. אמרי לב = Meditations and prayers for every situation & occasion in life/translated and adapted from the French by Hester Rothschild; revised and corrected by Isaac Leeser. — New York: Bloch, 1903.

    ix, 262 p. Original in French by Jonas Ennery. Copies: MH

639. מאגילניצקי'ס ליניען רע הילדים (קינדער פריינד): ספר-עזר לילדים להבין מעט מן התפלות והברכות והידיעות הנחוצות להם מלה במלה על פי שיטת-הטורים (ליניען סיסטעם); פיר קינדער אין שולע און אין הויז/מאת יוסף בן יהודה מאגילניצקי. — פילאדעלפיא: יוסף מאגילניצקי, תרס"ד. Copyright 1903 by Joseph Magil.

    175 p. [3] p. of music. Hebrew and Yiddish. Verso of t.p.: Magil's linear children's companion = רע הילדים. Deinard: 753. Copies: DLC (uncat) PP Gratz

640. ... מחזור = Form of prayers ... with English translation. — Rev. ed. — Brooklyn: Hebrew Pub. Co., 5663–1903.

    2 v. in 1. English and Hebrew. Pt. 1. Feast of New Year. — Pt. 2. Day of Atonement. Copies: MH

641. ... מחזור = Form of prayers ... with English translation. — New York: Hebrew Pub. Co., 1903.

v. English and Hebrew. Holdings: NNYI (v.1)

642. שלהבת יה = The Temple service ... Congregation Beth Miriam, Long Branch, N.J. — New York: P. Cowen, 1903–5664.

2 v. English and Hebrew. V.1. For the New Year's Day. — V.2. For the Day of Atonement. "Some of the English prayers ... are taken ... from the Union prayer book of the Central Conference of American Rabbis." Copies: NN NNJ

1904

643. Anthem: Praise ye the Lord this day / Alois Kaiser. — Baltimore: A. Kaiser, 1904.

Score (11 p.) For Soprano solo and chorus (SATB), with organ accompaniment. Sendrey: 7072. Copies: NNJ

644. The children's service for Rosh Ha-Shanah / Joseph Leonard Levy. — 2nd. ed. — Pittsburgh: Dick Press, 1904.

15 p. Copies: CLJ MH MWalA NN OCH

645. The children's service for use in religious schools / by J. Leonard Levy. — 2nd ed. — Pittsburgh: Dick Press, 1904.

259 p. Copies: CLJ MH NN OCH PPi

646. Evening service for the house of mourning: Congregation Rodeph Sholom, New York. — New York: P. Cowen, 1904.

32 p. English and Hebrew. English prayers are reprinted, in part, from the Union prayer book, with permission of the CCAR. Copies: MWalA NNJ OCH

647. Hymns and anthems for Jewish worship / edited by Isaac S. Moses. — New York: Bloch, 1904.

213, 1 p. English and German. Includes Deutsche Hymnen und Seelenfeier:

p. [167]–[214]. Copies: MH-AH MWalA NNJ OCH OCl RPB

648. Order of service appointed for laying the corner-stone of the Temple Congregation Beth Ahabah in the city of Richmond / by Fraternal Lodge, No. 53 A.F.& A.M., presided over by the Most Worshipful Grand Master of Masons in Virginia. Thomas N. Davis ... Friday March 4, 1904, at 4 o'clock p.m. — Richmond: Baptist & Picot, 1904.

15 p. Includes: "Sinai," a hymn by Rabbi Edward N. Calisch: p. 13. Copies: Vi

649. Order of worship for Sunday services: written and compiled for Temple Beth El, Detroit, Michigan / by Leo M. Franklin. — Detroit, Mich.: Jewish American Pub. Co., 1904.

22 p. Copies: MiD-B NNJ OCH

650. Sabbath music: complete evening and morning service according to the Union prayer book / S. Schlesinger. — New York: Bloch, 1904.

Score (3 v.) English and romanized Hebrew. For Cantor and chorus (SATB). Sendrey: 5964. Copies:

651. Sabbath-school hymnal: a collection of songs, services and responsive readings for the school, synagogue and home / edited and published by I.S. Moses. — 6th rev. and enl. ed. — New York: Bloch, 1904.

271 p. Includes music. Copies: CU DLC MH-AH MWalA NN NNAJHi OCl RPB

652. Schirai chinooch: confirmation hymns / Alois Kaiser. — Baltimore: A. Kaiser, 1904.

Score (19 p.) German and Hebrew. For chorus (SATB). Sendrey: 7451. Copies: NNJ

653. The service hymnal: with an introductory service/text compiled by Jos. Krauskopf; music compiled by Russell King Miller. — Philadelphia: E. Stern, 1904.

167 p. English and romanized Hebrew. Includes music. For Reform Congregation Keneseth Israel, Philadelphia, Pa. Sendrey: 6976. Copies: DLC MH-AH MiU NNHeb NNJ OCH PPGratz (Music) RPB

654. The service hymnal: with an introductory service/text compiled by Jos. Krauskopf; music compiled by Russell King Miller. — 2nd ed. — Philadelphia: E. Stern, c 1904.

167 p. English and romanized Hebrew. Includes music. For Reform Congregation Keneseth Israel, Philadelphia, Pa. Copies: NNHeb

655. The service hymnal: with an introductory service/text compiled by Jos. Krauskopf; music compiled by Russell King Miller. — 3rd ed. — Philadelphia: [E. Stern], c 1904.

167 p. English and romanized Hebrew. Includes music. For Reform Congregation Keneseth Israel, Philadelphia, Pa. Copies: PPGratz

656. The service hymnal: with an introductory service/text compiled by Jos. Krauskopf; music compiled by Russell King Miller. — 4th ed. — Philadelphia: Reform Congregation Keneseth Israel, c 1904.

167 p. English and romanized Hebrew. Includes music. For Reform Congregation Keneseth Israel, Philadephia, Pa. Holdings: ATLA (microform) CBGTU (microform) CtY-D (microform) DLC NNUT (microform)

657. "Shir Zion": a Friday night service arranged for use in American synagogues/ by the Society of American Cantors from the "Schir Zion" of S. Sulzer: souvenir of Society of American Cantors in commemoration of the one hundredth birthday and anniversary of S. Sulzer. — New York: Bloch, 1904.

Score (32 p.) English and romanized Hebrew. For Cantor and chorus, with organ accompaniment. Sendrey: 5981. Copies: InG KyLoS MH-Mu NFQC NNJ OCH PPGratz (Music)

658. Yom Kippur night: the original sacred Hebrew chorus as sung on the eve prior to the Day of Atonement: arranged for piano/Herman S. Shapiro. — Chicago: H. S. Shapiro, c 1904.

Score (8 p.). Second part of his Kol Nidre. Copies: OCH

659. הזכרת נשמות = Memorial service/by David Davidson. — New York: [s.n.], 1904.

p. Holdings: NNJ (Lost?)

660. זמירות ישראל = Ancient Jewish melodies/arranged by J. Benzion. — Chicago: [s.n.], c 1904.

Score (10 p.). Copies: OCH

661. סדר תפלות ישראל = The Union prayer-book for Jewish worship. Pt. I. Prayers for the Sabbath, the Three Festivals and the week days/edited and published by the Central Conference of American Rabbis. — New York: Bloch: Press of Stettiner Bros., 1904, c 1895.

110 p. English and Hebrew. Copies: NNHeb OCH

662. סדר תפלות ישראל = The Union prayer-book for Jewish worship. Pt. II. New Year's Day, Day of Atonement/edited and published by the Central Conference of American Rabbis. — New York: CCAR, 1904.

340 p. English and Hebrew. Copies: OCH

663. פֿאלשטענדיגער לינין-סדור לבתי-ספר: ולעם: אלע תפלות כסדר פֿיר א גאנץ יאהר: איבערזעצעט ווארט-ביי-ווארט אין נייעם לינין-סיסטעם פֿיר יעדע אידישע הויז חדרים און בתי-ספר מיט אריגינעלע און בעלעהרענדע קונסט בילדער און מוזיק, מיט וויכטיגע בעמערקונגען אין ספעציעלע סמנים, דורך וועלכע יעדער קען וויסן וואו עס איז א שוא נח, און וואו עס איז א שוא נע. — פֿילאדעלפֿיא, פא.: י. מאגילניצקי.

Copyright 1904 by Joseph Magil.

192, 272 p. Hebrew and Yiddish. Includes music. Copies: NNHeb

664. פֿאלשטענדיגער לינין-סדור לבתי-ספר: ולעם: אלע תפלות כסדר פֿיר א גאנץ יאהר: איבערזעצעט ווארט-ביי-ווארט אין נייעם לינין-סיסטעם פֿיר יעדע אידישע הויז חדרים און בתי-ספר מיט אריגינעלע און בעלעהרענדע קונסט בילדער און מוזיק... אלע תפלות פֿיר וואכען-טעג כסדר אויפֿן ארט. 2טה פֿערבעסערטע אויפֿלאגע. — פֿילאדעלפֿיא, פא.: י. מאגילניצקי.

Copyright 1904 by Joseph Magil.

192, 272 p. Hebrew and Yiddish. Includes music. Copies: CLU MH OCH

665. פֿאלשטענדיגער לינין-סדור לבתי-ספר: ולעם: אלע תפלות כסדר פֿיר א גאנץ יאהר: איבערזעצעט ווארט-ביי-ווארט אין נייעם לינין-סיסטעם פֿיר יעדע אידישע הויז חדרים און בתי-ספר מיט אריגינעלע און בעלעהרענדע קונסט בילדער און מוזיק... אלע תפלות פֿיר וואכען-טעג כסדר אויפֿן ארט. 2טה פֿערבעסערטע אויפֿלאגע. — פֿילאדעלפֿיא, פא.: י. מאגילניצקי.

Copyright 1904 by Joseph Magil.

192, 272, 139–176 p. Hebrew and Yiddish Includes music. Copies: CLJ DGW

666. תפלה לבית האבל = Evening service for the house of mourning: arranged for the use of the Congregation B'nai Jeshurun, N.Y./Joseph Mayer Asher, Rabbi of the Congregation. — New York: P. Cowen, 5664–1904.

59 p. English and Hebrew. Copies: NN NNHeb

667. תפלת ישראל = Prayers of Israel with English translation: according to the custom of the German and Polish Jews. — New York: Hebrew Pub. Co., 1904.

240, 236 [i.e. 230] p. Deinard: 938. Copies: DLC (uncat) MWalA

1905

668. Celebration by the Congregation Shearith Israel, Spanish and Portuguese Congregation in the City of New York: in commemoration of the 250th anniversary of the settlement of Jews in the United States: and the foundation of the Congregation in 1655. 5416–5666; 1655–1905 Sabbath Haye-Sara, Heshvan 27, 5666 November 25, 1905. — New York: Shearith Israel, 1905.

20 p. English with Hebrew. Contains: "Order of the service." Copies: DLC OCH

669. Central Conference of American Rabbis: union services in memory of the Russian martyrs of our faith: Isaiah Temple, Chicago, December Fourth, Nineteen Hundred Five. — Chicago: [s.n.], 1905.

6 leaves. Copies: OCH

670. Dedication ceremonies of the Congregation Beth-El, New York. — New York: [s.n.], 1905.

11 p. Copies: NNJ

671. Etz chajm: baritone solo and chorus/ Isadore H. Weinstock. — New York: Bloch, c1905.

Score (7 p.) romanized Hebrew. For Cantor and chorus (SATB), with organ accompaniment. Sendrey: 6456. Copies: OCH

672. The Lord is my light: anthem for soli and chorus, with organ accompaniment / E. J. Stark. — New York: Schirmer, c 1905.

Score (4 p.). Psalm 27. Copies: OCH

673. Memorial service in commemoration of the fifth anniversary of the death of the Rev. Dr. Isaac M. Wise: at Philadelphia, Pa., March 26th, 1905. — Philadelphia: S. W. Goodman, 1905.

14 p. Held at Reform Congregation Keneseth Israel, Philadelphia. Copies: DLC OCH

674. Order of service for use on the Sabbath before Thanksgiving Day Nineteen Hundred and Five: in commemoration of the 250th anniversary of the settlement of Jews in the United States / prepared by the Committee on Form of Prayer of the Executive Committee on the Celebration of the 250th Anniversary of the Settlement of Jews in the United States. — New York: Executive Committee, 1905.

15 leaves. English and Hebrew. Copies: DLC NNJ OCH

675. Shofar service / composed by E. J. Stark. — San Francisco: E. J. Stark, c 1905.

Score (13 p.) For chorus (SATB), with trombone and organ accompaniment. Copies: DLC OCH

676. Songs of Judah: hymns, Psalms and anthems / composed by C. Otto Weber. — New York: Bloch, c 1905.

Score (65 p.) For mixed voices with organ accompaniment. Sendrey: 7150.

Copies: LNT LNU NN NNJ OCH PPGratz (Music)

677. Young Israel's guide for home and the religious school / arranged and compiled by Bernard M. Kaplan. — San Francisco: M. L. Stern, 1905.

53 p. English and Hebrew. Includes Music. Compiled by the Rabbi of Ohabai Shalome Congregation, San Francisco. Copies: MWalA OCH WJHC

678. לינינען-סדור לבתי-ספר ולעם: סדר כל תפלות השנה, כלן על מקומן בשלמות... = פֿאלשטענדיגער סדור פֿיר א גאנץ יאהר: פֿיר יעדע אידישע הויז, חדרים און בתי ספר.../ פֿון יוסף בן יהודה מאגילניצקי. — פֿילאדעלפֿיא, פא., תרס״ו [1905 or 1906], c 1904 J. Magil.

192 p. Hebrew and Yiddish. Copies: DLC (uncat)

679. מחזור: חלק ראשון לראש השנה ויום הכפורים כמנהג ספרד: ע״פ מטה לוי ועברי דייטש. — ווילנא, תרס״ו [1905 or 1906] — New York: Europ. Hebrew Pub. Co.

1 v. (erratic paging) Hebrew and Yiddish. Commentary by Aaron ben Jehiel Michael, ha-Levi. Copies: MWalA

680. סדור לבתי-ספר ולעם: סדר כל תפלות השנה כלן על מקומן בשלמות... = פֿאלשטענדיגער סדור פֿיר א גאנץ יאהר...: /אלע תפלות פֿאלשטענדיג אויף איין ארט... פֿון יוסף בן יהודה מאגילניצקי. — פֿילאדעלפֿיא, פא.: י. מאגילניצקי, תרס״ו [1905 or 1906].

96, 136 p. Hebrew and Yiddish. Second part has separate t.p.: סדור לבתי-ספר ולעם: תפלות שבת ויום טוב בשלמותן... Copies: CLU MWalA NNJ OCH

681. סדר כל תפלות השנה = Magil's complete linear prayer book: comprising the prayers for the whole year: translated in the new linear system, with notes and original engravings: for the synagogue,

the home and the school. — Philadelphia: J. Magil, 1905.

192, 176 p. English and Hebrew. Includes music. Copies: MWalA PPGratz

682. סדר כל תפלות השנה = Magil's complete linear prayer book: comprising the prayers for the whole year: translated in the new linear system, with notes and original engravings: for the synagogue, the home and the school. — Philadelphia: J. Magil, 1905.

192 p. English and Hebrew. Includes music. Copies: DLC (uncat)

683. סדר כל תפלות השנה = Magil's complete linear prayer book: comprising the prayers for the whole year: translated in the new linear system, with notes and original engravings: for the synagogue, the home and the school. — 2nd improved ed. — Philadelphia: J. Magil, c1905.

192, 176 p. English and Hebrew. Includes music. Copies: CLHU MWalA NNYI NNJ OCH PPGratz RPB

683a. סדר תפלה לילדי בני אברהם = Temple B'nai Abraham Sabbath school ritual/ arranged by A. R. Levy. — Chicago: Temple B'nai Abraham, 1905.

24 p. English and Hebrew. Copies: OCH

684. סדר תפלות ישראל = The Union prayer-book for Jewish worship. Part I. Prayers for the Sabbath, the Three Festivals, and the week days/edited and published by the Central Conference of American Rabbis. — New York: Press of Stettiner Bros., 1905, c1895.

416 p. English and Hebrew. One of OCH's copies has: Addition to ritual for Sabbath Eve, Hebrew and English. 2 leaves inserted. Copies: OCH

685. עולת שבת: כולל תפלות לכל השבת ולשלש רגלים מן קבלת שבת אחר מוצ"ש... ונלוו עליו לקוטי מזמורים הנהוגים לאמרם קודם תפלת ערבית במוצאי שבת. — Brooklyn, N.Y.: Hebrew Pub. Co., 1905?

62 p. Deinard: 940. Copies: OCH

686. הרנה והתפלה = Songs and prayers for the Sabbath eve/composed and arranged by Solomon Baum. — New York: S. Baum, c1905.

Score (36 p., 2 leaves) English and romanized Hebrew. For Cantor and chorus (SATB), with piano or organ accompaniment. Sendrey: 6041. "Service for Sabbath eve": final 2 leaves. Copies: CLJ DLC MH MH-AH NN PPGratz (Music)

687. הרנה והתפלה = Songs and prayers for the Sabbath service/Solomon Baum. — [New York: S. Baum], c1905.

Score (36 p.) English and romanized Hebrew. For Cantor and chorus (SATB), with piano or organ accompaniment. Copies: CLHU MH-Mu NNJ

688. שירי זמרה: כולל תפלות כל השנה = Songs and chants for the prayers of the synagogue year/by H. Kleiner. — Philadelphia: H. Kleiner, 1905–1915.

Score (5 v.) English and Hebrew. For Cantor and chorus (SATB). Copies: NN

689. תפלת שבת = The Sabbath service: for Sabbath eve and Sabbath morning: arranged and revised with special English prayers and responsive readings/by Julius Silberfeld. — Brooklyn: Hebrew Pub. Co., 1905.

245 p. English and Hebrew. Copies: DLC MWalA

1906

690. Chants in the Sabbath services / composed by S. Sulzer and re-published by L. Grossmann for use in the Sabbath schools of the Plum Street Temple. — Cincinnati: L. Grossmann, 1906.

    Score (13 p.) Romanized Hebrew. Sendrey: 5980. Copies: OCH

691. Dedication services at the Temple of Bene Israel Congregation, Cincinnati, Ohio: Sept. 14 and 15, 1906. — Cincinnati: [Bene Israel], 1906.

    p. Copies: NNJ (Lost?)

692. The door of hope: a manual of prayers and devotional readings upon visiting the cemetery / prepared by the New York Board of Jewish Ministers 5658–1898. — 2nd ed. — New York: P. Cowen, 1906.

    92 p. Prepared primarily by Kaufmann Kohler. Copies: CLJ OCH

693. Evening service for the Sabbath / T. L. Krebs. — New York: Bloch, 1906.

    Score (24 p.) English and romanized Hebrew. For Cantor and chorus (SATB) Sendrey: 5937. Copies: OCH

694. "Order of service for use on the Sabbath before Thanksgiving Day, Nineteen Hundred and Five: in commemoration of the two hundred and fiftieth anniversary of the settlement of Jews in the United States"

    pp. 253–256. Prepared by a committee consisting of H. Pereira Mendes, M. H. Harris, Philip Klein, K. Kohler, S. Schechter, Samuel Schulman and Joseph Silverman for a celebration that took place at Carnegie Hall, New York, Thanksgiving Day 1905. In: *Two hundred and fiftieth anniversary of the settlement of Jews in the United States: 1655–1905.* New York: American Jewish Historical Society, 1906. Copies: CarP CSt CU DLC MiU CU

695. "Order of service for use on the Sabbath before Thanksgiving Day, Nineteen Hundred and Five: in commemoration of the two hundred and fiftieth anniversary of the settlement of Jews in the United States"

    pp. 253–256. Prepared by a committee consisting of H. Pereira Mendes, M. H. Harris, Philip Klein, K. Kohler, S. Schechter, Samuel Schulman and Joseph Silverman for a celebration that took place at Carnegie Hall, New York, Thanksgiving Day 1905. In: *Two hundred and fiftieth anniversary of the settlement of Jews in the United States: 1655–1905.* New York: New York Co-operative Society, 1906. Copies: CU CU-SB DCL FTaSU FU ICRL MiU MnU NAlU NBiSU NBuU NN NRU NSbSU PSt TJC

696. The Sabbath-school hymnal: a collection of songs, services and responsive readings for the school, synagogue and the home / I. S. Moses. — 7th rev. & enl. ed. — New York: Bloch, 1906, c1904.

    348 p. English with romanized Hebrew. Includes music. Copies: MH-AH NNJ

697. Supplement to the hymn book for use of Temple Emanu-El, New York / compiled by M. Spicker. — New York: Emanu-El, 1906.

    30 p. Copies: ATLA (microform) CBGTU (microform) CtY-D (microform) NNUT (microform) OCH PPGratz (Music)

698. Unveiling and consecration of the John Hay Memorial Window at the Temple of Reform Congregation Keneseth Israel, Philadelphia: Sunday, December

Second, Nineteen Six. — Philadelphia: [s.n.], 1906.

25, 3 p. Copies: MH OCH RPB

699. מאגיליניצקי׳ס לינינען רע הילדים: בבית ובבית הספר... = מאגיליניצקי׳ס קינדער פריינד: פיר קינדער אין שולע און אין הויז / מאת יוסף בן יהודה מאגילניצקי. — פילאדעלפיא: י. מאגילניצקי, c1906.

47, [2], 6–20 p. Hebrew and Yiddish. Includes music. Copies: PPGratz

700. מה טובו אהליך יעקב = How goodly are thy tents, O Jacob / Solomon Baum. — New York: S. Baum, 1906.

Score (9 p.) English and romanized Hebrew. For Cantor and chorus (SATB), with violin and piano or organ accompaniment. Sendrey: 7013. Copies: OCH

701. נגינות ברוך שור לימים נוראים = N'ginoth Baruch Schorr: Synagogen Gesänge für die hohen Feiertage / componiert von Baruch Schorr; herausgegeben von Israel Schorr. — New York: Bloch, 1906.

Score (250 p.) German and Hebrew. Deinard: 567 Sendrey: 5966. Copies: DLC OCH NN PPGratz (Music)

702. סדור כל בו: סדר תפלות מכל השנה עם תרגום אנגלית = Complete daily prayers: with a revised translation according to the custom of the Ashkenasim. — Brooklyn: Hebrew Pub. Co., 1906–תרס״ו.

735 p. English and Hebrew. Deinard: 936. Copies: CLU DLC MB MH NN NNJ OCH

703. סדור כל בו: סדר תפלות מכל השנה עם תרגום אנגלית = Complete daily prayers: with a revised translation according to the custom of the Ashkenasim. — New York: Hebrew Pub. Co., c1906.

735 p. English and Hebrew. Spine title: The form of daily prayers. Copies: DLC (uncat) OCH

704. סדר תפלות ישראל = The Union prayer-book for Jewish worship. Part I. Prayers for the Sabbath, the Three Festivals, and the days of the week / edited and published by the Central Conference of American Rabbis. — New York: Press of Stettiner Bros., 1906.

110 p. English and Hebrew. Copies: OCH

705. סדר תפלות ישראל = The Union prayer-book for Jewish worship / edited and published by the Central Conference of American Rabbis. — New York: Press of Stettiner Bros., 1906, c1894–1895.

2 v. (416, 340 p.) English and Hebrew. Pt. I. Prayers for the Sabbath, Three Festivals and the week days. — Pt. II New Year's Day, Day of Atonement. Copies: AzU (V.1) MH (V.2) NNJ (V.1) OCH (V.1) NNHeb (V.2)

706. ספר תנחומות = Book of consolation / by William Rosenau. — Baltimore: [s.n.], 1906.

65 p. English and Hebrew. Copies: NjP

707. פאלשטענדיגער לינינען-סדור לבתי ספר ולעם: אלע תפלות כסדר פיר א גאנץ יאהר: איבערזעטצט ווארט-ביי-ווארט אין נייעם לינין-סיסטעם פיר יעדע אידישע הויז, חדרים און בתי-ספר: מיט אריגינעלע און בעלעהרענדע קונסט בילדער און מוזיק, מיט וויכטיגע בעמערקונגען און ספעציעלע סמנים, דורך וועלכע יעדער קען וויסן וואו עס איז א שוא נח, און וואו עס איז א שוא נע. — פילאדעלפיא, פא.: י. מאגילניצקי. — Philadelphia: J. Magil, 1906.

192, 272 p. Hebrew and Yiddish. Includes music. Copies: DLC (uncat)

708. ראשית דעת שפת עבר: למוד הקריאה העברית על פי השטה הקולית בדרך חדשה עם ציורים ותפלות/מאת י. קרינסקי. — ניו יארק: ס. דרוקערמאן, 1906 = Reshith daath sephath Eber: elementary Hebrew reader according to a new system: with illustrations and prayers/by M. Krinski; explanations in English by J. Sprayregen. — New York, c1906.

80 p. English and Hebrew. Deinard: 745. Copies: DLC

709. רע הילדים = Magil's linear children's companion: for the school and the home: some of the prayers, benedictions and religious knowledge in Hebrew: with a linear translation in English/by Joseph Magil. — Philadelphia: J. Magil, c1906.

47, 6–20 p. English and Hebrew. Copies: MWalA

710. שירו לה׳ שיר חדש = Sing unto the Lord a new song: Sabbath eve service, according to the Union prayer book/composed by Ferdinand Dunkley. — New Orleans: Cable Co., c1906.

Score (31 p.) English and romanized Hebrew. For Cantor and choir (SATB), with organ accompaniment. Sendrey: 5883. Copies: CLJ OCH

711. שירו לה׳ שיר חדש = Sing unto the Lord a new song: Sabbath eve service, according to the Union prayer book/composed by Ferdinand Dunkley. — 2nd ed. — New York: Bloch, c1906.

Score (31 p.) English and romanized Hebrew. For Cantor and choir (SATB), with organ accompaniment. Copies: CLJ KyLoS LN NNJ PPGratz (Music)

712. שלהבת יה = Order of services ... as used by Temple Rodeph Sholom, N.Y.: adapted by Congregation Sh'erith Israel-Ahabath Achim. — Cincinnati, O.: Sherith Israel-Ahabath Achim, 5667–1906, c1897.

2 v. English and Hebrew. V.1. Service for Sabbaths and holidays. — V.2. Services for the New Year's Day and the Day of Atonement. Copies: NNHeb (V.2) OCH

713. תפלת ישראל = Prayers of Israel with an English translation: according to the custom of the German and Polish Jews. — New York: Hebrew Pub. Co., 1906.

240, 229 [1] p. English and Hebrew. Copies: MWalA NNJ OCH PPAnR

1907

714. The children's Psalm-book: a selection of Psalms with explanatory comments, together with a prayer-book for home uses in Jewish families/by Mrs. Nathaniel L. Cohen. — London: G. Routledge; New York: Bloch, 1907.

xii, 304 p. English and Hebrew. Copies: DLC MH

715. Children's service for the Day of Atonement/written and compiled by Marion L. Misch. — Providence, R.I.: Fox & Saunders, 1907.

23 p. Copies: OCH

716. Hymns and memoranda for Sunday school use: West End Synagogue, New York. — [New York: Printed for private circulation], 1907.

23 p. Compiled by F. de Sola Mendes for Cong. Shaaray Tefila, New York. Copies: OCH

717. Jiskor: Buch der Erinnerung: Gebete und Betrachtungen für die Seelenfeier, Jahrzeit und an den Grabern. — New York: Selbstverlag des Verfassers Philip Kraus, c1907.

20 p. German and Hebrew. Compiled by Philip Kraus. Cover title: Traver Album. Copies: MWalA

718. Kiddush: the consecration of the Sabbath eve at the family table / Joseph Krauskopf. — Philadelphia: [s.n], 1907.

15 p. Copies: NNJ OCH

719. Kol nidre: arranged for voice with violin and vioncello solo, with piano accompaniment / Henry A. Russotto. — New York: Hebrew Pub. Co., 1907.

Score (5 p.) romanized Hebrew. Sendrey: 7212. Copies:

720. The service manual / Joseph Krauskopf. — 6th ed. — Philadelphia: O. Klonower, 1907, c1892.

95, 256–564 p. English with Hebrew. Copies: OCH

721. אמרי לב = Meditations and prayers for every situation & occasion in life / translated and adapted from the French by Hester Rothschild; revised and corrected by Isaac Leeser. — New York: Bloch, 1907.

ix, 262 p. Original in French by Jonas Ennery. Copies: OCH

722. ... מחזור = Form of prayers ... with English translation. — Rev. ed. — New York: Hebrew Pub. Co., 5668–1907.

2 v. English and Hebrew. Copies: DLC (uncat) MWalA (V.1)

723. מחזור עבדת אהל מועד, כמנהג פולין / מוגה ומדויק היטב על ידי יעקב דעויס ונפתלי אדלר, עם תרגום אנגליש. — לונדון. = Service of the synagogue: a new edition of the Festival prayers with an English translation in prose and verse. — London: G. Routledge; New York: H. D. Buegeleisen, 1907–1909.

6 v. English and Hebrew. V.1. New Year. — V.2–3. Day of Atonement. — V.4. Tabernacles. — V.5. Passover. — V.6. Pentecost. Edited by Herbert M. Adler and Arthur Davis. Copies: CLU (V.5–6) DLC MH OClW

724. סדר ברכת המזון וקריאת שמע: עם עברי טייטש. — נוי-יארק: יוראפיאן היברו פאב. קא. — New York: Europ. Hebrew Pub. Co., 1907.

63 p. Hebrew and Yiddish. Copies: MWalA

725. סדר תפלות ישראל = The Union prayer-book for Jewish worship. Morning services / edited and published by the Central Conference of American Rabbis. — Provisional ed. — New York: CCAR: Press of Stettiner Bros., 1907.

86 p. English and Hebrew. Cover title: Morning services. Copies: CtY MH MH-AH MiDW MWalA NNHeb OCH

726. עבודת ישראל = A prayerbook for the services of the year at the synagogue / arranged by Benjamin Szold and Marcus Jastrow; English translation by Marcus Jastrow. — Rev. ed. of the translation. — Philadelphia: [s.n.], 1907.

2 v. English and Hebrew. Part 1. Services for the Year. — Part 2. Services for the New Year and the Day of Atonement. Copies: DLC MH (V.1) NNJ PPAp

727. הרנה והתפלה = Horinnoh wehatefilloh: songs and prayers for the Sabbath service / composed and arranged by Solomon Baum. — New York: S. Baum, c1907.

Score (36, 74 p.) English and romanized Hebrew. For Cantor and chorus (SATB), with organ accompaniment. Sendrey: 5863. Copies: NN PPGratz

1908

728. Adom olom [two versions] for choir, cantor or baritone solo with organ accompaniment / Max Helfère. — New York: Luckhardt & Belden, c 1908.

Score (11 p.) romanized Hebrew. Songs of Beth El — Closing anthems. Sendrey: 7060. Copies: OCH

729. Hymns and anthems: West End Synagogue ... New York. — [New York: Printed for private circulation only], 1908.

32 p. Compiled by F. de Sola Mendes? for Cong. Shaaray Tefila, New York. Sendrey: 6932. Copies: NN

730. Kiddush: the consecration of the Sabbath eve at the family table / Joseph Krauskopf. — Philadelphia: Reform Congregation Keneseth Israel, 1908.

15 p. Copies: OCH

731. Little daily helps for holy living / Council of Jewish Women, New York Section. — New York: The Council, 1908.

9 p. Copies: OCH

732. Morning service for the synagogue according to the Einhorn prayerbook / Arthur Dunham. — Chicago: C. F. Summy, Co., 1908.

Score (p.). Sendrey: 5882. Copies:

733. Sabbath afternoon service: arranged for the use of the children attending the Educational Alliance, New York. — New York: Stettiner Bros., 1908.

125 p. English and Hebrew. pp. 109–116: Music notes from the Union hymnal. Copies: NNJ OCH

734. Sabbath morning service / Edmund Serano Ender. — New York: Bloch, 1908.

Score (p.). Sendrey: 5887. Copies: OCH

735. Sabbath service according to the Union prayer book: for mixed quartette with organ accompaniment / Franz Wald. — New York: Bloch, 1908.

2 v. English and romanized Hebrew. Pt. 1. Evening service. Sendrey: 5985. Copies: OCH

736. Service for Friday evening / Edmund Serano Ender. — New York: Bloch, 1908.

Score (8 p.) English and romanized Hebrew. Copies: OCH

737. Services for children: prepared and collected for the use of religious schools / by Jacob Voorsanger; music composed by E. J. Stark. — San Francisco: Standing Committee on Religious Education of the Congregation Emanu-El, 1908.

69 p. English with romanized Hebrew. Includes music. Sendrey: 5977. Copies: CLHU CU DLC PPGratz (Music)

738. Tehilloth: service manual for Congregation Agudath Jeshorim, 86 Street Temple New York ... / arranged by D. Davidson. — New York: Baron, 1908.

63 p. Copies: NNJ OCH

739. מחזור ... כמנהג אשכנז עם פירוש מטה לוי: בו יפרש כל הפיוטים בסדר נכון ועם פירוש עברי דייטש לבאר פירוש המלות וכוונת המאמרים = דאס נייע מחזור מיט עברי דייטש האבין מיר געדרוקט מיט זעהר פיל מעלות אויף גרויסע אותיות און אלצדינג בסדר.
— New York: Hebrew Pub. Co., 1908.

2 v. Hebrew and Yiddish. Commentary attributed to Aaron ben Jehiel Michael, ha-Levi. V.1. ראש השנה ויום כפור — V.2. שלש רגלים. Copies: NNJ OCH

740. מחזור ... כמנהג ספרד עם פירוש מטה לוי...
— New York: Hebrew Pub. Co., 1908.

2 v. Hebrew and Yiddish. Commentary

attributed to Aaron ben Jehiel Michael, ha-Levi. V.1. ראש השנה — V.2. יום הכפורים. Copies: OCH

741. מחזור לראש השנה ויום הכפורים ושלש רגלים כמנהג אשכנז: עם ...תפלת מעריב ל"ה ופירוש מטה לוי עם העתקת עברי טייץ על כל התפלות שבפיוטי ראש השנה ויום כפור וטל וגשם ... — פֿערלאג פֿון היברו פאב. קא. — New York: Hebrew Pub. Co., 1908.

224 p. Hebrew and Yiddish. Commentary attributed to Aaron ben Jehiel Michael, ha-Levi. Copies: NNJ

742. מחזור עבדת אהל מועד, כמנהג פולין/ מוגה ומדויק היטב על ידי יעקב דעויס ונפתלי אדלר =

Service of the synagogue: a new edition of the Festival prayers with an English translation in prose and verse. — 2nd. ed. — London: G. Routledge; New York: Bloch, 1908.

6 v. English and Hebrew. V.1. New Year. — V.2–3. Day of Atonement. — V.4. Tabernacles. — V.5. Passover. — V.6. Pentecost. Edited by Herbert M. Adler and Arthur Davis. Copies: NNJ

743. סדור לבתי-ספר ולעם: סדר כל תפלות השנה כלן על מקומן בשלמות ... = פֿאלשטענדיגער סדור פֿיר א גאנץ יאהר: ... אלע תפלות פֿאלשטענדיג אויף איין ארט ... /פֿון יוסף בן יהודה מאגילניצקי. — פילאדעלפיא, פא.: י. מאגילניצקי, תרס"ח. Copyright by J. Magil. [Preface, 1908].

96, 176 p. Hebrew and Yiddish. Deinard: 302. Copies: NNJ

744. סדור לבתי-ספר ולעם: סדר כל תפלות השנה כלן על מקומן בשלמות ... = פֿאלשטענדיגער סדור פֿיר א גאנץ יאהר: ... /אלע תפלות פֿאלשטענדיג אויף איין ארט ... פֿון יוסף בן יהודה מאגילניצקי. — פילאדעלפיא, פא.: י. מאגילניצקי, תרס"ט, [1908 or 1909].

96, 176 p. Hebrew and Yiddish. Copies: OCH

745. סדר כל תפלות השנה = Magil's complete linear prayer book: with services for Sabbaths and Festivals. — 16th ed. — New York: Hebrew Pub. Co., c 1905. [Preface 1908].

176 p. English and Hebrew. Copies: CLJ OCoD

746. סדר כל תפלות השנה = Magil's complete linear prayerbook: comprising the prayers for the whole year: translated in the new linear system, with notes and original engravings: for the synagogue, the home and the school. — 2nd improved ed. — Philadelphia: Translated and published by Joseph Magil, c 1905, [Preface, 1908].

271, 192 p. English and Hebrew. Deinard: 937. Copies: Jewish Community Library of Los Angeles NNJ NNYI OCH

747. סדר תפלות ישראל = The Union prayer-book for Jewish worship/edited and published by the Central Conference of American Rabbis. — New York: Bloch., 1908, c 1894–1895.

2 v. English and Hebrew. Pt. I. Prayers for the Sabbath, Three Festivals and the week days. — Pt. II. New Year's Day, Day of Atonement. Copies: CLHU (V.1) NNHeb OCH

748. סידור יורה ומלקוש ומרוה ... חלק ראשון ... /מאתי שבתי בא"א הלל המכונה טשעק ... — נוארק: א.ח. ראזענבערג, תרס"ט. The newly improved prayer book entitled Yoreh-malkosh u'marveh: an improved guide for the teaching to young and old the art of properly reading the Hebrew language. Vol. 1./ by Sabbath Check. — New York: Power Printers, 1908.

12, 42, 10, [336], 8 p. Hebrew. No more published. Deinard: 934. Copies: DLC MWalA NN NNHeb

749. ספר חיים = Prayers for the dead/by B. Friedman. — Baltimore: Published by the Hebrew Friendship Cemetery Co.: Press of Emanuel & Hornstein, 1908, c 1907.

72 p. Copies: OCH

750. עבודת ישראל = A prayerbook for the services of the year at the synagogue/ arranged by Benjamin Szold and Marcus Jastrow; English translation by Marcus Jastrow. — Rev. ed. of the translation. — Philadelphia: [s.n.], 1908, c 1907.

2 v. English and Hebrew. Part 1. Services for the Year. — Part 2. Services for the New Year and the Day of Atonement. Copies: MH (V.1) NNJ (V.2)

751. תפלת שבת = The Sabbath service: for Sabbath eve and Sabbath morning: arranged and revised with special English prayers and responsive readings/by Julius Silberfeld, Rabbi, Congregation B'nai Abraham, Newark, N.J., for Temple Ansche Chesed, New York — New York: Bloch, 1908, c 1905 by Cong. B'nai Abraham, Newark, N.J.

276 p. English and Hebrew. Copies: NNHeb

1909

752. Adath Jeshurun hymnal. — Rev. — Philadelphia, Pa.: Adath Jeshurun, 1909.

36 p. Copies: MWalA NNJ

753. The children's service for Yom Kippur afternoon/by Joseph Krauskopf. — Philadelphia: Reform Congregation Keneseth Israel, 1909.

19 p. Cover title: A Kippur service for children. Copies: OCH

754. Children's services: arranged for each week of the month, for holidays and patriotic occasions/by Rudolph Grossman, rabbi of Temple Rodeph Sholom, New York. — New York: Bloch, 1909.

20 p. Copies: DLC (microfom) NN (microform) OCH

755. A child's ritual/by Abram Simon. — Washington, D.C.: [s.n.], 1909.

24 p. Copies: NN

756. Hymn book for Jewish worship. — Rochester, N.Y.: Daily Union & Advertiser Press, 1909.

3, 96 p. Compiled by M. Landsberg and S. Wile. Copies: OCH

757. Jewish hymnal for religious schools/ edited and compiled by Henry L. Gideon. — New York: Bloch, 1909.

Score (x, 91 p.) English and romanized Hebrew. Copies: NbU PPGratz PPStCH RPB

758. Lincoln centenary services, 1909. — Louisville, Ky.: Temple Adath Israel, 1909.

38 p. Copies: MiU NN

759. Morning services: Temple Mishkan Israel/prepared by David Levy. — New Haven, Conn.: [A.O. Steinbath Press], 1909.

32 p. English and Hebrew. Copies: NNHeb OCH

760. Order of service of Sabbath schools/ Louis Grossmann. — Cincinnati: May & Kreidler, 1909.

12 p. English and Hebrew. Copies: OCH

761. The Sabbath-school hymnal: a collection of songs, services and responsive readings for the school, synagogue and home/edited and published by I.S. Moses. — 9th ed. — New York: Bloch, 1909.

348 p. English and romanized Hebrew. Includes music. Copies: NN PPGratz

762. The service manual/by Joseph

Krauskopf. — 7th ed. — Philadelphia: O. Klonower, 1909.

95, 256–564 p. English with Hebrew. For Reform Congregation Keneseth Israel (Philadelphia, Pa.). Copies: NN PPGratz

763. Young Israel's guide for home and the religious school/arranged and compiled by B. M. Kaplan. — 2nd ed. — San Francisco: The Author at M. L. Stern, 1909, c1905.

3, 54, 2 p. English and Hebrew. Includes music. Compiled for Ohabai Shalome Congregation, San Francisco, Ca. Copies: CLHU OCH

764. אלה המזמורים והפסוקים לחנוכת בית הכנסת של ק״ק מקוה ישראל: פה פילאדילפיא, כ״ט לחדש אלול בשנת תרס״ט =
Dedication of the new synagogue of the Congregation Mikve Israel, at Broad and York Streets: on September 14, 1909, Elul 29 5669. — Philadelphia: Cahan Printing Co., 1909.

29, 19 p. English and Hebrew. Form of the service: pp. 1–19. Copies: ALTA (microform) CBGTU (microform) DLC FU MWalA NIC NN NNJ NNUT (microform)

765. ... מחזור = Form of prayers ... with English translation. — Rev. ed. — New York: Hebrew Pub. Co., 1909.

2 v. English and Hebrew. Copies: MH (V.1) NNJ PU (V.1)

766. מחזור כל בו: עם פירוש עברי טייטש בשם בית ישראל וילקוט פנינים יקרים ומעשה אלפס ... : נוסח ספרד. — ניו־יארק: היברו פאב. קא., 1909–

5 v. Holdings: MWalA (V.2-3)

767. סדר הדרת קדש: פֿארמאט קטן בהעתקת ענגליש: [קדיש מיט ענגליש לעטערס אין העברעאיש]

— New York: Hebrew Pub. Co., 1909.

18 p. Hebrew and Yiddish. Copies: OCH

768. סדר להדרת קדש: כולל תפלות כל השנה בהעתקת לשון ענגליש = ...
Form of prayers and blessings of Israel: with an English translation. — New York: Hebrew Pub. Co., 1909.

507 p. English and Hebrew. Copies: OCH

769. ספר אנעים זמירות = Sefer Anim zemiroth ... : musical service for the Sabbath morning according to the Union prayer book for Jewish worship/by E. J. Stark. — New York: Bloch, c1909.

Score (viii, 45 p.) English and romanized Hebrew (Preface in English and German) For Cantor, soli and chorus (SATB), with organ accompaniment. Copies: DLC OCH PPGratz (Music)

770. עבדת יום הזכרון; עבדת יום הכפורים = Holyday prayers: a new ritual for New Year and Day of Atonement. — New York: Bloch, 1909.

2 v. English and Hebrew. V.2 has title Holiday prayers. "This prayer book ... follows the traditional form ... omitting such portions of the piyutim as many American Conservative congregations do not include in their liturgy" — The Publishers. Copies: DLC MH-AH MWalA NN NNJ OCH PPD

191–?

771. Bircas Kohanim: für Cantor Solo und gemischten Chor/Josef Rosenblatt. — [New York: s.n., 191–?].

Score (4 p.) romanized Hebrew. Bound with: יהי רצון פֿון ראש חדש בענשן. — New York: Hebrew Pub. Co., 1917. (Entry 978). Copies: OCH

191–?

772. Children's harvest service / David Philipson. — [New York: Ark Pub. Co., 191-?].

11 p. Copies: OCH

773. Divine service for Sabbath schools: adopted from Dr. L. G.'s [Louis Grossmann] "Order of Service for Sabbath schools"/ by S. Schwartz. — Cleveland, O.: Ideal, [191-?].

8 p. English and Hebrew. Copies: OCH

774. Hymns from the New Union Hymnal / published by the Central Conference of American Rabbis. — New York: CCAR, [191-?] (Kansas City: Tiernan-Dart Printing Co.).

100 p. Copies: NNJ OCH

775. Memorial service. — Cincinnati, Ohio: May & Kreidler, [191-?].

12 p. English and German. For the Plum Street Temple (Bene Yeshurun). Bound with: Order of the memorial service at the Plum Street Temple (Entry 776). Page 12 differs from entry 776. Includes instructions for the choir to sing the hymn "Es jauchzen die Heere..." Copies: OCH

776. Order of the memorial service at the Plum Street Temple, Cincinnati, Ohio. — Cincinnati: May & Kreidler, [191-?].

12 p. For Bene Yeshurun. Bound with: Memorial service: (Entry 775). P. 12 differs from entry 775. Copies: OCH

777. Songs for congregational singing: Baltimore Hebrew Congregation. — Baltimore: The Congregation, [191-?].

16 p. Copies: OCH

778. Unsanneh tokef: for solo, choir and organ / Morris Goldstein. — New York: Bloch, [191-?].

Score (p.). Sendrey: 7052. Copies:

779. מחזור... עם תרגום אנגלית = Prayer book with a revised English translation / A. Th. Philips. — New York: Hebrew Pub. Co., [191-?].

2 v. English and Hebrew. V.1. New Year. — V.2. Day of Atonement. Copies: CLU (V.2) OCH

780. מחזור לראש השנה; מחזור ליום/ הכפורים מוגה ומדויק על ידי יעקב בן יצחק דעויס ונפתלי בן מרדכי אדלר הכהן, עם תרגום אנגלית. — נדפס כפי הוצאת לונדון. — ניו יארק: היברו פאב. קא. =

Service of the synagogue: a new edition of the Festival prayers with an English translation in prose and verse. — New York: Hebrew Pub. Co., [191-?].

267 [i.e. 534], 289 [i.e. 578] p. English and Hebrew. Copies: MWalB

781. מחזור לראש השנה ויום הכפורים ולשלש רגלים כמנהג אשכנז... עם העתקת עברי טייץ. — New York: Hebrew Pub. Co., [191-?].

368 p. Hebrew and Yiddish. Copies: OCH

782. מחזור לראש השנה ויום הכפורים ושלש רגלים כמנהג ספרד: ועתה הוספנו מטה לוי עם העתקת עברי טייץ על כל התפלות. — New York: Hebrew Pub. Co., [191-?].

368 p. Hebrew and Yiddish. Commentary attributed to Aaron ben Jehiel Michael, ha-Levi. Copies: MWalA

783. מחזור ראש השנה ויום הכפורים כמנהג אשכנז: עם פירוש מטה לוי: בו יפרש כל הפיוטים בסדר נכון עם פירוש עברית דייטש לבאר פירוש המלות וכוונת המאמרים = דאס נייע מחזור מיט עברי דייטש האבין מיר געדרוקט מיט זעהר פיל מעלות אויף גרויסע אותיות און אלצדינג כסדר. — New York: Hebrew Pub. Co., [191-?].

464 p. Hebrew and Yiddish. Commentary attributed to Aaron ben Jehiel Michael, ha-Levi. Copies: ICJS MWalA

191–? — 1910

784. מענה לשון: הוא סדר תחנות על בית עלמין.../מיוחסות...לר׳ אליעזר ליבמאן בן ליב, האבין מיר גישטעלט אויף עברי טייטש. — New York: Hebrew Pub. Co., [191-?].

192 p. Hebrew and Yiddish. Copies: OCH

785. סדור חנוך תפלה: באותיות גדולות מאד: כולל תפלות לכל השנה, גם ספירת העומר, וקדוש לבנה ואלפא ביתא עם גידול בנים... — ניו־יארק: פארלאג אייראפישע ספרים האנדלינג קא., [191-?].

288 p. Copies: DLC (uncat)

786. סדור חנוך תפלה עם חנוך לנער: כולל תפלות לכל השנה: נוסח אשכנז: באותיות גדולות. — ניו־יארק: היברו פאב. קא., [191-?].

1 v. (various pagings). Copies: OCH PPGratz

787. סדור לבתי־ספר ולעם = פאלשטענדיגער סדור פיר א גאנץ יאהר/פון יוסף בן יהודה מאגילניצקי. — 5טה פארמעהרטע און פערבעסערטע אויף. — פילאדעלפיא, פא.: י. מאגילניצקי; נוי יארק: הויפט־פארקויף היברו פאב. פא. [191-?].

96, 136 p. Hebrew and Yiddish. Copies: MWalA

788. סדור שפת אמת: כולל כל תפלות ישראל לכל השנה/מוגה ומסודר על ידי א. היימאן, עם תרגום ענגליש. — ניו־יארק: היברו פאב. קא., [191-?].

6, 214, 314 p. English and Hebrew. Copies: CLU NNYI

789. סדר להדרת קדש: כולל תפלות כל השנה וכל הברכות...בהעתקת ענגליש = Form of prayers and blessings of Israel: with an English translation. — New York: Hebrew Pub. Co., [191-?].

507 p. English and Hebrew. Copies: MWalA

790. סדר תפלות לאבלים: צדוק הדין, הזכרת נשמות, קדיש יתום, קדיש דרבנן, דינים ותפלות ליאהרצייט. — נויארק: היברו פאב. פא. = Mourners' prayers: Tzodok ha-din, memorial prayer, Kaddish, Jahrzeit laws and prayers. — New York: Hebrew Pub. Co., [191-?].

57 p. English and Hebrew. Copies: MWalA

791. סדר תפלת ישראל: כמנהג אשכנז: כולל תפלות מכל השנה...באותיות גדולות מאירות עינים. — New York: Hebrew Pub. Co., [191-?].

1 v. (various pagings). Copies: MWalA OCH

792. עולת שבת: כולל תפלות לכל שבת... ונלוו עליו ליפוטי מזמורים...לאמרם קודם תפלת ערבית במוצאי שבת... — New York: Hebrew Pub. Co., [191-?].

1 v. (various pagings). Copies: OCH

1910

793. Order of service for the New Year and the Day of Atonement/compiled and arranged by Jacob Nieto. — San Francisco: Congregation Sherith Israel, 1910 (Levison Printing Co.).

399 p. English and Hebrew. Copies: NN WJHC

794. Succoth revived: a manual of exercises for temple, synagogue or Sabbath school/by Solomon Schindler and M. M. Eichler. — New York: Bloch, 1910.

18 p. Copies: NN

795. The universal Lord (Adon olam)/by Maurice H. Harris. — Cincinnati: [M. H. Harris, 1910?].

Score (8 p.). Sendrey: 7055. Copies: NN

796. אמרי לב = Meditations and prayers for every situation & occasion in life/translated and adapted from the French

by Hester Rothschild; revised and corrected by Isaac Leeser. — New York: Bloch, 1910.

ix, 262 p. English, with final 2 pages in Hebrew. Original in French by Jonas Ennery. Copies: NNHeb

797. מחזור... כמנהג פולין: מוגה ומדויק כפי מחזור של החכם ואלף היידנהיים וכתבי יד ישנים/על ידי יעקב בן יצחק דעויס ונפתלי בן מרדכי אדלר הכהן, עם תרגום אנגלית. — ניו־יארק. =

Service of the synagogue: a new edition of the Festival prayers with an English translation in prose and verse. Reprinted from the latest and best London edition. — New York: Jewish Premium Pub. Co., 1910.

2 v. English and Hebrew. Edited by Herbert M. Adler and Arthur Davis. V.1. לראש השנה. — V.2. ליום הכפורים. Deinard: 464. Copies: CU DLC (uncat) MH NNJ NNYI (V.1) PPGratz

798. מחזור עבדת אהל מועד, כמנהג פולין: מוגה ומדויק... על ידי יעקב דעויס ונפתלי אדלר, עם תרגום אנגליש. — לונדון. =

Service of the synagogue, Day of Atonement: a new edition of the Festival prayers with an English translation: reprinted from the latest and best London ed. — New York: Hebrew Pub. Co., 1910.

76, 76, 77–83, 287, 287, 288–289 [2] p. English and Hebrew. Edited by Herbert M. Adler and Arthur Davis. Copies: DWT InNd KyWAT MiBsA MMet MoSpCB MsU NNF ScU TxAuCS TxFS

799. מענה לשון: סדר תחינות על בית עלמין. = Memorial prayers and meditations: translated with many original additions/by G. Selikovich — New York: Hebrew Pub. Co., 1910.

iv, 60, 63, 94 p. English and Hebrew. Copies: CLHU DLC MB MH MWalA NNYU

800. סדור חנוך תפלה עם חנוך לנער: כולל תפלות לכל השנה: נוסח אשכנז: באותיות גדולות מאד. — ניו־יארק: היברו פאב. קא., [1910?].

287 p. Copies: MWalA

801. סדר קבורה כפי מנהג ק"ק ספרדים שארית ישראל בנו יארק עם תרגום אנגלי. — מהד. תנינא. — נו יארק: נדפס בהוצאת חברה חסד ואמת, בשנת [תר"ע] =

Burial service as used in the Congregation Shearith Israel (Spanish and Portuguese) of New York. — New York: Published by the חברה חסד ואמת (Burial Society) of the above Congregation, 5670 [1910].

15, 19 p. English and Hebrew. Copies: MH MWalA NjP NNHeb OCH

802. סדר תפלות ישראל = The Union prayer-book for Jewish worship/edited and published by the Central Conference of American Rabbis. — New York: Bloch., 1910, c1894–1895.

2 v. English and Hebrew. Pt. I. Prayers for the Sabbath, Three Festivals and the week days. — Pt. II. New Year's Day, Day of Atonement. Copies: CLHU (V.2) OCH

803. סדר תפלות ישראל = The Union prayer-book for Jewish worship. Part II. New Year's Day, Day of Atonement/ edited and published by the Central Conference of American Rabbis. — New York: Bloch., 1910, c1894.

340 p. English and Hebrew. "The changes and additions in this book are made by the First Hebrew Congregation of Oakland, California, approved by the Central Conference of American Rabbis." — Label on cover. Copies: WJHC

804. ספר אנעים זמרות = Sefer anim zemiroth: musical service for the New Year according to the Union prayer book for

Jewish worship / Edward J. Stark. — New York: Bloch, c1910.

Score (120 p.) English and romanized Hebrew. For soli, with organ accompaniment. Sendrey: 5972. Copies: ICJS MWalA NN PPL

805. ספר נשמת חיים = The soul of life: מענה לשון book of prayer and devotion for the children of Israel as well as for all the regulations of women's life / by S. Bamberger. — New York: P. Friedman, 1910.

64 p. Copies: OCH

806. עבודת הקדש = Avodath hakodesh: works of sacred music: a complete edition of traditional and original compositions of synagogue music / Marcus Hast. — London: Bibliophile Press; New York: Bloch, c1910.

Score (4 v.) Engish and romanized Hebrew. For Cantor and chorus (SATB), with keyboard accompaniment. V.1. Sabbath liturgy for the whole year. — V.2. Hymns, prayers and praises for all the Festivals. — V.3. All Psalms incorporated in the liturgy and a large number for various occasions. V.4. Special services, consecration of synagogues, weddings ... Copies: CLU PPGratz

807. עבודת ישראל = A prayer book for the services of the year at the synagogue / arranged by Benjamin Szold and Marcus Jastrow; English translation by Marcus Jastrow. — Rev. ed. of the translation. — Philadelphia: [s.n.], 1910, c1907.

2 v. English and Hebrew. Part 1. Services for the year. — Part 2. Services for the New Year and the Day of Atonement. Cover title: Abodath Israel. Copies: CBGTU MH MWalA NNJ

808. קול רינה = Hebrew hymnal for school and home / edited by Lewis M. Isaacs and Mathilde S. Schechter. — New York: Bloch, 1910–5670.

61 p. English and Hebrew. Includes music. Sendrey: 6967. Copies: MH-AH MWalA OCH PPGratz (Music)

809. שירי זמרה, קבלת שבת = Shirei zimrah, Kabbalat Shabbat: Friday evening service = Synagogen Gesänge für Freitag Abends für Cantor, Solo und Chor und Orgel ... / composed by E. Schnipelisky. — New York: [s.n.], 1910.

Score (28 p.) romanized Hebrew. Sendrey: 5965, 6565. Copies: CLJ NB NNJ PBm PPGratz

1911

810. Evening prayers for the house of mourning: with thoughts on death and immortality. — New York: P. Cowen, 1911.

47 p. English and Hebrew. For Temple Emanu El, New York. Copies: OCH

811. Morning service for the synagogue according to the Union prayer book / Howard R. Thatcher. — New York: Bloch, 1911.

Score (72 p.) English and romanized Hebrew. For Cantor and chorus (SATB), with organ accompaniment. Copies: LN NN-Br NNJ PPGratz TxU

812. Personal prayers / Central Conference of American Rabbis. Committee on Personal Prayer. — [Philadelphia: CCAR], 1911.

ii, 59 p. Place of publication taken from a printed letter preceding the title page, sent out from Henry Berkowitz, Chair of the Committee on Personal Prayer, dated September 5, 1911. Copies: MH NNJ OCH

813. Prayers for private devotion from the Union prayer book/edited and published by the Central Conference of American Rabbis. — Cincinnati: CCAR, 1911.

   iv, 84 p. Compiled by the Committee on Personal Prayer, Henry Berkowitz, Chair. Copies: MH OCH

814. Ritual for Jewish worship/edited by Max Landsberg. — Rochester, N.Y.: D.R.Mann, 1911.

   2, 229 p. English and Hebrew. Copies: DLC OCH

815. The Sabbath-school hymnal: a collection of songs, services and responsive readings for the school, synagogue and home/edited and published by Isaac S. Moses. — 9th rev. and enl. ed. — New York: Bloch, 1911.

   348 p. English and romanized Hebrew. Includes music. Copies: PPGratz

816. אוהב שלום = Morning service for the synagogue according to the Union prayer book: composed for the choir of Oheb Shalom Temple, Baltimore, Maryland/Howard R.Thatcher. — New York: Bloch, 1911.

   Score (72 p.) English and romanized Hebrew. For Cantor, chorus (SATB), with organ accompaniment. Copies: OCH PPGratz

817. זמירות ישראל = Songs of Israel: responses, Psalms and hymns for worship in Jewish Congregations and schools/edited by Louis Grossmann. — Cincinnati: [s.n.], 1911.

   16 p. Includes music. Copies: CLHU OCH PPGratz (Music)

818. מחזור ... עם תרגום אנגלית = Prayer book ... with a revised English translation/by A.Th.Philips. — New York: Hebrew Pub.Co., 1911–תרע״ב.

   2 v. English and Hebrew. V.1. New Year. — V.2. Day of Atonement. Copies: MH-AH NNJ

819. מחזור ... עם תרגום אנגלית = Prayer book with a revised English translation/by A.Th.Philips. — New York: Hebrew Pub. Co., 1911–.תרע״ב

   4 v. English and Hebrew. V.1. ליום ראש השנה — V.2. ליום שני של ראש השנה — V.3. לערבית יום כפור — V.4. ליום כפור. Copies: MWalA (V.1–3) NNHeb NNJ

820. מחזור ... עם תרגום אנגלי: מוגה ומדויק כפי מחזור של החכם ואלף היידנהיים וכתבי יד ישנים/על ידי יעקב בן יצחק דעויס ונפתלי בן מרדכי אדלר הכהן ... = Service of the synagogue: a new edition of Festival prayers with an English translation in prose and verse. — New York: Hebrew Pub.Co., 1911.

   2 v. in 1. English and Hebrew. V.1. לראש השנה — V.2. ליום הכפורים. Copies: CLHU OCH

821. מחזור כל בו: עם פירוש עברי טייטש בשם בית ישראל וילקוט פנינים ומעשה אלפס ... : נוסח אשכנז. — ניו-יארק: היברו פאב. קא., תרע״ב [1911 or 1912].

   7 v. in 5. Hebrew and Yiddish. Copies: DLC (V.1–2, uncat) MWalA (V.1–2, 5) NNJ OCH

822. מחזור כל בו: עם פירוש עברי טייטש בשם בית ישראל וילקוט פנינים ומעשה אלפס ... : נוסח אשכנז. — ניו-יארק: היברו פאב. קא., תרע״ב [1911 or 1912].

   5 v. Hebrew and Yiddish. Copies: NNJ (V.1–4)

823. מחזור כל בו: עם פירוש עברי טייטש בשם בית ישראל וילקוט פנינים יקרים ומעשה

1911–1912

אלפס ... : נוסח ספרד. — ניו-יארק: היברו פאב. קא., תרע״ב [1911 or 1912].

5 v. Hebrew and Yiddish. Copies: MWalA (V.1–2)

824. סדור בית יהודה: סדר תפלת ישראל כמנהג אשכנז: כולל בו תפלות לכל השנה בשלשה חלקים עם העתקת עברית אשכנזית ... ועתה הוספנו בו אור חדש, והוא סדור הסטאטי המראה מקום כל ברכה ותפלה מקורן /... נעתק ונלקט מאת יהודה ליב ב״ר מאיר גארדאן. — ניוייארק: דזשואיש פרעס פאב. קא., תרע״ב [1911 or 1912].

3 v. in 1. Hebrew and Yiddish. Copies: MH MWalA NNJ OCH

825. סדר סליחות (השלמה) כמנהג ליטא, רייסן וזאמוט: אלע תפלות אויף עברי טייטש. — ניו יארק: היברו פאב. קא., תרע״ב [1911 or 1912].

286 p. Hebrew and Yiddish. Copies: ICJS MWalA

826. ספר אנעים זמירות = Sefer anim zemiroth: musical service for the Sabbath evening according to the Union prayer book for Jewish worship / by Edward J. Stark. — New York: Bloch, c1911.

Score (52 p.) English and romanized Hebrew. For Cantor, soli and chorus (SATB), with organ accompaniment. Sendrey: 5973. Copies: MH OCH PPGratz

827. ראשית דעת שפת עבר / מאת מ. קרינסקי; עם הערות בשפת אנגלית מאת י. שפרייערעגען.

Reshith daath sephath Eber: elementary Hebrew reader according to a new system: with illustrations and prayers / by M. Krinski; explanations in English by J. Sprayregen. — New York: Hebrew Pub. Co., 1911.

95 p. Copies: MH

828. תפלת מנחה לשבת = Sabbath afternoon service: arranged for young people's services. — New York: Bloch, 1911.

18, 18, 19–28 p. English and Hebrew. Copies: NNJ OCH

829. תפלת שבת = The Sabbath service: for Sabbath eve and Sabbath morning: arranged and revised with special English prayers and responsive readings / by Julius Silberfeld. — New York: Bloch, 1911.

244 p. English and Hebrew. Copies: NN

1912

830. Beth Ahabah hymnal: selected and arranged for Temple service and Sabbath schools. — Richmond, Va.: [Beth Ahabah], 1912.

122 p. English and Hebrew. Compiled by E. N. Calisch?. Copies: OCH ViU

831. Evening service for the synagogue. No. 1 / by W. H. Neidlinger. — Boston: O. Ditson, c1912.

Score (9 p.). Sendrey: 5946. Copies: PPGratz (Music)

832. Evening service for the synagogue. No. 2 / by W. H. Neidlinger. — Boston: O. Ditson, c1912.

Score (10 p.). Sendrey: 5946. Copies: PPGratz (Music)

833. In distress I called upon the Lord: Psalm CXVIII:5–25: adapted and arranged to the English version for solos and chorus, with organ accompaniment from Halevy's "Min-Hammetsar" / Edward J. Stark. — New York: Bloch, c1912.

Score (14 p.). For soli and chorus (SATB). Sendrey: 6894. Copies: CLJ MH-Mu

834. Memorial service: 3 Psalms for male voices / by S. Sulzer. — New York: The Cantors Association, c1912.

Score (7 p.) romanized Hebrew. Joshev b'seser — Shivisi — Ach E'lohim. Sendrey: 7475. Copies: NN

835. Memorial service: prepared for Congregation Ahawath Chesed Shaar Hashomayim. — New York: The Congregation, 1912.

19 p. Copies: NN OCH

836. Order of dedication service: September 8th, Elul 26th, 5672–1912: Congregation Adath Jeshurun, Philadelphia. — Philadelphia: Adath Jeshurun, 1912.

11, 11 p. English and Hebrew. Copies: NNJ

837. Prayers for private devotion from the Union prayer book / edited and published by the Central Conference of American Rabbis. — [Cincinnati: CCAR], 1912.

iv, 5–83 p. Copies: NNJ OCH

838. Rochmono d'one / Leo Low. — New York: Hebrew Pub. Co., 1912.

Score (5 p.) Romanized Hebrew. With piano accompaniment. Sendrey: 6261. Copies: NNJ

839. Service for Sabbath evening according to the Union prayer book: for chorus of mixed voices, with organ accompaniment / James H. Rogers. — New York: G. Schirmer, c1912.

Score (30 p.) English and romanized Hebrew. Sendrey: 5952. Copies: OCH PPGratz (Music)

840. The service manual / by Joseph Krauskopf. — 7th ed. — Philadelphia: O. Klonower, 1912, c1892.

95, 256–564 p. English with Hebrew. Copies MWalA

841. מאגילניצקי'ס לינינען רע הילדים: בבית ובבית הספר: עם תרגום בשיטת-הטורים... = מאגילניצקי'ס קינדער פריינד: פיר קינדער אין שולע און אין הויז.../מאת יוסף בן יהודה מאגילניצקי. — פילאדעלפיא, פא.: י. מאגילניצקי, תרע״ג [1912 or 1913, c1906].

47, 20 p. Hebrew and Yiddish. Copies: MWalA PPGratz

842. מחזור לראש השנה... עם תרגום אנגלי כמנהג פולין: מוגה ומדויק... על ידי יעקב דעויס ונפתלי אדלר... = Service of the synagogue. New Year: a new edition of the Festival prayers with an English translation in prose and verse, reprinted from the latest and best London edition. — New York: Hebrew Pub. Co., 1912.

289 p. English and Hebrew. Edited by Herbert M. Adler and Arthur Davis. Copies: IdPS OCl

843. סדור חנוך תפלה: כולל תפלות לכל השנה: ברכות הנהנין, סדר נשיאת כפים, ספירת העומר וקדוש לבנה... נדפס באותיות גדולות מאד... — ניו-יארק: דער מארגען זשורנאל, תרע״ג [1912 or 1913].

128 [i.e., 256] p. Copies: DLC (uncat)

844. סדור חנוך תפלה החדש: כולל תפלות ישראל לכל השנה: נוסח אשכנז: באותיות גדולות ובהירות מוגה בהגהה מדויקת על פי חקי הדקדוק... / מוגה ומסודר על ידי א. היימאן. — ניו-יארק: היברו פאב. קא., c1912.

vi, 311 p. On verso of t.p.: Sidur chinuch tefilah hechodosh / by A. Hyman. Copies: MWalA NNJ PPGratz UU

845. סדור חנוך תפלה החדש: כולל תפלות ישראל לכל השנה: נוסח אשכנז: באותיות גדולות ובהירות מוגה בהגהה מדויקת על פי חקי הדקדוק... / מוגה ומסודר על ידי א. היימאן. — ניו-יארק: היברו פאב. קא., c1912.

vi, 312 p. On verso of t.p.: Sidur chinuch tephilah hechodosh / by A. Hyman. Copies: DLC (uncat) OCH PPGratz

846. סדור תפארת יהודה: נוסח אשכנז: כולל

850. סדר תפלה לבתי ספר ולעם = Complete prayer book for synagogue, home & school: comprising all laws and customs relating to the sacred rites and ceremonies of the Jewish faith. — New York: S. Druckerman, 1912.

xxii, 376 p. English and Hebrew. Copies: MWalA

851. סדר תפלות ישראל = The Union prayer-book for Jewish worship / edited and published by the Central Conference of American Rabbis. — New York: Bloch., 1912, c1894–1895.

2 v. English and Hebrew. Pt. I. Prayers for the Sabbath, Three Festivals and the week days. — Pt. II. New Year's Day, Day of Atonement. Copies: CLHU (V.2) CoDI NNHeb OCH (V.2)

852. סדר תפלות ישראל = The Union prayer-book for Jewish worship / edited and published by the Central Conference of American Rabbis. — New York: Bloch., 1912, c1895.

416 p. English and Hebrew. Pt. I. Prayers for the Sabbath, Three Festivals and the week days. "The changes and additions in this book were made by the First Hebrew Congregation of Oakland, California, and approved by the CCAR." — Insert on end cover. Copies: OCH

853. סדר תפלות מכל השנה: מתורגם ללשון אנגלית / על ידי א. טה. פיליפס = Daily prayers with a revised English translation / by A. Th. Philips. — New York: Hebrew Pub. Co., 1912.

705 p. English and Hebrew. Copies: DLC (uncat) PU

854. ספר אהל שרה: כולל חובות הדת לבנות ישראל / אברהם עבר בן שמואל הירשאוויץ = Yohale Sarah: containing religious duties of the daughters of Israel, and moral helps /

כל תפלות ישראל וכל הברכות לכל השנה: נדפס באותיות גדולות ובהירות ובתבות מרוחות ובלתי צפופות זו לזו... / מסודר ומוגה על ידי א. היימאן חרלף. — ניו יארק: היברו פאב. קא.

x, 560 p. Hebrew, with English directions. On verso of t.p.: Sidur tifereth Jehudah / by A. Hyman Charlap. — New York: Hebrew Pub. Co., c1912. Copies: OCH

847. סדור תפארת יהודה: נוסח אשכנז: כולל כל תפלות ישראל וכל הברכות לכל השנה: נדפס באותיות גדולות ובהירות ובתבות מרוחות ובלתי צפופות זו לזו... / מסודר ומוגה על ידי א. היימאן חרלף. — ניו יארק: היברו פאב. קא.

x, 584 p. Hebrew, with English directions. On verso of t.p.: Sidur tifereth Jehudah / by A. Hyman Charlap. — New York: Hebrew Pub. Co., c1912. Deinard: 902. Copies: DLC

848. סדור תפארת יהודה: נוסח אשכנז: כולל כל תפלות ישראל וכל הברכות לכל השנה: נדפס באותיות גדולות ובהירות ובתבות מרוחות ובלתי צפופות זו לזו... / מסודר ומוגה על ידי א. היימאן חרלף. — ניו יארק: היברו פאב. קא.

x, 584 p. Hebrew, with English directions. On verso of t.p.: Sidur tifereth Judah / by A. Hyman Charlap. — New York: Hebrew Pub. Co., c1912. Copies: CLJ CLU DLC MH NNJ

849. סדור תפארת יהודה: נוסח ספרד: כולל כל תפלות ישראל וכל הברכות לכל השנה: נדפס באותיות גדולות ובהירות ובתבות מרוחות ובלתי צפופות זו לזו... / מסודר ומוגה על ידי א. היימאן חרלף. — ניו יארק: היברו פאב. קא.

620 p. Hebrew, with English directions. On verso of t.p.: Sidur tifereth Jehudah / by A. Hyman Charlap. — New York: Hebrew Pub. Co., c1912. Copies: DLC (uncat) NNJ

compiled and revised from authoritative sources by Abraham E. Hirschowitz. — 2nd ed. — New York: 5672–1912, c 1902.

xxvi, 77, 11 p. English and Hebrew. Meditations and prayers: pp. 47–77. Deinard: 20. Copies: DLC Jewish Community Library of Los Angeles TxDaM-P

855. עבודת ישראל = A prayerbook for the services of the year at the synagogue/ arranged by Benjamin Szold and Marcus Jastrow; English translation by Marcus Jastrow. — Rev. ed. of the translation. — Philadelphia: [s.n.], 1912, c 1907.

2 v. English and Hebrew. Part 1. Services for the year. — Part 2. Services for the New Year and the Day of Atonement. Copies: MWalA (V.1)

856. שירי תפלה = Song of prayer for Friday evening service/composed by Max Grauman. — New York: M. Grauman, c 1912.

Score (40 p.) English and romanized Hebrew. For Cantor and chorus (SATB), with organ accompaniment. Sendrey: 5905. Copies: CLHU NN OCH PPGratz (Music)

857. תפלת שבת = The Sabbath service: for Sabbath eve and Sabbath morning: arranged and revised with special English prayers and responsive readings/by Julius Silberfeld. — New York: Bloch, 1912., c 1905 Congregation B'nai Abraham, Newark, N.J.

245 p. English and Hebrew. Cover title: Sabbath and Festival service. Copies: MWalA

1913

858. Children's prayers for use in the school and home/by Ella Jacobs. — 2nd ed. — Philadelphia: [s.n.], 1913.

4 leaves. Copies: NN

859. Children's service for the Day of Atonement/written and compiled by Marion L. Misch. — New York: Bloch, 1913.

16 p. Copies: OCH

860. The children's service for use in religious schools/J. Leonard Levy. — 3rd ed. — Pittsburgh, Pa.: National Printing Co., 1913.

259 p. English and Hebrew. Copies: MH

861. Children's services: prayers and hymns for the religious school, Congregation Mickve Israel/George Solomon. — Savannah: [Mickve Israel], 1913.

61 p. Copies: OCH

862. Dr. David Einhorn's עלת תמיד: book of prayers for Jewish congregations: new translation after the German original. — [Chicago?: s.n.], 1913., c 1896 by Julie Einhorn.

166, 279 p. English and Hebrew. Pt. I. Services for the Sabbath, the Festivals and the days of the week. — Pt. II. Services for the New Year's Day and the Day of Atonement. Translation by Emil G. Hirsch. Copies: FU IHi MeLB NNHeb OCH

863. Evening and morning service for week days: reprint from the Union prayer book/ edited and published by the Central Conference of American Rabbis. — New York: Bloch, 1913.

64 p. English and Hebrew. Deinard: 972. Copies: CLU MH NN OCH PPGratz

864. Evening service for the synagogue according to the Union prayer book/ Howard R. Thatcher. — New York: J. Fischer and Bro., c 1913.

Score (50 p.) English and romanized

1913

Hebrew. For Cantor and chorus (SATB), with organ accompaniment. Sendrey: 5982. Copies: MiD

865. Hanukkah and Purim service: special reprint from the Sabbath school hymnal / by Isaac S. Moses. — New York: Bloch, 1913.

pp. 243–251, 16 p. of music. English and romanized Hebrew. Copies: MH OCH

866. Jewish home prayers / compiled by Menahem M. Eichler, Rabbi, Temple Ohabei Shalom, Boston, Mass. — Boston, Mass.: Daniels, 1913.

47 p., 1 p. of music. "Issued expressly for the Congregation." Copies: DLC (uncat) MWalA OCH

867. Kol nidre / R. A. Zagler. — New York: S. Schekter, c1913.

Score (5 p.) English and romanized Hebrew. For voice, with piano accompaniment. Sendrey: 7228. Copies: OCH

868. Sabbath morning service for the synagogue according to the Union prayer book / James H. Rogers. — Boston: O. Ditson, c1913.

Score (32 p.) English and romaninzed Hebrew. For Cantor and chorus (SATB), with organ accompaniment. Deinard: 833, 570? Sendrey: 5951. Copies: KyLos MH MoKU NNJ OCH OCl PPGratz (Music)

869. Sefer anim zemiroth: musical service according to the Union prayer book for Jewish worship / by Edward J. Stark. — New York: Bloch, 1913.

Score (2 v.) English and romanized Hebrew. For Cantor and chorus (SATB), with organ accompaniment. V.1 For the Eve of Atonement. — V.2. For the Day of Atonement. Sendrey: 5975 (V.1) 5974 (V.2). Copies: CLJ (V.2) DLC (V.2)

870. Sefer anim zemiroth: musical service according to the Union prayer book for Jewish worship / by Edward J. Stark. — New York: Bloch, 1913.

Score (2 v. in 1) English and romanized Hebrew. For Cantor and chorus (SATB), with organ accompaniment. V.1 For the Eve of Atonement. — V.2. For the Day of Atonement. Copies: NjN NNJ PPGratz (Music)

871. אוהב שלום = Evening service for the synagogue according to the Union prayer book: composed for the choir of Oheb Shalom Temple, Baltimore, Maryland / Howard R. Thatcher. — New York: Bloch, 1913.

Score (50 p.) English and romanized Hebrew. For Cantor and chorus (SATB), with organ accompaniment. Copies: NN NNJ OCH PlHs PPGratz (Music)

872. מגילת חנכה בהעתקת אנגליש: עם סדר הדלקת הנרות, הנרות הללו, מעוז צור ישועתי, שירים השייכים לחגיגת חנכה ושירי ציון, ותוי-נגינה (נאטען) לשירים אחדים / מוגה ומסודר על ידי א. היימאן (חרל״פ). — New York: Hebrew Pub. Co., 1913, תרע״ד.

26 p. [6] p. of music. Deinard 430? Copies: DLC (uncat)

873. מחזור ... עם תרגום אנגלית = Prayer book ... with a revised English translation / by A. Th. Philips. — New York: Hebrew Pub. Co., 1913–ג, תרע״ג.

2 v. English and Hebrew. V.1. New Year. — V.2. Day of Atonement. Copies: MH (V.1) MWalA NN NNHeb NNJ NNUT

874. מחזור לראש השנה ויום הכפורים: באותיות גדולות ובהירות: כל התפלות על מקומן כסדרן. שנת תרע״ג — New York: Hebrew Pub. Co., 1913.

332, 361 p. Copies: DLC (uncat) MH MWalA NNJ OCHi

875. מענה לשון: הוא סדר תחנות על בית עלמין לבקש ולחנן על קברי צדיקים... = דיעזען מענה לשון האבען מיר געדרוקט אויף עברי טייטש: כדי עס זאלען פֿערשטעהן... איך האב מיר צוגעגעבען די פֿאלגענדע תחינות און תפלות... און קדיש יתום וואס מען זאגט נאך דער קבורה. — ניו יארק: היברו פאב. קא., תרע״ד. [1913 or 1914]

192 p. Hebrew and Yiddish. Attributed to Eliezer Liebman ben Loeb. Copies: DLC (uncat) MH NNJ

876. סדור בית יהודה: סדר תפלת ישראל כמנהג אשכנז: כולל תפלות לכל השנה בשלשה חלקים עם העתקת עברית אשכנזית... ועתה הוספנו בו אור חדש, והוא סדור היסטארי המראה מקום כל ברכה ותפלה מקורן... / נעתק ונלקט מאת יהודה ליב ב״ר מאיר גארדאן. — ניו-יארק: דער מארגען זשורנאל, תרע״ד [1913 or 1914].

3 v. in 1. English, Hebrew and Yiddish. Holdings: CLU MH MWalA NNJ OCH

877. סדור חנוך תפלה: כולל תפלות לכל השנה: מנהג ספרד. — ניו-יארק: דער מארגאן זשורנאל, תרע״ג, 1913.

282 p. Hebrew and Russian. Deinard: 958. Copies: MH

878. סדור חנוך תפלה החדש: כולל תפלות ישראל לכל השנה: נוסח אשכנז: באותיות גדולות ובבהירות מוגה בהגהה מדויקת על פי חקי הדקדוק... /מוגה ומסודר על ידי א. היימאן. — ניו-יארק: היברו פאב. קא.

vi, 312 p. English and Hebrew. On verso of t.p.: Sidur chinuch tefilah hechodosh/ by A. Hyman. — Hebrew Pub.Co., c 1913. Copies: DLC MH NNJ NNYI

879. סדור חנוך תפלה החדש: כולל תפלות ישראל לכל השנה: נוסח ספרד: באותיות גדולות ובבהירות מוגה בהגהה מדויקת על פי חקי הדקדוק... /מוגה ומסודר על ידי א. היימאן. — ניו-יארק: היברו פאב. קא.

vi, 341 p. English and Hebrew. On verso of t.p.: Sidur chinuch tephilah hechodosh/ by A. Hyman. — Hebrew Pub.Co., c 1913. Copies: DLC MWalA NNJ OCH

880. סדור חנוך תפלה עם חנוך לנער: כולל תפלות לכל השנה: נוסח אשכנז: באותיות גדולות. — ניו-יארק: היברו פאב. קא., תרע״ד. [1913 or 1914]

— New York: Hebrew Pub. Co.

240 p. Copies: MH

881. סדר כל תפלות השנה = Magil's complete linear prayer book: comprising the prayers for the whole year: translated in the new linear system, with notes and original engravings: for the synagogue, the home and the school. — 5th improved ed. — Philadelphia: J. Magil, 1913–תרע״ד.

192, 174 p. English and Hebrew. Copies: NNJ OCH

882. סדר רחיצת המת: כפי מנהג ק״ק הספרדים שארית ישראל בנו יארק, עם תרגום אנגלי. — מהד. תנינא. — נו-יארק: נדפס בהוצאת חברה חסד ואמת, שנת תרע״ג. = Service for preparing the dead for burial: as used in the Spanish and Portuguese Congregation Shearith Israel, New York City. — New York: Published by the Society "Hebrew Hased Va-Amet" חברת חסד ואמת, founded in the City of New York, 5562–1802, 5673–1913.

11, 11 p. English and Hebrew. Copies: MH MWalA NN NNHeb OCH

883. סדר תפלות ישראל = The Union prayer-book for Jewish worship. Part I. Prayers for the Sabbath and the week days/edited and published by the Central Conference of American Rabbis. — New York: Bloch, 1913, c 1895.

110 p. English and Hebrew. Copies: CLHU (uncat) OCH

884. סדר תפלות ישראל = The Union prayerbook for Jewish worship. Part II. New Years Day, Day of Atonement/edited and published by the Central Conference of American Rabbis. — New York: Bloch., 1913, c1894.

340 p. English and Hebrew. Copies: MWalA OCH

885. עבודת ישראל = A prayerbook for the services of the year at the synagogue/arranged by Benjamin Szold and Marcus Jastrow; English translation by Marcus Jastrow. — Rev. ed. of the translation. — Philadelphia: [s.n.], 1913, c1907.

2 v. English and Hebrew. Part 1. Services for the year. — Part 2. Services for the New Year and the Day of Atonement. Copies: NNHeb

1914

886. Children's services for the New Year and Atonement Day. — New York: Bloch, 1914.

31 p. English and Hebrew. Publication/Jewish Religious School Union of New York; No. 1. Copies: OCH

887. How amiable are thy tabernacles: Opus 12./Edward Shippen Barnes. — New York: G. Schirmer, 1914.

Score (8 p.) For chorus (SATB), with organ accompaniment. Sendrey: 7011. Copies:

888. The Lord of all (Adon olam): old Hebrew melody/J. P. Donelly. — Boston: C. C. Birchard, 1914.

Score (4 p.) For chorus (SATB), with violin solo and piano or organ accompaniment. Sendrey: 7029. Copies:

889. Malchijos, Sichronos, Schof'ros: Rezitativen für Kantor-Solo/komponiert von D. Hornstein. — New York: Hebrew Pub. Co., c1914.

Score (16 p.) romanized Hebrew. Sendrey: 6517. Copies: OCH PPGratz (Music)

890. Prayer book for the Sabbath: order of service arranged for the use of the synagogue, Long Branch, N.J. — New York: [s.n.], 1914.

5, 6–64, 6–64 p. English and Hebrew. Compiled by Barnett A. Elzas. Copies: DLC NNHeb NNJ OCH

891. Psalm XXIX: Hovu Ladonoi = Ascribe unto God: for solo and choir ... adapted for congregational singing/by H. Meyer. — New York: Bloch, 1914.

Score (9 p.) romanized Hebrew. For Cantor and chorus (SATB), with organ accompaniment. Sendrey: 6861. Copies: OCH

892. Sabbath morning service/Abram Ray Tyler. — New York: Bloch, 1914.

Score (27 p.) English and romanized Hebrew. For Cantor and chorus (SATB). Sendrey: 5984. Copies: OCH

893. Sabbath prayer book: order of service/arranged by Barnett A. Elzas. — New York: Bloch, 1914.

64, 64 p. English and Hebrew. "Arranged for the use of the synagogue, Long Branch, N.J." — preface. Copies: NNJ OCH

894. Sabbath-school hymnal/revised and enlarged by I. S. Moses. — 11th ed. rev. and enl. — New York: Bloch, 1914.

348 p. English and romanized Hebrew. Includes music. Copies: NNHeb PPYH

895. The Union hymnal for Jewish worship. — [New York]: Published by the Central Conference of American Rabbis, 1914.

59 p. Text only. Copies: DLC (microform) NN NNJ OCH TcC

896. The Union hymnal for Jewish worship. — [s.l.]: Published by the Central Conference of American Rabbis, 1914.

xiv, 333 p. Includes text and music. "Anthem texts": p. 309–333. Some libraries catalog Hymnal as published in New York, while others claim Cincinnati. Copies: GEU-T IUG KyLxCB MoKU NNHeb NRU-Mus OCH PPAnR PPGratz (Music) PPULC RPB

897. ... מחזור = Form of prayers ... with English translation. — Rev. ed. — New York: Hebrew Pub. Co., 5675–1914.

2 v. in 1 English and Hebrew. V.1 לראש השנה — V.2. ליום כפור. Copies: MWalA NN NNHeb

898. סדור בית ישראל עברי-טייטש: כולל סדר התפלות לכל ימות השנה: עם ילקוט פנינים יקרים ומעשה אלפס יכיל שלשים ושנים באורים יקרים: נוסח אשכנז. — ניו יארק: היברו פאב. קא., 1914.

592 p. Hebrew and Yiddish. Bound with: ספר תהלים עם מעמדות. [New York: s.n., n.d.]. (Entry 1283). Copies: OCH

899. סדור בית ישראל עברי-טייטש: כולל סדר התפלות לכל ימות השנה: עם ילקוט פנינים יקרים ומעשה אלפס יכיל שלשים ושנים באורים יקרים: נוסח ספרד. — ניו יארק: היברו פאב. קא., 1914.

592 p. Hebrew and Yiddish. Copies: MWalA OCH

900. סדר סליחות לימים נוראים: כמנהג וואלין: גם הוספנו ... עברי טייטש. — ניו-יארק: היברו פאב. קא., 1914.

137 p. Hebrew and Yiddish. Copies: MWalA

901. סדר תפלות ישראל = The Union prayer-book for Jewish worship / edited and published by the Central Conference of American Rabbis. — New York: Bloch., 1914, c1894–1895.

2 v. English and Hebrew. Pt. I. Prayers for the Sabbath, Three Festivals and the week days. — Pt. II. New Year's Day, Day of Atonement. Copies: MWalA (V.1) NNHeb OCH

902. סדר תפלות כל השנה: כמנהג פולין/מוגה ומדויק היטב ומתורגם ללשון אנגליש על ידי שמעון בר יהודה סינגער, בהסכמת נתן אדלר הכהן. — הוצאת אמיריקנית = The authorized daily prayer book of the United Hebrew Congregations of the British empire: with a new translation by S. Singer; published under the sanction of the late Rabbi Nathan Marcus Adler. — 9th American ed. — London: Eyre and Spottiswoode; New York: Hebrew Pub. Co., [1914].

viii, 329, 337 p. English and Hebrew. Date taken from preface. Copies: Nhd NhMSA

903. סדר תפלות לשבת ויום טוב: כל התפלות של שבת ויום טוב נסדרו על מקומן לכל יצטרך המתפלל לחפש ... בהוראות אנגלית/מוגה ומסודר על ידי א. היימאן (חרלפ): עם עשרים ושמנה נומרים תוי-נגינה מאת ח.א. רוסאטא. — ניו יארק, תרע"ד = Music for Sabbath and Festival services: containing traditional selections / composed, selected and arranged by Henry Russotto. — New York: Hebrew. Pub. Co., 1914.

288 p., 31 p. of music. Hebrew. Deinard: 952. Sendrey: 6397. Copies: DLC MH MWalA OCH OrP

904. סדר תפלות מכל השנה: מוגה ומדויק היטב ומתורגם ללשון אנגלית/על ידי א. טה. פיליפס =
Daily prayers with a revised English translation/by A. Th. Philips. — 4th ed. — New York: Hebrew Pub. Co., 1914.

705 p. English and Hebrew. Copies: DLC (uncat) MH MWalA NNJ OCH PPGratz

905. ספר ברית יצחק: כולל א) דיני אירוסין ונשואין ... ב) דיני מילה ... ג) דיני פדיון הבן ... ד) דיני בר מצוה ... ה) דרושים לכל ענינים האלו ... בהעתקת אנגלית/מלוקט ע״י יצחק יהודה ליב קאדושין המוהל. — הוצאד ד. בהוספות רבות. — ניו-יארק: היברו פאב. קא., 1914, = c1897.
Brith Itzhak: a manual comprising the riti of marriage, circumcision, redemption of the first born, and confirmation, and the usual prayers for these ceremonies: also speeches designed for such occasions/by I. L. Kadushin.

81 p. English, Hebrew and Yiddish. Bound with: ספר ציון. Copies: DLC NNJ

906. ספר תנחומות = Book of consolation/by William Rosenau, Rabbi, Eutaw Place Temple, Baltimore, Md. — Baltimore: Lord Baltimore Press, 1914.

65 p. English and Hebrew. Copies: CLHU MWalA NNHeb OCH RPB

907. עבדת יום הזכרון: עבדת יום הכפורים = Holyday prayers: a new ritual for New Year and Day of Atonement. — 2nd ed. — New York: Bloch, 1914, c1909.

2 v in 1. (107, 210 p.) English and Hebrew. This prayer book ... follows the old traditional form ... omitting such portions of the piyutim as many American Conservative congregations do not include in their liturgy. — The publishers. Copies: MWalA

908. עבודת ישראל = A prayerbook for the services of the year at the synagogue/arranged by Benjamin Szold and Marcus Jastrow; English translation by Marcus Jastrow. — Rev. ed. of the translation. — Philadelphia: [s.n.], 1914, c1907.

2 v. English and Hebrew. Part 1. Services for the year. — Part 2. Services for the New Year and the Day of Atonement. Copies: MH (V.1) OCH (V.1) PPGratz

909. ראשית דעת שפת עבר/מאת מ. קרינסקי; עם הערות בשפת אנגלית מאת י. שפרייר׳עגען = Reshith daath sephath Eber: elementary Hebrew reader according to a new system: with illustrations and prayers/by M. Krinski; explanations by J. Sprayregen. — New York: Hebrew Pub. Co., 1914.

95 p. English and Hebrew. Holdings: MH

910. שירות ותשבחות = Selections from the prayer book for Sabbaths and Holy days: according to the custom of the Spanish and Portuguese Jews: for use of the pupils of the Mikve Israel School of Observation and Practice of Gratz College. — 2nd ed. — Philadelphia: [Cahan Printing Co.], 1914.

44 p. Hebrew with English headings. Copies: CLHU (uncat)

1915

911. Chanukas Habajis: Vier sämtliche Kompositione [sic] für Solo und gemischten Chor/S. Zemachson. — Chicago: S. Zemachson, 1915.

Score (20 p.) romanized Hebrew. For Cantor and chorus (SATB). Sendrey: 7272. Copies: NNJ OCH PPGratz

912. Children's services: arranged for use in religious schools/by J. M. Bazel. — Pittsburgh, Pa.: Glick Print, 1915.

24 p. Copies: DLC OCH

913. Complete musical service for Day of Atonement: evening, morning, afternoon, memorial and concluding, according to the Union prayer book/S. Schlesinger. — 3rd ed. — New York: Bloch, 1915.

Score (169 p.) English and romanized Hebrew. For Cantor and chorus (SATB), with organ accompaniment. Copies: OCH

914. Festival prayer book: order of service/ arranged by Barnett A. Elzas. — New York: Bloch, 1915.

5, 6–68, 6–68 p. English and Hebrew. "For the use of Conservative congregations." Copies: DLC MnU NN OCH

915. Festival prayer book: order of service arranged for the use of the synagogue, Long Branch, N.J. — New York: Bloch, 1915.

5, 6–68, 6–68 p English and Hebrew. Compiled by Barnett A. Elzas (preface). Copies: NN NNJ PPAnR

916. Kol nidre/Charles J. Roberts. — New York: C. Fischer, [1915].

Score (7, 7 p.) English and Hebrew. For Cantor and chorus, with piano or organ accompaniment. Sendrey: 7207. Copies: ABAu OCH

917. Songs of Israel: famous traditional Hebrew melodies (with text) for synagogue, school and home/compiled and arranged for piano by Martin Greenwald. — New York: Academic Music, c1915.

Score (46 p.) Interlinear words in romanized Hebrew. With piano accompaniment. Copies: CL NN

918. Songs of Zion: famous traditional Hebrew melodies (with text) for synagogue, school and home/compiled and arranged for piano by Martin Greenwald. — New York: Academic Music, 1915.

Score (52 p.) Romanized Hebrew. Copies: CLJ

918a. Ten choice Hebrew song classics (traditional) for voice and pianoforte/ compiled and edited by E. Kartschmaroff. — New York: Globe Music Co., c1915.

Score (32 p.) Romanized Hebrew. For voice, with piano accompaniment. Copies: ICJS. Kol nidre — Chad gadya — Olenu — Adir hu — Yigdal Elohim — En Kelohenu — Shir hama'alos — L'Dowid boruch — Mooz tsur y'shuosi. — Owinu malkenu.

918b. Ten choice Hebrew song classics (traditional) for voice and pianoforte/ compiled and edited by E. Kartschmaroff. — New York: Jos. W. Stern & Co., 1915.

Score (32 p.) Romanized Hebrew. For voice, with piano accompaniment. Copies: NBuU-Mu. Kol nidre — Chad gadya — Olenu — Adir hu — Yigdal Elohim — En Kelohenu — Shir hama'alos — L'Dowid boruch — Mooz tsur y'shuosi. — Owinu malkenu.

919. ברכת המזון עם סדר הברכות = Grace and blessings for various occasions. — New York: Hebrew Pub. Co., 1915.

63 p. English and Hebrew. Copies: CLH DLC (uncat) MH MWAlA NNJ OCH

920. זמירות ותפלות ישראל = Z'miroth ut'filoth Yisroel: a synagogue hymnal for Sabbath and Festivals: comprising songs for religious schools and junior services: compiled and adapted for the use of Cantor, choir and congregation/by M. Halpern. — Boston: Boston Music Co., c1915.

xii, 70, [70] p. Hebrew text with music. For Adath Jeshurun, Boston Mass. Deinard: 287. Sendrey: 6960. Copies: ICJS KyLoU MH NN OCH PPGratz (Music) RPB

1915

921. מחזור ... כמנהג פולון: מוגה ומדויק היטב כפי מחזור של החכם וואלף היידנהיים וכתבי יד ישנים/על ידי יעקב בן יצחק דעויס ונפתלי בן מרדכי אדלר הכהן: עם תרגום אנגלי. — ניו יארק =

Service of the synagogue: a new edition of the Festival prayers with an English translation in prose and verse. — New York: Jewish Premium Pub. Co., 1915.

2 v. English and Hebrew. V.1. לראש השנה. — V.2. ליום הכפורים. Deinard: 464. Copies: CLU MH MWalA NN NNJ

922. מחזור ... עם תרגום אנגלית/מוגה ומדויק היטב על ידי יעקב בן יצחק דעויס ונפתלי בן מרדכי אדלר הכהן. — נדפס כפי הוצאת לאנדאן=: ניו יארק: היברו פאב. קא., תרע"ו =

Service of the synagogue: a new edition of the Festival prayers with an English translation in prose and verse: reprinted from the best London ed. — New York: Hebrew Pub. Co., [1915 or 1916].

5 v. English and Hebrew. V.1. New Year. — V.2. Day of Atonement. — V.3. Tabernacles. — V.4. Passover. — V.5. Pentecost. Edited by Herbert M. Adler and Arthur Davis. Copies: NNJ

923. מקור חיים: סדר לבית האבל כפי מנהג האבל עם תהלים ותפלות ודברי נחמה ... ודיני אבלות ומנהגי תנחומין לק"ק שארית ישראל בניו יארק/הכל נערך ומסודר ממני חיים די אברהם פריירא מינדיז ודוד די סולה בן אליעזר פול. — ניו יארק: נדפס בהוצאת חברה חסד ואמת לק"ק שארית ישראל, שנת תרע"ו =

Fountain of life for those who mourn: containing prayers for the dying, prayers and services for the house of mourning, Psalms of comfort, prayers on visiting the burial ground, thoughts on the immortality of the soul, the laws and customs concerning mourning/compiled and edited by H. Pereira Mendes and David de Sola Pool, Ministers of the Spanish and Portuguese Congregation Shearith Israel, N.Y. — New York: Published by the Hebra Hased Va-Amet of the Congregation, 5676–1915.

135 p. English and Hebrew. Deinard: 535. Copies: MWalA NN OCH

924. סדור בית ישראל עברי-טייטש: כולל סדר התפלות לכל ימות השנה: עם ילקוט פנינים יקרים ומעשה אלפס: יכיל שלשים ושנים באורים יקרים: נוסח אשכנז. — ניו-יארק: היברו פאב. קא., תרע"ו [1915 or 1916].

1 v. (various pagings) Hebrew and Yiddish. Copies: DLC (uncat) ICJS NNJ OCH

925. סדור האר"י ז"ל: כולל תפלות לכל השנה ... ועוד הוספנו ברכות ראשונות ואחרונות בכל תפלה על מקומה ... — נויארק: היברו פאב. קא., תרע"ו [1915 or 1916].

128 p. Copies: NNYI

926. סדור חנוך תפילה: עם חנוך לנער וכללי הדקדוק: כולל תפלות לכל השנה באותיות גדולות מאד ... : נוסח אשכנז. — ניו-יארק: היברו פאב. קא., 1915.

303 p. Copies: DPC

927. סדור קרבן מנחה: כולל סדר התפלות לכל ימות השנה: עם ילקוט פנינים יקרים ומעשה אלפס יכיל שלשים ושנים באורים יקרים: נוסח אשכנז. — ניו-יארק: היברו פאב. פא., תרע"ה–1915.

780, 233, 88 p. Hebrew and Yiddish. Bound with: ספר תהלים עם מעמדות. [New York: s.n., 19 — ?]. (Entry 1283). Copies: NN OCH

928. סדור שפת אמת/מאת וואלף בר שמשון דוב איש היידנהיים =

Daily prayers with English instructions. — 1st new rev. ed., as correct as any ed. ever published in רעדעלהיים. — New York: Hebrew Pub. Co., 1915.

292 p. Copies: MWalA NNJ OCH

929. סדר תפלה לבתי ספר ולעם = Complete prayer book for synagogue, home and school: comprising prayers for the whole year: in strict conformity with the best authorities, giving the composers' names of the various prayers and all laws and customs relating to the sacred rites and ceremonies of the Jewish faith. — 2nd ed. — New York: S. Druckerman, 1915.

xxii, 376 p. English and Hebrew. Copies: MsSM OCH

930. סדר תפלות ישראל = The Union prayer-book for Jewish worship. Part I. Prayers for the Sabbath, the Three Festivals, and the weekdays / edited and published by the Central Conference of American Rabbis. — New York: Bloch., 1915, c1895.

110 p. English and Hebrew. Copies: MWalA NNJ OCH

931. סדר תפלות כל השנה = Daily prayers with English directions: Hebrew text from the Standard prayer book. — New York: Bloch, 1915.

469, 470 p. English and Hebrew. Copies: DLC MH OCH PPAnR

932. סדר תפלות כל השנה = The standard prayer book / authorized English translation by S. Singer. — Enl. American ed. — New York: Bloch, 1915.

469, 470 p. English and Hebrew. Copies: DLC MH NcD OCH PPGratz

933. סדר תפלות כל השנה כמנהג פולין: מוגה ומדויק היטב ומתורגם ללשון אנגליש / על ידי שמעון בר יהודה סינגער, הסכמת נתן אדלר הכהן. — הוצאת אמריקנית. — ניו-יארק, תרע"ה =

The authorised daily prayer book of the United Hebrew Congregations of the British empire: with a new translation by S. Singer; published under the sanction of the late Rabbi Nathan Marcus Adler. — 1st American ed. — London: Eyre and Spottiswoode; New York: Hebrew Pub. Co., 5675–1915, c1914.

viii, 329 p. English and Hebrew. Copies: CU MWalA NN OCH OClW

934. סידור תפלה יקרה: כמנהג אשכנז: עם זמירות, הושענות, סליחות, והגדה לפסח... וגם ספר תהלים עם כל הבקשות. — ניו-יארק: היברו פאב. קא., תרע"ו [1915 or 1916].

384, 142 p. Copies: DLC (uncat) OCH

935. סידור תפלה יקרה: כמנהג אשכנז: עם זמירות, ספירת העומר, נשיאת כפים, תפלת הדרך, שיר השירים, קדוש לבנה, קדיש ענגליש. — ניו-יארק: היברו פאב. קא., תרע"ו [1915 or 1916].

256 p. Copies: DLC (uncat) MWalA

936. ספר החיים = The book of life: services and ceremonies observed at the death bed, house of mourning and cemetery, together with prayers on visiting the graves: with an appendix containing the laws, rites and ceremonies concerning the dying and the dead and the usages of mourning / arranged by Barnett A. Elzas. — New York: Bloch, 1915.

86, 53 p. English and Hebrew. Deinard: 309. Copies: CLHU CLJ CoDU DLC FU MH MH-AH MWalA MWalB NNHeb OCH PPAnR

937. ספר החיים = The book of life: services and ceremonies observed at the death bed, house of mourning and cemetery, together with prayers on visiting the graves: with an appendix containing the laws, rites and ceremonies concerning the dying and the dead and the usages of mourning / arranged by Barnett A. Elzas. — New York: Bloch, 1915.

6 leaves. English and Hebrew. "Prospectus." Copies: OCH

938. רע הילדים = Magil's linear children's companion: for the school and the home: some of the prayers, benedictions and religious knowledge in Hebrew with a linear translation in English/by Joseph Magil. — 8th ed. — Philadelphia: J. Magil, 1915, c1906.

47, 6–20 p. English and Hebrew. Copies: MWalA

939. תפלה יקרה: כמנהג ספרד: עם זמירות, ספירת העומר, נשיאת כפים, תפלת הדרך, שיר השירים, קדוש לבנה, קדיש ענגליש. — ניו-יארק: היברו פאב. קא., תרע״ו [1915 or 1916].

142 p. Copies: CLHU MH NNJ OCH

940. תפלת יהושוע = Tfilath Jeschua: Synagogue Recitative/componiert von S. Weisser (Pilderwasser) — Brooklyn: Eagle Advertising and Novelty, 1915–1916.

Score (2 v.) Romanized Hebrew. For Cantor. V.2. Published: New York: The composer. V.1. High Holy days. — V.2. Shabbat and the Shalosh Regalim. Sendrey: 6595. Copies: DLC (V.1) PPGratz

941. תפלת מנחה לשבת = Sabbath afternoon service: arranged for young people's services. — 3rd ed. — New York: Bloch, 1915, c1911.

28 p. English and Hebrew. Copies: NNHeb

1916

942. Children's services arranged for use in religious schools/by Solomon M. Neches. — Pittsburgh, Pa.: Glick Print, 1916.

31 p. Copies: NN

943. Comfort ye, my people/Gottfried Heinrich Federlein. — New York: G. Schirmer, 1916.

Score (9 p.) For Cantor and chorus (SATB), with organ accompaniment. Sendrey: 7035. Copies:

944. Confirmation service/Isaac S. Moses. — New York: Bloch, 1916.

Score (46 p.) English and romanized Hebrew. For 1 voice or chorus (SATB). Sendrey: 7464. Copies: OCH

945. Divine service for the Congregation Ahawath Chesed Sha'ar Hashamayim/arranged by A. Huebsch; revised by Isaac S. Moses. — New York: The Congregation, 1916.

vii, 474 p. English and Hebrew. Copies: MWalA NN NNHeb OCH

946. Evening service for the New Year: recitatives for cantors/M. Halpern. — Boston: M. Halpern, 1916.

Score (5 p.) Romanized Hebrew. Copies: NNJ

947. Home service for 'Hanukkah: written for Congregation Rodef Shalom, Pittsburgh, Pa./by J. Leonard Levy. — 5th ed. — Pittsburgh: [s.n.], 1916, c1903.

33 p., 1 p. of music. "Hanukkah hymn" (words and music): p. 32–33. Copies: NN

948. Jewish science: divine healing in Judaism: with special references to Jewish scriptures and prayer book/by Alfred G. Moses. — [Mobile, Ala.: The Temple, c1916 by A.G. Moses].

149 p. Chapter VI (pp.75–146) contains prayers and meditations from the Bible, particularly from Psalms. Copies: Jewish Community Library of Los Angeles

949. Memorial exercises in memory of Solomon Schechter, president of the Jewish Theological Seminary of America: Monday evening, January 3, 1916, Aeolian Hall, New York. — [New York: s.n., 1916].

19 p. English and Hebrew. At head of title: זכר צדיק לברכה. Deinard: 285. Copies: DLC (uncat) MH NN OCH

950. Order of service for the evening of the Sabbath / Louis Grossmann. — Cincinnati, O.: [s.n.], 1916.

2 leaves. Copies: OCH

951. Sabbath morning service for the synagogue, according to the Union prayer book / C. Hugo Grimm. — Cincinnati: J. Church, c1916.

Score (60 p.) English and romanized Hebrew. For chorus (SATB), with organ accompaniment. Sendrey: 5907. Copies: OCH PPGratz (Music)

952. The Sabbath service and miscellaneous prayers adopted by the Reformed Society of Israelites: founded in Charleston, S.C. November 21, 1825: Reprinted with an introduction / by Barnett A. Elzas. — New York: Bloch, 1916.

69 p. Original by Isaac Harby, Abraham Moïse and D. N. Carvalho. Copies: CLJ DLC MWalA NN NNJ OCH TNJ

953. Temple service for the evening of the New Year / James Hotchkiss Rogers. — New York: G. Schirmer, c1916.

Score (39 p.) English and romanized Hebrew. For solo and chorus (SATB), with organ accompaniment. Sendrey: 5953. Copies: CLJ KyLoS MoS NNJ NRU-Mus OCH OCl PPGratz (Music)

954. במה מדליקין = Bame madlikin: für Cantor und Chor / Josef Rosenblatt. — New York: Hebrew Pub. Co., 1916.

Score (15 p.) romanized Hebrew. Sendrey: 6375. Copies: MH-Mu

955. יהי רצון פון ראש חדש בענשען = Yehi Rozon fon Rosh Chodesh Benschen / by Cantor Joseph Rosenblatt; arranged by H. A. Russotto. — New York: Hebrew Pub. Co., c1916.

Score (2 p.) romanized Hebrew. Copies: MH-Mu

956. יוצרות לארבע פרשיות עם הגדה לשבת הגדול. — נויארק: הובא לבית הדפוס ע״י דוד ראזענבערג מדינוב, תרע״ז, [1916 or 1917].

1 v. (unpaged). Copies: MWalA NNHeb

957. מחזור לראש השנה ויום הכפורים: כמנהג ספרד: עם קריאת הפרשיות וההפטרות בנגינים וטעמים... ועטה הוספנו מעריב לראש השנה ופירוש מטה לוי עם העתקת עברי-טייטש. — נוי-יארק: היברו פאב. קא., תרע״ז [1916 or 1917].

246 p. Hebrew and Yiddish. Commentary by Aaron ben Jehiel Michael, ha-Levi. Copies: PPGratz

958. סדור שפת אמת החדש: כולל כל תפלות ישראל לכל השנה / מוגה ומסודר על ידי א. היימאן. Daily prayer with English directions / revised and arranged by A. Hyman. — New York: Hebrew Pub. Co., c1916.

vi, 312 p. On verso of t.p.: Sidur sfath emeth hechodosh. Deinard: 973. Copies: DLC MWalA NNJ NNYI OCH

959. סדר ערבית לשבת = Sabbath eve service / arranged by Israel Herbert Levinthal, Rabbi, Temple Petach Tikvah, Brooklyn, N.Y.; published by the Petach Tikvah Junior Congregation, Brooklyn, N.Y. — New York: Bloch, 1916.

49, 49 p. English and Hebrew. Copies: CLJ DLC NN NNJ

960. סדר תפלות ישראל = The Union prayer-book for Jewish worship / edited and published by the Central Conference of American Rabbis. — New York: Bloch., 1916, c1894–1895.

2 v. English and Hebrew. Pt. I. Prayers

for the Sabbath, Three Festivals and the week days. — Pt. II. New Year's Day, Day of Atonement. Copies: OCH

961. סדר תפלות ישראל לבעלי מלחמה = A ritual for Jewish soldiers: compiled from volumes I and II of the Union prayer book and Prayers for private devotion. — [Rochester, N.Y.]: Central Conference of American Rabbis, 1916.

146 p. English and Hebrew. Copies: CLHU (uncat) NN PPAnR

962. סדר תפלות לאבלים: צדוק הדין, הזכרת נשמות, קדיש יתום, קדיש דרבנן, דינים ותפלות ליאהרצייט. — נויארק: היברו פאב. קא., תרע"ז = Mourning prayers: Tzodok ha-din, memorial prayer, Kaddish, Jahrzeit laws and practices. — New York: Hebrew Pub. Co., 1916.

57 p. English and Hebrew. Copies: DLC (uncat) MWalA

963. ש"ס תחינה החדשה: ענטהאלט הונדערט פינף און צוואנציג פערשיעדענע נייע און אלטע תחינות... אויסגערעכענט אין דעם אינהאלטס פערצייכעניס. — נו יארק: היברו פאב. קא. תרע"ו, c1916.

iii, 220 p. Yiddish with Hebrew. Copies: MWalA NNJ OCH

964. ש"ס תחנה החדשה (השלמה): ענטהאלט הונדערט זעקס און פערציג פערשיעדענע תחנות... — נוי יארק: היברו פאב. קא. תרע"ו, 1916.

ii, 252 p. Yiddish with Hebrew. Copies: CLHU DLC MH NNJ

965. ש"ס תחנה רב פנינים: מיט פיעלע פירושים און משלים און עברי טייטש... ענטהאלט הונדערט זעקס און זיבעציג נייע און אלטע תחנות און משלים, ארויסגענומען פון פיעלע מדרשים און ספרי מוסר. — New York: Hebrew Pub. Co., c1916.

iv, 314 p. Yiddish with Hebrew. Copies: DLC GEU MBrH MWalA MWalB NN NNJ OCH PU

966. תפלת שבת = The Sabbath service: for Sabbath eve and Sabbath morning: arranged and revised with special English prayers and responsive readings/by Julius Silberfeld, Rabbi, Congregation B'nai Abraham, Newark, N.J. — New York: Bloch, 1916, c1905.

244 p. English and Hebrew. Copies: NNJ

1917

967. Abridged prayer book for Jews in the Army and Navy of the United States. — Philadelphia: Jewish Publication Society of America, 5678–1917.

80, 85 p. English and Hebrew. Deinard: 955. Copies: CLU DLC MWalA NN OCH OU PP PPAnR PPGratz PPLT UU WaS

968. A book of prayer for Jewish girls/ compiled by the Committee on Religion of the New York Section of the Council of Jewish Women, 5678–1917. — New York: C.S. Nathan, 1917.

53 p. Copies: CLHU MWalA NNYU OCH

969. Eliyohu hanovi: arranged for voice and piano/by H. Lefkowitch. — New York: J.P. Katz, c1917.

Score (3 p.) romanized Hebrew. Copies: OCH

970. Evening and morning service for the New Year and the Day of Atonement/ Morris Goldstein. — Cincinnati: Willis Music, 1917.

Score (218 p.) English and romanized Hebrew. Synagogical music; no. 9. Copies: CLHU

971. Evening service for week days for the divine service to mark the beginning of the twenty-fifth Biennial Council of the

Union of American Hebrew Congregations: at Har Sinai Temple, Baltimore, Monday January 15, 1917. — [Baltimore: s.n., 1917].

7 leaves. English and Hebrew. Reprinted from סדר תפלות ישראל = The Union prayer-book for Jewish worship edited by the Central Conference of American Rabbis. Copies: OCH

972. Great is the Lord/Gottfried Heinrich Federlein. — New York: G. Schirmer, 1917.

Score (15 p.) For tenor solo and chorus (SATB), with organ accompaniment. Sendrey: 7036. Copies:

973. Minister's handbook/edited and published by the Central Conference of American Rabbis. — New York: Bloch, 1917.

65 p. English and Hebrew. Copies: NN OCH

974. New Jewish hymnal for religious schools and junior congregations: songs and anthems/edited and compiled by Henry L. Gideon; services compiled and adapted by Louis Weinstein. — New York: Bloch, 1917.

Score (viii, 173 p.) English and romanized Hebrew. Sendrey: 6947. Copies: COPL MH-AH NN NRU-Mus OCH RPB

975. Sabbath evening service for the synagogue, according to the Union prayer book/Franklin Pierce Fisk. — New York: Bloch, 1917.

Score (22 p.) English and romanized Hebrew. For Cantor and chorus (SATB), with piano or organ accompaniment. Sendrey: 5894. Copies: DLC OCH

976. Sabbath morning service/Morris Goldstein. — Cincinnati: Willis Music, 1917.

Score (52 p.) English and romanized Hebrew. Synagogical music; no. 3. Sendrey: 5902. Copies: CLHU

977. Sabbath school hymnal of K.K. Beth Elohim. — Charleston, S.C.: Beth Elohim, 1917.

9 p. Compiled by Jacob S. Raisin. Copies: DLC (microform) NN TcC (microform)

978. יהי רצון פֿון ראש חדש בענשן = Yehi rozon from Rosh Chodesh benschen/by Josef Rosenblatt; arranged for piano by H.A. Russotto. — New York: Hebrew Pub. Co., c1917.

Score (5 p.) romanized Hebrew. At head of title: Synagogue music = שירי תפלה. Bound with: Bircas Kohanim. — New York, [191-?] (Entry 771). Copies: OCH PPGratz

979. מחזור... עם תרגום אנגלית/מוגה ומדויק היטב על ידי יעקב בן יצחק דעויס ונפתלי בן מרדכי אדלר הכהן: נדפס כפי הוצאת לאנדאן. — ניו יארק: היברו פאב. קא., תרע״ז = Service of the Synagogue... : a new edition of the Festival prayers with an English translation in prose and verse: reprinted from the latest and best London edition. — New York: Hebrew Pub. Co., 1917.

2 v. in 1. English and Hebrew. V.1. New Year. — V.2. Day of Atonement. Copies: MWalA NNJ

980. סדור חנוך תפלה: כולל תפלות לכל השנה...: נוסח ספרד...: נדפס באותיות גדולות מאד... גם נלוה אליו סדר אלפא ביתא בצירוף הנקודות עם חנוכים לנסיון... נויארק: היברו פאב. קא., תרע״ח [1917 or 1918].

140 p. Copies: NNYI

981. סדור שפת אמת (הקטן): כולל כל תפלות ישראל לכל השנה/מוגה ומסודר על ידי א. היימאן =

Daily prayers with English instructions/ revised and arranged by A. Hyman. — New York: Bloch, 1917.

vi, 314 p. Deinard: 974. Copies: DLC (uncat) MH NNJ OCH

982. סדר תפלות ישראל = The Union prayer-book for Jewish worship. Pt. II. New Year's Day, Day of Atonement/edited and published by the Central Conference of American Rabbis. — New York: Bloch, 1917, c1894.

340 p. English and Hebrew. Copies: NNHeb

983. סדר תפלות כל השנה = Daily prayers with English directions: Hebrew texts from the Standard prayer book. — 12th thousand. — New York: Bloch, 1917, c1915.

470 p. English and Hebrew. Copies: OCH

984. סדר תפלות כל השנה = The standard prayer book: authorized English translation/ by S. Singer. — Enl. American ed., 3rd printing — New York: Bloch, 1917.

470 p. English and Hebrew. Copies: OCH PPAnR

985. ספר אהל שרה: כולל חובות הדת לבנות ישראל/אברהם עבר בן שמואל הירשאוויץ = Yohale Sarah: containing religious duties of the daughters of Israel and moral helps/ compiled and revised from authoritative sources by Abraham E. Hirschowitz. — 3rd ed. — New York: [s.n.], 1917.

3 p. leaves xxxv, A–E, 3–77, 2–8 p. English with Hebrew. Copies: CSt DLC MiGrC NNU PPGratz

986. עבדת יום הזכרון; עבדת יום הכפורים = Holyday prayers: a new ritual for New Year and Day of Atonement. — 3rd ed. — New York: Bloch, 1917, c1909.

2 v. in 1. English and Hebrew. "This prayer book...follows the old traditional form...omitting such portions of the piyutim as many American Conservative congregations do not include in their liturgy."— The Publishers. Copies: NNJ PPAnR

987. עבודת ישראל = A prayer book for the services of the year at the synagogue. First part./arranged by Benjamin Szold and Marcus Jastrow; English translation by Marcus Jastrow. — Rev. ed. of the translation. — Philadelphia: [s.n.], 1917.

227 p. English and Hebrew. Copies: MH

1918

988. Abridged prayer book for Jews in the Army and Navy of the United States: prepared and issued for the Jewish Welfare Board/ by the Jewish Publication Society of America. — Philadelphia: JPSA, 1918.

80, 85 p. English and Hebrew. Copies: MH MWalA NIC NN NRCR OCl OHi PPAnR

989. Abridged prayer book for Jews in the Army and Navy of the United States: prepared and issued for the Jewish Welfare Board/ by the Jewish Publication Society of America. — 3rd impression. — Philadelphia: JPSA, 1918.

80, 85 p. English and Hebrew. Reproduced in smaller size from the 1917 edition. Copies: DLC OCH

990. Abridged prayer book for Jews in the Army and Navy of the United States: prepared and issued for the Jewish Welfare Board/ by the Jewish Publication Society of America. — 4th impression. — Philadelphia: JPSA, 1918.

80, 85 p. English and Hebrew. "Jewish Welfare Board-U.S. Army and Navy, cooperating with aid under the supervision of the War Dept. Commission on Training Camp Activities." Copies: OCH

991. Abridged prayer book for Jews in the Army and Navy of the United States: prepared and issued for the Jewish Welfare Board/by the Jewish Publication Society of America. — 5th impression. — Philadelphia: JPSA, 1918.

    80, 85 p. English and Hebrew. Copies: DLC (uncat)

992. The blessing of peace/by L. Joachim and J. Koenigsberg. — New York: Star, 1918.

    62 p. English, Hebrew and Yiddish. Copies: DLC

993. Children's service: religious school of Hebrew Reform Congregation, Altoona Pennsylvania /compiled, arranged and transliterated by Moses J. S. Abels. — Altoona, Pa.: The Religious School, 1918.

    36 p. English and romanized Hebrew. Copies: OCH

994. Children's services for New Year and Atonement Day. — 2nd printing, 5th thousand. — New York: Bloch, 1917, c1915.

    31 p. English and Hebrew. Publication/ Jewish Religious School Union of New York; No. 1. Copies: OCH

995. The flower service: special reprint from the Sabbath school hymnal/Isaac S. Moses. — New York: Bloch, c1918.

    Score (pp. 186–199) For chorus (SATB), with piano accompaniment. Copies: OCH

996. Hallel Psalms 115, 116, 118/M. Forster. — St. Louis: M. Forster, 1918.

    Score (p.) English and romanized Hebrew. Sendrey: 6803. Copies:

997. The harvest service: special reprint from the Sabbath school hymnal/by Isaac S. Moses. — New York: Bloch, 1918.

    Score (pp. 212–225) For chorus (SATB), with piano accompaniment. Copies: MH OCH PPGratz

998. Order of service for the day of the New Year and Day of Atonement for junior congregations/by Louis Grossmann. — Cincinnati: [s.n], 1918.

    31 p. English and Hebrew. Copies: NNHeb OCH

999. Prayer book for the Day of Atonement: arranged for the use of the Congregation Beth Miriam, Long Branch, N.J./ by Barnett A Elzas. — New York: Publishers Printing Co., 1918.

    351 p. English and Hebrew. Copies: DLC NN TxU

1000. Prayer book for the New Year: arranged for the use of the Congregation Beth Miriam, Long Branch, N.J./by Barnett A. Elzas, Rabbi of the Congregation. — New York: Publishers Printing Co., 1918.

    94, 94 p. English and Hebrew. Copies: DLC MWalA NN NNJ

1001. Sabbath music: complete evening and morning service, according to the Union prayer book: for soprano, alto, tenor and bass, with organ accompaniment/ by S. Schlesinger. — 3rd ed. — New York: Bloch, 1918.

    Score (3 v.) English and romanized Hebrew. Copies: MBuG NNJ PPGratz (Music)

1002. Services for the New Year's day and the Day of Atonement for junior congregations/arranged by David Philipson. — Cincinnati: [s.n.], 1918.

    65 p. Copies: OCH

1918

1003. Special ritual of the High Steet Temple, Elmira, New York: for the first eve of the New Year 5679–1918/by J. Marcus. — [Elmira, N.Y.: The Temple, 1918].

6 leaves. Copies: OCH

1004. The strength of faith/by G. Taubenhaus. — [New York: s.n.], c1918.

90 p. Contents: Poems — Consolatories — Dedication — Rabbinics — Evening service — Prayer at grave. Copies: CLJ MH NN NNJ OCH

1005. אמרי לב = Meditations and prayers for every situation & occasion in life/translated and adapted from the French by Hester Rothschild; revised and corrected by Isaac Leeser. — New York: Bloch, 1918.

ix, 262 p. Original in French by Jonas Ennery. Copies: NjP

1006. ברכת שלום = Blessing of peace/by L. Joachim and J. Koenigsberg. — [New York: L. Schlanger], 1918.

1 v. (ca. 60 p.) English, Hebrew and Yiddish. Title on added t.p.: Prayer on the battlefield. Copies: MH

1007. טוב מעט בכונה = issued especially for the English-American בר מצוה/written, translated ... by H. Yaffee. — New York: Hebrew-English Scientific Pub. Co., c1918.

64 p. English and Hebrew. Deinard: 336. Copies: DLC (uncat)

1008. ... מחזור = Form of prayers ... with English translation. — Special ed. published by the Jewish Welfare Board-U.S. Army and Navy. — New York: Hebrew Pub. Co., 1918–5679.

2 v. in 1 (416, 480 p.) English and Hebrew. V.1. Feast of the New Year. — V.2. The Day of Atonement. Copies: MH MWalA NNJ ViW

1009. מחזור לראש השנה ויום הכפורים: כל התפלות על מקומן כסדרן. — New York: Hebrew Pub. Co., 1918.

2 v. in 1 (322, 361 p.). Copies: CLHU MWalA

1010. סדר תפלות ישראל = Evening services for the Sabbath and week-days: reprinted from the Union prayer-book/edited and published by the Central Conference of American Rabbis. — Special ed. published for the Jewish Welfare Board — U.S. Army and Navy. — New York: Bloch, 1918, c1895.

58 p. English and Hebrew. Copies: MWalA NNJ OCH

1011. סדר תפלות ישראל = The Union prayer-book for Jewish worship. Part II. New Year's Day, Day of Atonement/edited and published by the Central Conference of American Rabbis. — New York: Bloch, 1918, c1894.

340 p. English and Hebrew. Copies: CLHU (uncat) OCH

1012. סדר תפלות ישראל = The Union prayer-book for Jewish worship. Part II. New Year's Day, Day of Atonement/edited and published by the Central Conference of American Rabbis. — Special ed. published for the Jewish Welfare Board — U.S. Army and Navy, cooperating with and under the supervision of the War Dept. Commission on Training Camp Activities. — New York: Bloch, 1918, c1894.

340 p. English and Hebrew. Copies: NNJ OCH

1013. סדר תפלות ישראל = The Union prayerbook for Jewish worship/edited and published by the Central Conference of American Rabbis. — Rev. ed. — Cincinnati: [CCAR], 1918.

2 v. English and Hebrew. "Provisional ed." Pt. I. Services for the Sabbath, Services

for the Three Festivals, Services for week days. — Pt. II. Services for the New Year, Services for the Day of Atonement. Printed manuscript of the revision of the Union prayer book sent to the members of the CCAR. Copies: C DLC (V.1) MH MWalA (V.1) OCH

1014. סדר תפלות ישראל = The Union prayer-book for Jewish worship/edited and published by the Central Conference of American Rabbis. — Rev. ed. — Cincinnati: [CCAR], 1918–1922.

2 v. English and Hebrew. Pt. I. Services for the Sabbath, Services for the Three Festivals, Services for week days., Prayers for private devotion. — Pt. II. Services for the New Year, Services for the Day of Atonement. Copies: CLHU (V.1) CLJ DLC InIT MH MWalA NN OCH Pepperdine PSt RPB TxAuCS

1015. סדר תפלות כל השנה = The standard prayer book: authorized English translation/by S. Singer. — Enl. American ed., 18th thousand. — New York: Bloch, 1918, c 1915.

469, 470 p. English and Hebrew. Copies: NNJ

1016. ספר אהל שרה: כולל חובות הדת לבנות ישראל/אברהם עבר בן שמואל הירשאוויץ = Yohale Sarah: containing religious duties of the daughters of Israel and moral helps/compiled and revised from authoritative sources by Abraham E. Hirschowitz. — 4th ed. — New York: [s.n.], c 1918.

xxxv, A-E, 4–77, 2–8 p. English with Hebrew. Copies: IaAS Jewish Community Library of Los Angeles MiU

1017. קנות לתשעה באב = Sinagogue recitative for Tisha-Ba'v/by S. Weisser (Pilderwasser). — [New York?]: S. Weisser, 1918.

Score (12 p.) Romanized Hebrew. Copies: PPGratz (Music)

1018. רעווערענדס האנדבוך: סדור לחזנים: כולל כל התפלות והברכות וכל מיני מי שברך הנחוצים לחזנים בבתי התפלה ובסעודות מצוה... נוסחאי מצבות וגם לוח על מאה שנים. — נויארק: ש. דרוקערמאן, c 1918 = Reverend's hand book. — New York: S. Druckerman, 1918.

89, 56 p. Hebrew. Copies: DLC OCH

1019. שיר ושבחה: בקשות ופזמונים לשבתות ומועדים... נקבצו ובאו לבית הדפוס/מאת רפאל חיים הכהן בירושלים. — [נויארק]: וכעת נדפס על ידי חברי חברת עזרת אחים אנשי סוריה בנויארק, תרע״ט [1918 or 1919].

49 p. Deinard: 796. Copies:

1020. שירי ישראל לליל שבת = Friday evening melodies/composed by Israel Goldfarb and Samuel Eliezer Goldfarb. — New York: Bureau of Jewish Education, 1918.

Score (105 p.) Romanized Hebrew. Arranged in two parts for children's voices. Sendrey: 6953. Copies: CarP CU DLC FU MU MWalA PPGratz (Music)

1919

1021. Complete musical service for the Day of Atonement: evening, morning, afternoon, memorial and concluding, according to the Union prayer book/S. Schlesinger. — 4th ed. — New York: Bloch, 1919.

Score (169 p.) English and romanized Hebrew. For Cantor and chorus (SATB), with organ accompaniment. Copies: NN OCH

1022. Consecration of the Theodore Roosevelt Memorial Window at Temple Keneseth Israel ... November 2, 1919. — [Philadelphia: The Temple, 1919].

12 p. Copies: NN

1023. Deux psaumes pour chant et orchestre: Psaumes 114 et 137/musique de Ernest Bloch; version pour chant et piano par l'auteur; poèmes adaptés de l'hébreu par Edmond Fleg; traductions anglaises de Waldo Frank.— New York: G. Schirmer, 1919.

Score (20 p.) English and French. For Soprano, with piano accompaniment. Psalms 114 and 137. Copies: CU-SB FTaSU KWiU PU

1024. Deux psaumes pour chant et orchestre: Psaumes 114 et 137/musique de Ernest Bloch; version pour chant et piano par l'auteur; poèmes adaptés de l'hébreu par Edmond Fleg; traductions anglaises de Waldo Frank.— New York: G. Schirmer, 1919.

Score (2 v.) English and French. For Soprano, with piano accompaniment. Psalms 114 and 137. Copies: AzTes CHS CL CLS CLSU FU GCarrWG ICRC InU KyLoS LLafS MB MBCM MH-Mu MiDW MiEM MiHolH MnM MnManS MnU MoS NbU NjGbS NjP NRU-Mus NSbSU OCl OCu OrPR OrSaw PP PPULC TNBe

1025. New Jewish hymnal for religious schools and junior congregations: songs and anthems/edited and compiled by Henry L. Gideon; services compiled and adapted by Louis Weinstein.— 7th ed. — New York: Bloch, 1919, c1917.

Score (viii, 173 p.) English and romanized Hebrew. Copies: MWalA

1026. Order of service for the house of mourning/arranged and compiled by Jacob Nieto for the Congregation Sherith Israel, San Francisco.— 2nd ed.— [San Francisco: Levison Printing Co.], 1919–5680.

13 p. English and Hebrew. Copies: MWalA WJHC

1027. Order of service of religious schools/ Louis Grossmann.— Cincinnati: [s.n.], 1919.

8 p. Copies: OCH

1028. Out of the depths I cried/ L. M. Kramer.— New York: L. M. Kramer, c1919.

Score (8 p.) For soprano and tenor solo and chorus (SATB), with piano accompaniment. Sendrey: 6848. Copies: MH-Mu

1029. Prayer book for the New Year: arranged for the use of the Brooklyn synagogue.— New York: [s.n.], 1919.

351 p. English and Hebrew. Copies: NNJ

1030. Psaume 22: pour baryton et grand orchestre/réduction pour chant et piano par l'auteur; musique de Ernest Bloch; transcription française d'Edmond Fleg; traduction anglaise de Waldo Frank. — New York: G. Schirmer, 1919.

Score (17 p.) French and English. For baritone, with piano accompaniment. Sendrey: 6788. Copies: AzTes CLSU CoU CU FTaSU ICRC IU IWW KyLoS MBCM MiEM MiMarq NIC NN NNHuC OCl OrP PP PPCI PPULC TnBe TxSaT TxWB

1031. Psaume 114: pour chant et orchestre/ musique de Ernest Bloch; version pour chant et piano par l'auteur; poèmes adaptés de l'hébreu par Edmond Fleg; traductions anglaises de Waldo Frank. — New York: G. Schirmer, 1919.

Score (9 p.) English and French. For voice, with piano accompaniment. Sendrey: 6789? Copies: CLSU CSjU CU FTaSU MiMarq WM

1919

1032. Psaume 137: pour baryton et grand orchestre/réduction pour chant et piano par l'auteur; musique de Ernest Bloch; poèmes adaptés de l'hébreu par Edmond Fleg; traductions anglaises de Waldo Frank.— New York: G. Schirmer, 1919.

    Score (11 p.) English and French. For baritone, with piano accompaniment. Sendrey: 6790. Copies: CL CU FTaSU IWW NBu NN-Br PP WM

1033. Sabbath evening service for the synagogue: arranged according to the Union prayer book/Gottfried H. Federlein. — New York: Bloch, 1919.

    Score (24 p.) English and romanized Hebrew. For Cantor and chorus (SATB), with organ accompaniment. Copies: NNJ PPGratz (Music)

1034. Sabbath prayer book: arranged for Conservative congregations/by Barnett A. Elzas.— New York: Bloch, 1919.

    64, 72 p. English and Hebrew. Deinard: 915. Copies: DLC MH MWalA NNJ

1035. The service manual/by Joseph Krauskopf, of the Reform Congregation Keneseth Israel.— 10th ed.— Philadelphia: O. Klonower, 1919, c1892.

    95, 256–564 p. English with Hebrew. Copies: FMFIU ViNC

1036. The Sunday service/prepared by Harry Levi for Temple Israel, Boston. — Boston: Chapple Pub. Co., c1919.

    39 p. English and Hebrew. Copies: MWalA NN

1037. The Sunday service/prepared by Harry Levi for Temple Israel, Boston. — Boston: Stetson Press, c1919.

    39 p. English and Hebrew. Copies: DLC MH NNHeb OCH

1038. Synagogen-Gesänge für Kantor und gemischten Chor/componirt von S. Weisser (Pilderwasser), S. Kavetzky (Bedrokowetzky).— New York: J. P. Katz, 1919–

    Score (v.) Romanized Hebrew. For Cantor and chorus (SATB). v.1. לימים נוראים. Sendrey: 6461. Copies: MH MWalA NN NNJ

1039. V'shomru: a Sabbath eve chant (text from Ex. 31:16–17)/A.W. Binder. — New York: C. Fischer, c1919.

    Score (4 p.) English and romanized Hebrew. For 1 voice, with piano accompaniment. Sendrey: 7024. Copies NN OCH

1040. V'shom'ru: for four-part chorus of mixed voices with tenor and baritone (Cantor) solo and organ accompaniment/A.W. Binder. — New York: G. Schirmer, c1919.

    Score (5 p.) romanized Hebrew. For Cantor and chorus (SATB), with organ accompaniment. Sendrey: 7023. Copies: MH-Mu

1041. ...מחזור = Form of prayers ... with English translation.— Rev. ed.— New York: Bloch, 1919.

    2 v. in 1. English and Hebrew. V.1. לראש השנה — V.2. ליום כפור. Copies: NNJ

1042. ...מחזור = Form of prayers ... with English translation.— Rev. ed.— New York: Hebrew Pub. Co., 1919.

    2 v. English and Hebrew. V.1. לראש השנה — V.2. ליום כפור. Copies: MH (V.1) MWalA (V.2)

1043. מחזור ינייי: כפי מה שנמצא ממנו בגניזה אשר במצרים בהוספות פיוטי ינייי האחרים: עם הערות והגהות ומבוא אנגלי/מאת ישראל דאווידזאן; ועם הערות נוספות מאת לוי

גינצבורג. — נויארק: בית מדרש לרבנים אשר באמעריקא, תרע"ט =
Mahzor Yannai: a liturgical work of the VII century: edited from Genizah fragments, with notes and introduction by Israel Davidson; with additional notes by Louis Ginzberg. — New York: Jewish Theological Seminary of America, 1919.

xlix, 55 iv. English and Hebrew. Deinard: 463. Copies: CLU CSt DLC Jewish Community Library of Los Angeles MH MWalA NIC NNJ PPGratz RPB

1044. סדור דרך החיים: נהורא השלם ולקוטי צבי: נוסח אשכנז: עם ספר תהילים וסדר מעמדות. — ניו יארק: היברו פאב. קא. תר"ף [1919 or 1920].

1 v. (various pagings). Attributed to Jacob ben Jacob Moses, of Lissa. Copies: MWalB NN

1045. סדור כל בו: כולל תפלות לכל השנה עם תקוני שבת, זמירות, יום כפור קטן, הושענות, סליחות, יוצרות, הקפות, קריאת התורה. — New York: Hebrew Pub. Co., 1919.

940 p. Copies: DLC OCH

1046. סדור שפת אמת: כולל כל תפלות ישראל לכל השנה עם תרגום ענגליש/מוגה ומסודר על ידי א. היימאן =
Sephath emeth (Speach [sic] of truth): order of prayers for the whole year: Hebrew and English. — New York: Hebrew Pub. Co., 1919.

314, 314, [5] p. English and Hebrew. Copies: MWalA

1047. סדר תפלות ישראל = Prayer-book for Jewish deaf/compiled and adapted by the Committee on Welfare of Deaf, Council of Jewish Women. — Philadelphia: Council of Jewish Women, 1919.

28 p. English and Hebrew. Adapted from the Union prayer-book of the Central Conference of American Rabbis. Copies: NN OCH PPGratz

1048. סדר תפלות כל השנה = Daily prayers with English directions: Hebrew text from the Standard prayer book. — 20th thousand. — New York: Bloch, 1919, c1915.

470 p. English and Hebrew. Copies: NNJ OCH

1049. ספר צדה לדרך האמת: והוא מעבר יבק: ענטהאלט ווידוים אין אלע געביעטען ביי א גוסס און ביי א מת... די דינים ערקלעהרט אין זשארגאן... אויך די אורקוועלען פון די תפלות אויפגעקליבען און איבערזעצט/פון יהודה ליב גארדאן. — ניו יארק: בדפוס אמנות. תרע"ט. — New York: Omonuth, 1919.

78 p. Yiddish. Compiled by Aaron Berechiah ben Moses. Copies: DLC MBrH NN OCH

1050. עבודת ישראל = A prayer book for the services of the year at the synagogue/arranged by Benjamin Szold and Marcus Jastrow; English translation by Marcus Jastrow. — Rev. ed of the translation. — Philadelphia: [s.n.], 1919, c1907.

2 v. English and Hebrew. Part 1. Services for the year. — Part 2. Services for the New Year and Day of Atonement. Copies: MH (V.1) NNJ

1051. קריאה קדושה: א) כל התפלות של הוצאת ספר תורה ב) כל הלכות קריאת התורה איבערגעזעצט אין אידיש ג) כל כיוני שמות אנשים. — נויארק: ראזענבערג פרינט קא., תרע"ט. — New York, 1919.

64 p. Hebrew and Yiddish. Compiled by Judah Rosenberg. Deinard: 731. Copies: DLC NN

192-?

1052. V'shomru (Sabbath song); May the words: for choir and organ, or solo/Pinchos

Jassinowsky. — St. Louis: Raigor Art and Music Co., [192-?].

Score (7 p.) English and romanized Hebrew. Copies: OCH

1053. דריי רעטשיטאטיווען פאר ימים נוראים = Three recitatives for the High Holidays/ by Jacob L. Wasilkowsky. — Brooklyn: J. L. Wasilkowsky, [192-?].

Score (8 p.) Romanized Hebrew. For cantor. כמה יסרתנו — כי כשמך — אתה נתן יד לפושעים. Copies: CLJ PPGratz

1054. מחזור לראש השנה ויום הכפורים: כמנהג אשכנז... ועתה הוספנו תפלת מעריב לר״ה ופירוש מטה לוי עם העתקת עברי טייץ על כל התפלות שבפיוטי ראש השנה ויום כפור ... — New York: Hebrew Pub. Co., [192-?].

224 p. Hebrew and Yiddish. Commentary by Aaron ben Jehiel Michael, ha-Levi. Copies: MWalA

1055. מחזור לראש השנה ויום הכפורים: עם באורים בית לוי, מטה לוי, קרבן אהרן/חברו אהרן ב׳ יחיאל מיכל אב״ד דמקיילישאק: והוספנו בו לקוטי צבי ... הוספנו העתקות עברי טייטש ... באותיות גדולות. — ניו-יארק: היברו פאב. קא. [192-?].

400 p. Hebrew and Yiddish. Cover title: מחזור קרבן אהרן ולקוטי צבי. Copies: DLC (uncat) MWalA

1056. מחזור לראש השנה ויום הכפורים ושלש רגלים: כמנהג אשכנז ... ועתה הוספנו תפלת מעריב לר״ה ופירוש מטה לוי עם העתקת עברי טייץ על כל התפלות שבפיוטי ראש השנה ויום כפור ... — New York: Hebrew Pub. Co., [192-?].

368 p. Hebrew and Yiddish. Commentary by Aaron ben Jehiel Michael, ha-Levi. Copies: DLC (uncat)

1057. הנרות הללו = Haneros halolu/ L. Lewandowski. — New York: Metro, [192-?].

Score (3 p.) romanized Hebrew. For chorus (SATB), with organ accompaniment. Copies: OCH

1058. סדר תפלות ובקשות על החולה ר״ל ומקשה לילד ר״ל וספר מעבר יבק: כולל סדר הוידוי לחולה, ענייני המיתה, הטהרה הקבורה. — ניו יארק: א. קופטשיק, [192-?].

31 p. Hebrew with Yiddish instructions. Copies: NN (n.d) OCH ספר מעבר יבק by Aaron Berechiah ben Moses

1059. סידור ראבן חדש: נוסח ספרד: עם דרך חיים, הוא אסיפת דינים השייכים לסדר תפלה. — ניו יורק: היברו פאב. קא. [192-?].

1 v. (various paging). Commentary by Eliezer ben Nathan of Mainz; דרך החיים attributed to Jacob ben Jacob Moses, of Lissa. Copies: DLC OCH

1060. שבעה אופני הקדוש/מאת יוסף רוזענבלאטט. — ניו יארק: [י. ראזענבלאטט, [192-?].

Score (7 p.) Hebrew and romanized Hebrew. Sendrey: 6559. Copies: PPGratz (Music)

1061. שלהבת יה = Shalhevet Yah: the Temple service ... — New York: Congregation Rodef Sholom, [192-?].

2 v. English and Hebrew. V.1. For the Sabbath and the Festivals. — V.2. For the New Year's day and the Day of Atonement. Originally prepared by Aaron Wise and arranged by Rudolph Grossman. Copies: MH MWalA (V.2)

1062. תפלות למתחילים. חלק ראשון/נערך על ידי זאב גראסמאן = Prayers for beginners/by Wm. Grossman. — New York: Published by the Alliance of Israel, [192-?].

23, [8] p. Introduction in English and Yiddish, Text in Hebrew, with English explanations. Copies: MWalA

1920

1063. Evening service for the Sabbath: arranged with responsive readings, anthems and hymns. — New York: Bloch, 1920.

31, 31, 34–63 p. English and Hebrew. Copies: MWalA NNJ

1064. The Jewish songster/edited and transliterated by Israel and Samuel E. Goldfarb. — 3rd ed. — Brooklyn: Religious Schools of Congregation Beth Israel, 1920, c1918.

64 p. English, Hebrew and Yiddish, and romanized Hebrew and Yiddish. "A hand-book of Jewish song-texts in Hebrew, English and Yiddish with transliterations." Copies: CoDU MH PPGratz

1065. Order of service, with responses, Psalms and hymns: for use in Jewish Schools/Louis Grossmann. — Cincinnati: [s.n.], 1920.

55 p. Includes music. Copies: OCH

1066. Prayerbook and hymnal from the American Orthodox Jewish Youth: selected from various prayerbooks and hymnals/Benjamin Cohen. — El Paso, Texas: [s.n.], 1920.

p. English and Hebrew. Sendrey: 6925. Copies:

1067. Psalm 100/arranged by S. Zilberts. — New York: National Blue Print Co., [1920?].

Score (8 p.). Copies: MH-Mu

1068. The Sabbath-school hymnal: a collection of songs, services and responsive readings for the school, synagogue and home... /edited by Isaac S. Moses. — 14th ed., rev. and enl. — New York: Bloch, 1920.

Score (346 p.) English and Hebrew. Includes music. Copies: MWalA NN NNHeb

1069. Sukkos service for children/by Eli Mayer. — Albany, N.Y.: Sophreem Co., 1920.

32 p. English and romanized Hebrew. Copies: CLHU OCH

1069a. Ten choice Hebrew song classics (traditional) for voice and pianoforte/compiled and edited by E. Kartschmaroff. — New York: E. B. Marks, 1920.

Score (30 p.) Romanized Hebrew. For voice, with piano accompaniment. Copies: NNHeb. Kol nidre — Chad gadya — Olenu — Adir hu — Yigdal Elohim — En Kelohenu — Shir hama'alos — L'Dowid boruch — Mooz tsur y'shuosi. — Owinu malkenu.

1070. זמירות ותשבחות לליל שבת = Song and praise for Sabbath eve: for use at synagogue gatherings in connection with the late Friday evening sermon or discourse/arranged by Israel Goldfarb and Israel Herbert Levinthal. — Brooklyn: [s.n.], 1920.

Score (64 p.) English, Hebrew and romanized Hebrew. Copies: DLC FU MH OCH PPGratz (Music)

1071. זמירות ותשבחות לליל שבת = Song and praise for Sabbath eve: for use at synagogue gatherings in connection with the late Friday evening sermons or discourse/arranged by Israel Goldfarb and Israel Herbert Levinthal. — Brooklyn: [s.n.], 1920.

Score (120 p.) English, Hebrew and romanized Hebrew. Sendrey: 6956. Copies: AzU FTS FU NN-Br OCH PPGratz

1072. זמירות ותשבחות לליל שבת = Song and praise for Sabbath eve: for use at synagogue gatherings in connection with the late Friday evening sermon or discourse/arranged by Israel Goldfarb and Israel Herbert Levinthal. — 2nd ed. — Brooklyn: [s.n.], 1920.

Score (64 p.) English, Hebrew and romanized Hebrew. Sendrey: 6153. Copies: NN

1073. מחזור כל בו: עם פירוש עברי טייטש בשם בית ישראל וילקוט פנינים ומעשה אלפס... : נוסח אשכנז. — ניו-יארק: היברו פאב. קא., 1920.

5 v. Copies: MWalA (V.3)

1074. מחזור עבדת אהל מועד כמנהג פולין: מוגה ומדויק היטב כפי מחזור של וואלף היידנהיים וכתבי יד ישנים/על ידי יעקב בן יצחק דעויס ונפתלי בן מרדכי אדלר הכהן, עם תרגום אנגליש. — לונדון =

Service of the synagogue... : a new edition of the Festival prayers, with an English translation in prose and verse. — 5th ed. — London: G. Routledge; New York: Bloch, 1920.

6 v. English and Hebrew. V.1. New Year. — V.2–3. Day of Atonement. — V.4. Tabernacles. — V.5. Passover. — V.6. Pentecost. Copies: DLC

1075. מחזור עבדת אהל מועד כמנהג פולין: מוגה ומדויק היטב כפי מחזור של וואלף היידנהיים וכתבי יד ישנים/על ידי יעקב בן יצחק דעויס ונפתלי בן מרדכי אדלר הכהן, עם תרגום אנגליש. — לונדון =

Service of the synagogue... : a new edition of the Festival prayers, with an English translation in prose and verse. — 6th ed. — London: G. Routledge; New York: Bloch, 1920–1922.

6 v. English and Hebrew. V.1. New Year. — V.2–3. Day of Atonement. — V.4. Tabernacles. — V.5. Passover. — V.6. Pentecost. Copies: NNHeb

1076. מחזור עבדת אהל מועד כמנהג פולין: מוגה ומדויק היטב כפי מחזור של וואלף היידנהיים וכתבי יד ישנים/על ידי יעקב בן יצחק דעויס ונפתלי בן מרדכי אדלר הכהן, עם תרגום אנגליש. — לונדון =

Service of the synagogue... : a new edition of the Festival prayers, with an English translation in prose and verse. — 7th ed. — London: G. Routledge; New York: Bloch, 1920–1924.

6 v. English and Hebrew. V.1. New Year. — V.2–3. Day of Atonement. — V.4. Tabernacles. — V.5. Passover. — V.6. Pentecost. Copies: CLHU (V.2, 4–5) NNJ

1077. סדר תפלות ישראל = The Union prayer-book for Jewish worship. Part II. New Years' Day, Day of Atonement/edited and published by the Central Conference of American Rabbis. — New York: Bloch, 1920, c1894.

340 p. English and Hebrew. Copies: NNHeb OCH

1078. סדר תפלות ישראל = The Union prayer-book for Jewish worship. Part II. Services for the New Year, Services for the Day of Atonement/edited and published by the Central Conference of American Rabbis. — Rev. ed. — Cincinnati: CCAR, 1920.

353 p. English and Hebrew. Deinard: 917. Copies: MWalA OCH

1079. סדר תפלות כל השנה = The standard prayer book: authorized English translation/by S. Singer. — Enlarged American ed., 26th thousand. — New York: Bloch, 1920, c1915.

469, 470 p. English and Hebrew. Copies: NNHeb OCH

1080. סדר תפלות כל השנה כמנהג פולין: מוגה ומדויק היטב ומתרגם ללשון אנגליש/על ידי שמעון בן יהודה סינגער בהסכמת נתן אדלר

הכהן. — הוצאת אמריקנית, תר״ף =
The authorised daily prayer book of the United Hebrew Congregations of the British empire: with a new translation / by S. Singer; published under the sanction of the late chief Rabbi Nathan Marcus Adler. — American ed. — London: Eyre and Spottiswoode; New York: Hebrew Pub. Co., 5680–1920.

viii, 329, 329 p. English and Hebrew. Copies: NNJ

1081. עבדת יום הזכרון; עבדת יום הכפורים = Holyday prayers: a new ritual for New Year and Day of Atonement. — 4th ed. — New York: Bloch, 1920, c1909.

2 v. in 1. English and Hebrew. "This prayer book ... follows the old traditional form ... omitting such portions of the piyyutim as many American Conservative congregations do not include in their liturgy. — The Publishers. Copies: MWalA NNJ

1082. עבודת ישראל = A prayer book for the services of the year at the synagogue / arranged by Benjamin Szold and Marcus Jastrow; English translation by Marcus Jastrow. — Rev. ed of the translation. — Philadelphia: [s.n.], 1920.

2 v. English and Hebrew. Part 1. Services for the year. — Part 2. Services for the New Year and Day of Atonement. Copies: MH MWalA (V.2)

1083. תפלת שבת = The Sabbath service for Sabbath eve and Sabbath morning: arranged and revised with special English prayers and responsive readings / by Julius Silberfeld, Rabbi, Congregation B'nai Abraham, Newark, N.J. — New York: Bloch, 1920, c1905.

244 p. English and Hebrew. Copies: NN NNJ

1921

1084. The children's service for use in religious schools / J. Leonard Levy. — 4th ed. — Pittsburgh, Pa.: Press of J. Crawford Park, 1921.

259 p. Copies: MH

1085. Complete musical service for the Three Festivals, Pesah (Passover) Shabuoth (Pentecost) Succoth (Tabernacles), according to the Union prayer book / S. Schlesinger. — 3rd ed. — New York: Bloch, 1921.

Score (74 p.) English and romanized Hebrew. For Cantor and chorus (SATB), with piano accompaniment. Copies: DLC NN-Br

1086. Deux Psaumes pour soprano et orchestre: précédés d'un prelude orchestral: Psaumes 114 et 137 / musique de Ernest Bloch; poèmes adaptés de l'hebreu par Edmond Fleg; traductions anglaises de Waldo Frank. — New York: G. Schirmer, c1921.

Score (51 p.) English and French. G. Schirmer's edition of scores of orchestral works and chamber music; no. 145. Sendrey: 6791? Copies: AzFU CLSU CU CU-SB FPeU FTaSU GU InU MiDW MiRochOU MiU NII NN NNWML NRU-Mus OkU OYU PU

1087. Dr. David Einhorn's עלת תמיד: book of prayers for Jewish congregations: new translation after the German original. — [Chicago?: s.n.], 1921, c1896.

v, 166, 279 p. English and Hebrew. Edited by Emil G. Hirsch. Pt. 1. Services for the Sabbath, the Festivals, and the days of the week. — Pt. 2. Services for the New Year's day and the Day of Atonement. Copies: CLHU (uncat) Cst GEU-T ICNPT MWalA NcD WFonm

1088. The Emanu-El hymnal. — [Los Angeles: Emanu-El, 1921].

> Score (66 p.). Preface by Ernest Trattner. Copies: OCH

1089. Hallelujah: Psalm 113 / Joseph Rosenblatt. — New York: J. Rosenblatt, c 1921.

> Score (23 p.) English and romanized Hebrew. For chorus (SATB), with piano accompaniment. Copies: NNJ OCH PPBI

1090. Isaiah Congregation hymn book: dedicated to Joseph Stolz, who always advocated congregational singing. E. F. March 27, 1921. — Chicago: [Isaiah Congregation], 1921.

> 6 p. Copies: OCH

1091. Jaale: Hebrew Temple songs for Kol nidre: for solo Cantor and mixed chorus / music by Savel Zilberts. — New York: J. P. Katz, 1921.

> Score (14 p.) Romanized Hebrew. For Cantor and chorus (SATB). Sendrey: 6478. Copies: CL NNJ PPGratz (Music)

1092. Kiddush, or Sabbath sentiment in the home / by Henry Berkowitz; with special illustrations by Kathrine M. Cohen. — 2nd rev. ed. — Philadelphia: [s.n.], 1921, c 1898.

> 68 p., ill. 4 leaves of plates. See Singerman: 5310. Copies: InV1 MWalA NNJ PP

1093. Kol nidre / Arnold Perlmutter. — New York: A. Teres, c 1921.

> Score (5 p.) Romanized Hebrew. Sendrey: 7202. Copies: OCH

1094. Memorial service for the Day of Atonement: written for the Baltimore Hebrew Congregation / Morris S. Lazaron. — Baltimore: [s.n.], 1921.

> 34 p. Copies: NNJ OCH

1095. Prayers for use in the Jewish home: compiled on the occasion of the tenth anniversary of the rabbinate of Max D. Klein, and by him dedicated in affection to the households of Congregation Adath Jeshurun. — Philadelphia: [s.n.], 1921.

> 19, 20 p. English and Hebrew. Copies: DLC (uncat)

1096. Psaume 22 pour baryton et orchestre / musique de Ernest Bloch: poèmes adaptés de l'hebreu par Edmond Fleg; traductions anglaises de Waldo Frank. — New York: G. Schirmer, c 1921.

> Score (37 p.) English and French. For baritone and orchestra. Copies: CU FPeU FTaSU ICRC InU MiRoch OU NN NRU-Mus PU

1097. The Sabbath-school hymnal: a collection of songs, services and responsive readings for the school, synagogue and home / Isaac S. Moses. — 14th rev. and enl. ed. — New York: Bloch, 1921, c 1920.

> 346 p. English and romanized Hebrew. Includes music. Copies: MH NN NNJ

1098. The service manual / by Joseph Krauskopf, of the Reform Congregation Keneseth Israel. — 11th ed. — Philadelphia: O. Klonower, 1921, c 1892.

> 95, 256–564 p. English with Hebrew. Copies: NNYU

1099. A t'filoh = A prayer / words by A. Reisen; music by A. W. Binder. — New York: J. P. Katz, c 1921.

> Score (2 p.) English translation by D. L. Sprung. Copies: MH-Mu NNJ

1100. The Temple hymnal: arranged for Congregation Rodef Shalom, Pittsburgh, Pa. / by J. Leonard Levy. — 4th ed. — Pittsburgh: J. C. Park, 1921.

> pp. 110–256. Copies: OCH

1101. מחזור עבדת אהל מועד כמנהג פולין: מוגה ומדויק היטב כפי מחזור של וואלף היידנהיים וכתבי יד ישנים/על ידי יעקב בן יצחק דעויס ונפתלי בן מרדכי אדלר הכהן, עם תרגום אנגליש. — לונדון = Service of the synagogue ... : a new edition of the Festival prayers, with an English translation in prose and verse. — 8th ed. — London: G. Routledge; New York: Bloch, 1921–1925.

6 v. English and Hebrew. V.1. New Year. — V.2–3. Day of Atonement. — V.4. Tabernacles. — V.5. Passover. — V.6. Pentecost. Copies: CLHU (V.3, 6) MWalA (V.2) NNJ (V.1)

1102. סדור בית יהודה: סדר תפלות ישראל כמנהג אשכנז: כולל תפלות לכל השנה בשלשה חלקים עם העתקה עברית אשכנזית צחה וקלה: ועתה הוספנו בו אור חדש והוא סדור היסטארי ... /נעתק ונלקט מאת יהודה ליב ב״ר מאיר גארדאן (הנקרא חדש). — New York: G.E.B. Press, 1921.

3 v. in 1. Hebrew and Yiddish. Copies: CLU MH MiU MWalA MWalB NNJ NNYI

1103. סדור בית יהודה: סדר תפלות ישראל כמנהג אשכנז: כולל תפלות לכל השנה בשלשה חלקים עם העתקה עברית אשכנזית צחה וקלה: ועתה הוספנו בו אור חדש והוא סדור היסטארי ... /נעתק ונלקט מאת יהודה ליב ב״ר מאיר גארדאן (הנקרא חדש). — New York: G.E.B. Press, 1921–.

3 v. Hebrew and Yiddish. Copies: DLC

1104. סדור קרבן מנחה: כולל סדר תפלות לכל ימות השנה ושנים באורים ... נוסח אשכנז. — ניו-יארק: היברו פאב. קא. תרפ״ב [1921 or 1922].

780 p. Hebrew and Yiddish. Bound with: ספר תהלים עם מעמדות. (Entry 1283). Copies: NNYI

1105. סדור קרבן מנחה: כולל סדר תפלות לכל ימות השנה עם ילפוט פנינים ומעשה אלפס: נוסח ספרד. — ניו-יארק: היברו פאב. קא. תרפ״ב [1921 or 1922].

34, 16, 780 232 p. Hebrew and Yiddish. MH's copy bound with: ספר תהלים עם מעמדות. (Entry 1283) Copies: MH OCH

1106. סדור תפלת ישראל מכל השנה: עם פירוש נפלא "דברי שלמה" עם העתקה לעברי-טייטש/מאת שלמה יאנאווסקי. — New York: S. Janowski, 1921.

578, 164, 39 p. Hebrew and Yiddish. On verso of t.p.: Syder tefilas Israel/wyd. Szlama Janowski. Copies: NNJ

1107. סדר כל תפלות השנה = Magil's complete linear prayer book: comprising the prayers for the whole year: translated in the new linear system with notes and original engravings, for the synagogue, the home and the school. — 12th improved ed. — Philadelphia: Translated and published by J. Magil, 1921–א״תרפ, c1905.

2 v. in 1. English and Hebrew. Copies: NNJ

1108. סדר תפלות ישראל = The Union prayer-book for Jewish worship. Pt. I. Services for the Sabbath, Services for the Three Festivals, Services for week days, Prayers for private devotion/edited and published by the Central Conference of American Rabbis. — Rev. ed. — Cincinnati: [CCAR], 1921.

406 p. English and Hebrew. Copies: NNHeb OCH

1109. סדר תפלות ישראל = The Union prayer-book for Jewish worship. Pt. II. New Year's Day, Day of Atonement/edited and published by the Central Conference of American Rabbis. — New York: Bloch, 1921, c1894.

340 p. English and Hebrew. Copies: DLC KWiU MWalA NN NNHeb OCH

1110. ספר ידיד נפש: אין דיזען ספר געפֿינען זיך הנהגות התפלה און פרק שירה.../צו בעקומען בייא יונה בן דוב המכונה צוויקל. — ניו-יארק, תרפ״ב. — New York: J. Zwickel, [1921 or 1922].

56 p. Hebrew and Yiddish. Copies: DLC (uncat) MWalA NN OCH

1111. עבדת שלש רגלים = Festival prayers: a new ritual for Passover, Pentecost, Tabernacles. — New York: Bloch, 1921.

192, 194 p. English and Hebrew. Copies: DLC MH MWalA

1112. עבודת השלחן עם קריאת שמע על המטה = Home service with translation and transliteration/compiled by Rabbi and Mrs. Herbert S. Goldstein. — New York: Bloch, 1921.

75 p. English, Hebrew and romanized Hebrew. Copies: DLC MH

1113. עבודת ישראל = A prayer book for the services of the year at the synagogue/arranged by Benjamin Szold and Marcus Jastrow; English translation by Marcus Jastrow. — Rev. ed of the translation. — Philadelphia: [s.n.], 1921, c1907.

2 v. English and Hebrew. Part 1. Services for the year. — Part 2. Services for the New Year and Day of Atonement. Copies: MH (V.1) NNJ

1114. עבודת ישראל = A prayer book for the services of the year at the synagogue/arranged by Benjamin Szold and Marcus Jastrow; English translation by Marcus Jastrow. — Rev. ed of the translation. — Philadelphia: [s.n.], 1921, c1907.

2 v. English and Hebrew. Part 1. Services for Sabbaths, Festivals, and week days. — Part 2. Services for the New Year and Day of Atonement. "This edition differs from the regular addition of Abodath Israel by the insertion of prayers and responsive readings." Copies: MWalA

1115. תפלת שבת = The Sabbath service for Sabbath eve and Sabbath morning: arranged and revised with special English prayers and responsive readings/by Julius Silberfeld, Rabbi, Congregation B'nai Abraham, Newark, N.J. — New York: Bloch, 1921, c1905.

244 p. English and Hebrew. Copies: NNJ

1922

1116. B'zess Israel/Josef Rosenblatt. — New York: J. Rosenblatt, 1922.

Score (7 p.) romanized Hebrew. For chorus (SATB). Sendrey: 6376 Holdings:

1117. Chanukah songster: containing a complete children's musical service and other hymns in English and Hebrew/A.W. Binder. — New York: Bloch, 1922.

Score (16 p.). English and romanized Hebrew. For 1 voice, with piano accompaniment. Sendrey: 7238. Copies: MWalB NNJ OCH PPGratz WM

1118. "Consecration hymn for the consecration of Temple Sinai, November 13, 1872." In: Heller, Max, compiler. *Jubilee souvenir of Temple Sinai, New Orleans*. New Orleans, Temple Sinai, 1922. By James K. Gutheim. Copies: DLC FU LN RPB

1119. Evening service for the Sabbath: arranged with responsive readings, anthems, hymns. — 5th thousand. — New York: Bloch, 1922, c1920.

31, 31, 34–63 p. English and Hebrew. Copies: NN NNJ

1120. Friday evening service. No. 2: (short and of moderate difficulty)/by Edmund Serano Ender. — New York: Bloch, 1922.

Score (8 p.) English and romanized Hebrew. For Cantor and chorus (SATB). Sendrey: 5886. Copies: PPGratz (Music)

1121. Inspirational readings for the home/ Horace Wolf. — [Rochester: Berith Kodesh Sisterhood, 1922].

31 p. Copies: OCH

1122. A Purim songster: containing a tableau-ballade and other songs and hymns in English and Hebrew./A.W. Binder. — New York: Bloch, 1922.

Score (16 p.) English and romanized Hebrew. For 1 voice, with piano accompaniment. Sendrey: 7274. Copies: NNJ

1123. Service for confirmation/by A. Cronbach. — New York: Bloch, 1922.

23 p. Copies: DLC NN OCH

1124. The service-hymnal: with an introductory service/text compiled by Jos. Krauskopf; music compiled by Russell King Miller. — Philadelphia: E. Stern, c1922.

170 p. Includes music. For Reform Congregation Keneseth Israel, Philadelphia. Copies: MH-AH PNo PPGratz

1125. The service-hymnal: with an introductory service/text compiled by Jos. Krauskopf; music compiled by Russell King Miller. — Rev. ed. — Philadelphia: [Reform Congregation Keneseth Israel], 1922.

158 p. Includes music. For Reform Congregation Keneseth Israel, Philadelphia. Sendrey: 6984. Copies: PDoN PPGratz (Music)

1126. The service manual/by Joseph Krauskopf, of the Reform Congregation Keneseth Israel. — 12th ed. — Philadelphia: O. Klonower, 1922, c1892.

95, 256–564 p. English with Hebrew. For Reform Congregation Keneseth Israel, Philadelphia. Copies: NNHeb NNU OCH

1127. Shir Zion: Friday evening service arranged for use in American synagogues/ by the Society of American Cantors, from the "Schir Zion" of Salomon Sulzer. — 2nd ed. — New York: The Society, 1922, c1904.

Score (32 p.) English and romanized Hebrew. For Cantor and chorus (SATB), with organ accompaniment. "Souvenir of the Society of American Cantors in commemoration of the one hundredth birthday and anniversary of Salomon Sulzer." Copies: OCH PPGratz (Music)

1128. Two Cantor recitatives ... : Rozo deShabos ... Hamchabe es haner/S. Bernstein. — Brooklyn: S. Bernstein, 1922.

Score (7 p.) Romanized Hebrew. For 1 voice. Sendrey: 6495. Copies: OCH

1129. Uvnucho yomar/Josef Rosenblatt. — New York: J. Rosenblatt, 1922.

Score (7 p.) Romanized Hebrew. For Cantor and chorus (SATB). Sendrey: 6380. Copies:

1130. V'shom'ru, the Sabbath/A.W. Binder. — New York: C. Fischer, [ca. 1922].

Score (6 p.) English and romanized Hebrew. For solo (medium) and chrous (SATB), with piano or organ accompaniment. Copies: OCH

1131. זמירות ותשבחות לליל שבת = Song and praise for Sabbath eve: for use at synagogue gatherings in connection with the late Friday evening sermon or discourse/ arranged by Israel Goldfarb and Israel Herbert Levinthal. — 2nd ed. — Brooklyn: [s.n.], 1922 printing, c1920.

Score (64 p.) English, Hebrew and romanized Hebrew. Copies: PPGratz (Music)

1132. מחזור עבדת אהל מועד כמנטג פולין: מוגה ומדויק היטב כפי מחזור של וואלף היידנהיים וכתבי יד ישנים/על ידי יעקב בן יצחק דעויס ונפתלי בן מרדכי אדלר הכהן, עם תרגום אנגליש. — לונדון = Service of the synagogue ... : a new edition of the Festival prayers, with an English translation in prose and verse. — 9th ed. — London: G. Routledge; New York: Bloch, 1922–1925.

6 v. English and Hebrew. V.1. New Year. — V.2–3. Day of Atonement. — V.4. Tabernacles. — V.5. Passover. — V.6. Pentecost. Copies: CHLU (V.1) MBrH (V.5)

1133. סדור בית ישראל עברי-טייטש: כולל סדר התפלות לכל ימות השנה עם ילקוט פנינים יקרים ומעשה אלפס: יכיל שלשים ושנים באורים יקרים. — ניו-יארק: נוסח אשכנז: היברו פאב. קא., תרפ״ג [1922 or 1923].

592, 232, 88 p. Copies: OCH

1134. סדור שפת אמת/מאת וואלף בר שמשון דוב איש היידנהיים, שנת תרפ״ב = Daily prayers with English instructions — 1st new rev. ed. as correct as any ed. ever published in רעדעלהיים — New York: Hebrew Pub. Co., 1922.

293 p. Hebrew with English instructions. Copies: OCH

1135. סדר תפלות ישראל = The Union prayer-book for Jewish worship. Pt. I. Services for the Sabbath, Services for the Three Festivals, Services for week days, Prayers for private devotion/edited and published by the Central Conference of American Rabbis. — Rev. ed. — Cincinnati: [CCAR], 1922, c1918.

406 p. English and Hebrew. Copies: MH NNHeb OCH

1136. סדר תפלות כל השנה = The standard prayer book: authorized English translation/by S. Singer. — Enl. American ed., 34th thousand. — New York: Bloch, 1922, c1915.

469, 470 p. English and Hebrew. Copies: NN NNJ OCH PPGratz

1137. עבדת שבת = Sabbath prayers: a complete ritual for Sabbath eve, Sabbath morning, Sabbath afternoon. — New York: Bloch, 1922.

167, 167, 168–179 p. English and Hebrew. Copies: DLC MH MWalA NNJ

1138. עבודת ישראל = A prayer book for the services of the year at the synagogue/arranged by Benjamin Szold and Marcus Jastrow; English translation by Marcus Jastrow. — Rev. ed of the translation. — Philadelphia: [s.n.], 1922.

2 v. English and Hebrew. Part 1. Services for the year. — Part 2. Services for the New Year and Day of Atonement. Copies: MWalA (V.1)

1139. רנת עמך = Rinath amcho: arranged for Cantor and choir/composed by Jacob L. Wasilkowsky. — Brooklyn: J. L. Wasilkowsky, 1922.

Score (50 p.) Preface in Hebrew, romanized Hebrew words. For Cantor and 3 or 4 part chorus. Sendrey: 6580, 7148? Copies: PPGratz (Music)

1923

1140. Adon olam "Lord of the universe": hymn (for solo and choir with organ accompaniment)/by Michael Banner. — New York: Bloch, 1923.

Score (12 p.) English and romanized

Hebrew. For Cantor, soli and chorus (SATB), with organ accompaniment. Sendrey: 7009. Copies: OCH

1141. Al naharos Bovel: Männerchor/ Zavel Zilberts. — New York: The Cantors' Assn of America, 1923.

Score (22 p.) Romanized Hebrew. For 4 part male chorus, with piano or organ accompaniment. Psalm 137. Sendrey: 6907. Copies: NN

1142. A book of prayers for Jewish girls… / compiled by the Committee on Religion of the New York Section of the Council of Jewish Women. — 2nd ed. — New York: The New York Section of the Council of Jewish Women; Press of C.S. Nathan, 5684–1923.

51 p. Copies: DLC MWalA

1143. Children's services: arranged for each week of the month for holidays and patriotic occasions/ by Rudolph Grossman. — 7th printing. — New York: Bloch, 1923.

16 p. Copies: MWalA

1144. Complete musical service for New Year: evening and morning, according to the Union prayer book/ by S. Schlesinger. — New York: Bloch, 1923, c1901.

Score (64 p.) English and romanized Hebrew. For Cantor and chorus (SATB), with organ accompaniment. Copies: AzU CL CLJ MoKU NN-Br NN NNJ OCH PPGratz PPL

1145. Festival prayer book: order of service/ arranged by Barnett A. Elzas. — 2nd ed., enl. — New York: Bloch, 1923, c1915.

68, 68 p. English and Hebrew. Copies: MWalA

1146. Hebrew sacred chorus for mixed voices: No. 1. Ahavas olam. No. 2. Hashkivenu/ by G. Rabinowitz, Musical Director, Ohel Jacob Synagogue, Philadelphia, Pa. — [Philadelphia: G. Rabinowitz], c1923.

Score (15 p.) Hebrew. Copies: PPGratz (Music)

1147. Mogen ovos: for male choir and piano/ Leo Low. — New York: Cantors' Association of America, 1923.

Score (7 p.) Romanized Hebrew. Copies: NNJ

1148. New Jewish hymnal for religious schools and junior congregations: songs and anthems/ edited and compiled by Henry L. Gideon; services compiled and adapted by Louis Weinstein. — 8th ed. — New York: Bloch, 1923.

Score (viii, 173 p.) English and romanized Hebrew. Sendrey: 6946. Copies: NN PPGratz (Music)

1149. Sabbath-school hymnal: a collection of songs, services and responsive readings for the school, synagogue and home/ edited and published by Isaac S. Moses. — 14th rev. and enl. ed. — New York: Bloch, 1923, c1920.

Score (346 p.) English and romanized Hebrew. Includes music. Copies: ICJS NN

1150. Zwei Recitativen: I. Halben chatoeinu. II. M'loch: für Cantor und Chor/ von Jacob L. Wasilkowsky. — New York: J.P. Katz, c1923.

Score (16 p.) Romanized Hebrew. For Cantor and chorus (SATB). Sendrey: 6585. Copies: NNJ OCH PPGratz (Music)

1151. אמרי לב = Meditations and prayers for every situation & occasion in life/ translated and adapted from the French by Hester Rothschild; revised and corrected by Isaac Leeser. — New York: Bloch, 1923.

ix, 262 p. Original in French by Jonas Ennery. Copies: NNHeb

1152. ברכה ותפלה = Blessing and praise: a book of meditations and prayers for individual and home devotion/prepared and published by the Central Conference of American Rabbis. — Cincinnati: CCAR, 1923.

168 p. Copies: DLC Jewish Community Library of Los Angeles NN NNHeb OCH RPB TxU

1153. הבדלה = Havdoloh for solo, choir and piano/composed by Zavel Zilberts. — New York: Z. Zilberts: Printed by Radom and Neidorff, 1923.

Score (14 p.) Romanized Hebrew. Sendrey: 6579. Copies: NNJ OCl PPGratz (Music)

1154. היה עם פפיות = Heje im pifijos: for solo and male quartette/organ accompaniment specially composed by Zavel Zilberts for the Jubilee concert of the Cantors' Association of America, Feb. 3rd, 1924. — [New York]: Cantors' Association of America, 1923.

Score (25 p.) Romanized Hebrew. Sendrey: 7162. Copies: NNJ PPGratz (Music)

1155. הלכות נדה, חלה, הדלקת הנר, ברכת הנהנין בשפת אנגליש/על ידי יצחק ליב קאדושין = Sanitary law for married woman and man, law of aside cake, law of lighting candles, usual prayer for each meal/by J. L. Kadushin. — New Rochelle, N.Y.: Kadishin, 1923.

16 p. English and Hebrew. Copies: OCH

1156. ושמרו = 6 "V shomru's": a Sabbath Eve prayer for Reformed and Orthodox services: for chorus and organ/by Mark Silver. — New York: J. P. Katz, c 1923.

Score (24 p.) Romanized Hebrew. For chorus (SATB), with organ accompaniment. Sendrey: 7133. Copies: NN

1157. זמירות ברוך אל עליון = A Sabbath noon chant for mixed voices and piano accompaniment/ by Zavel Zilberts. — New York: Z. Zilberts; J. P. Katz, sole selling agent, c1923.

Score (9 p.) Romanized Hebrew. For chorus (SATB), with piano accompaniment. Copies: NNJ PPGratz (Music)

1158. זמירות ברוך אל עליון = Zemiros: Boruch El elyon/Zavel Zilberts. — New York: Metro Music Co., 1923.

Score (8 p.) Romanized Hebrew. For chorus (SATB), with piano accompaniment. Sendrey: 7416a. Copies: NNJ

1159. זמירות ברוך אל עליון = Zemiros: Boruch El elyon: for voice and piano accompaniment/Zavel Zilberts. — New York: J. P. Katz, c 1923.

Score (5 p.) Romanized Hebrew. Sendrey: 7416. Copies: OCH

1160. ישמחו במלכותך = Yismechu bemalchus'cho: Männerchor/composed by Zavel Zilberts. — New York: Cantors' Association of America, c1923.

Score (7 p.) Romanized Hebrew. 4 part male chorus. Sendrey: 6485. Copies: NNJ PPGratz (Music)

1161. מן המיצר = Min hamezar (Psalm 118) for solo, soli and male choir/ Leo Low. — [New York]: Cantors Association of America, c1923.

Score (18 p.) Romanized Hebrew. Sendrey: 6857. Copies: NN

1162. סדור קול יעקב: שירי תפלה סליחות/פון יעקב פראהמאן — New York: J. Frohmann, 1923.

Score (54 p.) Romanized Hebrew. Table of contents in Hebrew. Sendrey: 5897. Copies: PPGratz

1163. סדר תפלות ישראל = The Union prayer-book for Jewish worship/edited and published by the Central Conference of American Rabbis. — Rev. ed. — Cincinnati: [CCAR], 1923.

2 v. English and Hebrew. Pt.I. Services for the Sabbath, Services for the Three Festivals, Services for week days. — Pt.II. Services for the New Year, Services for the Day of Atonement. Copies: MWalA OCH (V.2)

1164. סדר תפלות ישראל = The Union prayer-book for Jewish worship. Pt. II. New Year's Day, Day of Atonement/ edited and published by the Central Conference of American Rabbis. — New York: Bloch, 1923, c1894.

340 p. English and Hebrew. Copies: CLHU MH NNHeb

1165. סדר תפלות ישראל = The Union prayer-book for Jewish worship. Pt. II. Services for the New Year, Services for the Day of Atonement/edited and published by the Central Conference of American Rabbis. — Rev. ed. — Cincinnati; Philadelphia: Conat Press, 1923.

370 p. English and Hebrew. Deinard: 925. Copies: NNHeb OCH

1166. סדר תפלות כל השנה = Daily prayers with English directions: Hebrew text from the Standard prayer book. — 24th thousand. — New York: Bloch, 1923, c1915.

470 p. English and Hebrew. Copies: OCH

1167. סדר תפלות מכל השנה: מוגה ומדויק היטב ומתורגם ללשון אנגלית/על ידי א. טה. פיליפס = Daily prayers with a revised English translation/by A.Th. Philips. — New York: Hebrew Pub. Co., 1923.

706 p. English and Hebrew. Copies: MWalB

1168. עבדת יום הזכרון: עבדת יום הכפורים = Holyday prayers: a new ritual for New Year and Day of Atonement. — 6th ed. — New York: Bloch, 1923, c1909.

2 v. in 1. English and Hebrew. "This prayer book … follows the old traditional form … omitting such portions of the piyutim as many American Conservative congregations do not include in their liturgy." — The Publishers. Copies: MH NNJ

1169. עבדת יום הזכרון: עבדת יום הכפורים = Holyday prayers: a new ritual for New Year and Day of Atonement. — 7th ed. — New York: Bloch, 1923.

2 v. in 1. English and Hebrew. "This prayer book … follows the old traditional form … omitting such portions of the piyutim as many American Conservative congregations do not include in their liturgy." — The Publishers. Copies: MWalA

1170. עבודת ישראל = A prayer book for the services of the year at the synagogue/ arranged by Benjamin Szold and Marcus Jastrow; English translation by Marcus Jastrow. — Rev. ed of the translation. — Philadelphia: [s.n.], 1923, c1907.

2 v. English and Hebrew. Part 1. Services for the year. — Part 2. Services for the New Year and Day of Atonement. Copies: MH

1171. רעוורענדס האנדבוך: סדור לחזנים: כולל כל התפלות והברכות וכל מיני מי שברך הנחוצים לחזנים בבתי התפלה ובסעודות מצוה… שמות של זכרים ונקבות ועוד… =

Reverend's handbook. — New rev. ed. — New York: S. Druckerman at Levant Press, c1923.

159 p. English, Hebrew, and Yiddish. Compiled by: א. האבמאן. Copies: OCH

1172. תפלת שבת = The Sabbath service for Sabbath eve and Sabbath morning: arranged and revised with special English prayers and responsive readings/by Julius Silberfeld, Rabbi, Congregation B'nai Abraham, Newark, N.J. — New York: Bloch, 1920, c1905.

244 p. English and Hebrew. Copies: MWalA WJHC

1924

1173. Confirmation service/arranged by Isaac S. Moses. — New York: Bloch, 1924.

46 p. English and Hebrew. Includes music. Copies: NNJ PPGratz

1174. Kedusha = Sanctification: for four-part chorus of mixed voices, with Cantor solo and organ accompaniment/ A.W. Binder. — New York: Bloch, 1924.

Score (7 p.) Romanized Hebrew. For Cantor and chorus (SATB), with organ accompaniment. Sendrey: 7017. Copies: NNJ OCH

1175. King David's Psalm of thanksgiving: for soli, chorus and orchestra/by Leon M. Kramer. — Brooklyn: L.M. Kramer, 1924.

Score (32 p.). Sendrey: 6847. Copies: NN-Br NNJ

1176. Let my prayer come unto Thy presence: sacred song for high voice, with piano accompaniment/A.W. Binder. — New York: G. Schirmer, 1924.

Score (7 p.). Sendrey: 7018. Copies:

1177. Order of service with responses, Psalms and hymns: for use in Jewish schools/Louis Grossmann. — Cincinnati: [s.n.], 1924.

55 p. Includes music. Sendrey: 5909. Copies: NNJ

1178. Prayers of the Jewish advance/by Abraham Cronbach. — New York: Bloch, 1924.

vii, 135 p. Includes: Prayers of the Jewish advance — The confirmation service — Miscellaneous prayers. Copies: CLJ DLC FU MH MWalA NN OCH OCl

1179. Sabbath evening service for the synagogue: arranged according to the Union prayer book/Gottfried H. Federlein. — 2nd ed. — New York: Bloch, 1924, c1919.

Score (24 p.) English and romanized Hebrew. For chorus (SATB) and organ accompaniment. Copies: OCH PPGratz

1180. The Sabbath evening service for the synagogue, according to the Union prayer book/by Franklin Pierce Fisk. — 2nd ed. — New York: Bloch, 1924, c1917.

Score (22 p.) English and romanized Hebrew. At head of title: To Rabbi H. Mayer and the Temple Sisterhood of Congregation B'nai Jehudah, Kansas City, Mo. Copies: PPGratz

1181. The Sabbath evening service for the synagogue. No. 2.: according to the Union prayer book/by Franklin Pierce Fisk. — 2nd ed. — New York: Bloch, 1924.

Score (23 p.) English and romanized Hebrew. Copies: DLC PPGratz (Music)

1182. Sabbath music: complete evening and morning service, according to the Union prayer book: for soprano, alto, tenor and bass, with organ accompaniment. Book II./S. Schlesinger. — 4th ed. — New York: Bloch, 1924.

Score (52 p.) English and romanized Hebrew. Copies: CU NN

1183. Sefer anim zemiroth: musical service for the New Year according the [sic] Union prayer book for Jewish worship/ Edward Josef Stark. — 2nd ed. — New York: Bloch, 1924, c1910.

Score (120 p.) English and romanized Hebrew. Copies: CLJ DLC NNJ

1184. Service for Sabbath eve and Sabbath morning: arranged for the use of Jewish camps/ by Barnett A. Elzas. — New York: Behrman, 1924.

36 p. English and Hebrew. Copies: NN

1185. Set me as a seal upon Thy heart (Song of Songs 8: 6–7): wedding song/ by A. Z. Idelsohn. — [New York?: s.n.], 1924.

Score (7 p.) For 1 voice, with piano accompaniment. Sendrey: 7449. Copies: IC NN-Br

1186. Synagogue service for Friday evening in E♭ Major: based on the ancient Pentateuchal mode utilizing the mode of Mogen avos/ by Abraham Zevi Idelsohn. — New York: National Council of Jewish Women, 1924.

Score (54 p.) English and romanized Hebrew. For Cantor and chorus (SATB) Sendrey: 5922. Copies: ABS CL MoSW NNJ OCH OCl PPGratz

1187. Synagogue service for Friday evening in F Major: based on the Ashkenazic mode of Adonoy moloch utilizing the mode of Mogen ovos/ by Abraham Z. Idelsohn. — New York: National Council of Jewish Women, 1924.

Score (43 p.) English and romanized Hebrew. For Cantor and chorus (SATB) Sendrey: 5923. Copies: CL ICACMu KyLoS NN-Br NNJ OCH PPGratz (Music)

1188. Synagogue service for Sabbath morning in E♭ Major: based on Psalm mode in major utilizing the mode of Ahavah rabba/ by Abraham Zevi Idelsohn. — Chicago: Sinai Congregation of Chicago, 1924.

Score (71 p.) English and romanized Hebrew. For Cantor and chorus (SATB). Sendrey: 5924. Copies: CL NN-Br NNJ OCH PPGratz (Music)

1189. Synagogue songs: personal, social, national: for synagogue and extra-congregational services/ compiled and edited by James Waterman Wise. — New York: [s.n.], 1924.

42 p. Includes music. English and Hebrew. Sendrey: 7005. Copies: CLJ CoDU InI MnU OCH PPGratz (Music)

1190. Temple service for Sabbath morning: arranged according to the Union prayer book/ by Rosalie Houseman; organ part edited by Wm. Carl. — New York: Bloch, 1924.

Score (36 p.) English and romanized Hebrew. For Cantor and chorus (SATB), with organ accompaniment. Sendrey: 5919. Copies: NBu NNJ OCH PPGratz (Music) RPB

1191. ברכת המזון עם סדר הברכות = Grace after meals: blessings for various occasions. — New York: North American Book Co., 1924.

59 p. English and Hebrew. Copies: NcU

1192. ושמרו = V, Schomru: a Sabbath eve prayer: for solo and piano accompaniment/ composed by Zavel Zilberts. — New York: Z. Zilberts, c1924.

Score (5 p.) Copies: PPGratz (Music)

1193. מזמור שיר חנוכת = Mismor schir chanukas: Psalm 30: cantata specially composed for the Cantors' Ass'n of American for their annual concert, February 15, 1925 / by Zavel Zilberts. — New York: Jewish Ministers' and Cantors' Ass'n of America, c1924.

    Score (36 p.) English and romanized Hebrew. For chorus (SATB). Sendrey: 6909. Copies: NNHeb NNJ PPGratz (Music)

1194. ממקומך = Mimkomcho / by Zavel Zilberts. — New York: J. P. Katz, c1924.

    Score (7 p.) Romanized Hebrew. Sendrey: 6481. Copies: NN OCH PPGratz (Music)

1195. סדור שפתי צדיקים...כמנהג ק״ק ספרדים...כאשר נדפס על ידי...דוד בן אהרן די סולה והגיה והמעתיק יצחק ליסר: ועתה נדפס בתוספות חדשות מועילות/מאת בנימין ארטום ראש ק״ק הספרדים בבריטאניא: והכל מסודר תחת השגחת הרב הנ״ל על ידי אברהם בן דוד די סולה, דורש טוב לעמו בק״ק שארית ישראל בעיר מנטריאל. — פילאדילפיא: שרמן, בשנת תרפ״ה-תרפ״ו.

The form of prayers according to the custom of the Spanish and Portuguese Jews: new edition based on the versions of D. A. De Sola and Isaac Leeser / edited and revised by Abraham De Sola, Minister of the Portuguese Congregation, Montreal ... printed with the authority of Benjamin Artom, Chief Rabbi of the Spanish and Portuguese congregations of England. — Philadelphia: Sherman, 5685–5686 [1924 or 1925–1925 or 1926].

    5 v. English and Hebrew. Copies: MWalA MWalB (V.2) NNJ PPAnR PPGratz

1196. סדור תפארת יהודה: נוסח אשכנז: כולל כל תפלות ישראל וכל הברכות לכל השנה: נדפס באותיות גדולות.../מסודר ומוגה על ידי א. היימאן חרלף. — ניו יארק: היברו פאב. קא. — New York, 1924.

    560 p. Copies: MH OCH

1197. סדר כל תפלות השנה = Magil's complete linear prayers for the whole year: translated in the new linear system with notes and original engravings for the synagogue, the home, and the school. — 14th improved ed. — Philadelphia: Translated and published by J. Magil, 1924–תרפ״ד, c1905.

    2 v. in 1. English and Hebrew. Copies: NNJ

1198. סדר תפלות כל השנה = The standard prayer book: authorized English translation / by S. Singer. — Enl. American ed., 44th thousand — New York: Bloch, 1924, c1915.

    469, 470 p. English and Hebrew. Copies: NNJ OCH

1199. סדר תפלות כל השנה כמנהג פולין: מוגה ומדויק היטב ומתרגם ללשון אנגלאיש/על ידי שמעון בן יהודה סינגער בהסכמת נתן אדלר הכהן. — הוצאת אמריקנית. תרפ״ה = The authorized daily prayer book of the United Hebrew Congregations of the British empire: with a new translation / by S. Singer; published under the sanction of the late chief Rabbi Nathan Marcus Adler. — London: Eyre and Spottiswoode; New York: Hebrew Pub. Co., 5685–1924.

    viii, 329, 329 p. English and Hebrew. Copies: MWalA

1200. סדר תפלות ישראל = The Union prayer-book for Jewish worship / edited and published by the Central Conference of American Rabbis. — Rev. ed. — Cincinnati: [CCAR], 1924, c1922.

    2 v. English and Hebrew. Pt. I. Services for the Sabbath, Services for the Three Festivals, Services for week days. — Pt. II. Services for the New Year, Services for the Day of Atonement. Copies: MH OCH (V.1) PPGratz (V.2)

1201. סדר תפלות ישראל = The Union prayer-book for Jewish worship. Pt. II. Services for the New Year, Services for the Day of Atonement/edited and published by the Central Conference of American Rabbis. — Rev. ed. — Cincinnati: CCAR; Philadelphia: Conat Press, 1924, c 1922.

370 p. English and Hebrew. Copies: OCH (V.2)

1202. סדר תפלות לשבת ויום טוב: ונוספו עליו לקוטי מזמורים למוצאי שבת/מוגה ומסודר על ידי א. היימאן (חרלפ). — New York: Hebrew Pub. Co., 1924.

319, 31 p. Copies: CLU

1203. סדר תפלות מכל השנה: מוגה ומדויק היטב ומתורגם ללשון אנגלית/על ידי א. טה. פיליפס = Daily prayers with a revised English translation/by A.Th. Philips. — New York: Hebrew Pub. Co., 1924.

705 p. English and Hebrew. Copies: CLJ MH OCH

1204. עבודת ישראל = A prayer book for the services of the year at the synagogue/arranged by Benjamin Szold and Marcus Jastrow; English translation by Marcus Jastrow. — Rev. ed of the translation. — Philadelphia: [s.n.], 1924, c 1907.

2 v. English and Hebrew. Part 1. Sabbaths, Festivals and week days. — Part 2. Services for the New Year and Day of Atonement. Slip inserted: This edition differs from the regular edition of Abodath Israel by the insertion of prayers and responsive readings prepared for Congregation Ohabei Shalom, Boston, Mass. by M. M. Eichler. Copies: MWalA (V.2) NNJ

1205. על חטא = For the sin/music by Pinchos Jassinowsky. — New York: Renanah Music Co., 1924.

Score (7 p.) English and Yiddish. For voice, with piano accompaniment. Copies: MH-Mu

1206. שירי תפלה = Recitativen für Kantor/komponirt fon Kantor Simon Zemachson. — New York: S. Zemachson, c 1924–1926.

Score (2 v., i.e. 50, 96 p.) Romanized Hebrew. For 1 voice. Pt. 1. Kobolos Shabbos Umariv. — Pt. 2. Morning service for the Sabbath and Festivals. Sendrey: 6600–6601. Copies: NN NNHeb (V.1) NNJ NNYI (V.2)

1207. תפלה לבית אבל = Evening service for the house of mourning: arranged for the use of the Congregation B'nai Jeshurun/Joseph Mayer Asher, Rabbi of the Congregation. — 2nd ed. — New York: P. Cowen, 5684–1924.

59 p. English and Hebrew. Copies: MWalA NNJ

1208. תפלת אליהו = Tefilas Eliyohu: cantorial recitatives for the Sabbath/E. Shnipelisky. — New York: Metro Music Co., c 1924.

Score (46 p.) Romanized Hebrew. For Cantor. Sendrey: 6566. Copies: MH-Mu PPGratz (Music)

1925

1209. Camp services for Jewish worship. — Cincinnati: Central Conference of American Rabbis, 1925.

20 p. Services compiled by Edward N. Calisch. Copies: NN

1210. Dedication of Temple Israel: September 13, 1925, Ellul 24th 5685. — Wilkes Barre, Pa.: [Temple Israel], 1925.

p. Copies: NNJ (Lost?)

1211. Dedication service of the new synagogue and Community Center of

Congregation Bnai Jeshurun of Philadelphia: September 10–13, 1925. — Philadelphia: [Bnai Jeshurun], 1925.

34, 8, 8 p. English and Hebrew. Copies: OCH

1212. Dedication services of the third Temple and first Community Centre of Congregation Beth Israel of Houston. — [Houston, Tex.]: Beth Israel, 1925.

[8] p. Copies: OCH

1213. Guide for the arrangement of young people's Friday evening service/compiled by the Religious Observance Committee of the Young People's League of the United Synagogue of America. — New York: United Synagogue of America, 1925.

16 p. Copies: OCH

1214. Music for the Sabbath evening service of the Temple: according to the Union prayer-book. Vol. II/by James H. Rogers. — New York: Behrman's Jewish Book-Shop, c1925.

Score (26 p.) Romanized Hebrew. For chorus (SATB), with organ accompaniment. Sendrey: 5950. Copies: PPGratz (Music)

1215. Prayers in the home for Jewish parents and children. — Mount Vernon, N.Y.: Distributed by the Religious School of Sinai Temple, 1925.

8 p. Arranged by J. I. Gorfinkle. Copies: OCH

1216. Prayers offered at the daily sessions of the Assembly/Rudolph I. Coffee, Rabbi, Temple Sinai, Oakland, California, Chaplain. — Sacramento, Ca.: California State Printing Office, 1925.

77 p. At head of title: California Legislature. Firty-sixth session, 1925. Cover title: Assembly prayers, 1925. Copies:

DLC WJHC (Collection of Temple Sinai, Oakland Ca. 67/53)

1217. Sabbath evening services: arranged for the South Shore Temple, The Chicago Free Synagog/by G. George Fox. — Chicago, Ill.: [s.n.], 1925.

47, 1 p. English and Hebrew. Presented to the Congregation by Reuben B. Horwish. — t.p. verso. Copies: CLHU CU NNHeb OCH

1218. Ten choice Hebrew song classics (traditional) for voice and pianoforte/compiled and edited by E. Kartschmaroff. — New York: E. B. Marks Music, c1925.

Score (32 p.) Romanized Hebrew. For voice, with piano accompaniment. Kol nidre — Chad gadya — Olenu — Adir hu — Yigdal Elohim — En Kelohenu — Shir hama'alos — L'Dowid boruch — Mooz tsur y'shuosi — Owinu malkenu. Copies: OCH

1219. Unesaneh toikef/Jacob L. Wasilkowsky. — New York: J. P. Katz, 1925.

Score (9 p.) Romanized Hebrew. For Cantor and chorus (SATB). Sendrey: 6584, 7149. Copies:

1220. V'shom'ru: traditional melody arranged for mixed choir and Cantor/Gottfried Heinrich Federlein. — New York: G. Schirmer, 1925.

Score (4 p.) Romanized Hebrew. For Cantor and chorus (SATB). Sendrey: 7038. Copies:

1221. אז ישיר = Oz joshir: contata: solo and male quartette, organ or piano accompaniment/Joseph M. Rumshinsky. — [New York]: Jewish Ministers' Cantors Association of America, 1925.

Score (45 p.). Copies: CLJ

1925

1222. ברכת כהנים = Bircath Kohanim (The Priestly benediction) for Sabbath and festive occasions: for Cantor and chorus/by Gershon Ephros.— New York: Bloch, 1925.

    Score (4 p.) Romanized Hebrew. For Cantor and chorus (SATB). Copies: NN

1223. ברכת כהנים/פנחס יאסינאווסקי = The blessing of the Priests: a prayer in Hebrew/music by Pinchos Jassinowsky.— New York: Renanah Music Co., c1925.

    Score (6 p.) Romanized Hebrew. English and Hebrew words precede music. For voice, with piano accompaniment. Copies: MH-Mu NN OCH

1224. ברכת כהנים/פנחס יאסינאווסקי. = The blessing of the Priests: a prayer in Hebrew/music by Pinchos Jassinowsky. — New York: [s.n.], c1925.

    Score (1 p.) Romanized Hebrew. For voice, with violin accompaniment. Copies: MH-Mu

1225. זמירות ותשבחות לליל שבת = Song and praise for Sabbath eve: for use at synagogue gatherings in connection with the late Friday evening sermon or discourse/arranged by Israel Goldfarb and Israel Herbert Levinthal. — 3rd rev. ed. — Brooklyn: [s.n.], 1925, c1920.

    Score (76 p.) English, Hebrew and romanized Hebrew. Copies: NN PPGratz

1226. זמירות ותשבחות לליל שבת = Song and praise for Sabbath eve: for use at synagogue gatherings in connection with the late Friday evening sermon or discourse/arranged by Israel Goldfarb and Israel Herbert Levinthal. — 3rd rev. ed. — Brooklyn: [s.n.], 1925, c1920.

    Score (120 p.) English, Hebrew and romanized Hebrew. Sendrey: 6956. Copies: NN PPGratz

1227. מחזור...עם תרגום אנגלית/מוגה ומדויק היטב על ידי יעקב בן יצחק דעויס ונפתלי בן מרדכי אדלר הכהן: נדפס כפי הוצאת לאנדאן. — ניו יארק: היברו פאב. קא., תרפ"ו = Service of the synagogue...: a new edition of the Festival prayers with an English translation in prose and verse: reprinted from the latest and best London edition. — New York: Hebrew Pub. Co., 1925.

    2 v. English and Hebrew. V.1. New Year. —V.2. Day of Atonement. Copies: MH

1228. מחזור לראש השנה = Form of the prayer for the Feast of New-Year, according to the custom of German and Polish Jews: with an English translation/carefully revised by Samuel Summer. — Vienna: J. Schlessinger; New York: North American Book Co., 1925.

    199, 260 (i.e. 160), 20 p. English and Hebrew. Copies: CNoS

1229. מחזור לראש השנה = The standard machsor for New Year/edited by Barnett A. Elzas. — New York: [s.n.], 1925.

    341, 341 p. English and Hebrew. Copies: PPAnR

1230. המנגן = The Jewish songster: music for voice and piano/edited by Israel Goldfarb and Samuel Goldfarb. — 4th rev. ed. — Brooklyn, N.Y.: Religious Schools of Congregation Beth Israel Anshe Emes, 1925.

    Score (221 p.) English and romanized Hebrew. Sendrey: 6954. Copies: GeU PPGratz (Music) TxU

1231. סדור חנוך תפלה: כולל תפלות לכל השנה...: נוסח ספרד...: נדפס באותיות גדולות מאד...גם נלוה אליו סדר אלפא ביתא בצירוף הנקודות עם חנוכים לנסיון... — New York: Hebrew Pub. Co., 1925.

    280 p. Copies: OCH

1232. סדור חנוך תפלה: עם חנוך לנער וכללי הדקדוק: כולל תפלות לכל השנה באותיות גדולות מאד: נוסח אשכנז. — New York: Hebrew Pub. Co., 1925.

1 v. (various pagings). Copies: CLU OCH

1233. סדור שפת אמת/מאת ואלף בר שמשון דוב איש היידנהיים = Daily prayers with English instructions — 1st new rev. ed. as correct as any ed. ever published in רעדעלהיים — New York: Hebrew Pub. Co., 1925–תרפ״ה.

293 p. Hebrew with English instructions. Copies: NNJ

1234. סדר תפלות ישראל = The Union prayer-book for Jewish worship/edited and published by the Central Conference of American Rabbis. — Rev. ed. — Cincinnati: CCAR, 1925, c1922–1924.

2 v. English and Hebrew. Pt. I. Services for the Sabbath, Services for the Three Festivals, Services for week days. — Pt. II. Services for the New Year, Services for the Day of Atonement. Copies: OCH

1235. סדר תפלות לשבת ויום טוב: עם דגושים ומתגים ועם ציונים לשוא-נע וסמני הפסקה/ מוגה ומסודר על ידי א. היימאן (חדלפ) = Sabbath and holiday prayer book. — New York: Hebrew Pub. Co., c1925.

326 p. Copies: DLC (uncat) NNJ

1236. סדר תפלות לשבת ויום טוב: עם דגושים ומתגים ועם ציונים לשוא-נע וסמני הפסקה/ מוגה ומסודר על ידי א. היימאן (חדלפ); ומתורגם ללשון אנגלית על ידי שמעון בן יהודה סינגער = Conservative Sabbath and holiday prayer book: English translation from S. Singer's Daily prayer book. — New York: Hebrew Pub. Co., c1925.

326, 325 p. English and Hebrew. Spine title: Sabbath and holiday prayers. Copies: DLC FU MH NjP NNHeb NNJ

1237. סדר תפלת ישראל כמנהג ספרד ... באותיות גדולות מאירות עינים. — New York: Hebrew Pub. Co., 1925.

1 v. (various pagings). Copies: OCH

1238. עבדת שבת = Sabbath prayers: a complete ritual for Sabbath eve, Sabbath morning, Sabbath afternoon. — 2nd ed. — New York: Bloch, 1925, c1922.

167, 167, 168–179 p. English and Hebrew. Copies: MWalA NNJ

1239. עבודת ישראל = A prayer book for the services of the year at the synagogue/ arranged by Benjamin Szold and Marcus Jastrow; English translation by Marcus Jastrow. — Rev. ed of the translation. — Philadelphia: [s.n.], 1925.

2 v. English and Hebrew. Part 1. Services for the year. — Part 2. Services for the New Year and Day of Atonement. Copies: MWalA MWalB

1240. תפלות ישראל לשבת ושלש רגלים = Prayers of Israel for the Sabbath and the Festivals: arranged and revised with the latest English translation, and responsive readings/by Jacob Bosniak, Rabbi, Ocean Parkway Jewish Center, Tifereth Israel, First Congregation of Kensington, Brooklyn, N.Y. — Brooklyn, N.Y.: Prayer Book Pub. Co., c1925.

124, 141 p. English and Hebrew. Copies: CLHU CLJ DLC MH MWalA NN NNJ PPGratz

No Date

1241. Additional responses for Sabbath eve service: as sung at Touro Synagogue, New Orleans, La./composed by F. Dunkley. — [New Orleans: Cable Co.?, n.d.]

Score (p.) English and romanized Hebrew. Sendrey: 6113. Copies:

1242. Adon olam/Ferdinand Dunkley. — New York: G. Schirmer, [n.d.]

Score (p.). Sendrey: 7030. Copies:

1243. Adonoy moh adom = O Lord! what is man: memorial anthem after a Hebrew melody of [Adolf] Grünzweig/William Sparger. — [New York: s.n., n.d.]

Score (8 p.) For alto or bass solo and chorus (SATB), with organ accompaniment. Sendrey: 7473. Copies:

1244. Chanukah service for Sabbath schools/arranged by William Rosenau and Alois Kaiser, of Temple Oheb Shalom, Baltimore, Md. — [Baltimore: Oheb Shalom, n.d.]

7 p. English and Hebrew. Copies: OCH

1245. Evening service for the New Year and Day of Atonement/M. Goldstein. — Cincinnati: Bloch, [n.d.]

Score (8 p.) English and romanized Hebrew. For Cantor and chorus (SATB). Sendrey: 5901. Copies:

1246. Jewish hymns for Jewish schools/arranged by H. Pereira Mendes. — New York: Masliansky Press, [n.d.]

20 p. Hebrew educational series; No. 4. Copies: MWalA OCH

1247. Memorial service: responsive readings, songs and hymns: arranged for use in religious services of Congregation B'nai Jeshurun. — [New York: B'nai Jeshurun, n.d.]

40 p. English and Hebrew. Copies: NNHeb NNJ

1248. Memorial service for the Day of Atonement, according to the Union prayer book: for 4 voices and organ accompaniment/S. Schlesinger. — [New York?: s.n., n.d.]

Score (1, 15 p.) For chorus (SATB), with organ accompaniment. Copies: DLC

1249. Morning service for the Temple Beth-El School of Buffalo/by Jacob Henry Landau. — Buffalo, N.Y.: [s.n., n.d.]

8 p. English and romanized Hebrew. Copies: OCH

1250. O day of God = Kol nidre: for solo voice, with brief four-voice choir and piano or organ a accompaniment/William Sparger and Alois Kaiser. — New York: Bloch, [n.d.]

Score (4 p.). Sendrey: 7137, 7189. Copies:

1251. Responses adapted for New Year and Atonement Eve: Borchu, Sh'ma, Boruch shem, Michomocho, Hapores, Tiku ki wayom/Fred. E. Kitziger. — New York: Bloch, [n.d.]

Score (p.) English and romanized Hebrew. For chorus (SATB), with organ accompaniment. Sendrey: 6222. Copies:

1252. Ritual for Friday evening service in the Temple Emanu-El of San Francisco. — [San Francisco: s.n., n.d.]

44 p. Copies: CU-SB NN

1253. Ritual for Friday evening service in the Temple Emanu-El of San Francisco. — [San Francisco: s.n., n.d.]

12 p. Copies: CU

1254. Sabbath song: How sweet upon this sacred day/composed by S. Hecht; arranged by M. Z. Tinker. — Cincinnati: Bloch, [n.d.]

Score (6 p.) For soli and chorus (SATB), with piano accompaniment. Sendrey: 6170. Copies:

1255. ברכת המזון עם סדר הברכות = Grace and blessings for various occasions:

No Date

Hebrew and English. — New York: Hebrew Pub. Co., [n.d.]

63 p. English and Hebrew. Copies: DLC (uncat)

1256. הזכרת נשמות = Complete memorial service for solo, mixed chorus with organ accompaniment/Gedaliah Rabinowitz. — New York: Bloch, [n.d.]

Score (23 p.) For Cantor and chorus (SATB), with organ accompaniment. Copies: PPGratz

1257. מחזור... עם תרגום אנגלי/מוגה ומדויק היטב על ידי יעקב בן יצחק דעויס ונפתלי בן מרדכי אדלר הכהן: נדפס כפי הוצאת לונדון = Service of the synagogue... : a new edition of the Festival prayers with an English translation: reprinted from the latest and best London edition. — New York: Hebrew Pub. Co., [n.d.]

2 v. English and Hebrew. V.1. New Year. — V.2. Day of Atonement. Copies: DeWi MB MH (V.1) MiGrC MnDUStS MoS NNJ OrPWB PPL (V.1) ViRuT

1258. מחזור החדש לראש השנה ויום הכפורים נוסח ספרד: באותיות גדולות כל התפלות על מקומן כסדרן. — ניו יארק: היברו פאב. קא., [n.d.].

361, 322 p. Copies: PPGratz

1259. מחזור כל בו: עם פירוש עברי טייטש בשם בית ישראל וילקוט פנינים ומעשה אלפס... : נוסח אשכנז. — ניו-יארק: היברו פאב. קא., [n.d.].

5 v. Hebrew and Yiddish. V.1 ראש השנה — V.2. יום כפור — V.3. סכות — V.4 פסח — V.5 שבועות. Copies: CLHU CLJ (V.1) DLC (V.2, uncat) MWalA (V.2,5) PPGratz

1260. מחזור כל בו: עם פירוש עברי טייטש בשם בית ישראל וילקוט פנינים ומעשה אלפס... : נוסח ספרד. — ניו-יארק: היברו פאב. קא., [n.d.].

5 v. Hebrew and Yiddish. V.1 ראש השנה — V.2. יום כפור — V.3. סכות — V.4 פסח — V.5 שבועות. Copies: CLHU (V.1) MH (V.2) MWalA (V.4,5) NNJ

1261. מחזור לראש השנה ויום הכפורים: נוסח ספרד: עם ביאורים בית לוי, מטה לוי ושם הכולל מהבאורים קרבן אהרן/חברם אהרן בהרב... יחיאל מיכל אב"ד דמיכיילישאק, עם העתקת בלשון יהודית אשכנזית עברי טייטש... — ניו-יארק: היברו פאב. קא., [n.d.].

400 p. Hebrew and Yiddish. Cover title: מחזור קרבן אהרן לקוטי צבי. Copies: MWalA

1262. א נייע ש"ס תחנה: פיר און אכציג פערשידענע נייטיגע תחינות פיר אגאנץ יאהר: מיט גרויסע ווערטער און אלעס כסדר. — Brooklyn: Hebrew Pub. Co., [n.d]

160 p. Hebrew and Yiddish. Copies: MH MWalA

1263. א נייע ש"ס תחנה: פיר און אכציג פערשידענע נייטיגע תחינות פיר אגאנץ יאהר: מיט גרויסע ווערטער און אלעס כסדר. — New York: Hebrew Pub. Co., [n.d.]

160 p. Hebrew and Yiddish. Copies: MH OCH

1264. א נייע ש"ס תחנה רב פנינים: איין און ניינציג פערשיעדענע תחינות פיר א גאנץ יאהר... אזיך סגולות נפלאות... — New York: L. Flohr, [n.d.]

156 p. Yiddish. Copies: OCH

1265. א נייע ש"ס תחנה רב פנינים: איין און ניינציג פערשיעדענע תחינות פיר א גאנץ יאהר... מיט גרויסע ווערטער און אלעס כסדר. — Brooklyn: A. Flohr, [n.d.]

150 p. Yiddish. Copies: DLC

1266. סדור בית ישראל עברי-טייטש: כולל סדר התפלות לכל ימות השנה עם ילקוט פנינים יקרים ומעשה אלפס: יכיל שלשים ושנים באורים יקרים: נוסח אשכנז. — New York: Hebrew Pub. Co., [n.d.]

1267. סדור בית ישראל עברי-טייטש: כולל סדר התפלות לכל ימות השנה עם ילקוט פנינים יקרים ומעשה אלפס: יכיל שלשים ושנים אורים יקרים: נוסח ספרד.
— New York: Hebrew Pub. Co., [n.d]

514, 34, 547–590 p. Hebrew and Yiddish. Copies: CLHU CLJ

1268. סדור האריז״ל: כולל תפלות לכל השנה... ועוד הוספנו ברכות ראשונות ואחרונות בכל תפלה על מקומה... באותיות מאירות עינים.
— New York: Hebrew Pub. Co., [n.d.]

128 p. Copies: NNYI

1269. סדור קרבן מנחה: נוסח אשכנז עם ... תחנות רבות ... כלם נעתקו בעברי-טייטש. — ניו-יארק: היברו פאב. קא. [n.d.]

615 p. Hebrew and Yiddish. Copies: NNYI

1270. סדור שפת אמת/מאת וואלף בר שמשון דוב איש היידנהיים =
Daily prayers with English instructions — 1st new rev. ed. as correct as any ed. ever published in רעדעלהיים — New York: Hebrew Pub. Co., [n.d.]

293 p. Hebrew with English instructions. Copies: OCH

1271. סדר סליחות לימים נוראים כמנהג אשכנז: נדפס מחדש בסדר נכון ... ובאותיות גדולות ויפות ... וגם הוספנו לתועלת ההמונים ונשים העתקת לשון אשכנזי ... המכונה עברי טייטש באותיות מרובעות ובנקודות. — ברוקלין: היברו פאב. קא. [n.d.]

162 p. Hebrew and Yiddish. Copies: NNHeb OCH

592, 232, 88 p. Some copies bound with: ספר תהלים עם מעמדות.(Entry 1283). Copies: Separate: Jewish Community Library of Los Angeles With ספר תהלים: MWalA NNHeb NNYI

1272. סדר קינות לתשעה באב: קינה היא וקוננה עם ישורון ...
— New York: L. Flohr, [n.d.]

62 p. Copies: OCH

1273. סדר קינות לתשעה באב: קינה היא וקוננה עם ישורון בדמעה שליש לחרבות בכי על חורבן בית המקדש ועל גלות בבל ...
— New York: Hebrew Pub. Co., [n.d.]

62 p. Copies: MH NNJ NNYI

1274. סדר קינות לתשעה באב: קינה היא וקוננה עם ישורון, וכל בית ישראל יבכו את שרפת בית מקדשנו אשר שרף ה׳: גם האבין מיר איבער גיזעצט אויף עברי-טייטש.
— New York: Hebrew Pub. Co., [n.d.]

161 p. Hebrew and Yiddish. Copies: CLHU (uncat) DLC (uncat) MWalA NNJ

1275. סדר קינות לתשעה באב: קינה היא וקוננה עם ישורון, וכל בית ישראל יבכו את שרפת בית מקדשנו אשר שרף ה׳: גם האבין מיר איבער גיזעצט אויף עברי-טייטש. — ברוקלין: היברו פאב. קא. [n.d.]

161 p. Hebrew and Yiddish. Copies: DLC (uncat) MH NNHeb

1276. סדר תפלות ובקשות על החולה ר״ל ומקשה לילד ר״ל וספר מעבר יבק: כולל ספר הוידוי לחולה, עניני המיתה, הטהרה והקבורה. — נו-יארק: בהוצאת מנורה רעלידזיס סופפלי קא.
— New York: Menorah Religious Supply Co., [n.d.]

32 p. Hebrew with Yiddish instructions. Copies: DLC (uncat) ספר מעבר יבק by Aaron Berechiah ben Moses

1277. סדר תפלות לכל השנה: נוסח אשכנז מתורגם אשכנזית. — פילאדעלפיא.
= Tägliche Gebete. [s.n., n.d.]

29, 462, 10 p. German and Hebrew. Deinard 954. Copies: DSI MH

No Date

1278. סדר תפלת ישראל כמנהג אשכנז: כולל תפלות מכל השנה... באותיות גדולות מאירות עינים.
— New York: Hebrew Pub. Co., [n.d.]

1 v. (various pagings). Copies: OCH

1279. סידור ברכות והודאות: נוסח אשכנז: עם דרך החיים הוא אסיפת דינים השייכים לסדר תפילה... — נויארק: היברו פאב. קא., [n.d.]

1 v. (various pagings). Commentary attributed to Jacob ben Jacob Moses, of Lissa. Bound with: סדר תהלים עם מעמדות (Entry 1283). Copies: DLC (uncat) MH OCH

1280. סידור חנוך תפלה: עם אלפא ביתא וגם גדול בנים. — נויארק: פֿארלאג אייראפישע ספרים האנדלינג קא., [n.d.].

144 p. Hebrew and Russian. Deinard: 960. Copies:

1281. סידור קרבן מנחה: נוסח אשכנז עם ... תחנות רבות... כלם נעתקו בעברי־טייטש. — ברוקלין: היברו פאב. קא., [n.d.]

615 p. Hebrew and Yiddish. Copies: MH MWalA OCH

1282. סליחות לימים נוראים: כמנהג אשכנז, ליטא, זאמוט ורייסין... גם... הסליחות ליום ט״ו כסלו, וגם התפלה על בית עלמין אשר הוחק לבני החברה קדישא גחש״א. — נויארק: א. פלאר, [n.d.]

48 p. Copies: NNYI

1283. ספר תהלים עם מעמדות... — ניו יארק: היברו פאב. קא. [n.d.]

234, 88 p. Hebrew and Yiddish. Found separate and bound with: סדור בית ישראל עברי־טייטש (Entry 898, 1266). Also bound with: סדור קרבן מנחה (Entry 927, 1104–1105). Also bound with: סידור ברכות והודאות (Entry 1279). Copies: Separate: DLC. With: סדור בית ישראל עברי־טייטש: MWalA NNHeb NNYI OCH With: סדור קרבן מנחה: MWalA With: סידור ברכות והודאות: MH

1283a. ספר מעבר יבק: כולל תפלות ותחנונים שיתפלל החולה בעד עצמו והתפלות המבקרים בעדו ותפלות לבני חברא קדישא: מיט עברי־טייטש/מסודר על ידי מ. שטרן. — ניו יארק: ההיברו פאב. קא., [19–]

128 p. Hebrew and Yiddish. Compiled by Aaron Berechiah ben Moses. Copies DLC

1284. קהלת/י.ל. פרץ. — ניו יארק: ארויסגעגעבן פֿון דער ״מארגען־פֿריידהייט״ מיט דער דערלויבעניש פֿון קלעצקין פֿארלאג, פוילן. [n.d.]

187 p. Contents: — אסתר — קהלת אקדמות — חד גדיא. Copies: OCH

Geographical Index

Albany, N.Y., 21, 31, 50, 129, 381, 1069
Altoona, Pa., 993

Baltimore, Md., 76, 81, 100, 103–105, 125, 133, 147, 150, 153, 164, 185, 193–195, 207, 211, 217–222, 226, 235, 240, 242–243, 250, 252, 262–263, 270, 274, 296, 312, 317, 343, 367–368, 401, 410, 455–458, 474, 552, 643, 652, 706, 749, 777, 816, 871, 906, 971, 1094, 1244
Berlin, Germany, 91–92
Boston, Mass., 15, 328, 547, 620–621, 623, 629, 831–832, 866, 868, 888, 920, 946, 1036–1037, 1204
British empire, see Great Britain
Brooklyn, N.Y., 99, 176, 233, 321, 344, 416, 523, 605–607, 625–627, 640, 685, 689, 702, 940, 959, 1029, 1053, 1064, 1070–1072, 1128, 1131, 1139, 1175, 1225–1226, 1230, 1240, 1262, 1271, 1275, 1281
Buffalo, N.Y., 130, 425, 1249

Cambridge, Mass., 14–16
Canada, 1
Charleston, S.C., 12, 20, 60, 86, 141, 152, 238, 261, 277, 952, 977
Chicago, Ill., 70, 96, 245, 248, 266, 290, 348, 358, 384, 389, 448, 455, 472–473, 477–480, 485–486, 490, 493–494, 496–498, 502–503, 505, 511, 518, 522, 526–527, 535, 590, 601, 631, 658, 660, 669, 683a, 732, 862, 911, 1087, 1090, 1188, 1217
Cincinnati, Ohio, 66, 69–70, 75, 102, 119–120, 142, 148, 154, 160, 163, 165, 180, 201–203, 223, 264, 266, 280, 339, 347, 354, 362–363, 370, 372, 376, 396, 402, 404, 407–408, 411, 421, 431–432, 435, 445, 451, 454, 468, 470–471, 473, 483, 502–503, 505, 512–513, 516, 524, 530, 548, 570, 592, 594, 632–633, 690–691, 712, 760, 775–776, 795, 813, 817, 837, 896, 950–951, 970, 976, 998, 1002, 1013–1014, 1027, 1065, 1078, 1108, 1135, 1152, 1163, 1165, 1177, 1200–1201, 1209, 1234, 1245, 1254
Cleveland, Ohio, 66, 69, 75, 114, 249, 261, 387, 492, 580, 773

Dallas, Tex., 557
Denver, Col., 431
Detroit, Mich., 156, 500–501, 636, 649

East Orange, N.J., 510
Egypt, 1043
El Paso, Tex., 1066
Elmira, N.Y., 1003
England, see Great Britain
Evansville, Ind., 160, 230, 253

Great Britain, 257, 320, 902, 933, 1080, 1195, 1199
Greenville, Miss., 408, 451

Harlem, New York, N.Y., 307, 459, 520, 578, 598
Haverstraw, N.Y., 558
Helena, Mont., 442
Houston, Tex., 1212

Jerusalem, Israel, 1019

Kansas City, Mo., 328, 774, 1180
Kingston, Pa., 309

Little Rock, Ark., 432
London, England, 10, 323, 549, 714, 723, 742, 780, 797–798, 806, 842, 902, 922, 933, 979, 1074–1076, 1080, 1101, 1132, 1199, 1227, 1257
Long Branch, N.J., 642, 890, 893, 915, 999–1000
Los Angeles, Ca., 1088
Louisville, Ky., 157, 556, 758

Milwaukee, Wis., 184, 255, 314, 323, 325, 369
Mobile, Ala. 561, 948
Montgomery, Ala., 615
Montréal, Québec, Canada, 257, 346, 432, 633, 1195
Mount Vernon, N.Y., 1215

New Haven, Conn., 57, 169, 759
New Orleans, La., 35, 38, 56, 72, 287, 315–316, 373, 422, 446, 466, 488, 532–533, 564, 710, 1118, 1241
New Rochelle, N.Y., 1155
New York, N.Y., 1–5, 8–11, 13, 19, 21–22, 27–28, 31–34, 36–37, 39–44, 47–49, 52–55, 57–58, 61–65, 74, 77–80, 82–85, 89, 91–95, 98–99, 106, 108–109, 111, 113, 115, 117–118, 122–124, 126–128, 131, 134–135, 137–140, 144–145, 149, 155, 158–159, 161–162, 166–170, 172–174, 176, 178–179, 182–183, 186, 188–192, 196–200, 204–206, 208–210, 212–213, 215–216, 224–225, 229, 231–232, 234, 237, 239, 241, 244, 247, 251, 254, 256, 258–259, 262–263, 265, 267–269, 272, 275–278, 281, 283–284, 286, 288, 291–295, 297–308, 310, 320, 324, 326–327, 329–330, 334–335, 340–342, 344–346, 349–353, 355–357, 359, 361, 364–366, 370, 374, 377–380, 382–383, 385–386, 388, 390, 392–395, 397–400, 403, 406, 412–415, 417–420, 423, 428–430, 433–434, 436–441, 443–444, 447, 449–450, 453, 459, 462, 467, 469, 471, 473, 481–482, 484, 489, 504, 506, 510, 514–515, 517, 519–521, 523, 528–531, 537–538, 540–544, 546, 549, 553–555, 558–560, 563, 565–568, 571, 573–579, 582–584, 589, 591, 593–602, 604, 608–610, 614, 617, 619, 624, 628, 630, 635, 637–638, 641–642, 646–647, 650–651, 657, 659, 661–662, 666–668, 670–672, 674, 676, 679, 684, 686–687, 692–697, 700–701, 703–705, 708, 711–714, 716–717, 719, 721–725, 727–729, 731, 733–736, 738–742, 745, 747–748, 751, 754, 757, 761, 765–772, 774, 778–792, 794, 796–806, 808–811, 815–816, 818–829, 833–835, 838–839, 842–854, 856–857, 859, 863–865, 867, 869–880, 882–884, 886–887, 889–905, 907, 909, 913–919, 918a, 918b, 921–937, 939, 941, 943–945, 949, 952–960, 962–966, 968–969, 972–975, 978–986, 992, 994–995, 997, 999–1001, 1004–1012, 1015–1021, 1023–1025, 1028–1034, 1038–1046, 1048–1049, 1051, 1054–1063, 1067–1068, 1069a, 1073–1077, 1079–1081, 1083, 1085–1086, 1089, 1091, 1093, 1096–1097, 1099, 1101–1106, 1109–1112, 1115–1117, 1119–1120, 1122–1123, 1127, 1129–1130, 1132–1134, 1136–1137, 1140–1145, 1147–1151, 1153–1154, 1156–1162, 1164, 1166–1169, 1171–1174, 1176, 1178–1187, 1189–1194, 1196, 1198–1199, 1202–1203, 1205–1208, 1213–1214, 1218–1224, 1227–1229, 1231–1233, 1235–1238, 1242–1243, 1246–1248, 1250–1251, 1255–1261, 1263–1264, 1266–1270, 1272–1274, 1276, 1278, 1280, 1282–1284, 1283a
Newark, N.J., 72a, 271, 452, 585, 751, 857, 966, 1083, 1115, 1172
Newton Centre, Mass., 331–332, 360, 409

Oakland, Ca., 803, 852, 1216

Paducah, Ky., 175, 279
Philadelphia, Pa., 7, 9, 17–18, 23–26, 30, 33, 45–46, 59, 67–68, 71, 73, 90, 101, 107, 112, 116, 121, 132, 136–137, 141, 143, 151, 171, 177, 194–195, 214, 218, 236, 240, 246, 257, 271, 289, 309, 311, 313, 333, 337–338, 371, 401, 426–427, 461, 463–465, 475–476, 491, 499, 508–509, 525, 532, 536, 550–551, 562, 581, 587, 622, 639, 653–656, 663–665, 673, 678, 680–683, 688, 698–699, 707, 709, 718, 720, 726, 730, 743–744, 746, 750, 752–753, 762, 764, 787, 807, 812, 836, 840–841, 855, 858, 881, 885, 908, 910, 938, 967, 987–991, 1022, 1035, 1047, 1050, 1082, 1092, 1095, 1098, 1107, 1113–

Geographical Index

1114, 1124–1126, 1138, 1146, 1165, 1170, 1195, 1197, 1201, 1204, 1211, 1239, 1277
Pittsburgh, Pa., 603, 611–613, 616, 634, 644–645, 860, 912, 942, 947, 1084, 1100
Poznan, Poland, 74
Prague, Czechoslovakia, 304
Providence, R.I., 715

Richmond, Va. 29, 487, 648, 830
Rochester, N.Y., 282, 319, 336, 424, 534, 756, 814, 961, 1121
Rödelheim, Germany, 85, 247, 265, 291, 300, 350, 364, 395, 414, 434, 627–628, 928, 1134, 1233, 1270
Russia, 669

Sacramento, Ca., 110, 460, 1216
Saint Louis, Mo., 375, 996, 1052
San Francisco, Ca., 51, 87, 97, 110, 146, 181, 187, 228, 273, 285, 295, 405, 495, 507, 539, 545, 572, 586, 588, 618, 675, 677, 737, 763, 793, 1026, 1252–1253
Savannah, Ga., 260, 318, 322, 450, 861
Spain, 553
Syracuse, N.Y., 61

Toledo, Ohio, 391
Toronto, Ontario, Canada, 244

United States, see also specific locales
United States, 5, 320, 668, 674, 694–695, 967, 988–991

Vienna, Austria, 1228
Vilnius, Lithuania, 568

Washington, D.C., 88, 569, 755
Wilkes-Barre, Pa., 309, 1210
Williamsburgh, Brooklyn, N.Y., 41

Hebrew

מצרים, ראה, Egypt
נו-יארק, ראה, New York, N.Y.
נוא-יארק, ראה, New York, N.Y.
נויארק, ראה, New York, N.Y.
נעוו-יארק, ראה, New York, N.Y.
פוזנא, ראה, Poznan, Poland
פילאדילפיא, ראה, Philadelphia, Pa.
פילאדעלפיא, ראה, Philadelphia, Pa.
צינציננאטי, ראה, Cincinnati, Ohio
קליוולאנד, ראה, Cleveland, Ohio
רעדעלהיים, ראה, Rödelheim, Germany

אלבני, ראה, Albany, N.Y.
בערלין, ראה, Berlin, Germany
ברוקלין, ראה, Brooklyn, N.Y.
ברטניא, ראה, Great Britain
ווילימסבארג, ראה, Williamsburgh, Brooklyn, N.Y.
ווילנא, ראה, Vilnius, Lithuania
ירושלים, ראה, Jerusalem, Israel
לאנדאן, ראה, London, England
לונדון, ראה, London, England
מאנטריאל, ראה, Montréal, Québec, Canada

Name Index

A.J.L., see Levi, Annie Josephine.
Aaron ben Jehiel Michael, ha-Levi, 626, 679, 739–741, 782–783, 957, 1054–1056, 1261
Aaron Berechiah ben Moses, 415, 1049, 1058, 1276, 1283a
Abels, Moses, J.S., see also Hebrew Reform Congregation (Altoona, Pa.)
Abels, Moses, J.S., 993
Adas Israel (Louisville, Ky.), 157, 758
Adath Israel (Louisville, Ky.), see Adas Israel (Louisville, Ky.)
Adath Jeshurun (Boston, Mass.), 920
Adath Jeshurun (New York, N.Y.), 131, 137, 168, 207, 568
Adath J'Shurun (New York, N.Y.), see Adath Jeshurun (New York, N.Y.)
Adath Jeshurun (Philadelphia, Pa.), 752, 837, 1095
Adereth El (New York, N.Y.), 111
Adler, Felix, 186
Adler, Herbert M., see also Service of the Synagogue=מחזור ... עם תרגום אנגלית Service of the Synagogue=מחזור עבדת אהל מועד
Adler, Herbert M., 723, 742, 780, 797–798, 820, 842, 921–922, 979, 1074–1076, 1101, 1132, 1227, 1257
Adler, Nathan Marcus, 902, 933, 1080, 1199
Adler, S. (Simon), see also Order of prayer for divine service=סדר תפלה
Adler, S. (Simon), 93, 108, 123–124, 173, 192, 216, 259, 276, 286, 294, 304, 351, 397, 449
Advisory Board of Jewish Ministers, 462
Aeolian Hall (New York, N.Y.), 949
Agudath Jeshorim (New York, N.Y.), 738
Ahabeth Achim (Cincinnati, Ohio), see also Sh'erith Israel-Ahabath Achim (Cincinnati, Ohio)
Ahabeth Achim (Cincinnati, Ohio), 548
Ahavath Chesed (New York, N.Y.), see Ahawath Chesed (New York, N.Y.)
Ahawath Chesed (New York, N.Y.), see also Ahawath Chesed-Shaar Hashomayim (New York, N.Y.)
Ahawath Chesed (New York, N.Y.), 167, 199, 204–205, 212, 225, 241, 306, 308, 366, 398, 467
Ahawath Chesed-Shaar Hashomayim (New York, N.Y.), see also Ahawath Chesed (New York, N.Y.)
Ahawath Chesed-Shaar Hashomayim (New York, N.Y.), see also Shaar-Hashomayim (New York, N.Y.)
Ahawath Chesed-Shaar Hashomayim (New York, N.Y.), 582, 835, 945
Alliance of Israel (New York, N.Y.), 1062
American Orthodox Jewish Youth, 1066
Ansche Chesed (New York, N.Y.), see Anshi Chesed (New York, N.Y.)
Anshe Emeth (Albany, N.Y.), see also Beth Emeth (Albany, N.Y.)
Anshe Emeth (Albany, N.Y.), 50
Anshe Temime Derekh, 417
Anshe Ma'ariv (Chicago, Ill.), 70
Anshi Chesed (New York, N.Y.), 161, 189–190, 213, 751
Artom, Benjamin, 257, 1195
Asher, Joseph Mayer, see also B'nai Jeshurun (New York, N.Y.)
Asher, Joseph Mayer, 666, 1207
Baltimore Hebrew Congregation (Baltimore, Md.), 474, 777, 1094
Bamberger, S., 805
Banner, Michael, 1140
Barnard, David, 41

Name Index

Barnes, Edward Shippen, 887
Baum, Solomon, *see also* הרנה והתפלה
Baum, Solomon, 686–687, 700, 727
Bayth Ahabah (Richmond, Va.), *see* Beth Ahabah (Richmond Va.)
Bazel, J. M., 912
Benai Israel (Sacramento, Ca.), *see* B'nai Israel (Sacramento, Ca.)
Bene Israel (Cincinnati, Ohio), 372, 445, 691
Bene Yeshurun (Cincinnati, Ohio), 142, 404, 690, 775–776
Benzion, J., 660
Berkowitz, Henry, *see also*
  Central Conference of American Rabbis. Committee on Personal Prayer. Kiddish, or Sabbath sentiment in the home.
Berkowitz, Henry, 278, 550–551, 812–813, 1092
Bernstein, S., 1128
Bertoni, Ferdinando, 24
Beth Ahabah (Richmond, Va.), 29, 487, 648, 830
Beth-El (Albany, N.Y.), 21, 129
Beth El (Detroit, Mich.), 636, 649
Beth El (New York, N.Y.), 62, 78–80, 281, 428, 440, 443–444, 447, 565, 584, 599, 670, 728
Beth-El Emeth (Philadelphia, Pa.), 67–68, 289
Beth-El School of Buffalo (Buffalo, N.Y.), 1249
Beth Elohim (Brooklyn, N.Y.), 99, 321
Beth Elohim (Charleston, S.C.), *see also* Reformed Society of Israelites (Charleston, S.C.)
Beth Elohim (Charleston, S.C.), 20, 60, 141, 152, 238, 261, 277, 977
Beth Emeth (Albany, N.Y.), *see also* Anshe Emeth (Albany, N.Y.)
Beth Emeth (Albany, N.Y.), 381
Beth Hamedrash Hagadol (New York, N.Y.), *see* Hungarian Congregation
Beth Hamedrah Hagadol (New York, N.Y.)
Beth Israel (Brooklyn, N.Y.). Religious Schools, 1064, 1230
Beth Israel (Houston, Tex.), 1212
Beth Israel (Philadelphia, Pa.), 33
Beth Israel Anshe Emes (Brooklyn, N.Y.). Religious School, *see* Beth Israel (Brooklyn, N.Y.). Religious Schools.
Beth Jacob (Albany, N.Y.), 31
Beth Miriam (Long Branch, N.J.), 642, 890, 893, 915, 999–1000
Beth-Or (Montgomery, Ala.), 615
Beth Zion (Buffalo, N.Y.), 130, 425
Bien, Herman M., 131
Bikur Cholim (Brooklyn, N.Y.), *see* Congregation Bikur Cholim (Brooklyn, N.Y.)
Binder, Abraham Wolf, 601, 1039–1040, 1099, 1117, 1122, 1130, 1174, 1176
Bingham, J. Foote, 183
Bloch, Ernest, 1023–1024, 1030–1032, 1086, 1096
B'nai Abraham (Chicago, Ill.), 683a
B'nai Abraham (Newark, N.J.), 751, 857, 966, 1083, 1115, 1172
B'nai Israel (Little Rock, Ark.), 432
B'nai Israel (Philadelphia, Pa.), 71, 136
B'nai Israel (Sacramento, Ca.), 110, 460
B'nai Jehudah (Kansas City, Mo.), 328
B'nai Jehudah (Kansas City, Mo.). Temple Sisterhood, 1180
B'nai Jeshurun (New York, N.Y.), 39, 98, 113, 128, 179, 310, 329, 345, 353, 390, 400, 666, 1207, 1247
B'nai Jeshurun (Newark, N.J.), 72a, 271, 585
B'nai Jeshurun (Philadelphia, Pa.), 1211
B'ne Israel (Cincinnati, Ohio), *see* Bene Israel (Cincinnati, Ohio)
B'ne Jeshurun (Milwaukee, Wis.), 184
Bogen, Joseph, *see also*
  Hebrew Union Congregation (Greenville, Miss.)
  Select prayers for the New Year and

Atonement days.
Prayerbook for Sabbath, Pesach, Shebuoth and Succoth=ענף יוסף
Bogen, Joseph, 408, 451
Bosniak, Jacob, 1240
Boston Academy of Music (Boston, Mass.), 15
Brandenstein, G., 99
Braun, Max, *see also* קול רינה
Braun, Max, 452
Brith Kodesh (Rochester, N.Y.), 319, 336
Brith Kodesh (Rochester, N.Y.). Sisterhood, 1121
B'rith Shalom Congregation (Louisville, Ky.), 556
Brock, Sallie, 170
Brooklyn Synagogue (Brooklyn, N.Y.), 1029
Browne, Edward B. M., *see also*
Gates of Hope (New York, N.Y.)
Prayers of Israel arranged for the American Reform…=תפלת ישראל
Browne, Edward B. M., 305, 327, 340, 380
Bureau of Jewish Education (New York, N.Y.), 1020

California. Legislature, 1216
Calisch, Edward N., *see also*
Beth Ahabah (Richmond, Va.)
Camp services for Jewish worship
תפלת בית אהבה
Calisch, Edward N., 487, 648, 1209
Campbell, Alexander, 554
Cantors' Association of America, *see also*
Jewish Ministers' Cantors Association of America.
Cantors' Association of America, 489, 834, 1147, 1154, 1160
Carl, Wm., 1190
Carnegie Hall (New York, N.Y.), 694–695
Carvalho, D. N., *see also* Reformed Society of Israelites (Charleston, S.C.)
Carvalho, D. N., 12, 952
Central Conference of American Rabbis, *see also*
Camp service for Jewish worship
Evening and morning serivces for week days
Evening service for week days
Minister's handbook
Prayers for private devotion
Temple service
Union hymnal
Blessing and praise=ברכה ותפלה
Evening services for the Sabbath and week days=סדר תפלות ישראל
Prayer-book for the Jewish deaf=
סדר תפלות ישראל
Union prayer book for Jewish worship=סדר תפלות ישראל
A ritual for Jewish soldiers=
סדר תפלות ישראל לבעלי מלחמה
Union prayer book=תפלות ישראל
Central Conference of American Rabbis, 472–473, 478, 485–486, 502–503, 505, 512, 516, 537–538, 570, 631–632, 642, 661–662, 669, 684, 704–705, 725, 747, 774, 802–803, 812–813, 837, 851–852, 863, 883–884, 895–896, 901, 930, 960–961, 971, 973, 982, 1010–1014, 1047, 1077–1078, 1108–1109, 1135, 1152, 1163–1165, 1200–1201, 1209, 1234
Central Conference of American Rabbis. Committee on Personal Prayer, 812–813
Central Conference of American Rabbis. Publications Committee, 632
Central Conference of American Rabbis. Ritual Committee, 455, 472–473, 478, 485–486
Charlap, A. Hyman, *see* Hyman, A.
Check, Sabbath, 748
Chicago Free Synagog, *see* South Shore Temple (Chicago, Ill.)
Church Street Synagogue, Zion's Holy Prophets (Boston, Mass.), 330
Clevelander Conferenz ernannten liturgisch Commission den Rabbinern, Kalisch, Rothenheim und Wise, *see*

Name Index

Committee of the Cleveland Conference.
Coffee, Rudolph I., 1216
Cohen, Asher D., 86
Cohen, Benjamin, 1066
Cohen, G. M., 114, 261
Cohen, Katherine M., 550–551, 1092
Cohen, M. S., 62
Cohen, Nathaniel L. (Mrs.), 714
Cohen, Raphael Ḥayim, 1019
Cohn, E. (Elkan), 50
Committee on Religion of the New York Section of the Council of Jewish Women, *see* Council of Jewish Women. New York Section. Committee on Religion.
Committee of the Cleveland Conference, 66, 69, 75
Congregation Bikur Cholim (Brooklyn, N.Y.), 344
Congregration B'nai Brith of Wilkes-Barre (Kingston, Pa.), 309
Congregation Moses Montefiore (New York, N.Y.), 383
Council of Jewish Women, 1186–1187
Council of Jewish Women. Committee on Welfare of Deaf, 1047
Council of Jewish Women. New York Section, 731
Council of Jewish Women. New York Section. Committee on Religion, *see also* Book of prayer for Jewish Girls.
Council of Jewish Women. New York Section. Committee on Religion, 968, 1142
Cronbach, A., *see also* Prayers for the Jewish advance.
Cronbach, A., 1123, 1178

Davidson, David, 582, 659, 738
Davidson, Israel, 1043
Davis, A. J., 239, 359, 547
Davis, Arthur, *see also* Service of the Synagogue= מחזור ... עם תרגום אנגלית

Service of the Synagogue= מחזור עבודת אהל מועד
Davis, Arthur, 723, 742, 780, 797–798, 820, 842, 921–922, 979, 1074–1076, 1101, 1132, 1227, 1257
Davis, David, 334
Davis, Thomas N., 648
De Leeuw, M. R., 111
De Sola, Abraham, 257, 1195
De Sola, D. A., 257, 1195
De Sola Mendes, Frederick, *see* Sola Mendes, Frederick de
De Sola Pool, David, *see* Sola Pool, David de
Dexter, Henry F., 331–332, 360, 409
Donnely, J. P., 888
Dunham, Arthur, 732
Dunkley, Ferdinand, 710–711, 1241–1242

Eckman, Julius, 87, 97
Educational Alliance (New York, N.Y.), 733
Eichler, Menahem M., *see also* Ohabei Shalom (Boston, Mass.).
Eichler, Menahem M., 794, 866, 1204
Einhorn, David, *see also* Beth El (New York, N.Y.) Dr. David Einhorn's עלת תמיד עלת תמיד
Einhorn, David, 76–80, 103, 207–208, 374, 448, 518, 522, 584, 732, 862, 1087
Einhorn, Julie, 862
Eisenstein, Judah David, *see also* פסוקי דזמרה
Eisenstein, Judah David, 567
Eliezer ben Nathan, of Mainz, 1059
Eliezer Liebman ben Loeb, *see also* מענה לשון
Eliezer Liebman ben Loeb, 574, 784, 875
Elzas, Barnett A., *see also* Beth Miriam (Long Branch, N.J.) Festival prayer book Prayer book for the Day of Atonement Prayer book for the New Year Prayer book for the Sabbath

175

Reformed Society of Israelites (Charleston, S.C.)
Sabbath service and miscellaneous prayers...
Service for sabbath eve and Sabbath mornng arranged for Jewish camps
Standard machsor for New Year= מחזור לראש השנה
Book of life=ספר החיים
Elzas, Barnett A., 890, 893, 914–915, 936–937, 952, 999–1000, 1034, 1145, 1184, 1229
Emanu-El (Helena, Mont.), 442
Emanu-El (Los Angeles, Ca.), 1088
Emanu-El (Milwaukee, Wis.), 325, 369
Emanu-El (Montréal, Québec, Canada), 633
Emanu-El (New York, N.Y.), 28, 36, 55, 93, 108, 123–124, 162, 186, 188, 239, 259, 276, 286, 294–295, 298, 351, 359, 388, 403, 423, 449, 506, 521, 553, 596, 600, 609, 697, 810
Emanu-El (San Francisco, Ca.), 51, 87, 146, 187, 295, 405, 572, 1252–1253
Emanu-El (San Francisco). Standing Committee on Religious Education, 588, 737
Emanuel (Dallas, Tex.), 557
Emanuel (Denver, Col.), 431
Ender, Edmund Serano, 734, 736, 1120
Ennery, Jonas, *see also* אמרי לב
Ennery, Jonas, 116, 143, 246, 592, 638, 721, 796, 1005, 1151
Ensel, Gustavus, S., 175, 279
Ephros, Gershon, 1222
Eppstein, E., *see also* Prayer and singing-book for the use of the rising generation...
Eppstein, E., 156, 184, 255
Eutaw Place Temple, *see* Oheb Shalom (Baltimore, Md.)
Executive Committee on the Celebration of the 250th Anniversary of the Settlement of Jews in the United States. Committee on the Form of Prayer, 674
Federlein, Gottfried Heinrich, 943, 972, 1033, 1179, 1220
Fellner, A., 406
Felsenthal, B. (Bernard), *see also* למען ילמדו
עלת תמיד
Felsenthal, B. (Bernard), 207, 290, 348
Ferguson, R. H., 331–332, 360, 409
Field Secretary of the Union of American Hebrew Congregations, *see* Union of American Hebrew Congregations. Field Secretary.
First Hebrew Congregation of Oakland (Oakland, Ca.), 803, 852
First Roumanian-American Congregation "שערי שמים" (New York, N.Y.), 617
Fischer, Wilhelm, 107, 132
Fisk, Franklin Pierce, 563, 975, 1180–1181
Fleg, Edmond, 1023–1024, 1030–1032, 1086, 1096
Foote, Arthur, 620, 623, 629
Forster, M., 996
Foster, Solomon, 637
Fox, G. George, *see also* South Shore Temple (Chicago, Ill.)
Fox, G. George, 1217
Frank, Waldo, 1023–1024, 1030–1032, 1086, 1096
Franklin, Leo M., *see also* Beth El (Detroit, Mich.)
Franklin, Leo M., 636, 649
Friedman, B., 749
Frohmann, Jacob, 1162
Fromental Halévy, Jacques, *see* Halévy, Jacques Fromental
Gates of Hope (New York, N.Y.), 305, 326, 340, 380
Gates of Mercy (New Orleans, La.), *see* Shangarai Chesed (New Orleans, La.)
Gates of Prayer (New Orleans, La.), 315

Gates of Prayer (New York, N.Y.), see Sha'aray Tefila (New York, N.Y.)
Gerold, Hermann, 548
Gesellschaft Brüder der Barmhezigeit (New York, N.Y.), 52
Gibson, S. Archer, 552
Gideon, Henry L., see also New Jewish hymnal
Gideon, Henry L., 757, 974, 1025, 1148
Ginzberg, Louis, 1043
Goldfarb, Israel, see also Jewish songster
Jewish songster = המנגן
זמירות ותשבחות לליל שבת
שירי ישראל לליל שבת
Goldfarb, Israel, 1020, 1064, 1070–1072, 1131, 1225–1226, 1230
Goldfarb, Samuel Eliezer, see also Jewish songster
Jewish songster = המנגן
שירי ישראל לליל שבת
Goldfarb, Samuel Eliezer, 1020, 1064, 1230
Goldstein, Herbert, 1112
Goldstein, Herbert (Mrs.), see Goldstein, Rebecca Fischel
Goldstein, Herman, 529
Goldstein, M. see Goldstein, Morris
Goldstein, Moritz, see Goldstein, Morris
Goldstein, Morris, 6, 197, 215, 280, 339, 407, 512, 778, 970, 976, 1245
Goldstein, Rebecca Fischel, 1112
Goetzl, Adolph L., 591
Gordon, Judah Leib ben Meir, see also
סדור בית יהודה
ספר צדה לדרך האמת
Gordon, Judah Leib ben Meir, 824, 876, 1049, 1102–1103
Gorfinkle, J. I., 1215
Gottheil, Gustav, see also
Emanu-El (New York, N.Y.)
Hymns and anthems adapted for Jewish worship
Morning prayers
Sun and shield
Temple Emanu-El hymn book for schools

Gottheil, Gustav, 239, 342, 357, 359, 386, 388, 481, 527–528, 583, 600
Gratz, Rebecca, 18
Gratz College. Mikve Israel School of Observation and Practice, see Mikve Israel School of Observation and Practice of Gratz College (Philadelphia, Pa.)
Graumann, Max, 856
Greenwald, Martin, see also
Songs of Israel
Songs of Zion
Greenwald, Martin, 917–918
Gries, Moses J., see also Tifereth Israel (Cleveland, Ohio)
Gries, Moses J., 492, 580
Grimm, C. Hugo, 951
Grossman, Rudolph, see also
Children's services
Rodeph Sholom (New York, N.Y.)
שלהבת יה
Grossman, Rudolph, 453, 543–544, 630, 754, 1061, 1143
Grossman, Wm., 1062
Grossmann, Louis, see also
Bene Yeshurun (Cincinnati, Ohio)
Chants in the Sabbath services
Order of serivce of Sabbath schools
זמרות ישראל
Grossmann, Louis, 500–501, 690, 760, 773, 817, 950, 998, 1027, 1065, 1177
Grünzweig, Adolph, 1243
Guinsburg, Th., 582
Gutheim, James K., 123, 186–187, 1118
Guttmacher, A., see also Baltimore Hebrew Congregation (Baltimore, Md.)
Guttmacher, A., 474

Haas, M., 387
Hahn, Aaron, see also
Tifereth Israel (Cleveland, Ohio)
קרבן אהרן
Hahn, Aaron, 249
Halévy, Jacques Fromental, 508, 833
Halpern, M. (Moses), see also Adath Jeshurun (Boston, Mass.)

Halpern, M. (Moses), 920, 946
Hand in Hand of Harlem (New York, N.Y.), 307
Har Sinai Temple (Baltimore, Md.), 58, 552, 971
Harby, Isaac, *see also* Reformed Society of Israelites (Charleston, S.C.)
Harby, Isaac, 12, 952
Harris, Maurice H., 694–695, 795
Harrison, William Henry, 19
Hast, Marcus, 806
Hay, John, 698
Hebra Bikur Holim Vekadisha (New York, N.Y.), 37
Hebrew Congregation Beth Elohim (Charleston, S.C.), *see* Beth Elohim (Charleston, S.C.)
Hebrew Congregation of Oakland (Oakland, Ca.), *see* First Hebrew Congregation of Oakland (Oakland, Ca.)
Hebrew Free Schools of New York, 234, 247, 265, 291, 300, 350, 364, 414, 433, 462, 627–628
Hebrew Friendship Cemetery Co. (Baltimore, Md.), 748
Hebrew Orphan Asylum (Brooklyn, N.Y.), 523
Hebrew Orphans' Asylum (Charleston, S.C.), 86
Hebrew Reform Congregation (Altoona, Pa.), 993
Hebrew Sunday School Society (Philadelphia, Pa.), 18
Hebrew Union Congregation (Greenville, Miss.), 408, 451
Hebrew Union-Veterans Association, 521
Hecht, Simon, *see also* זמירות ישראל
Hecht, Simon, 160, 230, 264, 280, 347, 376, 411, 483, 513, 530, 1254
Ḥeftsibah Hebrew School (San Francisco, Ca.), 87, 97
Heidenheim, Wolf, *see also*
מחזור עבדת אהל מועד
סדור שפת אמת

Heidenheim, Wolf, 40, 43–44, 82–85, 118, 145, 234, 247, 265, 291, 300, 350, 364, 414, 433, 627–628, 797, 820, 921, 928, 1074–1076, 1101, 1132, 1134, 1233, 1270
Helfère, Max, *see also* Beth El (New York, N.Y.)
Helfère, Max, 531, 728
Heller, Max, *see also* Prayer of repentance Sinai (New Orleans, La.)
Heller, Max, 493–494, 1118
Henry, H. A., 61, 110
Herxheimer, S., *see also* Israelitische Confirmand
Herxheimer, S., 160, 253
Ḥevrah ḥesed ve-emet, *see* Shearith Israel (New York, N.Y.). Ḥevrah ḥesed ve-emet
Ḥevrah Ḳadishah Gemilut Ḥasadim (New York, N.Y.), 206, 352
Ḥevrah Ḳadishah Gemilut Ḥasadim shel Emet de-Vilna (New York, N.Y.), 568
Ḥevrat 'Ezrat Aḥim Anshe Suryah be-Nu York, 1019
High Street Temple (Elmira, N.Y.), 1003
Hirsch, Emil, *see also* Dr. David Einhorn's עלת תמיד
Hirsch, Emil, 518, 862, 1087
Hirschowitz, Abraham E., *see also* Yohale Sarah = ספר אהל שרה
Hirschowitz, Abraham E., 619, 854, 985, 1016
Hochheimer, H. (Henry), *see also* Oheb Israel (Baltimore Md.) עבודת ישראל
Hochheimer, H. (Henry), 194–195, 218, 313, 337–338, 458, 581
Hochman, A., 1171
Home for Jewish Widows and Orphans of New Orleans (New Orleans, La.), 56
Hornstein, D. (David), 889
Horwich, Reuben B., 1217
House of Israel (Williamsburgh, Brooklyn, N.Y.), 41
Houseman, Rosalie, 1190
Huebsch, A. (Adolph), *see also*

Name Index

Ahawath Chesed (New York, N.Y.) Hymnen für den öffentlichen Gottesdienst der Tempel-Gemeinde...
סדר תפלה

Huebsch, A. (Adolph), 167, 204–205, 212, 225, 241, 306, 308, 366, 398, 452, 945

Hungarian Congregation Beth Hamedrash Hagadol (New York, N.Y.), 393

Hyman, A., *see also*
מגילת חנוכה בהעתקת אנגליש
סדור חנוך תפלה החדש
סדור שפת אמת (הקטן)
סדור תפארת יהודה
סדר תפלות לשבת וליום טוב

Hyman, A., 788, 844–849, 872, 878–879, 903, 958, 981, 1046, 1196, 1202, 1235–1236

Hyman Charlap, A. *see* Hyman, A.

Idelsohn, Abraham Z., 1185–1188

Imanu-El Congregation (New York, N.Y.), *see* Emanu-El (New York, N.Y.)

Imanu-El Gemeinde zu New York, *see* Emanu-El (New York, N.Y.)

Industrial School of the Hebrew Orphan Asylum (New York, N.Y.), 259, 298

Isaacs, Lewis M., *see also* קול רינה

Isaacs, Lewis M., 808

Isaacs, S. M., 99, 111

Isaiah Congregation (Chicago, Ill.), *see* Isaiah Temple (Chicago, Ill.)

Isaiah Temple (Chicago, Ill.), 669, 1090

Jackson, Solomon Henry, 10

Jacob ben Jacob Moses, of Lissa, 1044, 1059, 1279

Jacobs, Ella, 475–476, 858

Jacobs, Henry S., *see also* B'nai Jeshurun (New York, N.Y.)

Jacobs, Henry S., 86, 310, 345, 353, 390, 400

Jacobs, Solomon, 67

Janowski, Szlama, *see also* סדור תפלת ישראל מכל השנה

Janowski, Szlama, 1106

Jassinowsky, Pinchos, 1052, 1205, 1223–1224

Jastrow, M. (Marcus), *see also* Rodef Shalom (Philadelphia, Pa.) Songs and prayers and meditations
עבודת ישראל

Jastrow, M. (Marcus), 194–195, 214, 218, 236, 240, 313, 333, 337–338, 458, 491, 581, 726, 750, 807, 855, 854, 908, 987, 1050, 1082, 1113–1114, 1138, 1170, 1204, 1239

Jewish Ministers' Association of America, 370, 382, 420

Jewish Ministers' Cantors Association of America, *see also* Cantors' Association of America.

Jewish Ministers' Cantors Association of America, 1193, 1221

Jewish Publication Society of America, *see also* Abridged prayer book for Jews in the Army and Navy...

Jewish Publication Society of America, 967, 988–991

Jewish Religious School Union of New York (New York, N.Y.), 886, 994

Jewish Synagogue, Richmond Street, Toronto, Canada, *see* Richmond Street Synagogue (Toronto, Ontario, Canada)

Jewish Theological Seminary of America (New York, N.Y.), 949, 1043

Jewish Welfare Board, 988–991, 1008, 1010, 1012

Jewish Women's Congress (1893: Chicago), 477

Jews' Hospital (New York, N.Y.), 54

Jews' Synagogue (New York, N.Y.), *see* Shearith Israel (New York, N.Y.)

Jhudo Halewi, of Prague, *see* Judah Loew ben Bezalel

Joachim, L., 992, 1006

Judah Loew ben Bezalel, 304

K. K. B'ne Jeshurun (New York, N.Y.), *see* B'nai Jeshurun (New York, N.Y.)

Kadushin, I. L., 542, 905, 1155

Kahal Kadosh Mickvi Israel (Philadelphia, Pa.), *see* Mikveh Israel (Philadelphia, Pa.)
Kahal Kadosh Shearith Israel (New York, N.Y.), *see* Shearith Israel (New York, N.Y.)
Kaiser, Alois, *see also* Oheb Shalom (Baltimore, Md.)
Kaiser, Alois, 215, 220–221, 226, 235, 242–243, 250, 262–263, 270, 274, 317, 401, 410, 457, 477, 489, 589, 643, 652, 1244, 1250
Kaiser, Therese, 274
Kalisch, I., 69, 75
Kaplan, Bernard M., *see also* Ohabai Shalome (San Francisco, Ca.) Young Israe's guide for home and the religious school
Kaplan, Bernard M., 677, 763
Kartschmaroff, E., 1218
Kartschmaroff, E. (Edward), 918a, 918b, 1069a
Kavetzky (Bedrokowetzky), S., 1038
Kehilath Anshe Ma'ariv (Chicago, Ill.), *see* Anshe Ma'ariv (Chicago, Ill.)
Kenaises Israel (Syracuse, N.Y.), 61
Keneseth Israel (Philadelphia, Pa.), *see* Reform Congregation Keneseth Israel (Philadelphia, Pa.)
King Miller, Russell, *see* Miller, Russell King
Kitziger, Fred. E., *see also* Touro Synagogue (New Orleans, La.)
Kitziger, Fred. E., 373, 422, 446, 466, 488, 532–533, 564, 571
Kleeberg, Minna, 157
Klein, Max D., *see also* Adath Jeshurun (Philadelphia, Pa.)
Klein, Max D., 1095
Klein, Philip, 694–695
Kleiner, H., 688
Kneseth-Israel Gemeinde in Philadelphia, *see* Reform Congregation Keneseth Israel (Philadelphia, Pa.)
Koenigsberg, J., 992, 1006

Kohler, Kaufmann, *see also* Beth El (New York, N.Y.) New York Board of Jewish Ministers Sabbath eve service Union prayer book for Jewish worship = סדר תפלות ישראל
Kohler, Kaufmann, 443–444, 546, 565, 692?, 694–695
Kohn, S. S., 331
Kohut, Alexander, *see also* Ahawath Chesed (New York, N.Y.) אלון בכות Prayers for divine services of Congregation Ahawath Chesed = סדר תפלה
Kohut, Alexander, 398, 467
Kohut, George Alexander, 557
Kramer, Leon M., 1028, 1175
Kraus, Philip, 717
Krauskopf, Joseph, *see also* Kiddush Mourner's service Reform Congregation Keneseth Israel (Philadelphia, Pa.) School service Service hymnal Service manual Service ritual
Krauskopf, Joseph, 371, 427, 463–464, 499, 509, 525, 587, 622, 653–656, 718, 720, 730, 753, 762, 840, 1035, 1098, 1125–1126
Krebs, T. L., 693
Krinski, M., *see also* ראשית דעת שפת עבר
Krinski, M., 708, 827, 909
Kupchik, E., 415, 1058
Kurantmann, Joachim, 392, 566

Lamdan, Isaac, *see also* Emanu-El (Montréal, Québec, Canada)
Lamdan, Isaac, 633
Landau, Jacob Henry, 1249
Landsberg, Max, *see also* Brith Kodesh (Rochester, N.Y.) Hymn book for Jewish worship

Ritual for Jewish worship
Ritual for Jewish worship=סדר תפלות כל השנה
Landsberg, Max, 282, 319, 336, 424, 534, 756, 814
Lazaron, Morris S., *see also* Baltimore Hebrew Congregation (Baltimore, Md.)
Lazaron, Morris S., 1094
Lazarus, E. S., *see also* Shearith Israel (New York, N.Y.)
Lazarus, E. S., 8, 10
Leeser, Isaac, *see also*
 Mikveh Israel (Philadelphia, Pa.)
 אמרי לב
 סדור דברי צדיקים
 סדור שפתי צדיקים
Leeser, Isaac, 17, 25, 30, 45–46, 73, 116, 121, 143, 246, 257, 592, 638, 721, 796, 1005, 1151, 1195
Leeuw, M. R. de, *see* De Leeuw, M. R.
Lefkowitch, H., 969
Letteris, Meir, 42
Leucht, I. L., 287
Levenson, Louis, 334
Levi, Annie Josephine, 583
Levi, Harry, *see also* Sunday services
 Temple Israel (Boston, Mass.)
Levi, Harry, 1036–1037
Levinthal, Israel Herbert, *see also* זמירות ותשבחות לליל שבת
Levinthal, Israel Herbert, 959, 1070–1072, 1131, 1225–1226
Levy, A. R., 638a
Levy, Aaron, *see also* Shearith Israel (New York, N.Y.)
Levy, Aaron, 8
Levy, David, 277, 759
Levy, J. Leonard, *see also*
 B'nai Israel (Sacramento, Ca.)
 Book of prayer
 Children's service for use in religious schools
 Home service for Hanukkah
 Order of Thanksgiving service
 Rodef Shalom (Pittsburgh, Pa.)
Levy, J. Leonard, 460, 603, 611–613, 616, 644–645, 860, 947, 1084, 1100
Levy, Samuel Yates, 170
Lewandowski, Louis, 590, 1057
Lewin, Raphael D'C., *see also*
 American-Jewish ritual
 Temple Israel (Brooklyn, N.Y.)
Lewin, Raphael D'C., 176
Lincoln, Abraham, 131, 758
Loewenberg, William, *see also* Rodeph Shalom (Philadelphia, Pa.)
Loewenberg, William, 491
Lob, Otto, *see also* Israelitische Tempel-Gesänge
Lob, Otto, 245, 358
Low, Leo, 838, 1147, 1161
Lucas, Alice, 549
Luria, Isaac ben Solomon, *see also* סדור האר"י ז"ל
Luria, Isaac ben Solomon, 925, 1268
Magil, Joseph, *see also*
 לינען-סדור לבתי ספר ולעם
 מאגילניצקי'ס לינען רע הילדים
 סדור לבתי-ספר ולעם
 סדר כל תפלות השנה
 פאלשטענדיגער לינען סדור לבתי ספר ולעם
 רע הילדים
Magil, Joseph, 639, 663–665, 678, 680–683, 699, 707, 709, 743–746, 787, 841, 881, 938, 1107, 1197
Marcus, Alfred A., 330
Marcus, J., 1003
Masons. Fraternal Lodge No. 53 A.F. & A.M., 648
Mayer, Eli, 1069
Mayer, H., 1180
Mayer, Isaac, 232–233, 275, 514
Mayer, M., *see also* Hours of devotion
Mayer, M., 138–140, 158–159, 178, 186, 198, 237, 297, 341, 385, 519
McKinley, William, 599, 603

Mendelssohn, Felix, 532
Mendelssohn, Moses, 554
Mendes, Frederick de Sola, *see* Sola Mendes, Frederick de
Mendes, Henry Pereira, *see* Pereira Mendes, Henry
Mendes, Isaac P., 318
Mendes de Solla, J., 421
Merzbacher, L., *see also*
   Emanu-El (New York)
   סדר תפלה
Merzbacher, L., 55, 93, 108, 122–124, 146, 173, 186, 188, 192, 216, 259, 276, 286, 294, 351, 397, 449
Meyer, H., 891
Mickva Israel (Savannah, Ga.), 260, 318, 322, 450, 861
Micve Israel (Philadelphia, Pa.), *see* Mikveh Israel (Philadelphia, Pa.)
Micve Israel (Savannah, Ga.), *see* Mickva Israel (Savannah, Ga.)
Mikve Israel School of Observation and Practice of Gratz College, 910
Mikveh Israel (Philadelphia, Pa.), 7, 9, 17, 24–25, 30, 90, 764
Miller, Russell King, *see also* Service hymnal
Miller, Russell King, 653–656, 1124–1125
Miro, Heinrich, 42
Misch, Marion L., 715, 859
Mischkan Israel (New Haven Conn.), *see* Mishkan Israel (New Haven, Conn.)
Mishkan Israel (New Haven, Conn.), 57, 169, 759
Moïse, Abraham, *see also* Reformed Society of Israelites (Charleston, S.C.)
Moïse, Abraham, 12, 952
Moïse, Penina, *see also*
   Hymns written for the services of Congregation Beth Elohim
   Hymns written for the use of Hebrew congregations
Moïse, Penina, 20, 60, 141, 152, 238
Montefiore, Moses, 311, 315–316, 320–323, 330, 383

Moses, Alfred G., *see also* The Temple (Mobile, Ala.)
Moses, Alfred G., 948
Moses, Isaac S., *see also*
   Ahawath Chesed-Shaar Hashomayim (New York, N.Y.)
   Divine service for the Congregation Ahawath Chesed…
   Emanu-El (Milwaukee, Wis.)
   Hebrew reader containing the prayers of the Jewish ritual
   Hymns and anthems for Jewish worship
   Order of children's service for a Jewish Sabbath schools
   Sabbath-school hymnal
   Temple music
   תפלה למשה
   תפלות ישראל
Moses, Isaac S., 314, 325, 369, 384, 389, 455, 472–473, 479–480, 485–486, 490, 496–498, 511, 526, 535, 590, 635, 647, 651, 696, 761, 815, 865, 894, 944–945, 995, 997, 1068, 1097, 1149, 1173
Myers, Isidore, 539

Nachman, Abraham, 58
National Council of Jewish Women, *see* Council of Jewish Women
Naumbourg, S., 175
Neches, Solomon M., 942
Nefutsoth Jehudah (New Orleans, La.), *see also* Touro Synagogue (New Orleans, La.)
Nefutsoth Jehudah (New Orleans, La.), 35, 72
Neidlinger, W. H., 831–832
Neuda, Fanny Schmiedl, *see also*
   Hours of devotion
   Stunden der Andacht
Neuda, Fanny Schmiedl, 106, 115, 138–140, 158–159, 178, 191, 198, 229, 237, 297, 299, 341, 385, 482, 519
New York Board of Jewish Ministers, 546, 692

Name Index

Nieto, Jacob, *see also* Sherith Israel (San Francisco, Ca.)
Nieto, Jacob, 495, 586, 618, 793, 1026
Noelsch, Wm., 508

Ocean Parkway Jewish Center, Tifereth Israel, First Congregation of Kensington, (Brooklyn, N.Y.), 1240
Odeon (Boston, Mass.), 15
Ohabai Shalome (San Francisco, Ca.), 539, 677, 763
Ohabei Shalom (Boston, Mass.), 866, 1204
Oheb Israel (Baltimore, Md.), 194–195, 312
Oheb Israel-Gemeinde zu Baltimore, *see* Oheb Israel (Baltimore, Md.)
Oheb-Schalom Gemeinde zu Baltimore, *see* Oheb Shalom (Baltimore, Md.)
Oheb Shalom (Baltimore, Md.), 100, 104–105, 125, 153, 193–195, 252, 262–263, 456, 816, 871, 906, 1244
Ohel Jacob Synagogue (Philadelphia, Pa.), 1146
Orach Chaim Synagogue (New York, N.Y.), 559
Owst, W. G., 621

Pearl Street Synagogue, *see* Anshe Emeth (Albany, N.Y.)
Pereira Mendes, Henry, *see also* Shearith Israel (New York, N.Y.)
Pereira Mendes, Henry, 434, 694–695, 923, 1246
Peretz, I. L., 1284
Perlmutter, Arnold, 1093
Petach Tikvah (Brooklyn, N.Y.), 959
Petach Tikvah (Brooklyn, N.Y.). Junior Congregation, 959
Philips, A. Th., *see also*
מחזור ... עם תרגום אנגלית
סדר תפלות מכל השנה
Philips, A. Th., 779, 818–819, 853, 873, 904, 1167, 1203
Philipson, David, *see also* Bene Israel (Cinicnnati, Ohio)

Services for Sabbath and holidays
Philipson, David, 371, 445, 772, 1002
Piexotto, M. L. M., 8
Pinto, Israel, 2–4
Pinto, Joseph Yeshurun., 1
Pique, Rabbi, 8
Plum Street Temple, *see* Bene Yeshurun (Cincinnati, Ohio)
Polonies Talmud Torah School (New York, N.Y.), 272, 441
Pool, David de Sola, *see* Sola Pool, David de
Portuguese Congregation of Philadelphia, *see* Mikveh Israel (Philadelphia, Pa.)

Rabinowitz, Gedaliah, *see also* Ohel Jacob (Philadelphia, Pa.)
Rabinowitz, Gedaliah, 1146, 1256
Raisin, Jacob S., *see also* Beth Elohim (Charleston, S.C.)
Raisin, Jacob S., 977
Raphall, Morris Jacob, 42, 88, 111, 128
Raphell, M. J., *see* Raphall, Morris Jacob
Reform Congregation (Wilkes-Barre, Pa.), *see* Congregation B'nai Brith of Wilkes-Barre (Kingston, Pa.)
Reform Congregation Keneseth Israel (Philadelphia, Pa.), 59, 101, 112, 137, 151, 459, 463–464, 653, 656, 673, 698, 730, 753, 762, 1022, 1035, 1098, 1124–1126
Reform-Gemeinde Keneseth Israel (Philadelphia, Pa.), *see* Reform Congregation Keneseth Israel (Philadelphia, Pa.)
Reformed Congregation "Temple Beth Zion," *see* Beth Zion (Buffalo, N.Y.)
Reformed Society of Israelites (Charleston, S.C.), *see also* Beth Elohim (Charleston, S.C.)
Reformed Society of Israelites (Charleston, S.C.), 12, 952
Reisin, A., 1099
Religious Observance Committee of the Young People's League of the United Synagogue of America, *see* United

Synagogue of America. Young People's League. Religious Observance Committee.
Religious Schools of Congregation Beth Israel (Brooklyn, N.Y.), *see* Beth Israel (Brooklyn, N.Y.). Religious Schools.
Retter, Carl, 374
Rice, I. L., 215
Richmond Street Synagogue (Toronto, Ontario, Canada), 244
Roberts, Charles, J., 916
Rodef Shalom (New York, N.Y.), *see* Rodeph Sholom (New York, N.Y.)
Rodef Shalom (Philadelphia, Pa.), 23, 26, 171, 177, 194–195, 218, 311, 491
Rodef Shalom (Pittsburgh, Pa.), *see* Rodeph Shalom (Pittsburgh, Pa.)
Rodef Schalom (Philadelphia, Pa.), *see* Rodef Shalom (Philadelphia, Pa.)
Rodeph Shalom (New York, N.Y.), *see* Rodeph Sholom (New York, N.Y.)
Rodeph Shalom (Pittsburgh, Pa.), 603, 616, 947, 1100
Rodeph Sholom (New York, N.Y.), 22, 61, 453, 469, 543–544, 630, 646, 712, 754, 1061
Rodoph Scholom zu New-York, *see* Rodeph Sholom (New York, N.Y.)
Rogers, James H., 839, 868, 953, 1214
Roget, E., 24
Roosevelt, Theodore, 1022
Rosenau, William, *see also* Oheb Shalom (Baltimore, Md.)
Rosenau, William, 706, 906, 1244
Rosenberg, Judah, 1051
Rosenblatt, Josef, 771, 954–955, 978, 1060, 1089, 1116, 1129
Rothenheim, B., 69, 75
Rothschild, Hester, *see also* אמרי לב
Rothschild, Hester, 116, 143, 246, 592, 638, 721, 796, 1005, 1151
Roudafe Sholum (Philadelphia, Pa.) *see* Rodef Shalom (Philadelphia, Pa.)
Roudef Sholum (Philadelphia, Pa.) *see*

Rodef Shalom (Philadelphia, Pa.)
Roumanian-American Congregation "שערי שמים" (New York, N.Y.), *see* First Roumanian-American Congregation "שערי שמים" (New York, N.Y.)
Rumshinsky, Joseph M., 1221
Russotto, Henry A., 719, 903, 955, 978

Sachs, Michael, 91–92
Sapir, J.D., 554
Saxe, Joseph, 99
Schechter, Mathilde S., *see also* קול רינה
Schechter, Mathilde S., 808
Schechter, Solomon, 694–695, 949
Schindler, Solomon, 794
Schlesinger, Sebastian B., *see also* Complete musical service for...according to the Union prayer book Sabbath music
Schlesinger, Sebastian B., 524, 561, 594–595, 614, 650, 913, 1001, 1021, 1085, 1144, 1182, 1248
Schlessinger, W., *see also* Stunden der Andacht תחינות בנות ישורון
Israelitisches Andacht-buch=תפלת ישראל
Schlessinger, W., 63, 94, 106, 115, 191, 196, 209, 229, 299, 302, 436, 482
Schmiedl Neuda, Fanny, *see* Neuda, Fanny Schmiedl
Schnipelisky, E., 809, 1208
Schorr, Baruch, 701
Schorr, Israel, 701
Schulman, Samuel, 694–695
Schwartz, S., 773
Schwartzchild, Joseph (Mr. and Mrs.), 529
Seixas, Gershom, *see also* Shearith Israel (New York, N.Y.)
Seixas, Gershom, 5
Selikovich, G., *see also* מענה לשון
Selikovich, G., 799
Serano Ender, Edmund, *see* Ender, Edmund Serano
Shaar Hashomajim (New York, N.Y.), *see* Shaar Hashomayim (New York, N.Y.)

Name Index

Shaar Hashomayim (Montréal, Québec, Canada), 346
Shaar Hashomayim (New York, N.Y.) see also Ahawath Chesed-Shaar Hashomayim (New York, N.Y.)
Shaar Hashomayim (New York, N.Y.), 127, 540
Sha'aray Tefila (New York, N.Y.), 27, 34, 172, 254, 334, 716, 729
Sha'aray Tefilla (New York, N.Y.), see Sha'aray Tefila (New York, N.Y.)
Sha'are Shamayim (New York, N.Y.) see First Roumanian-American Congregation "שערי שמים"
Sha'are Tefilah (New York, N.Y.), see Sha'aray Tefila (New York, N.Y.)
Sha'arey Tefilah (New York, N.Y.), see Sha'aray Tefila (New York, N.Y.)
Shangarai Chesed (New Orleans, La.), 38
Shapiro, Herman S., 658
Sharay Tefila (East Orange, N.J.), 510
Shearith Israel (New York, N.Y.), 1, 8, 11, 13, 19, 89, 254, 541, 668, 801, 882, 923
Shearith Israel (New York, N.Y.) Hebra Hased Va-Amet, see Shearith Israel (New York, N.Y.). Hevrah Hesed ve-Emet
Shearith Israel (New York, N.Y.). Hevrah Hesed ve-Emet, 11, 801, 882, 923
Shearith Israel (Montréal, Québec, Canada), 257, 434, 1195
Sherith Israel (San Francisco, Ca.), 110, 181, 228, 273, 494, 586, 618, 793, 1026
Sherith Israel (San Francisco). Hebrew and Religious School, 273
Sh'erith Israel-Ahabath Achim (Cincinnati, Ohio), see also Ahabeth Achim (Cincinnati, Ohio)
Sh'erith Israel-Ahabath Achim (Cincinnati, Ohio), 712
Shippen Barnes, Edward, see Barnes, Edward Shippen
Shnipelisky, E., see Schnipelisky, E.
Shomer Emunim (Toledo, Ohio), 391

Silberfeld, Julius, see also תפלת שבת
Silberfeld, Julius, 689, 751, 829, 857, 966, 1083, 1115, 1172
Silver, Mark, 1156
Silverman, Joseph, 694–695
Simon, Abram, 755
Sinai (New Orleans, La.), 1118
Sinai (Oakland, Ca.), 1216
Sinai Congregation (Chicago, Ill.), 96, 448, 1188
Sinai-Gemeinde in Chicago, see Sinai Congregation (Chicago, Ill.)
Sinai Temple (Mount Vernon, N.Y.). Religious School, 1215
Singer, S., see also Standard prayer book = סדר תפלות כל השנה
Authorised daily prayer book = סדר תפלות כל השנה כמנהג פולין
Singer, S., 902, 932–934, 984, 1015, 1079–1080, 1136, 1198–1199, 1236
Society of American Cantors, 537–538, 657, 1127
Sola, Abraham de, see De Sola, Abraham
Sola, D. A. de, see De Sola, D. A.
Sola Mendes, Frederick de, see also Sha'ary Tefila New York (N.Y.)
Sola Mendes, Frederick de, 334, 361, 370, 716, 729
Sola Pool, David de, see also Shearith Israel (New York, N.Y.)
Sola Pool, David de, 923
Solla, J. Mendes de, see Mendes de Solla, J.
Solomon, Abraham, 285
Solomon, George, 861
Sonneschein, S. H., see also Temple Israel (Saint Louis, Mo.)
Sonneschein, S. H., 375
Sons of Israel Anshei Kalwarier, 619
Sons of Jacob (Haverstraw, N.Y.), 558
South Shore Temple (Chicago, Ill.), 1217
Spanish and Portuguese Congregation Shearith Israel, see Shearith Israel (New York, N.Y.)

Sparger, William, *see also* Emanu-El (New York, N.Y.)
Sparger, William, 477, 602, 609–610, 1243, 1250
Spicker, Max, *see also* Emanu-El (New York (N.Y.)
Spicker, Max, 560, 579, 602, 609–610, 624, 697
Sporberg, Joseph, 50
Sprayregen, Joshua, *see also* ראשית דעת
שפת עבר
Sprayregen, Joshua, 708, 827, 909
Sprung, D. L., 1099
Stanly Street Synagogue, *see* Shearith Israel (Montréal, Québec, Canada)
Stark, Edward Joseph, *see also* Emanuu-El (San Francisco, Ca.)
Stark, Edward Joseph, 507, 545, 672, 675, 735, 769, 804, 826, 833, 869–870, 1183
Stark, Josef, 507
Stein, Leopold, 261
Steinberg, Joel, 548
Stern, 42
Stern, D., *see also* Congregation B'nai Brith of Wilkes-Barre (Kingston, Pa.) Sunday services = קרבן תודה
Stern, D., 309
Stern, M., 1283a
Stiefel, Julius, 262
Stolz, Joseph, *see also* Isaiah Congregation (Chicago, Ill.)
Stolz, Joseph, 1090
Sulzer, S. (Salomon), *see also* Shir Zion
Sulzer, S. (Salomon), 657, 690, 834, 1127
Summer, Samuel, 1228
Synagogue, Long Branch, N.J., *see* Beth Miriam (Long Branch, N.J.)
Szold, Benjamin, *see also*
  Gebet-Ordnung für die Todten-Bestattung
  Gebete für Kinder für Haus und Schule
  Gebete und Gesänge aur Seelenfeier
  Gesänge und Gebete für den öffentlichen Gottesdienst der Israeliten
  Hebrew text for schools...
  Oheb Shalom (Baltimore, Md.)
  Songs and prayers and meditations
  הגיון לב
  עבודת ישראל
  ראשית דעת
Szold, Benjamin, 81, 104–105, 125, 133, 147, 150, 153, 164, 185, 193–195, 211, 214, 217–222, 235–236, 240, 242, 250, 252, 263, 296, 313, 317, 333, 337–338, 452, 458, 581, 726, 750, 807, 855, 885, 908, 987, 1050, 1082, 1113–1114, 1138, 1170, 1204, 1239

Taubenhaus, G., 1004
The Temple (Mobile, Ala.), 948
Temple Israel (Boston, Mass.), 1036–1037
Temple Israel (Brooklyn, N.Y.), 176
Temple Israel (Saint Louis, Mo.), 375
Temple Israel (Wilkes-Barre, Pa.), 1210
Temple Israel of Harlem (New York, N.Y.), *see also* Evening service at the house of mourning
Temple Israel of Harlem (New York, N.Y.), 459, 520, 578, 598
Thatcher, Howard R., *see also* Oheb Shalom (Baltimore, Md.)
Thatcher, Howard R., 811, 816, 864, 871
Tifereth Israel (Brooklyn, N.Y.), *see* Ocean Parkway Jewish Center, Tifereth Israel, First Congregation of Kensington, (Broolyn, N.Y.)
Tifereth Israel (Cleveland, Ohio), 249, 492, 580
Tinker, M. Z., 1254
Touro Synagogue (New Orleans, La.) *see also* Nefustoth Jehudah (New Orleans, La.)
Touro Synagogue (New Orleans, La.), 316, 422, 446, 1241
Trattner, Ernest, 1088
Tyler, Abram Ray, 892

Union of American Hebrew Congregations. Biennial (25th), 971

Union of American Hebrew Congregations. Field Secretary, 632
United Hebrew Congregations of the British empire, 902, 933, 1080, 1199
United States. Army, 967, 988–991, 1008, 1010, 1012
United States. Congress. House of Representatives, 88
United States. Navy, 967, 988–991, 1008, 1010, 1012
United States. President, 5, 131, 599, 603, 758
United States. War Department. Commission on Training Camp Activities, 1012
United Synagogue of America. Young People's League. Religious Observance Committee, 1213

Vidaver, H. (Henry), *see also* Book of life = ספר החיים
Vidaver, H. (Henry), 179, 266–268, 301, 324, 399, 484, 555, 607–608
Voorsanger, Jacob, *see also* Emanu-El (San Francisco, Ca.)
Voorsanger, Jacob, 588, 737

Wald, Franz, *see also* Temple service for New Year and Day of Atonement
Wald, Franz, 448, 734
Ware, Henry, 14–16
Wasilkowsky, Jacob L., 1053, 1139, 1150, 1219
Waterman Wise, James, *see* Wise, James Waterman
Weber, C. Otto, 676
Wechsler, Morris, *see also* Hungarian Congregation Beth Hamedrash Hagadol
Wechsler, Morris, 393
Weinstein, Louis, *see also* New Jewish hymnal
Weinstein, Louis, 974, 1025, 1148
Weinstock, Isadore H., 562, 671
Weisser (Pildewasser), S., 940, 1017, 1038
Welsch, Samuel, 174, 215, 225, 589
Werthheimer, Solomon Aaron, 504

West End Synagogue (New York, N.Y.), *see* Sha'aray Tefila (New York, N.Y.)
Wile, Solomon, *see also* Hymn book for Jewish worship
Wile, Solomon, 282, 424, 756
Wise, Aaron, *see also*
 Rodeph Sholom (New York, N.Y.)
 שלהבת יה
Wise, Aaron, 453, 469, 543–544, 630, 1061
Wise, Isaac M., *see also*
 Bene Yeshurun (Cincinnati, Ohio)
 מנהג אמעריקא
 שירי לה׳ שיר חדש
 תפלות בני ישורון
Wise, Isaac M., 66, 69, 75, 102, 119–120, 148, 154, 163, 165, 180, 201–203, 223, 261, 354, 362–363, 396, 402, 435, 454, 468, 471, 673
Wise, James Waterman, *see also* Synagogue songs
Wise, James Waterman, 1189
Wise, Morris S., 390
Wolf, Horace, *see also* Brith Kodesh (Rochester, N.Y.)
Wolf, Horace, 1121

Yaffee, H., 1005
Yannai (7th century Paytan), *see also* מחזור ייני
Yannai (7th century Paytan), 1043
Yates Levy, Samuel, *see* Levy, Samuel Yates
York, F. L., 500–501
Young Men's Hebrew Association (New York, N.Y.), 597

Zagler, R. A., 867
Zelig, Simon, 61
Zemachson, Simon, 911, 1206
Zeuner, Charles, 14–16
Zilberts, S., *see* Zilberts, Zavel
Zilberts, Zavel, 1067, 1091, 1141, 1153–1154, 1157–1160, 1192–1194
Zion Congregation (Chicago, Ill.), 448
Zwickel, J., 1110

Hebrew

Solomon, Abraham ראה שלום, ן' אביראל
Adler, Herbert M. ראה הכהן, מרדכי, בן נפתלי אדלר,
Adler, Nathan Marcus ראה הכהן, נתן, אדלר,
Aaron ben Jehiel Michael, ha-Levi ראה דמיכיילשאק, מיכל יחיאל בהרב אהרן
Eisenstein, Judah David ראה דוד, יהודה אייזענשטיין,
Lazarus, E.S. ראה שמואל, ב' אליעזר
Eliezer Liebman ben Loeb ראה ליב, בן ליבמאן אליעזר
Anshe Ma'ariv (Chicago, Ill.) ראה מעריב, אנשי
Committee of the Cleveland Conference ראה קליוולללאנד ק"ק בק הגדולה האסיפה
Artom, Benjamin ראה בנימין, ארטום,
Luria, Isaac ben Solomon ראה י, האר"
Beth-El (Albany, N.Y.) ראה אלבני, אל, בית
Hungarian Congregation Beth Hamedrash Hagadol (New York, N.Y.) ראה אונגארן אנשי הגדול מדרש בית הכנסת בית
Hungarian Congregation Beth Hamedrash Hagadol (New York, N.Y.) ראה אונגארן אנשי המדרש בית
Jews' Hospital (New York, N.Y.) ראה יארק, בנוא ליהודים אשר חולים בית
Beth Jacob (Albany, N.Y.) ראה אלבני, יעקב, בית
House of Israel (Williamsburgh, Brooklyn, N.Y.) ראה וויליאמסבארג, בעיר ישראל בית
Bene Yeshurun (Cincinnati, Ohio) ראה צינצינאטי, ישורון, בני
Rothenheim, B. ראה יצחק, ר"ב בנימין
Browne, Edward B.M. ראה יעקב, בן משה ברוין,
Gordon, Judah Leib ben Meir ראה מאיר בן יהודה גארדאן,
Ginzberg, Louis ראה לוי, גינצבורג,

Davidson, Israel ראה ישראל, דאווידזאן
De Sola, Abraham ראה דוד, בן אברהם סולה, די
De Sola, D.A. ראה אהרן, בן דוד סולה, די
Sola Pool, David de ראה פול, אליעזר בן דוד סולה, די
Davis, Arthur ראה יצחק, בן יעקב דעויס,
Hochman, A. ראה א., האכמאן,
Heidenheim, Wolf ראה וואלף, היידנהיים,
Hyman, A. ראה א., היימאן,
Hyman, A. ראה חרלפ, היימאן
Hirschowitz, Abraham ראה שמואל, בן עבר אברהם הירשאוויץ,
Cohen, Raphael Ḥayim ראה חיים, רפאל הכהן,
Heidenheim, Wolf ראה היידנהיים, איש דב, שמשון בר וואלף
Wechsler, Morris ראה מאריס, וויקסלער,
Werthheimer, Solomon Aaron ראה אהרן, שלמה ווערטהיימער,
Sachs, Michael ראה מיכל, זקש,
Gesellschaft Brüder der Barmherzigeit (New York, N.Y.) ראה רחמנים, אחים חברה
Ḥevrah Ḳadishah Gemilut Ḥasadim (New York, N.Y.) ראה חסדים, גמילות קדישה חברה
Ḥevrah Ḳadishah Gemilut Ḥasadim (New York, N.Y.) ראה אמת, של חסדים גמילות קדישה חברה
Ḥevrah Ḳadishah Gemilut Ḥasadim shel Emet de-Vilna (New York, N.Y.) ראה דווילנא, אמת של חסדים גמילות קדישה חברה
Ḥevrat 'Ezrat Aḥim Anshe Surya be-NuYork ראה בנויארק, סוריה אנשי אחים עזרת חברת

Name Index

Heftsibah ראה Hebrew School חפציבה
Hebrew School (San Francisco, Ca.)
Hyman, A. ראה, היימאן, א. חרלפ,
Check, Sabbath ראה, שבתי בן הלל טשעק,
Yannai (7th century Paytan) ראה, ינייַ
Janowski, Szlama ראה, שלמה יאנאווסקי,
Jassinowsky, ראה, פנחס יאסינאווסקי, Pinchos
Hand in Hand of Harlem ראה, יד ביד (NewYork, N.Y.)
Leeser, Isaac ראה, יצחק בן אורי ן׳ אליעזר
Wise, Isaac M. ראה, יצחק בן שמחה בונם
Kalisch, I. ראה, יצחק מאיר ב״ר יהודה
Kenaises Israel ראה, כנסת ישראל (Syracuse, N.Y.)
Magil, Joseph ראה, יוסף מאגילינצקי,
Montefiore, Moses ראה, משה מאנטיפיורי,
Pereira ראה, חיים די אברהם פריריא מינדיז,
Mendes, Henry
Mikveh ראה, מקוה ישראל לק״ק פילאדעלפיא
Israel (Philadelphia, Pa.)
De Sola, ראה, אברהם בן דוד די, סולה Abraham
De Sola, D. A. ראה, דוד בן אהרן די, סולה
Singer, S. ראה, שמעון בר יהודה סינגער,
Adath Jeshurun ראה, עדת ישורון, נו-יארק (New York, N.Y.)
Emanu-El (New ראה, עמנואל, נו-יארק York, N.Y.)
Sola Pool, ראה, דוד די סולה בן אליעזר פול, David de

Philips, A.Th. ראה, טה., א. פיליפס,
Pereira ראה, חיים די אברהם פרירא מינדיז,
Mendes, Henry
Peretz, I.L. ראה, ל., י. פרץ,
Zwickel, J. ראה, יונה בן דוב צוויקל,
Shearith ראה, ק״ק ספרדים שארית ישראל
Israel (New York, N.Y.)
ק״ק ספרדים שארית ישראל. חברה חסד ואמת, ראה .Shearith Israel. (New York, N.Y.)
Ḥevrah Ḥesed ve-Emet
Kadushin, I.L. קאדושין, יצחק יהודה ליב, המוהל, ראה
Sherith Israel (San ראה, ק״ק שארית ישראל Francisco, Ca.)
Kupchik, E. ראה, אליהו קופטשיק,
Krinski, M. ראה, מ., קרינסקי,
Eliezer ben Nathan, of Mainz ראה, ראבן
Rosenblatt, Josef ראה, יוסף ראזענבלאטט,
Shearith ראה, שארית ישראל במנטריאל
Israel (Montréal, Québec, Canada)
Shearith Israel ראה, שארית ישראל, נו-יארק (New York, N.Y.)
Schorr, Baruch ראה, ברוך שור,
Jackson, ראה, שלמה בן צבי מלונדון Solomon Henry
First Roumanian- ראה, שערי שמים, נו-יארק American Congregation "שערי שמים" (New York, N.Y.)
Sha'aray Tefila ראה, שערי תפלה, נו-יארק (New York, N.Y.)
Gates of Hope ראה, שערי תקוה, נו-יארק (New York, N.Y.)
Sprayregen, Joshua ראה, י., שפרייערעגען,

Title Index

2 Lieder nach der Confirmation, 225
6 "V,shomru's," see ושמרו
20 hymns for Jewish worship, 488
Der XXIV Psalm, 197

Abodath Israel, see עבודת ישראל
Abridged prayer book for Jews in the Army and Navy of the United States, 967, 988–991
Adath Jeshurun hymnal, 752
Additional responses for Sabbath eve service, 1241
Additions to the ritual, 474
Adon olam, see also אדון עולם
Adon olam, 610, 728, 1140, 1242
Adonoy moh adom = O Lord! what is man, 1243
Ahavas olam, see Hebrew sacred chorus for mixed voices
Al naharos Bovel, 1141
The American-Jewish ritual, 176
Ancient Jewish melodies, see זמירות ישראל
Andachtsbuch zum Gebrauche auf dem Friedhofe und in Trauerhause..., see ספר החיים
Andachtsbuch zum Gebrauche bei Krankheiten und Sterbfällen, see ספר החיים
Andachtsbüchlein für israelitische Kinder für Haus und Schule, 150
Anthem: Praise ye the Lord this day, 643
Anthems, hymns and responses for the Union prayer book, 489
Ascribe unto God, see Psalm XXIX: Hovu Ladonai
Assembly prayers, 1925, see Prayers offered at the daily sessions of the Assembly
Auswahl deutscher Gesänge zum Gebrauche im Temple der Imanu-El Congregation in New-York, 28

Auswahl israelitisch religiöser Lieder in Musik gesetzt, see זמירות ישראל
The authorised daily prayer book of the United Hebrew Congregations of the British empire, see סדר תפלות כל השנה כמנהג פולין
The authorized daily prayer book of the United Hebrew Congregations of the British empire, see סדר תפלות כל השנה כמנהג פולין
Avodath hakodesh, see עבודת הקדש
Bame madlikin, see במה מדליקין
Beth Ahabah hymnal, 830
Beth Emeth Sunday school hymns, 381
Bircas Kohanim, 771
Bircath Kohanim (The Priestly benediction), see ברכת כהנים
Birchas Cohanim, see ברכת כהנים
Blessing and praise, see ברכה ותפלה
The blessing of peace, see also ברכת שלום
The blessing of peace, 992
The blessing of the Priests, see ברכת כהנים
Book of consolation, see ספר תנחומות
The book of daily prayers for every day in the year according to custom of the German and Polish Jews, see סדור דברי צדיקים
The book of life, see ספר החיים
Book of prayer, 611–612
A book of prayer for Jewish girls, 968, 1142
A book of prayer for Jewish worship, see תפלת בית אהבה
Book of prayers for Israelitish Congregations, see עלת תמיד
Brith Itzhak, see ספר ברית יצחק
The burial of the dead, 420
Burial service as used in the Congregation Shearith Israel (Spanish and Portuguese) of New York, see סדר קבורה כפי

Title Index

מנהג ק״ק שארית ישראל בנו יארק עם תרגום אנגלי
B'zess Israel, 1116
Camp services for Jewish worship, 1209
Catechism designed for the religious instruction of Israelitish children, see ראשית דעת
Celebration by the Congregation Shearith Israel, Spanish and Portuguese Congregation, 668
Centennial anniversary: Sir Moses Montefiore, 311
Central Conference of American Rabbis: union services in memory of the Russian martyrs, 669
Ceremonies of the laying of the corner stone of the Temple of Oheb Shalom Congregation, 456
Chants in the Sabbath services, 690
Chanukah service for Sabbath schools, 1244
Chanukah songster, 1117
Chanukas Habajis, 911
Children's harvest service, 772
Children's prayers for all ages, 382
Children's prayers for use in the school and home, 475–476, 858
The children's Psalm-book, 714
Children's Sabbath service, 569
Children's service: religious school of Hebrew Reform Congregation, Altoona Pennsylvania, 993
The children's service for Rosh Ha-shanah, 644
The children's service for the Day of Atonement, 715, 859
Children's service for Yom Kippur afternoon, 753
Children's service for use in religious schools, 613, 645, 860, 1084
Children's services: arranged for each week of the month, 754, 1143
Children's services: arranged for use in religious schools, 912, 942
Children's services: prayers and hymns for the religious school, Congregation Mickve Israel, 862
Children's services for the New Year and Atonement Day, 886, 994
A child's ritual, 754
The Christian marriage ceremony, 183
The classified Psalter, see פסוקי דזמרה
Coll nidrey, 304
A collection of principal melodies of the synagogue, 477
Come, sons of the mighty, see Kommt, Söhne der Allmacht
Comfort ye, my people, 943
Compendium of the order of the burial service, 11
Complete daily prayers, see סדור כל בו
Complete memorial service for solo, mixed chorus with organ accompaniment, see הזכרת נשמות
Complete musical service for Day of Atonement, 594, 913, 1021
Complete musical service for New Year, 595, 1144
Complete musical service for the Three Festivals, 614, 1085
Complete prayer book for synagogue, home & school, see סדר תפלה לבתי ספר ולעם
Confirmant's guide to the Mosaic religion, 156, 184
Confirmation manual, 421
Confirmation service, 270, 944, 1173
Confirmation service: as sung at Touro Synagogue, 422
Consecration hymn for the consecration of Temple Sinai, 1118
Consecration of the Jewish synagogue, Richmond Street, Toronto, Canada, 244
Consecration of the Theodore Roosevelt Memorial Window at Temple Keneseth Israel, 1022
Consecration service, 136

Consecration service: synagogue of the Spanish and Portuguese Congregation Shearith Israel, see סדר העבודה לחנוכת הבית לק״ק שארית ישראל

Conservative Sabbath and holiday prayer book, see סדר תפלות לשבת ויום טוב

Consolation, 457

The crown of a good name, 278

Daily prayer with English directions, see סדור שפת אמת החדש

Daily prayers, see מנהג אמעריקא תפלות בני ישורון

Daily prayers for American Israelites, see מנהג אמעריקא

The daily prayers, see also Gebet-Buch für den öffentlichen Gottesdienst und die Privat Andacht

The daily prayers, see also מנהג אמעריקא, תפלות בני ישורון

The daily prayers, 66

Daily prayers with a revised English translation, see סדר תפלות מכל השנה

Daily prayers with English directions, see סדר תפלות כל השנה

Daily prayers with English instructions, see סדור שפת אמת, סדור שפת אמת (הקטן)

Day of God = Tag des Herrn, 545

Dedication ceremonies: Temple Emanuel, Dallas Texas, 557

Dedication ceremonies of the Congregation Beth-El, New York, 670

Dedication of Temple Israel, 1210

The dedication of the Home for Jewish Widows and Orphans of New Orleans, 56

Dedication of the new synagogue, 328

Dedication of the new synagogue Beth-El Emeth, 67

Dedication of the new synagogue of the Congregation Mikve Israel, see אלה המזמורים והפסוקים לחנוכת בית הכנסת של ק״ק מקוה ישראל

Dedication of the new Temple Adas Israel, 157

Dedication of the new Temple Beth-El, 440

Dedication of the synagogue of the Congregation Sons of Jacob, Haverstraw, N.Y., 558

Dedication of the Temple Gates of Hope, 305

Dedication service, Congregation Moses Montefiore, 383

Dedication service for the new synagogue Beth-El Emeth, 68

Dedication service of the new synagogue and Community Center of Congregation Bnai Jeshurun of Philadelphia, 1211

Dedication services at the Temple of Bene Israel Congregation, 691

Dedication services of the third Temple and first Community Centre of Congregation Beth Israel of Houston, 1212

Dedicatory services of Orach Chaim synagogue, 559

Deux psaumes pour chant et orchestre: Psaumes 114 et 137, 1023–1024

Deux psaumes pour soprano et orchestre, 1086

Devotional exercises for the use of the daughters of Israel, see רחמה

Divine consoler, see אלון בכות

Divine service for Sabbath schools, 773

Divine service for the Congregation Ahawath Chesed Sha'ar Hashamayim, 945

The divine service of American Israelites, see תפלות בני ישורון כפי מנהג אמעריקא

The door of hope, 546, 692

Dr. David Einhorn's עלת תמיד, see also עלת תמיד

Dr. David Einhorn's עלת תמיד, 518, 862, 1087

Draft of a revised ritual for Temple Emanu-El, New York, 403

Title Index

Einweihung der Synagoge der Gemeinde Rodef Schalom, 177
Eliyohu hanovi, 969
The Emanu-El hymnal, 1088
Etz chajim, 671
Evening and morning service for the New Year and the Day of Atonement, 970
Evening and morning service for the week days, 505
Evening and morning service for week days, 631, 863
Evening prayers for the house of mourning, 423, 506, 596, 810
Evening service at the house of mourning, 478, 570, 578
Evening service for the house of mourning, *see*
תפלה לבית האבל
תפלת ערבית לבית האבל
Evening service for the house of mourning: Congregation Rodeph Sholom, New York, 646
Evening service for the New Year, 946
Evening service for the New Year and the Day of Atonement, 1245
Evening service for the Sabbath, 693
Evening service for the Sabbath: arranged with responsive readings, anthems, hymns, 1063, 1119
Evening service for the Sabbath and week-days, *see* סדר תפלות ישראל
Evening service for the synagogue: according to the Union prayer book, *see also* אוהב שלום
Evening service for the synagogue: according to the Union prayer book, 547, 864
Evening service for the synagogue. No. 1, 831
Evening service for the synagogue. No. 2, 832
Evening service for week days for the divine service to mark the beginning of the twenty-fifth Biennial Council of the Union of American Hebrew Congregations, 971

Evening service for week-days and the Sabbath, 632
Evening service of Roshashanah, and Kippur, 2

Fear not, O Israel, 579
The feast of Tabernacles, 14–16
Festival prayer book, 914–915
Festgebete der Israeliten, *see* מחזור לכל מועדי השנה
Festival prayer book: order of service, 1145
Festival prayers, *see* עבדת שלש רגלים
Fiftieth anniversary services of the Temple, Cleveland Ohio, Tifereth Israel Congregation, 580
The flower service, 995
For little children, 633
For the sin, *see* על חטא
Form of blessings of Israel with an English translation, *see* סדר להדרת קדש
Form of daily prayers according to the custom of the Spanish and Portuguese Jews, *see* סדר התפילות כמנהג ק״ק ספרדים
The form of prayers according to the custom of the Spanish and Portuguese Jews, *see* סדור שפתי צדיקים
Form of prayers and blessings of Israel with an English translation, *see* סדר להדרת קדש
Form of prayers for the ... according to the custom of the German Jews, *see* מחזור ... כמנהג אשכנז
Form of prayers for the ... according to the custom of the German and Polish Jews, *see*
מחזור ...
מחזור ... כמנהג אשכנז
Form of prayers for the ... according to the custom of the Polish Jews, *see* מחזור ... כמנהג פולין
Form of service at the consecration of the new synagogue Benai Israel, Sacramento, Cal., 110
Form of service at the consecration of the

193

new synagogue Kenaises Israel, *see* סדר חנוכת הבית דקהלה החדשה כנסת ישראל

Form of service at the consecration of the synagogue Adereth El, 111

Form of service at the consecration of the synagogue Beth Elohim, Brooklyn N.Y., 99

Form of service at the consecration of the synagogue Mishkan Israel, 57

Form of service for the dedication of the new synagogue of the Portuguese Congregation "Mikve Israel," *see* אלה המזמורים אשר שרו להקת המשוררים לחנוכת בית הכנסת של ק״ק מקוה ישראל

Form of service for the dedication of the new synagogue of the Portuguese Hebrew Congregation "Shearith Israel," *see* אלה המזמורים אשר שרו להקת המשוררים לחנוכת בית הכנסת שבנו היחידים בשם ק״ק שארית ישראל

Form of the prayer for the Feast of New Year, *see* מחזור לראש השנה

The form of the prayer which was performed at the Jews' synagogue, 1

Form of the service at the dedication of the new synagogue of Kahal Kadosh "Mickvi Israel," *see* אלה השירים והפסוקים מהקפות מהספרים לחנוכת בית הכנסת מקוה ישראל

Form of the service at the dedication of the new synagogue of Kahal Kadosh "Shearith Israel," 8

Form of the service at the dedication of the new synagogue of Kahal Kadosh "Shearith Israel" in Crosby Street, *see* אלה השירים והפסוקים מהקפות מהספרים לחנוכת בית הכנסת שארית ישראל

Form of the service for the consecration of the new synagogue of Congregation Mickva Israel, 260

Fountain of life for those who mourn, *see* מקור חיים

Friday evening melodies, *see* שירי ישראל לליל שבת

Friday evening religious exercises of the Young Men's Hebrew Association, New York, 597

Friday evening service, 6

Friday evening service. No. 2, 1120

Fünfzigjähriges Stiftungsfest der Gemeinde Ahabeth Achim (Bruderliebe), 548

Das Gebetbuch der Israeliten, *see* סדור תפלת ישראל

Gebet-Buch fuer Sabbath, Pesach, Schebuoth, Succoth und Rosh Hashana, *see* קרבן אהרן

Gebet-Buch für den öffentlichen Gottesdienst und die Privat-Andacht, *see* מנהג אמעריקא תפלות בני ישרון

Gebet-Buch für den öffentlichen Gottesdienst und die Privat-Andacht, *see also* The daily prayers

Gebet-Buch für den öffentlichen Gottesdienst und die Privat-Andacht, *see also* תפלות בני ישורון, מנהג אמעריקא

Gebet-Buch für den öffentlichen Gottesdienst und die Privat-Andacht, 69

Gebetbuch für israelitische Reform-Gemeinden, 58

Gebetbuch für israelitische Reform-Gemeinden, *see* עלת תמיד

Gebete bei Leichenbegängnissen auf dem Friedhof der Oheb-Israel zu Baltimore, 312

Gebete der Israeliten in Amerika, *see* תפלות ישראל

Gebete für den öffentlichen Gottesdienst der Tempelgemeinde Ahawath Chesed, *see* סדר תפלה

Gebete für Kinder für Haus und Schule, 236

Gebete-Ordnung der Congregation Ahawath Chesed für ראש השנה und יום כפור, 167

Gebet-Ordnung für die Todten Bestattung, 252

Title Index

Gebete und Gesänge zur Seelenfeier, see הזכרת נשמות

Gebete und Gesänge zur Seelenfeier (Szold), 81

Gebete zur öffentlichen und häuslichen andacht, 223

Gedenkbuch ... für alle ihre verstorbenen Mitglieder, 100

Gemilus chasodim, see סדר גמלות חסדים

Gesänge für den öffentlichen jüdischen Gottesdienst aus verschiedenen Liedersammlungen zusammengetragen, 101, 137, 168, 281

Gesänge für israelitischen Reform Gemeinden aus verschiedenen Liedersammlung zusammengetragen, 151

Gesänge und Gebete, 22

Gesänge und Gebete für den öffentlichen Gottesdienst der Israeliten, 185, 211

Gesänge zum Gebrauche beim Gottesdienst der Reform-Gemeinde "Keneseth Israel" zu Philadelphia, 59

Gesänge zur feierlichen Einweihung des Versöhnungstage, 1854, 50

Golden jubilee services and dedication ceremonies, 615

Gottesdienst für Sabbath, Fest- und Wochentage und Gebete für Kinder, 271

Gottesdienst-Ordnung der Gemeinde Mischkan Israel in New Haven, Conn., 169

Grace and blessings for various occasions, see ברכת המזון עם סדר הברכות

Great is the Lord, 972

Guide for the arrangement of young people's Friday evening service, 1213

Halben chatoeinu, see Zwei Recitativen

Hallel Psalms 115, 116, 118, 996

Hallelujah: Psalm 113, 1089

Hamchabe es haner, see Two cantor recitatives

Haneros halolu, see הנרות הללו

Hanukkah and Purim service, 865

Hanukkah festival, 479

The harvest service, 997

Hashkivenu, see Hebrew sacred chorus for mixed voices

Havdoloh for solo, choir and piano, see הבדלה

Hebrew first reader, see מלמד להועיל

Hebrew hymnal for school and home, see קול רינה

A Hebrew reader containing the daily prayers of the Jewish ritual, 384

Hebrew reader containing the daily prayers of the Union prayer book, 480

A Hebrew reader containing the prayers and Psalms of the Jewish ritual, 490

The Hebrew reader for schools, 313, 581

Hebrew sacred chorus for mixed voices, 1146

The Hebrew text for schools from the prayerbook of B. Szold, 296, 458

Heje im pifijos, see היה עם פפיות

Der Herr ist Koenig, 174

Holyday prayers, see עבדת יום הזכרון; עבדת יום הכפורים

Home service for Hanukkah, 634, 947

Home service with translation and transliteration, see עבודת השלחן עם קריאת שמע על המטה

Horinnoh wehatefilloh, see הרנה והתפלה

Hours of devotion, see also Stunden der Andacht

Hours of devotion, 138–140, 158–159, 178, 198, 237, 297, 341, 385, 519

Hovu Ladonai, see Psalm XXIX: Hovu Ladonai

How amiable are thy tabernacles, 887

How goodly are thy tents, 531–532, 623

How goodly are thy tents, O Jacob, see מה טובו אהליך יעקב

Hymn book for Jewish worship, 282, 424, 756

Hymnen, 96

Hymnen für den öffentlichen Gottesdienst

der Tempelgemeinde Ahawath Chesed, 212, 306
Hymns, 272, 441
Hymns and anthems, 298
Hymns and anthems: West End Synagogue, 729
Hymns and anthems adapted for Jewish worship, 342, 357, 386, 481
Hymns and anthems for Jewish worship, 635, 647
Hymns and memoranda for Sunday school use, 716
Hymns and prayers for the religious school of Congregation Ahawath Chesed-Shaar Hashomayim, 582
Hymns and prayers in English and German, see שירו לה׳ שיר חדש
Hymns and responses from Jastrow's prayer book, 491
Hymns collected from various sources and selections from the Psalms, 459, 520, 598
Hymns for divine service in Temple Emanu-El, 186–187, 276, 294, 351, 449
Hymns for Jewish worship, 343
Hymns for Jewish worship (Gottheil), see Hymns and anthems adapted for Jewish worship
Hymns from the New Union hymnal, 774
Hymns of Beth El Emeth Congregation, 289
Hymns, Psalms and prayers in English and German, see שירו לה׳ שיר חדש
Hymns written for the service of the Hebrew Congregation, Beth Elohim, 20
Hymns written for the use of Hebrew Congregations, 60, 141, 152, 238

In distress I call upon the Lord, 833
In Thee, O God, do I put my trust, 560
Inauguration of the Hebrew Orphans' Asylum in Charleston, S.C., 86
Inspirational readings for the home, 1121
Isaiah Congregation hymn book, 1090
Der israelitische Confirmand, 160, 253

Israelitische Tempel-Gesänge, 245, 358
Israelitisches Andachts-buch, see תפלת ישראל
Israelitisches Gebetbuch für den öffentlichen Gottesdienst im ganzen Jahre, see עבודת ישראל
Israelitisches Gebetbuch für die häusliche Andacht, see הגיון לב
Israelitish prayer book for all the public services of the year, see עבודת ישראל

Jaale, 1091
The Jewish home prayer-book, 370
Jewish home prayers, 866
Jewish hymnal for religious schools, 757
Jewish hymns for Jewish schools, 1246
Jewish hymns for Sabbath schools and families, see זמירות ישראל
זמרות ישראל
The Jewish prayer book, see תפלות ישראל
תפלת ישראל
Jewish science, 948
The Jewish songster, see also המנגן
The Jewish songster, 1064
The Jewish year, 549
Jiskor, 717

Kedusha = Sanctification, 1174
Kiddush: the consecration of the Sabbath eve at the family table, 718, 730
Kiddush, or Sabbath sentiment in the home, 550–551, 1092
King David's Psalm of Thanksgiving, 1175
A Kippur service for children, see The children's service for Yom Kippur afternoon
Kol nidre, see O day of God
Kol nidre, see Yom Kippur night
Kol nidre (Perlmutter), 1093
Kol nidre (Roberts), 916
Kol nidre (Russotto), 719
Kol nidre (Zagler), 867
Kol rinah, see קול רינה
Kol zimroh, see קול זמרה

Kommt, Söhne der Allmacht, 226
Kranken Gebete des Hebra Bikur Holim Vekadisha, *see* תפלות החולה
Kranken-Gebete für die חברה אחים רחמנים Gesellschaft Brüder der Barmhezigeit, *see* תפילות החולה

Lema'an yilmedu, *see* למען ילמדו
Let my prayer come unto Thy presence, 1176
Lincoln centenary services, 1909, 758
Little daily helps for holy living, 731
The Lord is my light, 672
The Lord is ruler, *see* Der Herr ist Koenig
The Lord of all (Adon olam), *see also* Adon olam
The Lord of all (Adon olam), 888

Machsor, *see* מחזור לפסח שבועות וסוכות
Magil's complete linear prayer book, *see* סדר כל תפלות השנה
Magil's linear children's companion, *see* רע הילדים
Maḥzor Yannai, *see* מחזור ינייי
Malchijos, Sichronos, Schof'ros, 889
Meditations and prayers for every situation in life, *see* אמרי לב
Meditations of the heart, 583
Memorial exercises in memory of Solomon Schechter, 949
Memorial hymn (Why are thou cast down), *see also* Why art thou cast down my soul?
Memorial hymn (Why are thou cast down), 507
Memorial prayers and meditations, *see* מענה לשון
Memorial service, *see* הזכרת נשמות
Memorial service: 3 Psalms for male voices, 834
Memorial service (Plum Street Temple), *see also* Order of the memorial service at the Plum Street Temple
Memorial service (Plum Street Temple), 775

Memorial service: prepared for Congregation Ahawath Chesed Shaar Hashomayim, 835
Memorial service: responsive readings, songs and hymns, 1247
Memorial service after Dr. Einhorn's prayer book, 584
Memorial service for the Day of Atonement: according to the Union prayer book, 561, 1248
Memorial service for the Day of Atonement: written for Congregation Rodeph Shalom, 616
Memorial service for the Day of Atonement: written for the Baltimore Hebrew Congregation, 1094
Memorial service for the dead, *see* הזכרת נשמות
Memorial service in commemoration of the fifth anniversary of the death of the Rev. Dr. Isaac M. Wise, 673
Memorial service held in honor of our dearly beloved and much lamented President William McKinley, 599
Memorial service of the Hebrew Union-Veterans Association, 521
Memorial service (Seelenfeier) for the Day of Atonement, 531
Mimkomcha, *see* ממקומך
Min hamezar, 387
Min hamezar (Psalm 118) for solo, soli and male choir, *see* מן המיצר
Minhammezar, 507
Minister's handbook, 973
Mismor schir chanukas, *see* מזמור שיר חנוכת
M'loch, *see* Zwei Recitativen
Mogen ovos, 1147
Morning prayers, 388, 600
Morning service for the synagogue according to the Einhorn prayerbook, 732
Morning service for the synagogue according to the Union prayerbook, *see also* אוהב שלום

Morning service for the synagogue according to the Union prayerbook, 811
Morning service for the Temple Beth-El School of Buffalo, 1249
Morning services: Temple Mishkan Israel, 759
Mourners' prayers, see סדר תפלות לאבלים
The mourner's service, 509
Music for Sabbath and Festival services, see סדר תפלות לשבת וליום טוב
Music for the Sabbath evening service of the Temple: according to the Union prayer book, 1214
Music to the hymns and anthems for Jewish worship by G. Gottheil, 359
My strength and song in the Lord, see עזי וזמרת יה

New Festival service: specially composed for the Reformed Hebrew ritual, 552
New Jewish hymnal for religious schools and junior congregations, 974, 1025, 1148
New Year's hymn, 571
The newly improved prayer book entitled Yoreh-malkosh u'marveh, see סידור יורה ומלקוש ומרוה
N'ginoth Baruch Schorr, see נגינות ברוך שור לימים נוראים
O day of God = Kol nidre, 1250
O Lord! what is man, see Adonoy moh adom
Opening services of the Temple, Wilson & Central Aves.: Tifereth Israel Congregation, 492
Order of children's service for Jewish Sabbath schools, 314, 389
Order of consecration of the synagogue "House of Israel" Williamsburgh, see סדר חנוכת בית הכנסת בית ישראל בעיר ווילימסבארג
Order of consecration service of the Congregation Beth Jacob, at Albany, see סדר חנוכת הבית והשירים אשר ישוררו קהל בית יעקב

Order of dedication service, 836
Order of exercises at the consecration of the new synagogue of the Congregation Shaar Hashomajim, 127
The order of prayer for divine service, see סדר תפלה
Order of prayer for the Israelitish divine service, see עבודת ישראל
Order of prayer in the house of mourners, 188, 276, 294
Order of prayers adopted by the Congregation Mickva Israel, Savannah, Georgia, see סדר תפלה
Order of prayers and responsive readings for Jewish worship, see תפלה למשה תפלת ישראל
Order of prayers established by the Congregation, אנשי מעריב Chicago, Illinois, 70
Order of prayers for חפציבה Hebrew School, 87, 97
Order of Selihot to be recited on Yom Kippur, see סליחות ליום כפור
The order of service, 213
Order of service and the consecration of the synagogue Shangarai Chesed, 38
Order of service appointed for laying the corner-stone of the Temple Congregation Beth Ahabah, 648
Order of service at the consecration of the new synagogue of Congregation Bnai Jeshurun, 128
Order of service at the consecration of the new synagogue of the Congregation "Bnai Israel," 71
Order of service at the consecration of the new synagogue "Shaar Hashomayim" see זמרות ושירות
Order of service at the consecration of the synagogue Nefutsoth Jehudah of New Orleans, 35
Order of service at the consecration of the

synagogue Rodef Sholum, of Philadelphia, 26

Order of service at the consecration of the synagogue Roudafe Sholum, of Philadelphia, 23

Order of service at the dedication of the Congregation Beth El, see רינה ותפילה

Order of service at the dedication of the synagogue Hungarian Congregation Beth Hamedrash Hagadol, see חנוך בית הכנסת בית המדרש הגדול אנשי אונגארן

Order of service at the dedication of the synagogue Nefutsoth Jehudah of New-Orleans, 72

Order of service at the dedication of the synagogue of Cong. Sharay Tefila, 510

Order of service at the dedication of the synagogue of Congregation "B'nai Jeshurun," 329

Order of service at the dedication of the Temple of Congregation Bikur Cholim, 344

Order of service at the inauguration of the Jews' Hospital, New York, see סדר העבודה ביום חנוכת בית החולים אשר ליהודים

Order of service at the re-opening celebration of the Temple Anshi Chesed, 161

Order of service for Shabuoth and confirmation, see חג השבועות תרנ״ז

Order of service for the consecration of the Temple Ahawath Chesed, 199

Order of service for the consecration of the Temple Emanu-El, 162

Order of service for the day of solemn fast and humiliation, see סדר העבודה

Order of service for the day of the New Year and the Day of Atonement for junior congregations, 998

Order of service for the evening of the Sabbath, 950

Order of service for the house of mourning, 1026

Order of service for the New Year and the Day of Atonement, 793

Order of service for use on the Sabbath before Thanksgiving Day Nineteen Hundred and Five, 674, 694–695

Order of service for ראש השנה ויום כפור and הזכרת נשמות, 228

Order of service in honor of the hundredth birthday of Sir Moses Montefiore, Bart., 315

Order of service in honor of the one hundredth birthday of Sir Moses Montefiore, Bart., 316

Order of service in the synagogue of the Congregation שארית ישראל, 19

Order of service of religious schools, 1027

Order of service of Sabbath schools, 760

Order of service on laying the first stone of the synagogue K. K. B'ne Jeshurun, 39

Order of service, Thanksgiving Day, 254

Order of service to be performed at the consecration of the new synagogue "The Gates of Prayer," see סדר חנוכת הבית והשירים אשר ישוררו קהל שערי תפלה

Order of service to be performed at the consecration of the synagogue Beth Israel, see סדר חנוכת הבית

Order of service to be performed at the consecration of the synagogue, Washington Street, Newark, N.J., 72a

Order of service, with responses, Psalms and hymns, 1065, 1177

Order of services at the dedication of the new synagogue First Roumanian-American Congregation "שערי שמים," 617

Order of services at the house of mourning, burial and setting of tombstones, see שערי חסד

Order of services for the dedication of Temple Beth Zion, 425

Order of services . . . as used by Temple Rodeph Sholom, N.Y. adapted by Con-

gregation Sh'erith Israel-Ahabath Achim, see שלהבת יה
Order of services for the house of mourning, 618
Order of Thanksgiving service, 460
Order of the burial of the dead and service in the house of mourning, 522
Order of the consecration of the synagogue Beth-El at Albany, see סדר חנוכת הבית והשירים אשר שרו קהל בית אל
Order of the memorial service at the Plum Street Temple, see also Memorial service (Plum Street Temple)
Order of the memorial service at the Plum Street Temple, 404, 776
Order of the service for Sabbath evening, 7
Order of the service for the consecration of the new Stanly Street synagogue, see סדר חנוכת הבית
Order of worship for Sunday services, 649
Ordnung der Gebete beim Gottesdienst der Gemeinde Anschi Chesed, 189
The Orpheus, 261
Out of the depths, 1028
Oz joshir, see אז ישיר

Personal prayers, 812
Pijutim, Gebete ung Gesänge zum Gebrauche, see קדש הלולים
A prayer, see A tefilah
Prayer and singing-book for the use of the rising generation of Hebrew Congregations, 255
Prayer at the opening of the House of Representatives, 88
Prayer book ... with revised English translation, see מחזור ... עם תרגום אנגלית
Prayer book for the Day of Atonement: arranged for the use of the Congregation Beth Miriam, 999
Prayer book for the New Year: arranged for the use of the Brooklyn synagogue, 1029
Prayer book for the New Year: arranged for the use of the Congregation Beth Miriam, 1000

Prayer book for the Sabbath, 890
"A prayer for peace," 170
A prayer of repentance for the afternoon of the Day of Atonement, 493–494
Prayer of the repentant, 562
Prayerbook and hymnal from the American Orthodox Jewish Youth, 1066
Prayer-book for Sabbath, Pesach, Shebuoth and Succoth, see ענף יוסף
Prayer-book for Jewish deaf, see סדר תפלות ישראל
A prayerbook for the services of the year at the synagogue, see עבודת ישראל
Prayers and hymns for divine service, 585
Prayers and hymns for the use of religious school attached to the Congregation B'nai Jeshurun, 390
Prayers for beginners, see תפלות למתחילים
Prayers for mourners, see אלון בכות
Prayers for private devotion from the Union prayer book, 813, 837
Prayers for the dead, see ספר חיים
Prayers for the divine services of Congregation Ahawath Chesed, see סדר תפלה
Prayers for the house of mourning, 572
Prayers for the Sabbath, Rosh-Hashanah, and Kippur, 3–4
Prayers for the sick and the dead, see הזכרת נשמות
Prayers for use in the Jewish home, 1095
Prayers, hymns and exercises, 273
Prayers in commemoration of the dead, 405
Prayers in the home for Jewish parents and children, 1215
Prayers of Israel, (Temple "Gates of Hope" שערי תקוה) see
תפלת ישראל = Prayers of Israel:
תפלות לכל השנה
תפלת ישראל: התפלות מכל השנה כמנהג ק"ק שערי תקוה
תפלת ישראל כולל התפלות מכל השנה כמנהג ק"ק שערי תקוה
Prayers of Israel for the Sabbath and the

Festivals, *see* תפלות ישראל לשבת ולשלש רגלים

Prayers of Israel with an English translation, *see* תפלות ישראל
תפלת שראל

Prayers of the Jewish advance, 1178

Prayers offered at the daily sessions of the Assembly, 1216

Predigt-Lieder, 190

The priestly blessing, 175

Proceedings of the laying of the cornerstone for the synagogue of the Congregation Rodef Shalom, 171

Programm für das Einweihungs-fest der neuen Synagoge der Gemeinde Beth-El, 129

Programm für das Einweihungsfest des neuens Tempels der Reforme-Gemeinde "Keneseth Israel," 112

Programm für das Einweihungs-fest des Tempels der Reform-Gemeinde "Temple Beth Zion," 130

Programm of the ceremonies of the consecration of the Temple of the Reformed Congregation "Temple Beth Zion" *see* Programm für das Einweihungs-fest des Tempels der Reform-Gemeinde "Temple Beth Zion"

Programme of ceremonies at the dedication of the Temple K.K. Bene Yeshurun, of Cincinnati, 142

Programme of the consecration services of the synagogue of the Congregation Rodef Shalom, *see* Einweihung der Synagoge der Gemeinde Rodef Schalom

Programme of the dedication service of the synagogue Emmanu-El, 51

Programme of the dedication services at the Temple of Congregation Emanu-El, 442

Programme of the dedication services at the Temple of Congregation Shomer Emunim, 391

Programme of the dedication services of Reform Congregation Keneseth Israel, 461

Programme of the exercises on the laying of the corner-stone, 113

Psalm I, verses 1, 2, and 3, 317

Psalm XXIX: Hovu Ladonoi, 891

Psalm 100, 1067

Psalm CXII. Heil dem Manne, 262

Psalm CXXV. We sich auf Gott verlässt, 263

The Psalmists, 406

Psaume 22: pour baryton et grand orchestre, 1030

Psaume 22: pour baryton et orchestre, 1096

Psaume 114: pour chant et orchestre, 1031

Psaume 137: pour baryton et grand orchestre, 1032

Pure words, 318

A Purim songster, 1122

Rebecca Gratz prayers, 18

Recitativen für Kantor, *see* שירי תפלה

Religiöse Betrachtungen und Gebete für Israel Frauen und Mädchen, *see* תחינות בנות ישורון

Religious discourse delivered in the synagogue in this city, 5

Religious duties of the daughters of Israel, *see also* ספר אהל שרה

Religious duties of the daughters of Israel, 619

Requiem for the Day of Atonement, *see* הזכרת נשמות

Reshith daath sephath Eber, *see* ראשית דעת שפת עבר

Response to silent prayer, 623

Responses adapted for New Year and Atonement Eve, 1251

Responses, Psalms and hymns for worship in congregations and schools, *see* זמרות ישראל

Rest in the Lord, my soul, 601, 629

Reverend's hand book, *see* רעווערעדס האנדבוך

Rinath amcho, see רנת עמך
Ritual for children's Sabbath services and Sabbath school devotions, 636
Ritual for Friday evening service in the Temple Emanu-El of San Francisco, 1252–1253
Ritual for funerals and prayers in the house of mourning... see ספר החיים
A ritual for Jewish soldiers, see סדר תפלות ישראל לבעלי מלחמה
Ritual for Jewish worship, see also Ritual for Jewish worship = סדר תפלות כל השנה
Ritual for Jewish worship, 319, 534, 814
Rochmono d'one, 838
Rozo deShabos, see Two cantor recitatives

Sabbath afternoon service, see תפלת מנחה לשבת
Sabbath afternoon service, 462, 523, 733
Sabbath and holiday prayer book, see סדר תפלות לשבת וליום טוב
Sabbath and holiday prayers, see סדר תפלות לשבת וליום טוב
Sabbath eve service, see מעריב של שבת סדר ערבית לשבת
Sabbath eve service, Temple Beth-El, New York, 443–444
Sabbath eve services and hymns and anthems for Sabbath and holidays, 494, 586
Sabbath evening service for the synagogue: arranged according to the Union prayer book, 1179
Sabbath evening service for the synagogue, according to the Union prayer book, 975, 1033, 1180
Sabbath evening service. No. 1., 563
Sabbath evening service. No. 2., 1181
Sabbath evening services: arranged for the South Shore Temple, 1217
Sabbath hymn, 407
Sabbath morning service, 620, 734, 892, 976
Sabbath morning service for the synagogue, according to the Union prayer book, 868, 951
Sabbath music, 524, 650, 1001, 1182
A Sabbath noon chant for mixed voices and piano accompaniment, see זמירות ברוך אל עליון
Sabbath prayer book, 893
Sabbath prayer book: arranged for Conservative congregations, 1034
Sabbath prayers, see עבדת שבת
The Sabbath service according to the Union prayer book, 735
The Sabbath service and miscellaneous prayers adopted by the Reformed Society of Israelites, 12, 952
Sabbath service for children, 637
The Sabbath service: for Sabbath eve and Sabbath morning, see תפלת שבת
Sabbath service of the Reformed Hebrew ritual, 621
Sabbath song: How sweet upon this sacred day, 1254
Sabbath-school hymnal, 496–498, 511, 535, 651, 696, 761, 815, 894, 1068, 1097, 1149
Sabbath-school hymnal of K. K. Beth Elohim, 977
The sacred harp of Judah, 114
Sacred memorial services in memory of the late משה מאנטיפיורי Sir Moses Montefiore, 330
Sanitary law for married woman and man, see הלכות נדה, חלה, הדלקת הנר, ברכת הנהנין...
Schirai chinooch, 652
The school service, 499, 587
Sefer Anim zemiroth, see also ספר אנעים זמירות ספר אנעים זמרות
Sefer Anim zemiroth, 869–870, 1183
Select prayers for the New Year and Atonement days, 408
Selected hymns and prayers for divine service, 307

Title Index

Selected hymns for Hebrew Sunday school, 426, 536

Selections from the prayer book for Sabbaths and Holy days, *see* שירות ותשבחות

Sephath emeth, *see* סדור שפת אמת

Service and sermon held on the day of lamentation, 131

Service for confirmation, 1124

Service for Friday evening, 736

Service for preparing the dead for burial: as used in the Spanish and Portuguese Congregation Shearith Israel, New York City, *see* סדר רחיצת המת: כפי מנהג ק"ק הספרדים שארית ישראל בנו יארק

Service for Sabbath eve and Sabbath morning: arranged for the use of Jewish camps, 1184

Service for Sabbath evening according to the Union prayer book, 839

Service for the burial of the dead, *see* צדוק הדין

Service for the dead, *see* הזכרת נשמות

The service hymnal, 653–656, 1124–1125

The service manual, 463–464, 720, 762, 840, 1035, 1098, 1126

Service of prayer and thanksgiving as used in all the synagogues of the British empire, 320

Service of the sanctuary for the Sabbath and Festivals, *see* עבודת הקדש

Service of the synagogue, *see* מחזור... מחזור עבדת אהל מועד, כמנהג פולין

A service of the synagogue in the time of Jesus Christ, 331–332, 360, 409

Service on the occasion of the one hundredth birthday of Sir Moses Montefiore, 321

The service-ritual, 371, 427, 465, 525, 621

Services at the installation of David Philipson, 372

Services for children, 588, 737

Services for Sabbath and holidays, 445

Services for the New Year's day and the Day of Atonement for junior congregations, 1002

Services of B'rith Shalom Congregation, *see* עבודת ברית שלום

Set me as a seal upon Thy heart (Song of Songs 8: 6–7), 1185

Shalhevet Yah, *see* שלהבת יה

Sherai Israel, *see* שירי ישראל

"Shir Zion," 657, 1127

Shirai chinooch, *see* שירי חנוך

Shirai tehilloh, *see* שירי תהילה

Shire Yehudah, 373, 446, 466, 564

Shirei zimrah, Kabalat Shabbat, *see* שירי זמרה, קבלת שבת

Shofar service, 675

Sidur chinuch tefilah hechodosh, *see* סדור חנוך תפלה החדש

Sidur chinuch tephilah hechodosh, *see* סדור חנוך תפלה החדש

Sidur tifereth Jehudah, *see* סדור תפארת יהודה

Sidur tifereth Judah, *see* סדור תפארת יהודה

Simchath Torah, *see* שמחת תורה

Sinagogue recitative for Tisha-Ba'v, *see* קנות לתשעה באב

Sing unto the Lord a new song, *see* שירו לה׳ שיר חדש

Sir Moses Montefiore, Centennial, 322

Sir Moses Montefiore, Centennial celebration, 323

Song and praise for Sabbath eve, *see* זמירות ותשבחות לליל שבת

The song book for Jewish worship, 526

Song of prayer for Friday evening service, *see* שירי תפלה

Songs and chants for the prayers of the synagogue year, *see* שירי זמרה

Songs and prayers and meditations for divine services of Israelites, 214, 333

Songs and prayers for the Sabbath eve, *see* הרנה והתפלה

Songs and prayers for the Sabbath service, *see* הרנה והתפלה

Songs for congregational singing, 777

Songs of Israel, see זמירות ישראל
Songs of Israel (Greenwald), 917
Songs of Judah, see Shire Yehudah
Songs of Judah: hymns, Psalms and anthems, 676
Songs of the synagogue for Sabbath morning according to the ritual of D. Einhorn, 374
Songs of Zion, see A collection of principal melodies of the synagogue
Songs of Zion (Greenwald), 918
The soul of life, see ספר נשמת חיים
Source of salvation, see מעין הישועה
Special prayer during the time of our war with Spain, 553
Special ritual of the High Steet Temple, Elmira, New York, 1003
The standard machsor for New Year, see מחזור לראש השנה
The standard prayer book, see סדר תפלות כל השנה
The strength of faith, 1004
Stunden der Andacht, see also Hours of Devotion
Stunden der Andacht, 106, 115, 191, 229, 299, 482
Succoth revived, 794
Sukkos service for children, 1069
Sun and shield, 527–528
The Sunday service, 1036–1037
Sunday service: Temple Beth-El, New York, 565
Sunday services for Jewish Reform congregations, see קרבן תודה
Supplement to the hymn book for use of Temple Emanu-El, New York, 697
Syder tefilas Israel, see סדור תפלת ישראל מכל השנה
Synagogen-Gesänge für Kantor und gemischten Chor, 1038
The synagogical service, see עמנואל
Synagogue and school, 361
Synagogue dedication service, see סדר חנוכת הבית

The synagogue service arranged for the Congregation B'nai Jeshurun of New York, see עבדת הקדש
Synagogue service for Friday evening in E♭ Major, 1186
Synagogue service for Friday evening in F Major, 1187
Synagogue service for Sabbath morning in E♭ Major, 1188
Synagogue service for the use of the Congregation "Shaaray Tefilla" see בית תפלה
Synagogue songs, 1189

Tag des Herrn, see Day of God
Tägliche Gebete, see: סדר תפלות לכל השנה נוסח אשכנז, מתורגם אשכנזית
A tefilah = A prayer, 1099
Tefilas Eliyohu, see תפלת אליהו
Tehilloth, 738
The Temple Beth-El hymn book for the use of religious schools, 428, 447
Temple B'nai Abraham Sabbath school ritual, see סדר תפלה לילדי בני אברהם
Temple Emanu-El hymn book for schools, 239
The Temple hymnal, 1100
Temple Israel — New ritual, see Trial issue of the new ritual for "Temple Israel" St. Louis
Temple music, 590
The Temple service, 512
The Temple service arranged for the Congregation Rodeph Sholom of New York, see שלהבת יה
The Temple service ... Congregation Beth Miriam, Long Branch, N.J., see שלהבת יה
Temple service for the evening of the New Year, 953
Temple service for New Year and Day of Atonement, 448
Temple service for Sabbath morning: arranged according to the Union prayer book, 1190
Ten choice Hebrew song classics (tradi-

Title Index

tional) for voice and pianoforte, 918a, 918b, 1069a, 1218
Tfilath Jeschua, see תפלת יהושוע
Three Psalms, Nos. 77, 121, 129, 554
Three recitatives for the High Holidays, see דריי רעטשיטאטיווען פאר ימים נוראים
Torah service, 410
Tov le hodos, 602
Traditional hymn for the Day of Atonement, see אותך אדרש
Translation of the order of service at the consecration of the synagogue Beth Ahabah, 29
Trial issue of the new ritual for "Temple Israel" St. Louis, 375
Tunes for the Israelitish school, 220–221, 235, 242, 250
Two cantor recitatives... Rozo deShabos... Hamechabe es haner, 1128
Two responses, 623

Union hymnal, 537–538, 895–896
Union prayer book, see תפלות ישראל
The Union prayer-book for Jewish worship, see סדר תפלות ישראל
The universal Lord (Adon olam), see also Adon olam
The universal Lord (Adon olam), 795
Unesaneh toikef, 1217
Union services in memory of the Russian martyrs of our faith, see Central Conference of American Rabbis: Union services in memory of the Russian martyrs of our faith
Unsane taukef, see ונתנה תוקף
Unsanneh tokef, 778
Unveiling and consecration of the John Hay Memorial Window, 698
Uvnucho yomar, 1129

V, Schomru: a Sabbath eve prayer, see ושמרו
V'shomru: a Sabbath eve chant, 1039
V'shom'ru: for four-part chorus, 1040
V'shom'ru: traditional melody arranged for mixed choir and Cantor, 1220
V'shomru (Sabbath song); May the words, 1052
V'shom'ru, the Sabbath, 1130

Why art thou cast down my soul?, see also Memorial hymn (Why are thou cast down?)
Why art thou cast down my soul?, 529
Why art thou cast down, O, my soul?, 624
Wm. McKinley memorial service, 603

Yehi Rozon fon Rosh Chodesh Benschen, see יהי רצון פון ראש חדש בענשען
Yehi Rozon from Rosh Chodesh benschen, see יהי רצון פון ראש חדש בענשען
Yismechu bemalchus'cho, see ישמחו במלכותך
Yohale Sarah, see ספר אהל שרה
Yom Kippur night, 658
Young Israel's guide for home and the religious school, 677, 763

Zimrath Yah, see זמרת יה
Z'miros: Baruch El elyon, see זמירות ברוך אל עליון
Z'miroth ut'filoth Yisroel, see זמירות ותפלות ישראל
Zwei Recitativen. I. Halben Chatoeinu. II. M'loch, 1150

Hebrew

Evening service for ראה גם prayer book the synagogue according to the Union prayer book

אדון עולם, ראה גם Adon olam
אדון עולם, 24
אוהב שלום = Evening service for the synagogue according to the Union

הבדלה, 1153
הגיון לב = 153, 240
הזכרת נשמות = Complete memorial service for solo, mixed chorus with organ accompaniment, 1256
הזכרת נשמות = Gebete und Gesänge zur Seelenfeier, 36
הזכרת נשמות = Memorial service, 659
הזכרת נשמות = Memorial service for the dead, 539
הזכרת נשמות = Prayers for the sick and the dead, 345
הזכרת נשמות = Requiem for the Day of Atonement, 274
הזכרת נשמות = Service for the dead, 179
היה עם פפיות, 1154
הלכות נדה, חלה, הדלקת הנר, ברכת הנהנין בשפת אנגליש, 1155
ונתנה תוקף, 392
ושמרו = "V shomru's", 6, 1156
ושמרו = V, Schomru, 1192
זכר צדיק לברכה, ראה Memorial exercises in memory of Solomon Schechter
זמירות ברוך אל עליון = A Sabbath noon chant, 1157
זמירות ברוך אל עליון = Zemiros: Baruch El elyon, 1158–1159
זמירות ושירות, 346
זמירות ותפלות ישראל, 920
זמירות ותשבחות לליל שבת, 1070–1072
1131, 1225–1226
זמירות ישראל = Ancient Jewish melodies, 660
זמירות ישראל = Auswahl israelitisch-religiöser Lieder in Musik gesetzt, 107, 132
זמירות ישראל = Jewish hymns for Sabbath schools and families, 230, 264
זמירות ישראל = Songs of Israel, 817
זמירות ישראל = Jewish hymns for Sabbath schools and families, 347, 376, 411, 483,
513, 530
זמירות ישראל = Responses, Psalms and

אוהב שלום = Evening service for the according to the Union synagogue prayer book, 871
אוהב שלום = Morning service for the synagogue according to the Union prayer book
ראה גם Morning service for the synagogue according to the Union prayer book
אוהב שלום = Morning service for the synagogue according to the Union prayer book, 816
אותך אדרש, 279
אז ישיר, 1221
אלה המזמורים אשר שרו להקת המשוררים בחנוכת בית הכנסת שבנו היחידים בשם ק"ק שארית ישראל, 89
אלה המזמורים אשר שרו להקת המשוררים לחנוכת בית הכנסת של ק"ק מקוה ישראל, 90
אלה המזמורים והפסוקים לחנוכת בית הכנסת של ק"ק מקוה ישראל, 764
אלה השירים והפסוקים מהקפות מהספרים לחנוכת בית הכנסת מקוה ישראל, 9
אלה השירים והפסוקים מהקפות מהספרים לחנוכת בית הכנסת שארית ישראל, 13
אלון בכות = Divine consoler, 591
אלון בכות = Prayers for mourners, 467
אמרי לב, 116, 143, 246, 592, 638, 721, 796,
1005, 1151
אתה נתן יד לפושעים, 1053

בית תפלה, 334
במה מדליקין, 954
ברכה ותפלה, 1152
ברכת המזון עם סדר הברכות, 919, 1191, 1255
ברכת כהנים = Bircath Kohanim, 1222
ברכת כהנים = Birchas Cohanim, 566
ברכת כהנים = The blessing of the Priests, 1223–1224
ברכת שלום = Blessing of peace
ראה גם The blessing of peace
ברכת שלום = Blessing of peace, 1006
דברי צדיקים, ראה סדור דברי צדיקים
דריי רעטשיטאטיוועין פֿאר ימים נוראים, 1053

Title Index

hymns for worship in congregations
and schools, 500–501
חג השבועות תרנ"ז = Order of service for
Shabuoth and confirmation, 540
חנוך בית הכנסת בית המדרש הגדול אנשי
אונגארן, 393
טוב מעט בכונה, 1007
יהי רצון פון ראש חדש בענשען = Yehi Rozon
fon Rosh Chodesh Benschen, 955
יהי רצון פון ראש חדש בענשען = Yehi Rozon
from Rosh Chodesh benschen, 978
יוצרות לארבע פרשיות עם הגדה לשבת
הגדול, 956
ישמחו במלכותך, 1160
כי כשמך, 1053
כמה יסרתנו, 1053
למען ילמדו, 290, 348
לינען-סדור לבתי-ספר ולעם, 678
מאגילניצקי'ס לינען רע הילדים, ראה גם רע
הילדים
מאגילניצקי'ס לינען רע הילדים, 639, 699, 841
מאגילניצקי'ס קינדער פֿריינד, ראה
מאגילניצקי'ס לינען רע הילדים
מגילת חנכה בהעתקת אנגליש, 872
מה טובו אהליך יעקב, ראה גם How goodly
are thy tents
מה טובו אהליך יעקב, 700
מזמור שיר חנוכת, 1193
מחזור ...Form of prayers...with English
translation, 53, 117, 200, 231, 256,
283–284, 335, 349, 377, 394, 412–413,
428–430, 604–605, 625, 640–641, 722,
765, 1008, 1041–1042
מחזור ...Service of the synagogue, 797,
820, 842, 921–922, 979, 1227, 1257
מחזור: חלק ראשון לראש השנה ויום הכפורים
כמנהג ספרד, 679
מחזור ...כמנהג אשכנז = Form of prayers,
43, 82–83
מחזור ...כמנהג אשכנז עם פירוש מטה לוי, 739

מחזור ...כמנהג ספרד עם פירוש מטה לוי, 740
מחזור ...כמנהג פולין = Form of prayers,
44, 84, 144
מחזור ...עם תרגום אנגלית = Prayer book
with a revised English translation, 779,
818–819, 873
מחזור החדש לראש השנה ויום הכפורים, 1258
מחזור יניי, 1043
מחזור כל בו: עם פירוש עברי טייטש בשם בית
ישראל וילפוט פנינים ומעשה אלפס, 766,
821–823, 1073, 1259–1260
מחזור ליום א' וב' של ראש השנה (ליום כפור),
573
מחזור ליום כפור כמנהג אשכנז ופולין, 395
מחזור לכל מועדי השנה, 91
מחזור לפסח שבעות וסוכות = Machsor, 145
מחזור לראש השנה = Form of prayer for the
Feast of New-Year, 1228
מחזור לראש השנה = The standard machsor
for New Year, 1229
מחזור לראש השנה; מחזור ליום הכפורים,
780
מחזור לראש השנה ויום הכפורים: באותיות
גדולות ובהירות, 874
מחזור לראש השנה ויום הכפורים: כל התפלות
על מקומן כסדרן, 1009
מחזור לראש השנה ויום הכפורים:
כמנהג אשכנז, 1054
מחזור לראש השנה ויום הכפורים: כמנהג
ספרד, 957
מחזור לראש השנה ויום הכפורים: נוסח ספרד:
עם באורים בית לוי, מטה לוי..., 1261
מחזור לראש השנה ויום הכפורים ושלש רגלים
כמנהג אשכנז, 741, 781, 1056
מחזור לראש השנה ויום הכפורים ושלש רגלים
כמנהג ספרד, 782
מחזור לראש השנה ויום הכפורים עם באורים
בית לוי, מטה לוי ..., 626, 1055
מחזור לראש השנה ויום כפור, 118
מחזור עבדת אהל מועד, כמנהג פולין = Service
of the synagogue, 723, 742, 798,
1074–1076, 1101, 1132
מחזור קרבן אהרן ולקוטי צבי, ראה מחזור
לראש השנה ויום הכפורים עם באורים בית
זמרת יה, 215

לוי, מטה לוי ...
מחזור קרבן אהרן לקוטי צבי, ראה מחזור לראש
השנה ויום הכפורים: נוסח ספרד: עם
באורים בית לוי, מטה לוי ...
מחזור ראש השנה ויום הכפורים: כמנהג
אשכנז, 783
מלמד להועיל, 285
ממקומך, 1194
מן המיצר, 1161
המנגן = The Jewish songster
ראה גם The Jewish songster
המנגן = The Jewish songster, 1230
מנהג אמעריקא = Daily prayers for
American Israelites, 201–203, 362–363,
396, 468
מנהג אמעריקא תפלות בני ישרון, ראה גם
תפלות בני ישרון מנהג אמעריקא
מנהג אמעריקא תפלות בני ישרון = Daily
prayers, 102, 119, 154, 163, 180
מנהג אמעריקא תפלות בני ישרון =Gebet-
Buch für den öffentlichen
Gottesdienst..., 120
מעין הישועה = Source of salvation, 232–233,
275, 514
מענה לשון, 574, 784, 875
מענה לשון = Memorial prayers and
meditations, 799
מעריב של שבת, 431–432
מקור חיים, 923

נגינות ברוך שור לימים נוראים, 701
דאס נייע מחזור מיט עברי דייטש, ראה מחזור
ראש השנה ויום הכפורים: כמנהג אשכנז
אנייד ש״ס תחנה, 1262–1263
א נייע ש״ס תחנה רב פנינים, 1264–1265
הנרות הללו, 1057

סדור בית יהודה, 824, 876, 1102–1103
סדור בית ישראל עברי-טייטש, 898–899, 924,
1133, 1266–1267
סדור דברי צדיקים, 30
סדור דרך החיים, 1044
סדור האריז״ל, 925, 1268
סדור חנוך תפילה, 926
סדור חנוך תפלה: באותיות גדולות מאד, 785

סדור חנוך תפלה: כולל תפלות לכל השנה,
843, 877, 980, 1231
סדור חנוך תפלה החדש = Sidur chinuch
hechodosh tefilah, 844, 878
סדור חנוך תפלה החדש = Sidur chinuch
tephilah hechodosh, 845, 879
סדור חנוך תפלה עם חנוך לנער, 575, 786, 800,
880, 1232
סדור כל בו, 1045
סדור כל בו = Complete daily prayers,
702–703
סדור לבתי-ספר ולעם, 680, 743–744, 787
סדור קול יעקב, 1162
סדור קרבן מנחה, 576, 927, 1104–1105, 1269
סדור שפת אמת, 40, 85
סדור שפת אמת = Daily prayers with English
instructions, 234, 247, 265, 291, 300, 350,
364, 414, 432, 627–628, 928, 1134, 1233, 1270
סדור שפת אמת = Sephath emeth, 1046
סדור שפת אמת (היימאן), 788
סדור שפת אמת החדש = Daily prayer with
English directions, 958
סדור שפת אמת (הקטן) = Daily prayers with
English directions, 981
סדור שפתי צדיקים, 17, 25, 45–46, 73, 121, 257,
1195
סדור תפארת יהודה, 1196
סדור תפארת יהודה = Sidur tifereth Jehudah,
846–847, 849
סדור תפארת יהודה = Sidur tifereth Judah,
848
סדור תפלת ישראל, 92
סדור תפלת ישראל מכל השנה, 1106
סדר ברכת המזון וקריאת שמע, 724
סדר גמלות חסדים, 248
סדר הדרת קדש, 767
סדר הסליחות ליום ב׳ פרשת שמות לחברה
ביקור חולים וקדישה, 74
סדר העבודה, 98
סדר העבודה ביום חנוכת בית החולים
אשר ליהודים, 54
סדר העבודה לחנוכת הבית לק״ק שארית
ישראל, 541

Title Index

סדר התפילות כמנהג ק״ק ספרדים, 10
סדר חנוכת בית, 434
סדר חנוכת בית הכנסת בית ישראל בעיר ווילימסבארג, 41
סדר חנוכת הבית, 33, 172
סדר חנוכת הבית דקהלה החדשה כנסת ישראל, 61
סדר חנוכת הבית החדשה, 181
סדר חנוכת הבית והשירים אשר ישוררו קהל בית יעקב, 31
סדר חנוכת הבית והשירים אשר ישוררו קהל שערי תפלה, 27
סדר חנוכת הבית והשירים אשר שרו קהל בית אל 21
סדר כל תפלות השנה = Magil's complete linear prayer book, 681–683, 745–746, 881, 1107, 1197
סדר להדרת קדש = Form of blessings of Israel, 258, 292–293
סדר להדרת קדש = Form of prayers and blessings of Israel, 365, 378, 515, 606, 768, 789
סדר סליחות (השלמה) כמנהג ליטא, רייסן, וזמוט, 825
סדר סליחות לימים נוראים: כמנהג וואלין, 900
סדר סליחות לימים נוראים כמנהג אשכנז, 1271
סדר סליחות לימים נוראים כמנהג פולין גדול ופולין קטן, 577
סדר ערבית לשבת, 959
סדר קבורה כפי מנהג ק״ק ספרדים שארית ישראל בנו יארק עם תרגום אנגלי, 801
סדר קינות לתשעה באב, 1272–1275
סדר רחיצת המת: כפי מנהג ק״ק הספרדים שארית ישראל בנו יארק עם תרגום אנגלי, 882
סדר תפלה = Gebete für die öffentlichen Gottesdienst der Tempelgemeinde Ahawath Chesed, 204–205, 241, 308, 366
סדר תפלה = Order of prayer for divine service, 55, 93, 108, 122–124, 146, 173, 192, 216, 259, 276, 286, 294–295, 351, 397, 449
סדר תפלה = Order of prayers adopted by the Congregation Mickva Israel, Savannah, Georgia, 450

סדר תפלה = Prayers for the divine services of Congregation Ahawath Chesed, 398
סדר תפלה לבתי ספר ולעם = Complete prayer book for synagogue, home & school, 850, 930
סדר תפלה לילדי בני אברהם, 683a
סדר תפלות ובקשות על החולה, 415, 1058, 1276
סדר תפלות ישראל = Evening services for the Sabbath and week-days: reprinted from the Union prayer-book, 1010
סדר תפלות ישראל = Prayer-book for Jewish deaf, 1047
סדר תפלות ישראל ראה גם, תפלות for Jewish worship = The Union prayer-book
ישראל = Union prayer book
סדר תפלות ישראל = The Union prayer-book, for Jewish worship, 502–503, 516, 661–662, 684, 704–705, 725, 747, 802–803, 851–852, 883–884, 901, 930, 960, 982, 1011–1014, 1077–1078, 1108–1109, 1135, 1163–1165, 1200–1201, 1234
סדר תפלות ישראל לבעלי מלחמה = A ritual for Jewish soldiers, 961
סדר תפלות כל השנה = Daily prayers with English directions, 931, 983, 1048, 1166
סדר תפלות כל השנה = Ritual for Jewish worship ראה גם Ritual for Jewish worship
סדר תפלות כל השנה = Ritual for Jewish worship, 336
סדר תפלות כל השנה = The standard prayer book, 932, 984, 1015, 1079, 1136, 1198
סדר תפלות כל השנה כמנהג פולין = The authorised daily prayer book of the United Hebrew Congregations of the British empire, 933, 1080
סדר תפלות כל השנה כמנהג פולין = The authorized daily prayer book of the United Hebrew Congregations of the British empire, 902, 1199
סדר תפלות לכל השנה: נוסח אשכנז, מתורגם אשכנזית, 1277
סדר תפלות לאבלים, 790, 962
סדר תפלות לשבת ויום טוב, 903, 1202

Ritual for funerals and prayers = ספר החיים
in the house of mourning… 368, 469
ספר חיים = Prayers for the dead, 749
ספר ידיד נפש, 1110
ספר מעבר יבק, 1283a
ספר נשמת חיים, 805
ספר צדה לדרך האמת, 1049
ספר ציון, 542, 905
ספר שיר ציון, 504
ספר תהלים עם מעמדות, 1283
ספר תנחומות = Book of consolation, 706, 906

עבדת הקדש, 400
עבדת יום הזכרון; עבדת יום הכפורים, 770, 907, 986, 1081, 1168–1169
עבדת שבת, 1138, 1238
עבדת שלש רגלים, 1111
עבודת ברית שלום, 556
עבודת הקדש = Avodath hakodesh, 806
עבודת הקדש = Service of the sanctuary, 277
עבודת השלחן עם קריאת שמע על המטה, 1112
עבודת ישראל = Israelitisch Gebetbuch für den öffentlichen Gottesdienst im ganzen Jahre, 125, 193–195, 217
עבודת ישראל = Israelitish prayer book for all the public services of the year, 218, 337–338
עבודת ישראל = The order of prayer for the Israelitish divine service, 133, 164
עבודת ישראל = A prayerbook for the services of the year at the synagogue, 726, 750, 807, 855, 885, 908, 987, 1050, 1082, 1113–1114, 1138, 1170, 1204, 1239
עולת שבת, 685, 792
עזי וזמרת יה, 629
על חטא, 1205
עלת תמיד, ראה גם עלת תמיד Dr. David Einhorn's
עלת תמיד = Book of prayers for Israelitish Congregations, 207–208
עלת תמיד = Gebetbuch für israelitische Reform-Gemeinden, 76–80, 103

סדר תפלות לשבת ויום טוב = Conservative Sabbath and holiday prayer book, 1236
סדר תפלות לשבת ויום טוב = Sabbath and holiday prayer book, 1235
סדר תפלות מכל השנה = Daily prayers with a revised English translation, 853, 904, 1167, 1203
סדר תפלת ישראל: כמנהג אשכנז, 791, 1278
סדר תפלת ישראל: כמנהג ספרד, 1237
סידור ברכות והודאות, 1279
סידור חנוך תפלה: עם אלפא ביתא וגם גדול בנים, 1280
סידור יורה ומלקוש ומרוה, 748
סידור קרבן מנחה: נוסח אשכנז עם…תחנות רבות, 1281
סידור ראבן חדש, 1059
סידור תפלה יקרה, 934–935
סליחות ותפלות ליום ט״ו כסלו, 206, 352
סליחות ליום כפור, 34
סליחות לימים נוראים כמנהג אונגארן, מעהרען, בעהעמען שלעזיען וכל גלילות, 416
סליחות לימים נוראים כמנהג אשכנז, ליטא, זאמוט ורייסין, 1282
ספר אהל שרה = Yohale Sarah ראה גם Religious duties of the daughters of Israel
ספר אהל שרה = Yohale Sarah, 854, 985, 1016
ספר אנעים זמירות, ראה גם Sefer Anim zemiroth
ספר אנעים זמירות, 769, 826
ספר אנעים זמרות, 804
ספר ברית יצחק, 542, 905
ספר החיים = Andachtsbuch zum Gebrauche auf dem Friedhofe und in Trauerhause… 367
ספר החיים = Andachtsbuch zum Gebrauche bei Krankheiten und Sterbfällen…, 147
ספר החיים = The book of life (Elzas), 936–937
ספר החיים = The book of life (Vidaver), 266–268, 301, 324, 399, 484, 555, 607–608

Title Index

עמנואל, 609
ענף יוסף, 451
פֿאלשטענדיגער לינין־סדור לבתי־ספר ולעם, 665–663, 707
פֿאלשטענדיגער סדור פֿיר א גאנץ יאהר, ראה לינין־סדור לבתי־ספר ולעם סדור לבתי־ספר ולעם
פסוקי דזמרה, 567
צדוק הדין, 353
קבוץ סליחות ותפלות ליום חמשה עשר לחדש כסלו, 568
קדש הלולים, 105–104
קהלת, 1284
קול זמרה, 339
קול רינה = Hebrew hymnal for school and home, 808
קול רינה, Kol rinah, 452
קנות לתשעה באב = Sinagogue recitative for Tisha-Ba'v, 1017
קרבן אהרן, 249
קרבן תודה, 309
קריאה קדושה, 1051
ראשית דעת = Catechism designed for the religious instruction of Israelitish children, 219–222, 235, 242, 250
ראשית דעת שפת עבר, 708, 827, 909
רחמה, 42
רינה ותפילה, 62
הרנה ותפילה = Horinnoh wehatefilloh, 727
הרנה ותפילה = Songs and prayers for the eve Sabbath, 686
הרנה ותפילה = Songs and prayers for the Sabbath service, 687
רנת עמך, 1139
רע הילדים, ראה גם מאגילניצקי'ס לינין רע הילדים
רע הילדים, 709, 938
רעווערענדס האנדבוך, 1018, 1171
שבעה אופני הקדוש, 1060
שיר ושבחה, 1019
שירו לה' שיר חדש = Hymns and prayers in English and German, 435

שירו לה' שיר חדש = Hymns, Psalms and prayers, 165
שירו לה' שיר חדש = Sing unto the Lord a new song, 710–711
שירות ותשבחות, 910
שירי זמרה, 688
שירי זמרה, קבלת שבת, 809
שירי חנוך, 243
שירי ישראל = Sherai Israel, 280
שירי ישראל לליל שבת, 1020
שירי תהילה, 470
שירי תפלה = Recitativen für Kantor, 1206
שירי תפלה = Song of prayer for Friday evening service, 856
שלהבת יה = Order of services…as used by Temple Rodeph Sholom, N.Y. adapted by…, 712
שלהבת יה = Shalhevet Yah, 1061
שלהבת יה = Temple service: arranged for the Congregation Rodeph Sholom, 543–544, 630
שלהבת יה = Temple service… Congregation Beth Miriam, 642
שמחת תורה, 401
ש״ס תחינה החדשה, 963
ש״ס תחינה רב פנינים, 965
ש״ס תחנה החדשה (השלמה), 964
שערי חסד, 287
שפת אמת, ראה סדור שקת אמת
שפתי צדיקים, ראה סדור שפתי צדיקים
תחינות בנות ישורון, 94, 196, 209, 302, 436
תפילות החולה, 52
תפלה זכה חדשה לימים נוראים ולכל ימות השנה, 417
תפלה יקרה, 939
תפלה לבית האבל, 666, 1207
תפלה למשה, ראה גם תפלת ישראל = Order of prayer and responsive readings for Jewish worship
תפלה למשה, 325
תפלות בני ישורון…כפי מנהג אמעריקא = Divine service of American Israelites, 148, 354, 402, 454, 471

211

American Jewish Liturgies

תפלת ישראל = The Jewish prayer book, 455
תפלת ישראל = Order of prayers and responsive readings for Jewish worship ראה גם תפלה למשה
תפלת ישראל = Order of prayers and responsive readings for Jewish worship, 369
תפלת ישראל = Prayers of Israel with English translation, 64–65, 95, 109, 126, 134–135, 149, 155, 166, 182, 210, 224, 251, 269, 288, 303, 326, 355–356, 379, 418–419, 437–439, 517, 593, 667, 713
תפלת ישראל = Prayers of Israel: תפלות לכל השנה containing the divine services of the entire year arranged for the American Reform services in the "Temple Gates of Hope"…, 380
תפלת ישראל: התפלות מכל השנה כמנהג ק״ק שערי תקוה, 340
תפלת ישראל כולל התפלות מכל השנה כמנהג ק״ק שערי תקוה, 326
תפלת מנחה לשבת, 828, 941
תפלת ערבית לבית האבל, 310
תפלת שבת = The Sabbath service, 689, 751, 829, 857, 966, 1083, 1115, 1172

תפלות בני ישורון, מנהג אמעריקא, ראה גם, The daily prayers Gebet-Buch für den öffentlichen Gottesdienst und die Privat-Andacht
תפלות בני ישורון, מנהג אמעריקא, ראה גם מנהג אמעריקא תפלות בני ישורון
תפלות בני ישורון, מנהג אמעריקא, 75
תפלות החולה, 37
תפלת ישראל = Gebete der Israeliten in Amerika, 223
תפלת ישראל = Jewish prayer book, 472
תפלת ישראל = Prayers of Israel with English translation, 32, 47–49, 224
תפלת ישראל = Union prayer book
תפלת ישראל = The Union prayer-book for Jewish worship ראה גם, סדר תפלות ישראל
תפלת ישראל = Union prayer book, 473, 485–486
תפלת ישראל לשבת ולשלש רגלים = Prayers of Israel for the Sabbath and the Festivals, 1240
תפלות למתחילים, 1062
תפלת אליהו, 1208
תפלת בית אהבה, 487
תפלת יהושוע, 940
תפלת ישראל = Israelitisches Andachts-Buch, 63, 94, 209, 302, 436

Liturgical Index

Siddurim

Siddur/Seder Tefilah, including Siddur with Maḥzor (סדור/סדר תפלה), 10, 17, 25, 30, 32, 40, 45–49, 55, 63–66, 69–70, 73, 75–80, 85, 92–95, 102–103, 108–109, 119–126, 133–135, 146, 149, 154–155, 163–164, 166, 173, 176, 180, 182, 192–195, 201–205, 207–210, 216–218, 223–224, 234, 241, 247, 251, 257–259, 265, 269, 271, 276, 286, 288, 291–295, 300, 302–303, 308, 319, 325–327, 336–338, 340, 350–351, 355–356 362–365, 369, 371, 375, 378–380, 396, 398, 403, 414, 418–419, 427, 433, 436–439, 449–450, 465, 468, 472–473, 487, 502–503, 515–518, 525, 534, 575–576, 593, 606, 611–612, 622, 627–628, 639, 661, 663–665, 667, 678, 680–684, 699, 702–705, 707, 709, 713, 726, 738, 743–748, 750, 767–768, 785–789, 791, 800, 802, 807, 814, 824, 840, 843–853, 855, 862, 876–881, 883, 885, 898–899, 901–902, 904, 908, 924–935, 945, 958, 960–961, 967, 980–981, 983–984, 987–991, 1013–1015, 1044–1048, 1050, 1059, 1066, 1079–1080, 1082, 1087, 1102–1108, 1113–1114, 1133–1135, 1138, 1163, 1166–1167, 1170, 1178, 1195–1200, 1203–1204, 1231–1234, 1237, 1239, 1266–1270, 1277–1281

Siddur. Daily Prayers, 480

Siddur. Daily Prayers. Evening Service (ערבית), 310, 423, 478, 505–506, 570, 578, 596, 631–632, 646, 666, 810, 863, 971, 1004, 1010, 1207

Siddur. Daily Prayers. Evening Service. Ahavat ʻolam (אהבת עולם), 1146

Siddur. Daily Prayers. Evening Service. Hashkivenu (השכבנו), 1146

Siddur. Daily Prayers. Morning Service (שחרית), 388, 505, 600, 631, 725, 759, 863

Siddur. Daily Prayers. Morning Service. Mah ṭovu ohalekha (מה טובו אהליך), 531–532, 623, 629, 700, 887

Siddur. Daily Prayers. Morning Service. Az yashir (אז ישיר), 1221

Siddur. Daily Prayers. Morning Service. ʻAmidah. Ḳedushah. Mimkomkha (ממקומך), 1194

Siddur. Daily Prayers. Sunday Services. 309, 565, 649, 1036–1037

Siddur. Sabbath, 3–4, 12, 58, 249, 277, 331–332, 334, 360, 400, 409, 445, 451, 453, 455, 463–464, 543–544, 556, 630, 685, 712, 720, 762, 792, 840, 890, 893, 903, 910, 952, 1034–1035, 1061, 1098, 1126, 1137, 1202, 1235–1236, 1238, 1240

Siddur. Sabbath. Evening Service, 431–432, 443–444, 495, 586, 597, 632, 689, 751, 829, 857, 959, 966, 1010, 1063, 1083, 1115, 1119, 1172, 1184, 1213, 1217, 1252–1253

Siddur. Sabbath. Evening Service. Ve-shamru (ושמרו), 629, 1039–1040, 1052, 1130, 1156, 1192, 1220

Siddur. Sabbath. Evening Service. Magen avot (מגן אבות), 1147

Siddur. Sabbath. Morning Service, 689, 751, 829, 857, 966, 1083, 1115, 1172, 1184

Siddur. Sabbath. Musaf. Yiśmeḥu (ישמחו), 1160

Siddur. Sabbath. Afternoon, 462, 523, 733, 828, 941

Benedictions (ברכות)

Birkhot ha-nehenin, 365, 378, 515, 606, 768, 789, 843, 846–849, 919, 925, 1018, 1155, 1171, 1191, 1196, 1255, 1268, 1279

Grace after meals (ברכת המזון)/Benschers, 504, 724, 919, 1191, 1255

Havdalah, 1153
Havdalah. Eliyahu ha-Navi (אליהו הנביא), 969
Kiddush (All versions), 1060
Kiddush. Friday Night, 550–551, 718, 730, 1092
Tefilat ha-derekh (תפלת הדרך), 935, 939

Maḥzorim

Maḥzor. Full Year Cycle (מחזור לכל השנה), 53, 83, 91, 117, 144, 200, 231, 256, 283–284, 334–335, 349, 377, 394, 400, 412–413, 429–430, 453, 543–544, 625, 630, 712, 723, 739, 741–742, 766, 781–782, 821–823, 922, 1056, 1061, 1073–1076, 1101, 1132, 1259–1260

Maḥzor. High Holidays (מחזור לימים הנוראים), 3–4, 43–44, 82, 84, 87, 118, 148, 167, 189, 228, 366, 408, 454, 471, 485–486, 573, 604–605, 626, 640–642, 662, 679, 722, 740, 765, 770, 779–780, 783, 793, 797, 803, 818–820, 873–874, 884, 897, 907, 921, 957, 979, 982, 986, 998, 1002, 1008–1009, 1011–1012, 1041–1042, 1054–1055, 1077–1078, 1081, 1109, 1164–1165, 1168–1169, 1201, 1227, 1257–1258, 1261

Maḥzor. High Holidays. Evening Service, 2

Maḥzor. High Holidays. Rosh ha-Shanah (מחזור לראש השנה), 249, 842, 1000, 1029, 1228–1229

Maḥzor. High Holidays. Rosh ha-Shanah. Evening Service, 1003

Maḥzor. High Holidays. Rosh ha-Shanah. Morning. Shofar Service, 675

Maḥzor. High Holidays. Rosh ha-Shanah. Hymns, 571, 585

Maḥzor. High Holidays. Yom Kippur (מחזור ליום כפור), 354, 395, 397, 402 798, 999

Maḥzor. High Holidays. Yom Kippur. Memorial Service, 36, 100, 228, 274, 533, 561, 616, 1094, 1247

Maḥzor. High Holidays. Yom Kippur. Afternoon Service. Prayer of Repentance, 493–494

Maḥzor. High Holidays. Yom Kippur. Seliḥot, 34

Maḥzor. High Holidays. Yom Kippur. Hymns, 50, 279, 562, 585

Maḥzor. Pilgrim Festivals (מחזור לסוכות, לפסח, ולשבועות), 58, 145, 249, 277, 445, 451, 455, 556, 685, 792, 903, 914–915, 1111, 1145, 1202, 1235–1236, 1240

Maḥzor. Pilgrim Festivals. Sukkot, 87, 772, 794, 997, 1069

Maḥzor. Pilgrim Festivals. Sukkot. Hoshanot, 934, 1045

Maḥzor. Pilgrim Festivals. Sukkot. Hymns, 14–16

Maḥzor. Pilgrim Festivals. Shemini Atseret. Musaf. Geshem, 741

Maḥzor. Pilgrim Festivals. Śimḥat Torah, 401

Maḥzor. Pilgrim Festivals. Śimḥat Torah. Hakafot, 1045

Maḥzor. Pilgrim Festivals. Passover. Musaf. Tal, 741

Maḥzor. Pilgrim Festivals. Shavu'ot, 995

Maḥzor. Pilgrim Festivals. Shavu'ot. Akdamut millin, 1284

Other Holiday Liturgy

Birkat ha-Ḥodesh (Rosh Ḥodesh Benshen ברכת החדש), 955, 978
Ḳidush levanah (קדוש לבנה), 785, 843, 935, 939
Yom Kippur Kaṭan, 1045
Ḥanukah, 479, 634, 865, 872, 947, 1117, 1244
Ḥanukah. Ha-Nerot halalu (הנרות הללו), 872, 1057
Ḥanukah. Ma'oz tsur (מעוז צור), 872, 918a, 918b, 1069a, 1218
Purim, 865, 1122
Sefirat ha-'Omer, 785, 843, 934–935, 939

Liturgical Index

Piyyuṭim

Piyyuṭim, 1043
Zemirot (זמרות), 407, 504, 660, 686–687, 727, 920, 934–935, 939, 1019, 1045, 1254
Zemirot. Friday Night, 550–551, 1020, 1070–1072, 1092, 1131, 1225–1226
Zemirot. Saturday Afternoon, 685, 792, 1157–1159, 1199
Yotserot (יוצרות), 956, 1044
Ma'amadot (מעמדות), 1044, 1283
Perek shirah (פרק שירה), 1110
Kinot for Tish'ah be-Av קינות לתשעה (באב), 1017, 1272–1275
Seliḥot (סליחות), 74, 206, 352, 417, 568, 825, 934, 1045
Seliḥot before the High Holidays, 416–417, 577, 900, 1162, 1271, 1282

Psalms (תהלים)

Collections/Selections, 215, 280, 406, 459, 470, 472, 490, 500, 520, 567, 598, 676, 714, 806, 817, 934, 948, 1044, 1065, 1175, 1177, 1283
Psalm 1, 317
Psalm 16 (שויתי), 834
Psalm 22, 1030, 1096
Psalm 24, 197
Psalm 27, 672
Psalm 29, 226, 891
Psalm 30 (מזמור שיר חנוכת הבית), 1193
Psalm 49 (אך אלהים), 834
Psalm 71, 560
Psalm 77, 554
Psalm 91 (יושב בסתר עליון), 834
Psalm 92 (מזמור שיר ליום השבת), 602, 629
Psalm 93, 174
Psalm 100, 1067
Psalm 112, 262
Psalm 113, 1089
Psalm 114 (בצאת ישראל), 1023–1024, 1031, 1086, 1116
Psalm 115, 996
Psalm 116, 996
Psalm 118 (מן המיצר), 387, 508, 833, 996, 1161
Psalm 121, 554
Psalm 125, 263
Psalm 126 (שיר המעלות), 918a, 918b, 1069a, 1218
Psalm 129, 554
Psalm 130, 1028
Psalm 137 (על נהרות בבל), 1023–1024, 1032, 1086, 1141
Psalm 144 (לדוד ברוך), 918a, 918b, 1069a, 1218

Special Prayers or Prayer Books

Camp Services, 1184, 1209
Children's Prayer Books/Readers with Prayers/Prayer Books for Religious School, 87, 97, 150, 156, 160, 184, 219–222, 230, 232–236, 239, 242–243, 247, 250, 253, 265, 270–273, 275, 278, 285, 290–291, 296, 298, 300, 313–314, 339, 343, 347–348, 350, 361, 364, 381–382, 384, 389–390, 411, 414, 421, 426, 428, 433, 441, 447, 458–459, 462, 475–476, 480, 483, 490, 496–501, 511, 513, 520, 523, 526, 530, 535–536, 569, 575, 581–582, 587–588, 598, 613, 627–628, 633, 636–637, 639, 644–645, 651–652, 663–665, 677–678, 680–683, 683a, 690, 696, 699, 707–709, 714–716, 733, 737, 743–745, 753–755, 757, 760–761, 763, 772–773, 785–787, 794, 800, 808, 815, 817, 827–828, 830, 841, 843–845, 850, 858–861, 865, 877–881, 886, 894, 909–910, 912, 917–918, 920, 926, 929, 938, 941–942, 944, 950, 974, 977, 980, 993–995, 997–998, 1002, 1007, 1020, 1025, 1027, 1062, 1064–1066, 1068–1069, 1084, 1099, 1107, 1117, 1122–1123, 1143, 1147–1149, 1177, 1197, 1213, 1215, 1230–1232, 1244, 1246, 1249, 1280
Home Prayer Books, 153, 223, 240, 370,

550–551, 677, 714, 763, 808, 850, 866, 947, 1092, 1095, 1112, 1152, 1215
Hymnals/Gesänge/Songs/Anthems, 20, 28, 59–60, 96, 101, 104–105, 107, 114, 123, 132, 137, 141, 151–152, 165, 168, 173, 185–187, 190, 211–212, 214–215, 220–221, 227, 230, 238–239, 242, 245, 250, 255, 261, 264, 272–273, 276, 280–282, 289, 294, 298, 306–307, 333, 339, 342–343, 347, 351, 357–358, 361, 373, 376, 380–381, 386, 411, 424, 426, 428, 435, 441, 447, 449, 457, 459, 462, 470, 477, 481, 483, 487–489, 491, 495–498, 500–501, 511, 513, 520, 526, 530, 535–538, 579, 582, 585–586, 589, 598, 601, 623, 635, 643, 647, 651, 653–656, 660, 672, 676, 688, 696–697, 716, 729, 752, 756–757, 761, 774, 777, 806, 808, 815, 817, 830, 838, 861, 894–896, 911, 917–918, 918a, 918b, 920, 943, 972, 974, 977, 1025, 1053, 1064–1066, 1068, 1069a, 1088, 1090, 1097, 1099–1101, 1117, 1119, 1122, 1124–1125, 1128, 1139, 1148–1150, 1154, 1176–1177, 1189, 1208, 1218, 1230, 1246–1247

Musical Services

Siddur. Sabbath. Evening Service, 6, 215, 371, 446, 452, 466, 512, 524, 547, 563–564, 590, 609, 621, 629, 650, 657, 686–687, 693, 710–711, 727, 736, 806, 809, 826, 831–832, 839, 856, 864, 871, 940, 975, 1001, 1033, 1070–1072, 1120, 1127, 1131 1179–1182, 1186–1187, 1206, 1208, 1214, 1225–1226, 1241

Siddur. Sabbath. Morning Service, 215, 373–374, 446, 466, 512, 524, 564, 590, 609, 620, 650, 686–687, 727, 732, 734–735, 769, 806, 811, 816, 868, 892, 940, 951, 975, 1001, 1182, 1188, 1190, 1206

Mahzor. High Holidays, 215, 448, 512, 701, 940, 970, 1038

Mahzor. High Holidays. Avinu malkenu, 918a, 918b, 1069a, 1218

Mahzor. High Holidays. Musaf. U-netaneh tokef (ונתנה תוקף), 392, 778, 1219

Mahzor. High Holidays. Rosh ha-Shanah, 595, 804, 1144, 1183

Mahzor. High Holidays. Rosh ha-Shanah. Evening Service, 946, 953, 1245, 1251

Mahzor. High Holidays. Rosh ha-Shanah. Musaf. Malkhuyot, Zikhronot, Shofarot, 889

Mahzor. High Holidays. Yom Kippur, 594, 869–870, 913, 1021

Mahzor. High Holidays. Yom Kippur. Al het (על חטא), 1205

Mahzor. High Holidays. Yom Kippur. Evening Service, 658, 1091, 1245, 1251

Mahzor. High Holidays. Yom Kippur. Evening Service. Kol nidre (כל נדרי), 304, 545, 658, 719, 867, 916, 918a, 918b, 1069a, 1091, 1093, 1218, 1250–1251

Mahzor. Pilgrim Festivals, 215, 512, 552, 614, 806, 940, 1085

Mahzor. Pilgrim Festivals. Morning Service, 1206

Prayer Books for the Deaf, 1047
Prayer Books for Soldiers, 961, 967, 988–992, 1006, 1008, 1010, 1012
Prayer for the Hazan, 5, 1154

Prayers for the Government, 5
Prayer at the Opening of the House of Representatives, 88
Prayers at the California State Legislature, 1216

Prayers for Peace, 170, 553, 992, 1006
Prayers for the Sick, 37, 52, 147, 248, 345, 415, 1058, 1276, 1283a
Rabbis'/Cantors' Manuals, 420, 546, 692, 973, 1018, 1171

Tehinnot/Devotionals/Women's Prayer Books, 18, 42, 65, 94, 106, 115–116, 138–140, 143, 158–159, 178, 191, 196, 198, 209, 223, 229, 237, 246, 297, 299, 302, 318, 341,

Liturgical Index

385, 436, 453, 482, 519, 527–528, 549, 583, 592, 619, 638, 721, 731, 796, 805, 812–813, 837, 854, 948, 963–965, 985, 1005, 1016, 1121, 1151–1152, 1155, 1262–1265, 1269

Prayer Books for Girls, 968, 1142

Life Cycle Events

Circumcision (ברית מילה), 542, 905
Redemption of the First-born Son (פדיון הבן), 542, 905
Bar Mitzvah, 257, 421, 542, 905, 1007
Confirmation, 156, 160, 184, 225, 232–233, 243, 253, 270, 275, 278, 421–422, 514, 540, 652, 944, 1123, 1173, 1178
Marriage Ceremonies, 183, 542, 806, 905, 1185
Funerals/Prayers at the Grave/Prayers in the House of Mourning, 11, 147, 188, 190, 248, 252, 259, 266–268, 276, 287, 294, 301, 310, 312, 324, 352, 367–368, 399, 415, 420, 423, 467, 469, 478, 484, 506–507, 509, 522, 546, 555, 570, 572, 574, 578, 591, 596, 607–608, 618, 646, 666, 692, 706, 717, 749, 784, 790, 799, 801, 805, 810, 875, 882, 906, 923, 936–937, 962, 1004, 1018, 1026, 1049, 1058, 1207, 1276, 1282
Memorial Services (הזכרת נשמות)/Seelenfeier, 36, 81, 179, 345, 404–405, 539, 584, 647, 659, 717, 775–776, 790, 799, 834–835, 962, 1247, 1256
Memorial Services. Adonai mah adam (אדני מה אדם), 1243
Memorial Services. Hymns. Why art thou cast down, my soul, 507, 529, 624

Special Events/One Time Events

Anniversary Services, 548, 580, 615
Dedication Ceremonies (חנוכת הבית), 8–9, 13, 21–23, 26–27, 29, 31, 33, 35, 38–39, 41, 50–51, 54, 56–57, 61–62, 67–68, 71–72, 72a, 86, 89–90, 99, 110–113, 127–130, 136, 142, 157, 161–162, 171–172, 177, 181, 199, 213, 244, 260, 305, 328–329, 344, 346, 383, 391, 393, 425, 434, 440, 442, 456, 461, 492, 510, 541, 557–559, 615, 617, 648, 670, 691, 698, 764, 836, 1022, 1118, 1210–1212
Fast Day Service, January 4th, 1861, 98
Lincoln Centenary Services, 758
Memorial Services for One Individual or One Event, 19, 131, 330, 521, 599, 603, 669, 673, 949
Prayers for the Dedication of a New Torah, 7
Prayers for the Installation of a New Rabbi, 372
Service in Honor of the 100th Birthday of Moses Montefiore, 311, 315–316, 320–323
Service in Honor of the 250th Anniversary of Jewish Settlement in the United States, 668, 674, 694–695
Service in Honor of the 400th Anniversary of Columbus' Journey, 460
Thankgiving Services, 1, 254

Individual Prayers

Adon ʿolam (אדון עולם), 24, 610, 629, 728, 795, 888, 1140, 1242
Alenu, 629, 918a, 918b, 1069a, 1218
ʿAmidah. Ḳedushah, 629, 1174
Ba-meh madliḳin (במה מדליקין), 954
Barkhu, 629, 1251
En Kelohenu, 629, 918a, 918b, 1069a, 1218
Ḳaddish, 574, 767, 790, 875, 935, 939, 962
Mi khamokha (מי כנוך), 629, 1251
Priestly blessing (ברכת כהנים, דוכן, נשיאת כפים), 175, 566, 771, 843, 935, 939, 1222–1224
Shemaʿ (קריאת שמע), 629, 724, 1112, 1251
Shir ha-yiḥud, 573
Torah Service (סדר הוצאת התורה/סדר קריאת התורה), 410, 629, 1045, 1051
Torah Service. Uve-nuḥo yomar (ובנוחו יאמר)/ʿEts ḥayim (עץ חיים), 671, 1129

Yehiyu le-ratson imre fi (May the words), 1052
Yigdal, 918a, 918b, 1069a, 1218

Different Liturgical Rites

Ari Rite/Nusaḥ Sefarad/Ḥasidic Rite, 679, 740, 766, 782, 823, 849, 877, 879, 899, 925, 939, 957, 980, 1059, 1105, 1231, 1237, 1258, 1260–1261, 1267–1268
Conservative Rite, 666, 770, 808? 890, 893, 907, 914–915, 949, 986, 999–1000, 1034, 1081, 1145, 1168–1169, 1207, 1210, 1213, 1229, 1236, 1240
German Rite/Minhag Ashkenaz, 21–23, 26, 31–33, 39–40, 43, 47–52, 62–65, 71, 82, 85, 91–92, 94–95, 98, 109, 113, 117–118, 126–129, 134–135, 145, 149, 155, 166, 179, 182, 189–190, 196, 200, 206, 209–210, 224, 231, 234, 247, 251, 256, 258, 265, 269, 271, 283–284, 288, 291–293, 300, 302–303, 326, 329, 334–335, 345, 347–350, 352, 355–356, 364–365, 377–378, 390, 394, 400, 412–415, 417–419, 429–430, 433, 436–439, 515, 517, 542, 573–576, 593, 604–606, 625–628, 639–641, 663–665, 678, 680–683, 685, 688–689, 699, 702–703, 707–709, 722, 724, 739, 741, 743–746, 748, 751, 763, 765, 767–768, 779, 781, 783–792, 799–800, 818–822, 824, 828–829, 841, 843–848, 850, 853, 857, 873–876, 878, 880–881, 897–898, 903–905, 924, 926–929, 931–932, 934–935, 939, 941, 958–959, 962–966, 979, 981, 983–984, 1009, 1015, 1030, 1041–1042, 1044–1046, 1048, 1054–1056, 1058, 1063, 1066, 1073, 1079, 1083, 1102–1104, 1107, 1111, 1115, 1119, 1133–1134, 1136–1137, 1166–1167, 1172, 1196–1198, 1202–1203, 1232–1233, 1235, 1238, 1247, 1259, 1266, 1269–1271, 1277–1282
German and Polish Rite, 30, 53, 83, 393, 577, 667, 713, 1228
Hungarian Rite (מנהג אונגארן, מעהרען), 393, 416
Lithuanian Rite (מנהג ליטא, רייסן וזאמוט), 568, 825
Polish Rite, 44, 74, 84, 144, 577, 723, 742, 780, 797–798, 842, 902, 921–922, 933, 1074–1076, 1080, 1101, 1106, 1132, 1199, 1227, 1257
Reform Rite, 6, 12, 20, 28–29, 36, 55, 58–60, 66, 69, 75–81, 93, 99–105, 108, 112, 114, 119–120, 122–125, 130, 133, 137, 141–142, 146–148, 150–154, 156, 160, 162–165, 167–168, 173, 176–177, 180, 184–188, 192–195, 199, 201–205, 207–208, 211–212, 214, 216–223, 225, 232–233, 235–236, 238–243, 249–250, 252–253, 259, 261, 270, 274–278, 280, 282, 286, 294–296, 298, 305–306, 308–314, 318–319, 321–322, 325, 327, 333, 336–340, 342–343, 347, 351, 354, 357, 359, 362–363, 366, 369, 371–375, 380–381, 384, 386, 388–389, 396–398, 401–405, 407–408, 410, 421–424, 427–428, 431–432, 435, 440, 443–458, 460–461, 463–469, 471–474, 477–481, 485–492, 496–503, 505–506, 509, 511–514, 516, 518, 521–522, 524–526, 532–535, 537–539, 543–545, 547, 550–553, 557, 561, 563–565, 570–572, 580–582, 584, 587–590, 594–596, 599–600, 603, 611–614, 616, 621–622, 624, 629–632, 634–636, 642, 644–656, 661–662, 669–670, 673, 683a, 684, 690–691, 693, 696–698, 704–706, 710–712, 718–720, 725–726, 730, 732–737, 747, 750, 753, 756, 760–762, 769, 772–777, 794, 802–804, 807, 810–817, 826, 830, 835, 837, 839–840, 851–852, 855, 860–866, 868–871, 883–885, 894–896, 901, 906, 908, 913, 930, 944–945, 947–948, 950–953, 960–961, 967, 970–971, 973, 975–977, 982, 987–991, 993, 995, 997–998, 1001–1002, 1008, 1010–1014, 1021–1022, 1027, 1033, 1035–1037, 1047, 1050, 1061, 1065, 1068–1069, 1077–1078, 1082, 1084–1085, 1087–1088, 1090, 1092, 1094,

1097–1098, 1100, 1108–1109, 1113–1114,
1118, 1120–1121, 1123–1126, 1135, 1138,
1143–1144, 1149, 1152, 1163–1165, 1170,
1173, 1177–1183, 1186–1190, 1200–1201,
1204, 1209, 1214, 1216–1217, 1234, 1239,
1241, 1244–1245, 1248–1253
Roumanian Rite, 617
Sephardic Rite (Spanish and Portuguese),
    1–5, 7–11, 13, 17, 19, 25, 35, 38, 45–46, 72–
    73, 89–90, 121, 254, 257, 361? 434, 541,
    668, 764, 801, 882, 910, 923, 1193
Syrian Rite, 1019
Vohlin Rite. (מנהג וואלין), 900

Cross References

Adonoi mah adam. *see* Life Cycle Events.
    Memorial Services. Adonai mah adam
Ahavat 'olam, *see* Siddur. Daily Prayers.
    Evening Service. Ahavat 'olam
Akdamut millin, *see* Mahzor. Pilgrim Festivals. Shavu'ot. Akdamut millin
'Al het, *see* Special Prayers and Prayer
    Books. Musical Services. Mahzor. High
    Holidays. Yom Kippur. 'Al het
'Al naharos Bavel, *see* Psalms. Psalm 137
'Arvit, *see* Siddur. Daily Prayers. Evening
    Service
Az yashir, *see* Siddur. Daily Prayers.
    Morning Service. Az yashir
Barkhu, *see* Individual prayers. Barkhu.
Birkat ha-Mazon, *see* Benedictions. Grace
    after meals
Birkhot ha-nehenin, *see* Benedictions.
    Birkhot ha-nehenin
Eliyahu ha-Navi, *see* Benedictions. Havdalah. Eliyahu ha-Navi
'Ets hayim, *see* Individual Prayers. Torah
    Service. Uve-nuho yomar/Ets hayim
Hakafot, *see* Mahzor. Pilgrim Festivals.
    Simhat Torah. Hakafot
Hashkivenu, *see* Siddur. Daily Prayers.
    Evening Service. Hashkivenu
Hosh'anot, *see* Mahzor. Pilgrim Festivals.

Sukkot. Hosh'anot
How Goodly are Thy Tents, *see* Siddur.
    Daily Prayers. Morning Service. Mah
    tovu ohalekha
Kaddish, *see* Individual Prayers. Kaddish
Kidush levanah, *see* Other Holiday
    Liturgy. Kidush levanah
Kol nidre, *see* Special Prayers or Prayer
    Books. Musical Services. Mahzor. High
    Holidays. Yom Kippur. Kol nidre
Ma'ariv, *see* Siddur. Daily Prayers. Evening
    Service
Magen avot, *see* Siddur. Sabbath. Evening
    Service. Magen avot
Mah tovu ohalekha, *see* Siddur. Daily
    Prayers. Morning Service. Mah tovu
    ohalekha
Mahzor le-Rosh ha-Shanah, *see* Mahzor.
    High Holidays. Rosh ha-Shanah
Mahzor le-Yamim Nora'im, *see* Mahzor.
    High Holidays
Mahzor le-Yom Kippur, *see* Mahzor. High
    Holidays. Yom Kippur
Mahzor le-Yom ha-Kipurim, *see* Mahzor.
    High Holidays. Yom Kippur
Mahzor le-Sukot, la-Pesah, ule-Shavu'ot,
    see Mahzor. Pilgrim Festivals
Ma'oz Tsur, *see* Other Holiday Liturgy.
    Hanukkah. Ma'oz tsur
May the words, *see* Individual prayers.
    Yehiyu le-ratson imre fi.
Memorial Service for the Day of Atonement, *see* Mahzor. High Holidays. Yom
    Kippur. Memorial Service
Min ha-metsar (Min hammezar), *see*
    Psalms. Psalm 118
Minhah le-Shabat, *see* Siddur. Sabbath.
    Afternoon Service
Ha-Nerot halalu, *see* Other Holiday
    Liturgy. Hanukkah. Ha-Nerot halalu
Oz Jashir, *see* Siddur. Daily Prayers.
    Morning Service. Az yashir
Pidyon ha-ben, *see* Life Cycle Events. Redemption of the First-born Son

American Jewish Liturgies

Rosh Ḥodesh benshen, *see* Other Holiday Liturgy. Birkat ha-Ḥodesh
Seder Tefilah, *see* Siddur
Sefirat ha-'Omer, *see* Other Holiday Liturgy. Sefirat ha-'Omer
Shaḥarit, *see* Siddur. Daily Prayers. Morning Service
Shir ha-ma'alot, *see* Psalms. Psalm 126
Shofar Service, *see* Maḥzor. High Holidays. Rosh ha-Shanah. Shofar Service
Sidur, *see* Siddur
Sidur le-Ḥol, *see* Siddur. Daily Prayers
Sidur le-Shabat, *see* Siddur. Sabbath
Tefilat ha-derekh, *see* Benedictions. Tefilat ha-derekh
Tehilim, *see* Psalms
Tov le hodos, *see* Psalms. Psalm 92
Traveler's prayer, *see* Benedictions. Tefilat ha-derekh
U-netaneh toḳef, *see* Special Prayers or Prayer Books. Musical Services. Maḥzor. High Holidays. Musaf. U-netaneh toḳef
Universal Lord, *see* Individual Prayers. Adon 'olam
Uve-nuḥo yomar, *see* Individual Prayers. Torah Service. Uve-nuḥo yomar/'Ets ḥayim
Ve-shamru, *see* Siddur. Sabbath. Evening Service. Ve-shamru.
Why art thou cast down, my soul, *see* Life Cycle Events. Memorial Services. Hymns. Why art thou cast down, my soul
Yizkor, *see* Life Cycle Events. Memorial Services
Yizkor le-Yom Kipur, *see* Maḥzor. High Holidays. Yom Kippur. Memorial Service
Zemirot, *see* Piyyuṭim. Zemirot

Hebrew Cross References

גשם, ראה Maḥzor. Pilgrim Festivals. Shemini atseret. Musaf. Geshem

הבדלה, ראה Benedictions. Havdalah

הושענות, ראה Maḥzor. Pilgrim Festivals. Sukkot. Hosha'not

הזכרת נשמות, ראה Life Cycle Events. Memorial Services

הקפות, ראה Maḥzor. Pilgrim Festivals. Simḥat Torah. Haḳafot

השכבנו, ראה Siddur. Daily Prayers. Evening Service. Hashkivenu

ונתנה תוקף, ראה Special Prayers or Prayer Books. Musical services. Maḥzor. High Holidays. Musaf. U-netaneh Toḳef

ושמרו, ראה Siddur. Sabbath. Evening Service. Ve-shamru

אדון עולם, ראה Individual Prayers. Adon 'olam

אדני מה אדם, ראה Life Cycle Events. Memorial Services. Adonoi mah adam

אהבת עולם, ראה Siddur. Daily Prayers. Evening Service. Ahavat 'olam

אז ישיר, ראה Siddur. Daily Prayers. Morning Service. Az yashir

אליהו הנביא, ראה Benedictions. Havdalah. Eliyahu ha-Navi

אקדמות מלין, ראה Maḥzor. Pilgrim Festivals. Shavu'ot Aḳdamut millin

ברכת החדש, ראה Other Holiday Liturgy. Birkat ha-Ḥodesh

ברכת המזון, ראה Benedictions. Grace after meals

ברכת כהנים, ראה Individual Prayers. Priestly Blessing